Doing *Style*

Doing *Style*

Youth and Mass Mediation in South India

CONSTANTINE V. NAKASSIS

The University of Chicago Press   Chicago and London

CONSTANTINE V. NAKASSIS is assistant professor of anthropology at the University of Chicago.

The University of Chicago Press, Chicago 60637
The University of Chicago Press, Ltd., London

Printed in the United States of America

25 24 23 22 21 20 19 18 17 16 1 2 3 4 5

ISBN-13: 978-0-226-32771-6 (cloth)
ISBN-13: 978-0-226-32785-3 (paper)
ISBN-13: 978-0-226-32799-0 (e-book)

DOI: 10.7208/chicago/9780226327990.001.0001

Library of Congress Cataloging-in-Publication Data
Names: Nakassis, Constantine V., 1979– author.
Title: Doing style : youth and mass mediation in South India / Constantine V. Nakassis.
Description: Chicago ; London : University of Chicago Press, 2016. | ©2016 | Includes bibliographical references and index.
Identifiers: LCCN 2015043778| ISBN 9780226327716 (cloth : alkaline paper) | ISBN 9780226327853 (paperback : alkaline paper) | ISBN 9780226327990 (e-book)
Subjects: LCSH: College students—India—Tamil Nadu—Social life and customs—21st century. | Fashion—Social aspects—India—Tamil Nadu. | Popular culture—India—Tamil Nadu.
Classification: LCC GT1470.T36 N35 2016 | DDC 391.00954/82—dc23
LC record available at http://lccn.loc.gov/2015043778

⊚ This paper meets the requirements of ANSI/NISO Z39.48-1992 (Permanence of Paper).

Dedicated to the arrival of Carmen Cassandre Dominique Nakassis and to the memory of Radha Viswanathan, a mother and friend to me since my first arrival in Madurai

. . . sweating in the sun
that melted
the wings' wax . . .

—William Carlos Williams

Contents

Acknowledgments

This is a book about the cultural phenomenology of college youth in urban Tamil Nadu, about such youths' experiences of liminality and ambivalence and how those experiences materialize in various mass-mediated ways. To share their liminal time and space, to be able to live alongside them and partake of their everyday was not a small thing to ask. The myriad young people with whom my research brought me in contact—who shared living space with me, who let me bend their ear, hang out with them, and who went out of their way to make me feel part of their lives and worlds—these young men and women showed a warmth and generosity for which I am ever grateful and heartened.

This research project had a long gestation, with its ups and downs, wrong turns and U-turns. Many people during my ongoing education have helped move it along toward its present form. Asif Agha inspired me to pursue the path of linguistic anthropology. He is a brilliant and dynamic teacher and advisor, and now a colleague and friend, who has impacted my thinking in innumerable, fundamental ways. Greg Urban, my first teacher of anthropology as a college freshman, has been a generous reader and interlocutor of my research, always encouraging me—through example and pointed intervention—to think about the big picture. I am indebted to them both.

This manuscript gelled while I was a postdoctoral fellow and then assistant professor at the University of Chicago. My colleagues here have provided immense academic stimulation and encouragement. Susan Gal, Hussein Ali Agrama, Shannon Lee Dawdy, Judith Farquhar, William Mazzarella,

Andrew Graan, Elina Hartikainen, Stephen Scott, Elizabeth Brummel, Sean Dowdy, Amy Leia McLachlan, and E. Annamalai and the Tamil Studies Workgroup all helped shape the arguments in this book. Many of the book's chapters were worked out and worked over with my wonderful writing group: E. Summerson Carr, Julie Chu, and Jennifer Cole. I owe a special debt to Michael Silverstein, a fount of intellectual generosity, mentorship, and friendship since my arrival at the University of Chicago. I thank him for his advice, both scholarly and professional, and for his support of and interest in my work.

Paul Manning has been a constant source of encouragement and criticism in my writing about brands. Early on, he forced me to reconsider my own voice—something I rather needed at the time. Alexander Dent provided wonderful feedback that helped clarify my thinking regarding brand piracy. As I later found out, he also provided incredibly detailed comments on the book manuscript as a whole that significantly helped bring it to its current shape. His generosity with his time and intellectual energy is amazing, and I am extremely grateful for it. Bernard Bate, Kedron Thomas, and Amanda Weidman read chapter drafts of the manuscript, providing detailed comments to improve them. Chris Gregory, Richard Bauman, Francis Cody, Hilary Dick, Sara Dickey, Joseph Hankins, John Haviland, Matthew Hull, Judith Irvine, Elise Kramer, Alaina Lemon, Ritty Lukose, Brent Luvaas, Bruce Mannheim, Sasha Newell, Anand Pandian, David Pedersen, Swarnavel Eswaran Pillai, Susan Seizer, Kristina Wirtz, and Kathryn Woolard all read or listened to various arguments that appear in in the book, providing helpful feedback. I thank them all.

Dr. E. Annamalai, Dr. Vasu Renganathan, Dr. Bharathy Lakshmana Perumal, and Mrs. Jayanthi Kannan were absolutely essential to this project. In addition to their helpful insights into and discussion about the materials and arguments in the book (which they never hesitated to provide over the course of many years and countless e-mails), I am indebted to each of them for being, in one way or another, at one time or another, my teachers of Tamil. நன்றி.

My classmates from the University of Pennsylvania—Luke Fleming and Melanie Dean (discussions with whom produced many of the book's key ideas), Michael Lempert (who helped me articulate the book's bigger picture), Llerena Searle (who graciously read the whole manuscript at a time of need), Rebecca Pardo (who provided critical feedback and insight on a number of chapters), Kyung-Nan Koh, Seran Schug, and Teresa Raczek (who took me to India for the first time)—have long been a source of support, both intellectual and personal.

For sustaining my spirits while conducting fieldwork and providing me with a second home and family, I express my love and gratitude to the late Radha Viswanathan (to whom this book is dedicated) and her wonderful family, as well as to my dearest friend and research assistant, K. Saravana Senthil Kumar and his incredibly warm family, whose laughter, food, and affection always rejuvenated me in times of need. This project would not have been possible without Radhamma's and Senthil's generous help, keen insights, and unflagging support. Thanks also go to Uma Devi and Georgina, who helped as research assistants, as well as to my amazing friends in Madurai and Chennai, who, each in their own way, furthered my research: Vijayasree Mathan, John Paul, Robinson Samuel, Tony James, M. Yuvaraj, Aravind Kumar, Anjiet Singh, Guru Vikram, Bruce Obenin, Ram Prabhu, Vijay Ananth, Kingsley Pandian, Stanley Sahayam, Vignesh Waran, Santhosh, Anten Edilbert, Kedharnath Sairam, Shaktisree Gopalan, Anusha Hariharan, and Srinitti Jayagopal. Special acknowledgment and thanks are due to Aravind, Vijayasree, and Kedharnath, who patiently fielded countless follow-up questions over the years.

My research in film and television would not have been possible without the help of "Film News" Anand, Hariharan Krishnan, B. Lenin, Father S. Rajanayagam, Venkat Prabhu and his team, Kalyana Devan, Kalyan Kumar, Karunas, Nithil Dennis, Suriya Narayanan, Anuradha Huggler, G. V. Prakkash, John Fernandes, Mr. Bhoopathi, Pooja Gallyot, Craig Gallyot, Paloma Rao, Sunita Raghu, and Gokul Dhanapal. Thanks to Carola Kroeber and Chezhiyan for helping me with contacts in and advice on textile production.

My research in colleges was facilitated by countless administrators, professors, and other staff. I am grateful to all of them for their help. Professor Suka Joshua went out of her way to assist me in the field and in following up on certain facts afterward. For his intellectual support, encouragement, and friendship while in the field, I owe a special debt to Dr. Madhavan Raghavendran.

T. David Brent, Priya Nelson, and Ellen Kladky have guided this manuscript through the most recent phase of its life. I thank them for the time and energy that they have devoted to it. The manuscript was much improved by two excellent reviewers, who provided engaged, critical feedback. Critique from reviewers of article versions of chapters 2 and 3 greatly improved them. Scott Henson expertly copyedited the manuscript, cleaning it up and improving its clarity. Thanks to Sunitha Raghu and Mr. Nataraj for help procuring images, to Nora Sweeney and Naoko Ataka for permissions to use their images, and to Sean Maher for ably collecting together the film stills for the book.

To my family: my brother Dimitri shows a seemingly endless capacity to read, reread, comment on, and correct my work. He even made a map for me along the way (figure 1). He has long been a mentor to me, his advice seeing me through all stages of my intellectual and professional life. I am ever thankful for his insight, his fine attention to detail, and his willingness to spend time to help me. My sister Magda provided her keen eye and expertise as an editor on numerous occasions, even on the day before the arrival of her son, and my nephew, Victor. I thank her for helping me clarify my ideas and prose as well as for her endless questions. My parents, Anastasios and Carmen, were my first intellectual role models—curious and critical, tenacious and creative. I thank them for their support and love.

My deepest thanks are to Julie Cousin for her patience, her levelheadedness, her engagement with my scholarly work (at all the odd and inconvenient times I would bring it up), and her willingness to share life in the field and beyond with me. I know it hasn't always been easy. Thank you.

This book would not have been possible without research and writing support from the American Institute of Indian Studies, the Zwicker Fund at the University of Pennsylvania, the Marion R. and Adolph J. Lichtstern Fund for Anthropological Research, the Committee on Southern Asian Studies, and the Franke Institute for the Humanities at the University of Chicago. Significant portions of chapter 3 have been published in *Anthropological Quarterly* (Nakassis 2012a). They are used here with permission.

Note on Transliteration, Quotation, and Pseudonyms

As I discuss in more detail in chapter 4, what constitutes a Tamil lexical item is not always self-evident. Indeed, many of the Tamil terms in this text (e.g., *style, local, decent,* and even *English*), while of English origin, have become normalized (and transformed) as part of everyday spoken Tamil, though even such a distinction is complex and problematic. There is an indeterminate and shifting threshold between these "codes," to say nothing of the registers they comprise. As Chaise LaDousa (2014:108–36) has discussed in another Indian context, this can make the graphic form of print problematic, as it can convey a sense of rigidity and clarity that simplifies a much more complex linguistic reality. With this caveat in mind, I indicate Tamil linguistic forms in the expansive sense noted above with *italics*, with words of English origin retaining their canonical English spellings (e.g., *local* instead of *lōkkal*) and all others transliterated following the Madras Lexicon scheme (with some slight changes, see below). When used within otherwise Tamil speech, linguistic forms of (perceived) English origin that are not normalized as Tamil are left unitalicized. In my own discussion, unitalicized English words (e.g., style, local) retain their American English meanings. For the transliteration of Tamil proper names (e.g., of people, places, films), I follow general usage in unitalicized font (e.g., Madurai instead of *Maturai*), unless they are titles for works of art, in which case I italicize them (e.g., *Pokkiri* instead of *Pōkkiri*).

Tamil script	Roman script	International Phonetic Alphabet (IPA)
Consonants		
க்	*k*	Initial, geminated: k Initial, postnasal (*ṅ*): g Intervocalic, postliquids: γ
ங்	*ṅ*	ŋ
ச்	*c*, *s*	Initial, geminated: tʃ Postnasal (*ñ*): d͡ʒ Initial, intervocalic: s
ஞ்	*ñ*	ɲ
ட்	*ṭ*	Initial, geminated: ʈ Initial, intervocalic, postnasal (*ṇ*): ɖ
ண்	*ṇ*	ɳ
த்	*t*	Initial: t̪, d̪ Geminated: t̪ Intervocalic: ð Postnasal (*n*): d̪
ப்	*p*, *b*	Initial, geminated: p Initial, intervocalic, postnasal (*m*): b
ம்	*m*	m
ய்	*y*	j
ர்	*r*	ɾ
ல்	*l*	l
வ்	*v*	ʋ
ழ்	*ḻ*	ɻ
ள்	*ḷ*	ɭ
ற்	*ṟ*	ɾ Geminated: ɖɾ
ந், ன்	*n*	n
ஜ்	*j*	d͡ʒ
ஷ்	*ṣ*	ʂ

Tamil script	Roman script	International Phonetic Alphabet (IPA)
Vowels		
அ	*a*	ɐ
ஆ	*ā*	ɑː
இ	*i*	i
ஈ	*ī*	iː
உ	*u*	Initial: u, Noninitial: ʉ, ɯ
ஊ	*ū*	uː
எ	*e*	e
ஏ	*ē*	eː
ஒ	*o*	o
ஓ	*ō*	oː
ஐ	*ai*	aɪ
ஔ	*au*	aʊ

For direct quotations in the original language, I use double quotation marks. For glosses or translations of quoted discourse, I use single quotation marks. Except for place names and publicly known figures, all names in this book are pseudonyms.

List of Symbols and Abbreviations

In certain transcripts, I use the following symbols:

(#)	# second pause
(.)	short pause (fewer than 0.2 seconds)
//. . . //	overlapping speech
=	no pause between turns of talk
-	interruption, break in speech
a::	elongated vowel
-h	in-breath
↑	rising intonation
SMALL CAPS	louder volume
( )	implied or elided word or phrase
[ ]	referent of anaphor or other term, full spelling or missing letters of contracted word, IPA transcription
< >	description of nonlinguistic action
(( ))	speech that is unclear in the original recording
. . .	elided speech
*	disfluent speech

In interlinear glosses, I use the following abbreviations:

1pers.pl.	first-person plural verb ending
2pers.pl.	second-person plural verb ending (honorific with singular referent)
3pers.pl.	third-person plural verb ending (honorific with singular referent)
ABL.	ablative case
ADJ.	adjectival ending (*-āna*)
ADV.	adverbial ending (*-āka*)

AVP.	adverbial participle
COMP.	complementizer
COMPL.	completive aspectual verb (*viṭu*)
DAT.	dative case
FUT.	future tense
HON.	honorific
IMP.pl.	imperative mood, plural (honorific with singular addressee)
INST.	instrumental case
INT.	yes/no question marker
NEG.	negation
NEUT.	neuter verb ending
NOM.	nominalization of verb
OBL.	oblique case
PRES.	present tense
PST.	past tense

Introduction

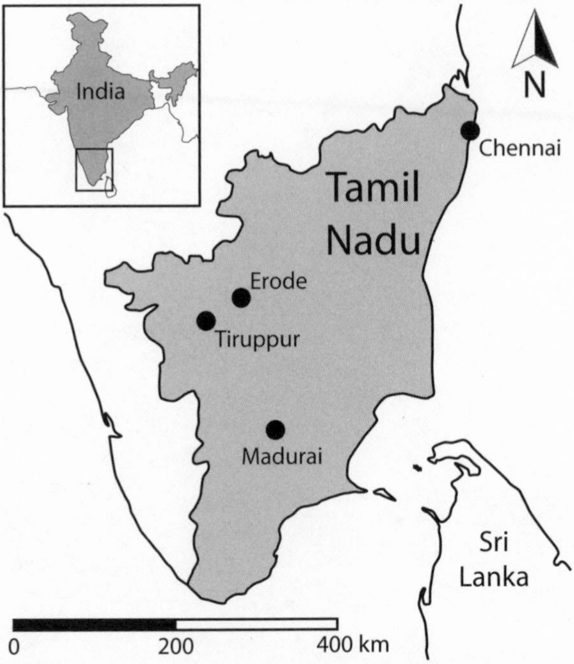

Figure 1. Tamil Nadu, India

ONE

Doing *Style*

"Āmbiḷḷaikki mīsai tān a<u>l</u>aku."

'For a man, a mustache is beauty.'

—TAMIL SAYING, SAID TO MY BARE FACE

I'd never seen a mustache like Anthony's on a college student. Nor have I since. Anthony was a middle-class young man studying in an elite arts and science college in Chennai, the cosmopolitan capital of the south Indian state of Tamil Nadu where I was conducting research (figure 1). The mustache ran across Anthony's upper lip, dipped down at the corners of his mouth, halted at his chin, and then moved outward along his jaw line, stopping midway and curling upward. When I asked Anthony about his mustache, he smirked and simply said "*style*," which was to say that it was, like other objects of youth status (such as brand apparel and English speech), different, attention-grabbing, transgressive, cool. Not everyone felt that way. For some, such a mustache was too much, too ostentatious. It was hostile, arrogant and uppity. It *over*did *style* (*style over-ā paṇṟatu*).

A curling mustache like Anthony's is typically associated with the Madurai region from which he hailed—a sign of traditional, if rugged, adult masculinity.[1] Such an abundant mustache is iconic of power, aggression, dominance and thus of particular authority figures—police officers, soldiers, politicians—and certain dominant martial castes. More generally, for young men like Anthony, healthy mustaches are taken as stereotypical of 'big men' (*periya āḷuṅka*): high-status adults who inhabit and uphold the *mariyātai* ('respect') of "society" and "culture" (*kalāccāram*) and thus command respect and 'prestige' (*kauravam*) themselves.[2]

Anthony's mustache was anomalous because within the gendered age hierarchy that defined his liminal place as a young man (*iḷaiñar*), he was excluded from commanding such adult respectability and authority. Not that most youth like Anthony wanted such a status. As Prabhu, a slight, middle-class college student with only a soft dusting of facial hair, said to me, 'At this age, one shouldn't look like a *periya āḷ* ('big man,' 'adult'). We are youth. What does a college kid need a mustache for? You can't expect us to act like serious people!' As he explained, an adult-looking mustache on a young man is old-fashioned, age- and status-inappropriate, and in the case of a mustache like Anthony's, too rural and aggressive.[3] It would be embarrassing. At the same time, as if to excuse his own (lack of) facial hair, Prabhu noted that not being able to grow any facial hair was also embarrassing. You'd look like a *cinna paiyan*, a 'little boy' or 'child' whose masculinity was deficient. One needed some facial hair.

Young men's faces, then, betrayed exclusion and ambivalence, liminality. But they produced it as well. Many young men preferred "different" grooming styles that navigated the child's smooth skin and the adult's beautiful mustache: a "goatee" (just the chin), a "French beard" (goatee plus mustache), a pencil-thin, sculpted beard (inspired by American hip-hop fashion), a "trim" (five o'clock shadow) or a light beard (both associated with the *rowdy*, or 'thug'), or a clean shave (associated with foreigners, urban elites, and north Indians; only worn by students who could grow sufficient facial hair to shave; cf. Srinivas 1976:152).[4] Such grooming styles reinscribed normative adult masculinity and age hierarchy (by differentiating "mature" hirsute youth from hairless 'little boys'), even as they bracketed such hierarchy with alternate grooming patterns, which, importantly, reached toward other, exterior social worlds and subjects: foreigners, US hip-hoppers, urban elites, north Indians, *rowdies*. Doing so did (or at least tried to do) *style* (*style paṇṟatu*).

But if most youths' facial hair did *style* by implicitly invoking normative adult masculinity while explicitly refashioning it, Anthony's mustache was seemingly identical to what youth *style* otherwise eschewed. And yet, Anthony's mustache also harbored its own metamarks of difference. Anthony kept his whiskers trimmed close and neat, rather than letting them grow out, as if a mere outline of the real thing. But not only was his mustache not quite that of the rugged 'big man'; it was recognizably taken from a recent film, *Singam* (2010), whose rowdy police-officer hero, played by the film star Suriya, has just such a mustache (figure 2).[5]

By reanimating the filmic representation of this manly mustache,

Figure 2. Three mustachioed men: Anthony (2010), Suriya in *Singam* (2010), and a *periya āḷ* from Kambam town in Theni district (2009). The photo of this 'big man' from Kambam was taken on a film set in rural Theni where I was conducting research as an assistant director on the Venkat Prabhu film *Goa* (2010). This man was a "junior artist" ('extra') typecast for his mustache to function as a rural 'big man.' Men with mustaches like this (*mīsaikkāraṅka*, or 'mustache men'), while a widely circulated cinematic stereotype, were also not uncommon in this region of southern Tamil Nadu.

Anthony simultaneously sported and disavowed the very hair on his face, capturing something of its social value even as he put it in quotes. His mustache was and was not the mustaches he was citing. And thus it was and was not his own.[6] As with all *style*, as we will see, to not brook such difference is to risk becoming too similar to what is cited. This is why, in fact, some of Anthony's classmates saw his attempt at *style* as excessive and contrived, as *over style*. It came too close to those hierarchies and inequalities of age, respectability, caste, and urbanity that socially located these youth and kept them liminal and subordinate; it came too close to those hierarchies that these youth, through *style*, attempted to suspend.

preciseness of styling

From Style to *Style*

This book presents an ethnography of the pragmatics and metapragmatics of youth cultural practice in south India. I focus on how practices of *style* encapsulate and produce experiences of hierarchy, liminality, and ambivalence for college students like Anthony and his peers. Navigating a horizon of avoidance and desire, embarrassment and aspiration, intimacy and status, solidarity and individuation, youth cultural practices of *style* are performative of youth subjectivity and sociality, of the not quite and the not yet, a semiotic of difference and deferral cast in material form. This book theorizes this sociological and semiotic dynamic, this push and pull of *style* and its excesses and lacks. I explore how this dynamic underwrites the ways in which youth sociality unfolds in, and constitutes, the peer group and how, in this unfolding, such sociality reaches out to and becomes entangled with the various media forms and social worlds that youth reanimate in their everyday lives: global brands and elite fashion, English and its cosmopolitan ecumene, Tamil film heroes and their film worlds (and mustaches), among others still. Such a study of *style* is an account of the poetics of liminality as the central feature of youth cultural practice and its mass mediation.

This is familiar terrain for scholars of youth culture. Foundational work on youth subcultures by the Birmingham school of cultural studies in the 1970s also analyzed what they called "style," theorizing how youth subcultural styles expressed, and symbolically resolved, the larger class and age conflicts of postwar Britain (Hebdige 1979; Cohen 1993[1972]; Clarke et al. 1997[1975]). In this vein of work, "style" had two senses, describing the aesthetic forms and social practices linked to particular subcultural identities ("punk," "mod," etc.) while at the same time analytically drawing these diverse subcultural styles together as part of the more general phenomenon of youth cultural expression under conditions of capitalism. The analysis of style in both its senses was part of British cultural studies' attempt to recover an expressive youth politics of resistance that both demonstrated the authentic response of working-class cultures to capitalism and drew out the ideological and institutional processes by which class inequality was glossed over and naturalized.

In this book, my interest concerns something different, if uncannily so: *style*, a particular local discourse among youth in contemporary Tamil Nadu. Neither a gloss for an aestheticized subculture nor an analytic to reveal class reproduction and resistance, *style* is an ethnographic datum, a term used by Tamil youth to typify a diverse congeries of objects and activities associated with youth sociality and status, aesthetics and value. My point of departure in this book, then, is how youths' discourses and practices of *style* reflexively explicate and intervene in their own life worlds and social projects. As an ethnographic object, *style* provides the book's analytic entry into the pragmatics of these life worlds and social projects. My use of the word "pragmatics" here is important, for less a question of the expressive or ideological aspects of youth culture—that is, how we might treat *style* as allegorically reflecting something of the larger political economy (say, post-1991 liberalization) and thus needing to be read or decoded by the analyst (Nakassis 2013d:245–46, 266–67)—my interest is how *style* acts in the world as a kind of performative, constituting youth culture in its various manifestations.

The term "*style*," importantly then, is not (quite) my own. It is a youth word, concern, and tool, just as it is, as the analytic lens of this book, a borrowing from my friends' everyday talk about status, value, and aesthetics in the college and beyond. The term is not quite theirs either though. For them too, it is a borrowing. But while the etymon of *style*—or *style-u* as it is typically pronounced in colloquial Tamil, with an epenthetic, or "enunciative," *-u* [ɯ] appended—is English, the site of its borrowing is to be found elsewhere. In fact, it is to be found in multiple elsewheres. Most famously and visibly, *style* invokes the so-called Superstar of Tamil cinema: the "King of *Style*," Rajinikanth. As I discuss in chapters 6 and 7, Rajinikanth is an important source for *style*, its veritable embodiment and origin, its definition made performative flesh. The word *style*, as far as my friends knew, was first used in Tamil to talk about Rajinikanth. *Style*, however, is more than Rajinikanth, and acts of *style* draw on many other sites of borrowing: global brands (chapters 2–3), music-television VJs (chapter 5), and other film actors (like Surya, as we saw above), among other sites.[7]

Always marked in my text by italics, *style* cites some other social imaginary while being necessarily marked as distinct from it, like a quotation that repeats another's words while framing those words as not quite themselves anymore and not quite those of their current animator. This does not mean, of course, that *style* is exogenous to youth practices, that *style*'s origins, material forms, and logics are only ever to be found elsewhere. Quite the opposite. Much of the work of the book is to show how *style* is an irreducibly local phenomenon only ever analyzable relative to the particular contexts and concerns of the youth for whom it is consequential, even as those acts reach outward and away from their here-and-now. As a form of reflexive practice about the liminality and ambivalence of youth by youth, *style* performatively brings such liminality and ambivalence into being, instating modes of youth subjectivity and sociality that radiate outward from youths' peer groups, entangling, most importantly for this study, the very producers of the social forms that young people take up and reanimate in doing *style*. I call the semiotic form of this performativity "citationality."

Theoretical and methodological concerns drive my close attention to the reflexivity and citationality of *style*. This book details how the liminal phenomenology and citational semiotics of *stylish* youth practices come to be manifest in particular material and textual forms, a process of becoming and (de)stabilization mediated by the reflexivity of those very practices *and* by the entanglements that such practices forge with other social projects like garment design and manufacture, music-television production, and film production.[8] In order to capture the tangled relationships that *style* reflexively mediates and materializes, this book moves between research with young people in colleges and research with those involved in the design, production, and circulation of the *stylish* forms that populate youth peer groups. I focus on how "producers" of ("counterfeit") brand garments (retailers, distributors, wholesalers, designers, and manufacturers in Madurai, Chennai, Tiruppur, and Erode; chapters 2–3), televised Tamil-English speech (music-television VJs and producers in Chennai; chapters 4–5), and commercial Tamil film (actors, directors, producers, and other technicians in Chennai; chapters 6–7) come to be entangled with youth "consumers" of such forms through the idiom of *style*. By situating *style* on both sides of the screen and commodity chain, I show how the dynamics of doing *style* in the college perforate the media object—shaping its genesis, and hence its very materiality and textuality—and, in doing so, prefigure and invite its citational use by youth to do *style*.[9]

In tacking between these different sites, this book builds on and attempts to articulate various literatures that have theorized the relationship between youth practice and mass media. On the one hand, this book looks to scholars who have shown how, under conditions of late capitalism, contemporary media and marketing practices have shifted their focus to representing, targeting, and addressing youth demographics (e.g., Frank 1998; Mazzarella 2003:215–49; Lukács 2010)—that is, the "production" of mass media. On the other hand, this book draws on scholars who have demonstrated the creative ways in which young people engage with media objects (e.g., Hebdige 1979; Bucholtz 2002; 2011; Weiss 2002; Liechty 2003; de Boek and Honwana 2005; Lukose 2009; Newell 2012)—that is, the "reception" or "consumption" of mass media. In traversing such approaches, I suggest that the issue is not simply the necessity of presenting complementary points of view on the "same" media object (i.e., its production and reception). Rather, my aim is to underscore that the primary ethnographic datum about mass mediation is the complex *entanglement* that media coordinate between multiple social actors as they come to mutually (if only partially) orient themselves to the material and semiotic forms that, by this very orientation, they bring into being. As I show, such a view of mass mediation, ironically perhaps, requires us to decenter—and to attend to how the citationality of *style* decenters—those very forms. Focusing on this entanglement requires us to analytically bracket, and thus put in question, the stability and coherence of things like brands, mediatized English, and film texts and instead focus on empirical moments when those things are themselves bracketed, suspended, and deformed. Doing so, I suggest, offers a fresh perspective on the study of mass mediation and youth culture.

In what follows in this chapter, I contextualize how liminality and social hierarchy were experienced by the young people with whom I lived and spent time, focusing on the ambivalent practices that reflexively register and performatively enact that liminality. As I show, the citationality of youth practices of *style* emerges out of and responds to experiences of liminality and hierarchy, even as these practices produce and transform such experiences. I pay particular attention to the role of the college in framing such experiences and practices and in rendering them particularly acute. In order to set up this discussion, I first situate my ethnographic research with college students, locating the institutions in which they matriculated within a wider set of historical shifts that have changed the face of higher education in contemporary India. I then turn to an ethnographic account of how the college—as social imaginary, institution, and space of social activity—shapes the peer group, a site of sociality marked by a fundamental tension between, on the one hand, the transgression of adult norms through acts of *stylish* individuation and, on the other hand, modes of intimacy and solidarity that problematize those very *stylish* acts. It is this particular ambivalence and tension, I argue, that shapes the phenomenology and semiotics of doing *style*, making acts of *style* take on a particular "double-voiced" (Bakhtin 1982), or citational, form. Finally, the chapter discusses how the citationality of *style* entangles the media forms (and subjects) that youth reanimate in their own peer-group activities, in turn rendering those forms (and subjects) citational.

The Colleges Where I Worked

Conducted from 2007 to 2009, with follow-up trips in 2010, 2011, and 2014, my research with college students took place in five predominantly English-medium colleges in two cities, Madurai and Chennai.[10] Madurai is a city in the south of Tamil Nadu comprising about one million residents (with the greater metropolitan area nearing 1.5 million).[11] Known for its numerous temples and its "pure" Tamil, it is often described as a big village due to the amount of in-migration from neighboring rural and peri-urban areas and its relatively conservative public culture. In Madurai, I conducted research in three colleges: a historically elite, but now perhaps best described as semielite, coeducational, but largely men's, college founded by Protestant missionaries in the late nineteenth century (approximately 2,800 students, undergraduate and postgraduate); a semielite women's college founded by an American missionary and educator in the late 1940s (approximately 3,000 students); and a reputable coeducational college founded by a Hindu industrialist in the 1940s that, relative to the other two colleges, had a relatively greater amount of lower-middle-class students and students from rural backgrounds (approximately 2,200 students).[12] All three colleges were "autonomous," which is to say that they had the right to maintain a degree of curricular and administrative autonomy from government universities, including the right to create "self-financing" departments (i.e., departments solely funded by relatively expensive student tuitions) for new, in-demand courses.[13]

In the coeducational Christian college, I lived in two "hostels" (or dormitories) over the 2007–2008 academic year. I first stayed in a hostel for undergraduate students enrolled in self-financing departments and roomed with two Christian third-year students: Stephan, a hip and fashionable, near-fluent English-speaking young man from Kodaikanal (a "hill station" to the northwest of Madurai), and Sebastian, a relatively more conservative young man from a village in Tirunelveli district (about 200 kilometers south of Madurai) whose English was relatively basic. After three months in the self-financing hostel, for the rest of the year, I lived in a hostel for undergraduate students enrolled in "aided" departments (i.e., departments whose costs were subsidized by the government and thus whose tuitions were relatively cheap). I roomed with two first-year Hindu students: Yuvaraj, a quiet but friendly young man from Dindugul (a medium-sized town north of Madurai), and Shanmugam, an even quieter young man from Devakottai (a small town east of Madurai) who spent much of his time practicing hip-hop dancing, at which he excelled. All four students would have described themselves as middle class, but by my observations, Yuvaraj and Stephan came from relatively more affluent families. All four were native Tamil speakers with the exception of Stephan who, while fluent in Tamil, came from a Malayalam ethnolinguistic background. In this college and in the coeducational Hindu college, I spent time on campus with both hostel students and "day scholars" (commuting students), went on outings (to movie theaters, shops, restaurants, parks, bars, and other colleges' "culturals" competitions), attended classes, and conducted interviews with them. In the aided hostel of the coeducational Christian college, I screened films and music-television programs for students, which were followed by group discussions. In the women's college, while I enjoyed comparatively limited access to student life (more on this below), I was able to spend time with students on campus and conduct semiformal interviews. I also screened films and held discussions with students afterward. In all the colleges, I interviewed administrators and professors.

In Chennai (also known by its colonial name, Madras), a city of 4.7 million inhabitants (with the larger metropolitan area nearing 8.7 million), I conducted research in two colleges during the 2008–2009 academic year: an elite autonomous Catholic college founded in the 1920s (approximately 7,000 students) and a historically prestigious government college founded by a Hindu philanthropist in the mid-nineteenth century, the student body of which is now predominantly working class and lower caste (approximately 4,500 students). Certain departments of both colleges were coeducational, though the Catholic college had more female students than the government college, which was almost exclusively male at the undergraduate level.[14] The Catholic college had the most affluent student body of the five colleges that I worked in, and the government college had the least. I stayed in the Catholic college's hostel, which housed both aided and self-financing students, for five months of the academic year. I lived very briefly with an upper-middle-class young man from the northeastern state of Bihar and then with Sam, a gregarious, upwardly mobile, middle-class young man from Salem (a small city in the northwest of Tamil Nadu). Sam was a native speaker of Tamil, and he had a relatively strong command of English. As in Madurai, in both colleges, I went to classes, spent time with day scholars and hostel students on and off campus, and interviewed students, administrators, and professors. I also accompanied the third-year students of one coeducational department from the Catholic college on their weeklong "college tour" (field trip). In all these colleges, while I interacted with both undergraduate and postgraduate students, I predominantly write about undergraduate students, given that the dynamics I describe in the book were most pronounced among them. In addition to the students in these Madurai and Chennai colleges, I also selectively conducted research with students from other colleges in the state as well as with youth and adults who did not attend college.

During the time of my research, all the colleges that I worked in were adjusting to significant, and in many ways deleterious, changes brought on by the privatization of higher education, a process that began in Tamil Nadu in the late 1970s and intensified with the liberalization of the Indian economy in the 1980s and 1990s (Sebastian 2008; Tilak 2013a). These changes, which I discuss in the next section, have shaped the shifting forms of inequality and heterogeneity that mark the student bodies of the colleges where I worked, providing a fertile, and fraught, ground for the complex dynamics of doing *style* that are the focus of this book.

The Changing Face of Higher Education in India

The first modern colleges in India were established under colonial rule as institutions for British Orientalist scholarship about India, scholarship that would help the East India Company (and later the British Raj) rule indigenous subjects by their own customs and laws.[15] With the anti-Orientalist turn in the early nineteenth century, higher education in India became increasingly, if contentiously, figured as a tool to create a loyal class of elite Indians through modern English education (Basu 1991; Srivastava 2003; Chandra 2012), "English" here comprising the English language (chapter 4), Western canon and "modern" epistemologies (Seth 2007), as well as an anglicized habitus including, for example, British fashions of dress (Tarlo 1996; chapter 2). This early phase of higher education was unabashedly, if not unproblematically, elitist (largely availed by urban, upper-class and upper-caste men, predominantly Brahmin; see Fuller and Narasimhan 2014:61–89), even if the university system was understood to be open and secular in principle (Béteille 2010). Higher education was the access point to coveted civil service jobs, and in contrast to more recent patterns discussed below, this period saw relatively large growth in arts and science colleges with little growth in professional and engineering colleges (Basu 1991).

With India's national independence in 1947, higher education was increasingly framed by the mandate to expand its demographic base by class, caste, and gender,[16] largely through reservation policies (though caste reservations had already been in place in the Madras Presidency by the 1920s, given colonial concerns about Brahmin monopolization of education and civil service posts and, relatedly, the emergence of an indigenous, non-Brahmin movement).[17] Even if higher education remained a bastion for elites of various kinds, guided by a Nehruvian developmentalist dispensation to "uplift" the nation, the democratization of higher education in the postindependence period did lead to both the expansion of higher education (in terms of number of students and institutions) and its demographic diversification.

If higher education during colonial rule was oriented toward the colonial apparatus and its civilizing project and if, in the postindependence period, it was oriented toward modernizing the nation through "socialistic" development and democratization, since at least the 1980s, but in particular since the 2000s, higher education has come to be increasingly oriented toward the "global knowledge economy" (Fernandes 2006; Chanana 2013[2007]). With liberalization, the growth of Information Technology (IT) and related private sectors—particularly in south Indian cities such as Bangalore, Hyderabad, and Chennai—has led to a seemingly bottomless demand for engineering, applied science, and commerce degrees. To meet this demand, new institutions—private engineering and other technical and professional colleges (Fuller and Narasimhan 2006), private arts and science colleges, and "parallel colleges" and other private tutoring and certificate centers (Fernandes 2006:96–99, 131–33; Lukose 2009)—have proliferated at astonishing rates, while existing institutions have attempted to keep pace by expanding their offerings.[18] Overall, this demand has resulted in decreased enrollments in arts and science colleges of those belonging to what the professors and administrators where I worked called the "creamy layer": elites who, in the past, would have leveraged their liberal arts education to secure coveted civil service employment. Today this creamy layer predominates in elite engineering and other professional institutions, many of which are privately run (Fernandes 2006:88ff.; Fuller and Narasimhan 2014:93–96). As a result of this shift, arts and science colleges overall have seen increased enrollments of working-class students, lower-caste students, first-generation students, and students from less-prestigious Tamil-medium schooling backgrounds.[19]

Within arts and science colleges, demand has significantly grown for relatively more expensive self-financing courses in computer science, commerce, and natural sciences—courses that can lead to master's degrees in IT or business and jobs in IT-related fields or multinational corporations—and, to a lesser degree, courses in English literature, which are seen by some to offer advantage in accessing call-center and other multinational corporate job opportunities (LaDousa 2014). This shift has been to the detriment of other departments within these colleges. Because admissions to these arts and science colleges are by department and because, by and large, parents and other elder kin choose the departments to which students apply by speculating on future job prospects, departments that are seen as less likely to get one a job in the neoliberal, white-collar workforce—such as history, sociology, Tamil, philosophy, and economics—have suffered massively in enrollments. Most students joined these departments simply because they could not get into other departments or other colleges (Annamalai 2004:190). The result is that students from privileged class, caste, and regional backgrounds were more likely to be found in (self-financing) courses like commerce, computer science, and the like, while first-generation students, rural students, and lower-class and lower-caste students were more likely to be found in (aided) arts and sciences courses that were considered to lack "market value." These hierarchies mirror linguistic differences as well, with students in more prestigious colleges and departments being more likely to have been schooled (or schooled for longer) in English-medium schools, while less prestigious colleges and departments have more Tamil-medium students.

As a result of such changes, the colleges where I worked were heterogeneous social spaces that were internally crosscut by various axes of social difference (class, caste, region, language, department, funding type).[20]

This, in turn, has created overlaps *across* arts and science colleges, making the various colleges where I worked in some ways more alike overall than they would have been in the past, even as their student bodies were perhaps more unlike those of a generation or two ago.

The students with whom I socialized, and on whom I focus discussion in this book, were located, in one way or another, somewhere in between the extremes of these intersecting axes of social difference and inequality. Just as important, their peer groups had their centers of gravity somewhere in the middle of these continua of class, caste, and language. They were neither the most elite nor the poorest, neither the most nor the least fluent in English; rather, they comprised a range of class positions and linguistic fluencies. They were always mixed in terms of caste and community.

This in-betweenness wasn't simply a descriptive, demographic fact. It was a reflexively experienced state of ambivalence about one's place within such hierarchies. This ambivalence was all the more acute, of course, because the college institution promised class and linguistic mobility, because the college plotted a trajectory toward one privileged pole of these tangled hierarchies—the urban, English-speaking, (upper-) middle-class, "modern" subject—that was *not* who these youth and their peers in their here-and-now could claim to be.

My focus on the middle is important to underscore because the dynamics of *style* that concern this book are most acute and visible among such youth. The tensions and ambivalence of their liminality were the most experientially palpable, and thus the most likely to take citational form in acts of and metadiscourse about *style*. Indeed, the discourse and practice of *style* was of less importance for students in the least-prestigious departments of the government college, who tended to be the least affluent (though they too did and talked about *style*),[21] and it was near absent in the rarefied circles of elite, English-fluent students in the most prestigious, self-financing departments in the Catholic college, for whom *style* (in the sense used, and in the ways performed, by other students) would be considered gauche and "*local*" (a term denoting low status that I discuss in chapter 2). As a result of this focus on the middle, much of my discussion centers on the commonalities across the colleges rather than the extremes or differences, though I occasionally take them up for comparative reference.

Finally, it is important to highlight that the anchor of my discussion is young men. This is for a number of reasons, not the least of which is my relatively restricted access to female students and their peer groups as compared with the intimacies and proximity I had with young men, as noted above. But more than this, though not unrelated to it, the dynamics of *style* and the very cultural category of youth that *style* attempted to perform were most elaborated and visible among young men. As elsewhere (Liechty 2003:233–34; Comaroff and Comaroff 2005; Jeffrey 2010), the figure of youth is masculinized in Tamil Nadu. In popular Tamil imaginaries, the category of youth is stereotypically associated with transgressiveness, ostentation, exteriority, self-centeredness, and the publicly displayed individual body. These associations are central to the pragmatics of *style*, and they are resolutely problematic for normative femininity.

This is not to say, of course, that *style* is exclusively the domain of young men. As numerous conversations and friendships with young college women showed me, they did talk about and do *style*, transgressing normative bounds and experimenting with new subjectivities through dress, language, and film, among other media. College was, in fact, a privileged space for young women to do so, even more so than for young men, whose public movements were not as restricted and whose behaviors were not as contained by the patriarchal kin group and its proxies as women's. What it is to say, however, is that what *style* presupposes and does is much more likely to be policed and violently censured for young women by both their female and male peers and by their kin and college administrators who, given increasing coeducation driven by privatization, felt it necessary to ensure patriarchal norms of public, feminine comportment in the college. The problematics of *style* for women are, as I discuss in more detail in chapters 2 and 6, a function of the way in which the control and containment of the young woman's body, and her sexuality more particularly, underwrite the patriarchal economies and hierarchies of men's status and respectability that *style* plays with, undermines, and refashions. This makes the stakes of young women's *style* more extreme and thus makes *style*, in certain ways, less visible and less likely to be (felicitously) performed by young women. Or at least, it makes *style* manifest in other, relatively less sexualizing modalities (such as English use, as suggested in chapter 4).

Liminality and Youth

As noted above, the college students with whom I worked experienced an acute sense of being in between, an experience conditioned by multiple axes of social difference and inequality that came together in the college. While in various chapters of the book, I discuss particular manifestations, experiences, and productions of hierarchies of class, language, and gender—the most important of which for *style*, perhaps, is class—below I focus on the relationship between age hierarchy and liminality precisely because age was the predominant idiom within which such various in-betweens took shape and were experienced and expressed. Which is to say that the various sociodemographic axes of difference that organized students and their ambivalent expectations of the future were wrapped up in the very cultural category of youth, that liminal subject position that *style* performed and attempted to open for inhabitance—that is, performatively bring into being.[22]

To say that young people are liminal is perhaps to state the obvious. In contemporary Tamil Nadu, as elsewhere, the age category of youth (denoted in Tamil as "*iḷamai paruvam*," "*vāliba vayasu*," "youth," or "teen-age") is construed as a transitory status in the lifecycle.[23] Youth are neither children nor adults, neither dependents nor quite independent. They are not fully subordinate to adult authority, as are children, yet they are also excluded from institutions and economies of adult authority and status, often located in nonpermanent jobs or, as for the students that I worked with, educational institutions like colleges. Indeed, as I discuss below, the college is perhaps the liminal institution par excellence in Tamil Nadu (as it is elsewhere): a time and space set apart that affords the possibility to be liminal and to produce liminality, and thus youth.

While we typically think of liminality, and hence the category of youth, as being in between sociodemographic categories, times, or spaces, in my discussion, liminality encompasses much more. For me, liminality is a reflexive orientation to the experience of being beholden to multiple mandates at the same time, which is to say that if liminality takes flesh in and through a particular configuration of space, time, and sociality (a Bakhtinian chronotope of youth, as it were), it is crucially because of young people's reflexive attunement to the ambivalences and contradictions that place them in that very sociospatiotemporal order of things. Liminality is, in this sense, a production and an achievement of a particular kind of reflexive, affective stance to the in-between and in-transit or, as I would put it more generally, to multiplicity and contradiction. Liminality is as much about attempts to act on social time-spaces as it is about attempts to act in social time and space. I am particularly interested in liminality, then, as a relationship between seeming incommensurables, as the experience of opposing social forces and discourses as they are encountered by the subject (chapter 2), of the necessity to be or not be more than one thing at once. Sometimes this is framed and experienced as a trajectory in the lifecycle but not always.[24]

Below I discuss two ways in which such liminality manifests itself for and is produced by the college youth with whom I worked and lived: first, as an experience of age hierarchy that prompts forms of transgression, including acts of *style*, that attempt to open up alternate spaces of youth aesthetics, value, status, and authority and, second, as an experience of age hierarchy that prompts forms of egalitarian sociality that problematize such transgressions and acts of *style*, even as such forms of sociality make acts of *style* possible. In the first case, liminality is produced as the necessity to be at once neither an adult nor a child and thus, simultaneously, to be *like* both. In the second, liminality is produced as the necessity to simultaneously do *style* without doing either too much or too little *style*. These intersecting liminalities set the stage for my discussion of citationality and mass mediation in later sections of this chapter as well as for understanding the more general dynamics of *style* that are at issue in the rest of the book.

Hierarchy and *Style*

The students with whom I worked experienced and produced themselves as youth through their relationship to the forms of authority to which they were subordinate and excluded, to what they sometimes simply referred to as "society" (or in Tamil, "*samūkam*" or "*samutāyam*"): one's kin and caste group and, more generally, high-status male adults ('big men') who set the rules for legitimate social interaction.[25] Such students performed youth and thus produced youth status through acts that transgressed adult authority and respectability (*mariyātai*)—in particular, middle-class norms of respectability aligned with the college institution—by availing and instating alternate normativities, socialities, gendered subjectivities, aesthetics, and values. While *style* was not the only way this was done, it was one of its predominant idioms.

The texture of everyday college life was filled with performances of transgression on and off the campus. For young men, this included horsing around in the college canteen, mocking teachers when they were out of earshot, writing graffiti on classroom and bathroom walls, engaging in provocative youth fashion, skipping class and getting drunk, smoking cigarettes outside of the college, fighting with rival cliques, teasing and romancing female classmates, or hopping the college wall after curfew to catch the "second show" (the last film screening of the night; cf. Willis 1977). Such transgressions were often direct reactions to what students felt to be the excessive rules and restrictions of the college (or "society" more generally), the way the college treated them like 'little boys' (*cinna pasaṅka*), curbing their freedom and assuming that they weren't "mature" enough to think or fend for themselves; they were, they insisted.[26] And they demonstrated this to themselves and their peers through such transgressions.[27]

By transgressing norms of adult authority, *decency*, and respectability—which is to say the very basis upon which age hierarchy subordinated and excluded students as not yet and not quite—students reinscribed the very coordinates of the hierarchy that they attempted to suspend and stand apart from through their transgressions. Acts of *style* perspectivally divided students into 'big men' and 'little boys.' Students who didn't do *style*, who didn't transgress by disregarding hostel rules and jumping the wall, who didn't smoke and drink or display flashy Western fashions were considered by those who did to be 'little boys' who were too afraid of the hand of authority, who didn't have the "maturity" or *tairiyam* ('boldness,' 'courage') to skirt authority, do what they felt like, or assert their own alternate authority and sense of aesthetics and value. At the same time, acts that demonstrated such "maturity," importantly if contradictorily, were understood positively as childlike in their conspicuous lack of seriousness. As Prabhu noted at the outset of the chapter, one can't expect youth to act like serious people, like 'big men'!

For those typified by others as 'little boys,' the same discourse of maturity could be inverted: what about jumping the hostel wall after hours makes one mature? All that it would accomplish would be getting them in trouble. Acting as if they were a bunch of 'big men' (*periya āḷuṅka*), such youth would only manage to show how childish (*cinnappuḷḷettanam*) they really were. There was a limit to transgression (a statement all would agree on, even if they disagreed on where that limit was located) and a limit to *style*.

What is important to notice is that it is precisely in relation to adult normativities of authority and age hierarchy that youth "maturity," and hence social status, is calibrated and negotiated among students in and between their peer groups (for indeed, peer groups formed around emergent local norms about what was considered to be acceptable deviation from adult authority). This is accomplished through the experience and production of a double mandate: to be simultaneously neither a child nor an adult and thus *like* both a child (playful, unserious) and an adult (bold, independent, authoritative).[28] A sociologically grounded experience of age and generational difference prompts productions of liminality as the felt necessity to be both and neither, to be multiple. Doing *style* does just this. And it does so as a reflexive commentary on and intervention into the very hierarchies that it uncannily reinscribes as the coordinates of youth status, sociality, and subjectivity.

These dynamics took a particularly visible and elaborated form within the college, a "modern" space that was spatially, temporally, and socially set off from the everyday experiences of hierarchy outside of the college that underwrote what these youth called "society." For administrators, professors, hostel "wardens," and especially for students, the college was supposed to be a space for experimentation with new freedoms and modes of being in the world (Parameswaran 2001; 2002; Lukose 2009).[29] (Hence my friends' annoyance when they felt they weren't being accorded such freedoms.) In college, students could do all the things that could not always be easily done at home, in the space and presence of elder kin and neighbors: speak in new languages, dress fashionably, romance and flirt, roam around town, and the like.[30] This made college a place for novelty, transgression, and play. At the same time, this freedom had its limits inscribed by the college itself. Administrators, professors, and hostel wardens also saw their role as a surrogate (if altered) patriarchal authority. Even as the college kept adulthood and the seriousness of the future in abeyance, it also brought both closer by attempting to socialize and discipline students to the *decent* middle-class subjectivity that, it was hoped, would afford students mobility in the postcollege, white-collar economy. The college, not unlike the peer group (as I discuss below), bracketed "society," even as it reinscribed and stood in for it. And through that doubling, the college afforded its students a space for transgression that was not quite transgression, a place to enact youth subjectivities in ways that allowed college, and thus adult, authority to be suspended, if only for a time. This doubling allowed for, and in a sense invited, *style*. It called for students' active production of transgressive experiences of liminality, for the need to assert their distance from an adult order of things by keeping it close, but not too close.

Hierarchy and *Over Style*

Youth practices in the college didn't simply repudiate or bracket adult respectability and propriety through cheeky facial hair or late-night escapades. They also turned on engaging and bracketing the very idea of hierarchy itself, on attempting to instate forms of egalitarian sociality that suspended and inverted, if only temporarily, the hierarchies of kinship, caste, class, and age and generation that shaped the very experience and production of youth as an inhabitable subjectivity (Osella and Osella 1998; 2004:245–46; Nisbett 2007). This came out in a conversation about caste with Vignesh, a student at the Madurai college where I lived. Vignesh explained, with conviction, that in the college, caste was not observed.

Caste was something that happened out there in villages or back then in the past but not here and now in the college. In the college, one was free to socialize with whomever one wanted, regardless of class, caste, or religious community. He didn't even know his friends' castes, he insisted. Without missing a beat but with an air of regret, Vignesh went on to say that he fully expected to have to orient himself to caste after college and after marriage. 'Growing up' meant going 'into' caste. There was no choice, he noted, 'Because that is how society is here. It makes you observe caste. After marriage, we all have to go inside society/caste' ("*Kalyāṇattukku appuṟam samūkattukkuḷḷē pōkaṇum*"). Whether or not Vignesh's account of caste in the college or postmarriage life is accurate, he understood himself, as a college youth, to be outside of caste and adult "society." And this imagined exteriority to caste and community structured his social interactions in the college. As he noted, and as I also observed, it was generally proscribed and in bad taste to explicitly align with or even to talk about caste with college peers (Lukose 2009:177). Invidious distinctions of caste and community, to say nothing of class (chapters 2, 6) and linguistic difference (both of which were surrounded by this very same disavowing discourse; chapter 4), were always deferred: never us, here, now.

Of course, caste, community, class, and linguistic difference did matter in these youths' lives. They pervaded their home lives, their ability to move through public space, and even the college campus itself, particularly at the level of administrative politics.[31] Precisely because of this fact, such distinctions had to be disavowed and kept at bay through practices that acted *as if* such distinctions didn't matter. If and when distinctions of caste, class, religion, or language inserted themselves, it was always as a disruption of what these young men and women understood as how youth sociality in the college—a "modern" institution—ought to work (Jeffrey 2010). Such hierarchies were to be suspended, a suspension that was the very foundation of peer-group sociality.

This suspension of hierarchy was also enabled by the ways in which the college organized students into year cohorts by department and hostel, irrespective of age—that key principle of respect and authority in Tamil Nadu.[32] Year cohorts (for undergraduate students, first years, second years, and third years),[33] in effect, neutralized age difference within and across years, hierarchically ranking year cohorts by the relative relation of "juniors" and "seniors" (i.e., those of lower or higher years). Such ranked cohorts were formed in a number of ways. They were inscribed and produced by hazing practices in which seniors "ragged" their juniors (chapter 2). Further, with very few exceptions, one did not take classes with students of other years or other departments. Within hostels, one normally lived with one's year mates. As a result, students' intimate social circles were formed precisely by the fault lines of inequality and hierarchy that shot through the college (most important, year, but also department, funding type, and in certain colleges, hostel), exteriorizing such hierarchies as the outer boundary of the otherwise relatively flattened, age-neutralized peer group. As subsequent chapters show, it is precisely where such differences were not institutionally flattened—as with class and language—that one found the most interactional work to level them. This is not to say that, as with caste distinctions, such inequalities of language or class (or hostel or department) did not cut across peer groups. Rather, it is to stress that the college, as an ideologically invested and institutionally organized space, tended to bracket such hierarchies as the basis for peer-group sociality, conditioning the ways in which and with whom youth interacted (and thus did or did not do *style* with or for). This was despite, or rather because of, the fact that students experienced the college as a heterogeneous space shot through with difference.

Youth peer groups are spaces of intense intimacy, reciprocity, and peer pressure. Such intimacy and solidarity is expressed through the sharing of food, words of abuse and fictive kinterms (see below), class notes, clothing, cigarettes, and other kinds of property, as well as through physical displays of homosociality—rough housing, holding hands, running fingers through each other's hair, and sleeping in the same beds—all of which are otherwise, outside the college, normatively contained within the caste and kin group. Youth peer groups bracket and transgress these lines by figuratively replicating them within the peer group, reanimating and suspending forms of caste and kin intimacy and solidarity by recasting friendship through them (Nakassis 2013d; 2014; cf. Osella and Osella 2000a:230; Alex 2008:535). Adults often find such physical and linguistic intimacy disturbing, even insolent, precisely because it crosses the boundaries drawn by "society" (Osella and Osella 1998; Nisbett 2007).

The important point here is that sociality in the college is founded on the bracketing and reinscription, and thus transformation, of forms of hierarchy and that in this case, such experiences and engagements with hierarchy organize the peer group around a tension: on the one hand, the peer group affords—and in certain cases, demands—individuating status-raising acts of *style* that transgress norms of adult authority, respectability, and propriety by figurating them in alternate forms; on the other hand, the peer group demands deference to its own alternate norms, norms that require eschewing precisely the social differences that the former affordance/demand portends. The peer group comprises a centrifugal and centripetal push and pull (cf. Simmel 1998[1904]), a productive tension between egalitarianism and hierarchy, solidarity and differentiation, intimacy and individuation, and between *style* and its lacks and excesses—*style* that is *over*, that tries too hard, that shows off too much or not enough. The peer group makes *style* possible, for it provides youth with the breathing room necessary for its display (for in other contexts and for other audiences, *style* is likely to be policed and even proscribed by higher-status individuals), even as it makes doing *style* problematic (for every *stylish* act risks being seen as invidiously reinscribing hierarchical difference, and thus tipping into *over style* by acting too much like a 'big man,' by coming too close to what one's acts should only ever figuratively represence). Remember that Anthony's *Singam* 'stache was not simply seen by some of his peers as hokey. By being too similar to what it cited, it was also seen as arrogant and uppity, as presuming he was a bigger man than he was, as showing off too much. Teasing, gossip, social ostracization, and even physical altercation were all modes of dealing with the excesses of *style*, of continually reconstituting the peer group as a relatively egalitarian space, a space itself opened by the suspension of those perduring modes of adult status and respectability from which youth were excluded and by which they were subordinate.

There is a kind of performative contradiction to doing *style*, then, precisely because the quality of excess, of being *over* is immanent in and implied by *style* as a mode of ostentatious self-differentiation and individuation. As this book's various chapters show, in order for *style* to be felicitous, it must hedge on itself, constantly mitigating its interpretation as *over*. As Gregory Bateson (1972:182) pointed out in a different context, there must always be some metacommunicative framing that mitigates the descent of play fighting into actual melee or, as in this case, that mitigates self-individuation devolving into invidious hierarchy. Caught and constituted in this dialectic, doing *style* is required, to invoke Georg Simmel's (1984[1909]:151) reflections on flirtation, to split itself into a "playful approach and withdrawal," to be a "tentative turning toward something on which the shadow of its own denial already falls." Doing *style* is required to be citational.

Citationality and *Style*

Here, then, are two intersecting liminalities that emerge from college students' reflexive experiences of their sociological status as youth: the double mandate to simultaneously not be an adult and not be a child yet be like both *and* to do *style* without doing too much or too little *style* (and thus tentatively resolve the former mandate). These liminalities entail what performance theorist Richard Schechner (1985:111–13) refers to as "not [. . .], not not [. . .]" or the "twiceness" of the "as if"—that is, what happens when something or someone is beholden to two or more mandates that are not easily resolvable to each other but that willy-nilly must be (or must be attempted to be). Here liminality manifests itself as multiplicity harnessed in a unified, if internally complex, act. In Anthony's case, for example, it manifested as the very hair on his face—a grooming *style* that figured him as being not and not not a child and not and not not an adult, not and not not a film star and not and not not a rural 'big man.' These interlocked liminalities and multiplicities, as I show throughout the book, inflect nearly every domain of youth practice in the college, which is to say that such liminalities give college youth culture, and the very category of youth, in Tamil Nadu its particular ethnographic texture.

The semiotic form of such liminality is citational. Citations manage the necessity to speak with two voices in the same breath, to inhabit numerous roles and identities at once, to abide by multiple, potentially contradictory mandates or points of view simultaneously. Citations enable the "playful approach and withdrawal" of flirtation, as Simmel puts it. Like canonical citations such as quotations, citational acts re-present some other social form or discursive event through one's own voice but keep it in quotes, simultaneously reanimating and bracketing what is cited as not quite one's own (Nakassis 2013b).

Take, for example, youths' address practices, a central mode by which youth mark and create intimacy and solidarity in their peer groups (Nakassis 2014). As noted above, college students' speech is peppered with kinterms for male cross kin and affines. In Madurai and Chennai, terms like *māms* and *māpps* (derived from kinterms for mother's brother and brother-in-law/cross cousin, respectively) are *stylish* ways of addressing friends. Such "fictive," or tropic (Agha 2007), kinterms invoke in the here-and-now of their utterance an elsewhere, an absent kinship, even as they keep it in abeyance. They cite kinship. The *style* of such citational kinterms turns on their nonnormative, even transgressive quality—that is, that they are "incorrect" uses, that they disregard (some of) the kinship norms and affects that they invoke, bringing kinship into the peer group even as they keep it at arm's length. The citationality of such address practices materializes the very liminality of youth sociality in the college, articulating the fact that students are not kin and yet are not not kin, that they share intimacies reserved for certain cross kin relations (in distinction, tellingly, to the relatively hierarchical patriline) in a space otherwise predicated on the absence and negation of kinship logics and hierarchies—namely, the college.

This simultaneous reanimation and disavowal of what is, not coincidentally, the central kernel of "society," kinship, is materialized in the very lexical realization of these terms: *māms* and *māpps* are *stylish*ly truncated, deformed versions of the kinterms they cite—*māmā(n)* and *māppiḷḷai*, respectively—their lexical alteration being a reflexive sign of their status *as* citations, or the "shadow of (their) own denial," as Simmel put it. In their rematerialization, *māms* and *māpps* are and are not kinterms. Such terms decenter kinship through a detour and an elsewhere. Moreover, this elsewhere is itself already doubled, for such youth uses harken to another mediatized site of borrowing. These terms are seen as *style* in Madurai, for example, because they are associated with Chennai youth and, more to the point, with their stereotyped depiction in film and television (see chapter 5), just as English address terms like "dude" and "bro"—glossed to me by Chennai friends as "the same as" fictive cross kinterms in Tamil—are *stylish* in Chennai, given mediatized association with American youth worlds.

Important to the performativity and citationality of doing *style* is how it does something to what it cites, decentering and negating it, simulating and hybridizing it. Citational acts are, to appropriate a term from Judith Butler (1993:175), "deformative." In disavowing what they otherwise seem to be, citations alter what they reanimate and thus also transformatively entangle the act and agent of citation with what and who is cited. A closely trimmed mustache, an abbreviated kinterm, a misspelled brand name (chapters 2–3), English sprinkled into Tamil or vice versa (chapters 4–5), and playful quotations of films (chapters 6–7)—all such *stylish* forms cite their "original" sources, appropriating their value while reflexively marking their deforming difference from them. Such double-voiced signs do *style* through the "close distance" (Mazzarella 2003) they achieve with what they cite, a semiotic liminality that figurates participation in, for example, rural masculinity, cosmopolitan fashion, the global linguistic ecumene, and filmic imaginaries, even as these imaginaries (and youths' pretensions to participate in them) are bracketed and refashioned. The citation harbors multiple stances and voices (Bakhtin 1982; Voloshinov 1986) and, in doing so, attempts to manage multiple mandates and desires, to embody liminality and engage hierarchy.

Central to the felicity of *style* is this citational reflexivity: the act of *style*'s framing of itself *as* citational through the material traces of its deformativity. Without quotation marks, acts of *style* come too close to what they cite, too close to that which, as we saw above, must be repudiated and distanced from so as to do *style* in the first place. Without quotation marks, citations become the literal acts they purport to only reanimate (Nakassis 2013b): acts of invidious distinction and hierarchical difference. Without such metamarks of difference, doing *style* falters. It *over*does *style* (or underdoes it) such that acts figurating exteriority go too far (or not far enough), either by being seen as illegitimately asserting oneself as the 'big man' or by being seen as coming too close to the figure of the 'child,' as with acts of filmic citation that approach 'childish' subaltern practices of fandom (chapter 6). The citationality of youth practices constitutes an attempt to have one's cake and eat it too, to both individuate from and defer to one's peers, to be like but not to be children and adults, to come close to exterior objects of alternate value but not too close.

As I show in chapter 2, this means that citationality—a term that I have appropriated from Jacques Derrida (1988)—is not simply a function of what Derrida calls "iterability," the identity (or "ideality") and difference that every repetition entails; rather, citational acts are reflexively mediated by their figuration and interpretation *as* iterations, *as* citations. Not all semiotic acts are marked, or taken, as citations. Only some come to be. This implies that theoretical questions surrounding citationality—such as questions of subjectivity (chapter 2)—can productively be posed as empirical issues about how particular acts figure themselves and their contexts and come to be taken up as such (or not). Such questions, as the book shows, are best answered ethnographically.

To be like but not to be, to co-opt what is not one's own and to be seen as doing just that, to pass near the scorching sun and the dark-blue sea without melting or drowning one's wings all require the reflexive semiotics of the citation, its ability to hold diverse voices in suspended animation, to put what is (re)presenced in quotes, to bracket it even as it is reanimated, and to draw attention to that very fact. Citationality brings what is just out of reach close but not too close. The citational act and subject of youth practice is and is not quite (yet). It is this doubled quality that allows the tensions of the peer group to be managed, that allows adulthood to be deferred and childhood transcended and thus allows youth to be inhabitable (which is to say, produced), if only for a time. And it is, as I discuss below, what entangles youth with mass-mediated social forms and those who "produce" them and what allows global brands, south-Indian music-television English, and commercial Tamil film texts to be domesticated for use in the peer group, to be formed and deformed through the push and pull of *style*. It is such citational interlinkages that constitute, I suggest below, a central object for the study of mass mediation.

Mass Mediation and *Style*

In navigating the multiple mandates of performing youth and doing *style* in the college, media forms have a pride of place in youth peer groups: the mustache of a film star, a global designer brand, a swatch of English borrowed from music television, and the like. Such forms are sites of aesthetic engagement and entertainment. They are objects of value, imagination, and desire. And this also makes them foci of youth sociality, tools for youths' status work. In this book, I intentionally, if unconventionally, treat these various social forms as instances of mass media. In doing so, I follow Asif Agha's (2011a; 2011b) call to expand and refocus the category of media around what he calls "mediatization."[34] Agha (2011a:163) defines mediatization as those "institutional practices that reflexively link processes of communication to processes of commoditization." What is at issue in this book, however, is not so much the commoditized nature of communication (though the media forms discussed in the book are, indeed, commoditized) but Agha's expansive treatment of mass media as involving interdiscursive connections across "phases" of mediation. I am interested in framing mass mediation from the perspective of the coordination of otherwise disparate events of discursive interaction at scales that involve, but also exceed, face-to-face exchange. From this point of view, objects of *style*, like brand garments, filmic mustaches, on-air English-Tamil speech, and the like, are all media forms in the sense that they mediate, or coordinate, and thus produce large-scale, dispersed social relations (to wit, youth culture) in ways irreducible to single, local events of interaction. Mass mediation, for me, requires attending to the interdiscursively forged *relations* between events and sites of social practice—between the campus and the textile workshop, the tea stall and the film set, the hostel television room and the television studio, but also among the college campus, the tea stall, and the hostel; between television stations and their VJs; between actors and their films; between local textile producers and global brand manufacturers. I treat such relations as the constituting social fact of mass media.

While social forms like brands, youth slang, and film are not typically grouped together as mass media, they operate and are organized in ways whose similarity benefits from a singular methodological and analytic framework. This book provides one such framework. I ask how we might see media objects as the precipitates of the entanglements between youth peer groups and the "producers" of such objects. The semiotic form of this sociomaterial mode of entanglement is the citation; its cultural substance is *style*. As I show, through its citational semiotics, *style* mediates the materialization and entextualization of particular media objects by calibrating the social projects of those who come to be commonly oriented vis-à-vis those very forms.

While the study of mass mediation necessitates attention to each of these social projects and their interrelationships, in this book, my primary departure point and ethnographic anchor is the youth peer group; secondarily, it is those involved in the "production" of the media that youth draw on in their everyday social practices.[35] The primacy given to youth, and young men in particular, follows from my emphasis on how the various media forms that are reanimated in youth peer groups to do *style* are themselves already marked and re-marked by the dynamics of the peer group, by its liminality and citationality. Youths' citational practices do something to the media forms they cite, not simply in the post hoc moment of their "reception" or "consumption," but in the way in which they are made and unmade at the sites of their creation and circulation. By grounding my analysis in the youth peer group, then, I aim to demonstrate how the very constitution of media must always be situated beyond the canonical, and proximate, contexts of their "production" (and, it turns out, their "reception"). I show how those involved in the making of brand garments, music television, and films come to be entangled with youth (their "consumers"), just as youth are with each other, an entanglement that results from producers' citations and imaginations of youth practice, from their own common aesthetic orientation to *style*, and from the ways in which the market viability of their productions depend on their addressing and being citationally taken up by youth. Media materialize such multiple entanglements, simultaneously registering and anticipating them.

This way of framing mass mediation complicates the way we typically think of media. As I show in the various sections of this book, if we take such citational relationships as our primary datum, then the basic categories upon which our theories of brand, language, and film presume—namely, brand, linguistic code, and text—are rendered problematic precisely because the citational relations that I discuss in this book themselves turn on bracketing the ontological status, fixity, and coherence of these categories. Each pair of chapters focuses on this problematization and interrogates these ontologies: What and when is a brand (chapters 2–3)? What and when is a linguistic code (chapters 4–5)? What and when is a film text (chapters 6–7)? How does *style*—in mediating the various sites and social projects that conspire to materialize the media forms that acts of doing *style* seize upon—depend on these ontologies, even as it deforms and decenters them? What might the citation tell us about what is being cited, the deformed about the norm that it reanimates and brackets?

Answers to these questions raise larger issues for theorizing mass mediation. Work on mass media has long tended to implicitly assume the stability, autonomy, and coherence of the media object as being what producers "produce" and consumers "consume" (or audiences "receive"), setting up each as distinct, if not independent, with regard to the others. It is on this linear imaginary of a media division of labor that a division of academic labor is based: some scholars read and decode media objects, others elicit "reception," others study their "production." In such a view, the relationships between these sites become an aporia, a gap created by fixing, and fixating on, the stable media object.

While in some ways, this way of talking about mass mediation is unavoidable (indeed, these terms appear in various guises in the chapters that follow) and certainly generative in certain moments, as a whole, this book attempts to problematize such ways of treating media—and thus notions of "production," "consumption," and "reception"—by taking the citational relationships between garment manufacturers and youth, music-television VJs and youth, and film actors and youth as its object of analysis. I show how such entanglements are the conditions upon which particular media artifacts and genres are intelligible and materialized. From this point of view, media forms can fruitfully be seen not simply as tools taken up by youth or the outcomes of media producers' creative efforts but as barometers of citational interactions stretched across social space and time, as dynamic materializations whose very citational forms bear the past and anticipatory traces of various social actors' citational engagements.

Similar theoretical moves and critiques have been raised in the study of so-called new or digital media through concepts such as "interactivity" (Gane and Beer 2008), "prosumption" (Manovich 2001; cf. Toffler 1980), "produsage" (Bruns 2008), "convergence culture" (Jenkins 2008), and "spreadability" (Jenkins, Ford, and Green 2013). However, as this book suggests and as I discuss in the concluding chapter, a methodological and analytic framework that undermines discrete categories of production and consumption is required even to understand how so-called old media work (Lukács 2010:22–23), and even social forms not typically included in the category of "the media."[36] Whether old or new, canonically considered media or not, the question remains: how are social relations between various noncopresent social parties mediated over space and time? This basic question is hindered by assuming the self-same stability and autonomy of media forms.

The question this book raises, then, is under what conditions do such ontologies—brand, code, text—and thus the media forms that come to instantiate them come to be intelligible as such, materialized in such a way that their analysis is even possible at all? And if such coherences are the achievements of the very processes being studied, how are we to think those processes? Can analytics like brand, code, and text be presumed upon in a coherent analysis of the citational semiotics of *style*, a semiotics that animates such ontologies even as it decenters and deforms them? Or do such ready-at-hand analytics (namely, brand, code, and text) instate their own ideologies of semiosis that obscure that citationality and hence obscure what they purport to elucidate in the first place (namely, what and when a brand, linguistic code, or film text "are")? Is it, then, the very (in) coherence of such ontologies and analytics that has to be theorized? To invert Richard Schechner's (1985:296) proposition, is it precisely because everything is in quotation marks that the categories are not settled?

PART I

Brand

TWO

Brand and Brandedness

Fresher's Day

On a midsummer evening in 2007, the Madurai college hostel that I had moved into the week before was bustling with activity. For this and the coming weeks, in fact, the campus was abuzz: every department and hostel was having a function to officially welcome the "freshers" (first-year students). It was our hostel's "welcome function," or "fresher's day." In addition to celebrating hostel solidarity and "welcoming" the incoming students, this function signaled the end of "ragging," a colonial inheritance from British educational and military institutions (akin to US college hazing rituals) during which second- and third-year "seniors" force freshers (who most often, but not exclusively, belong to their departments or hostels) to perform exaggerated and often absurd acts of subservience and deference to them.[1]

The previous two weeks had been punctuated with quotidian events of ragging that had led up to this function. Seniors would call freshers to where they were sitting, make them stand in front of them with submissive bodily demeanor, bombard them with personal questions in intimidating and demeaning language, and force them to engage in embarrassing acts—for example, singing love songs to unknown persons of the opposite sex or performing the "college salute" (grabbing one's crotch, gyrating one's hips, then stamping one's foot and saluting copresent seniors). During this ragging period, various proscriptions might be levied on freshers. For men, using cell phones; going to the movies, parks, or malls; talking to young women; smoking cigarettes; drinking alcohol; and generally being loud and visible were all likely to be policed. Those who engaged in such activities risked censure, and more ragging, from their seniors. Generally, any act or sign of youth status, anything that broke the rules and asserted independence, anything that called positive attention to oneself—in short, anything these young men called "*style*"—was off-limits. Loud mouths, show offs, the fashion conscious, and generally richer freshers were all more likely to be made examples of, made to be equal to their same-year peers, something reminiscent of the rites of passage classically discussed by Victor Turner (1967:103).

Sartorially, freshers were often made to forsake their fashionable clothing, including their branded garments, and instead were forced to dress "*decent*" by wearing shabby "formals": button-down dress shirts and slacks. Nathan, a middle-class friend who had completed his bachelor of arts at the Madurai college where I was living, for example, relayed to me how the seniors in his master of business administration program in Coimbatore ordered him to stop wearing his preferred hip-hop-inspired clothing (baggy jeans, sneakers, and T-shirts) and physically forced him to remove his prized Livestrong bracelet. Instead, he was told to wear dowdy formals. When I asked why, Nathan said that his seniors found his *stylish* dress arrogant, his name-brand apparel uppity and presumptuous. They thought he was trying to stand out too much. Similarly, at a Chennai college that an acquaintance, Kumar, attended, freshers were made to wear cheap, tailored button-down shirts left untucked, plain polyester slacks, and ratty bathroom slippers. By forcing freshers to wear shabby formals and forsake their brand gear, seniors attempted to deny incoming students like Nathan and Kumar access to *style*. Such students were forced to dress like those who they were not and desired not to be: low class (hence shabby), adult, and working (hence formals). By being figuratively put in another's sartorial place, such students were put in their place, at least for a while.

The ragging practices at my Madurai college were occasional, generally playful, and considered very mild by all involved. They were a far cry from the more extreme and sadistic forms of ragging that have received much press in recent (and past) years and that have resulted in the criminalization of ragging in Indian colleges (Saqaf 2009). While officially there was an active attempt by college administrators to stamp ragging out, the kinds of ragging that I describe here continued on, often with the implicit consent of the administration. As one hostel warden confided, "I'm not supposed to say this, but ragging is necessary in the college." Indeed, the officially sanctioned welcome function was a public part of the ragging ritual, its end point and its culmination. Even if its relation to ragging was officially disavowed, the welcome function itself was a form of ragging that required incoming freshers to perform onstage—to sing, dance, or show some other talent—while their seniors hooted, hollered, booed, interrupted, and otherwise gave them a hard time.

Like the warden, students also saw ragging as a necessary practice. Freshers anticipated it with a mix of fear and delight. It was exciting. It was what college was supposed to be about. Without it, college life would be boring (*bore aṭikkutu*), one incoming fresher told me. Older students took a more functionalist perspective on things. Sebastian, one of my Madurai roommates in his third and final year, observed that without ragging, year cohorts would lack solidarity and intimacy, leading to "groupism" (i.e., cliques and factions) among hostel students of the same year.[2] To avoid such groupism and promote year, and ultimately hostel, unity (for ragging also forced a form of hierarchical intimacy with seniors), students had to be ragged.[3] And indeed, it was the common experience of ragging that formed the boundaries of the year-equal cohort, a space wherein social difference was putatively flattened and within which forms of intimacy and egalitarian norms of sociality could be instated and experienced (chapter 1). This required bracketing and transforming those social hierarchies from outside the college, which otherwise located these youth.

Ragging negates age difference and converts it into year difference. It reinscribes that hierarchy by which youth are subordinated to adults—namely, age and generation—within the student population as a hierarchy of year, as the relative relation of "juniors" and "seniors." Hence a junior who is older than a senior would still be ragged by him and would still be required, during and after ragging (and even after college), to give him deference, to address him with honorific address forms (second-person plural verb endings and pronouns, the kinterm for older brother [see note 3 in this chapter]), to do what he asks, and the like.[4] Ragging allowed seniors to usurp the college administration's authority, figuratively acting like 'big men' who lorded their *gettu* ('dominance,' 'prestige') over freshers—who were thereby figurated as 'little boys'—by enforcing the otherwise relatively lax college and hostel rules (such as dress codes, bans on cell phone usage, and hostel curfews) and then some. Suspended in the college, hierarchically ranked lifecycle categories reappear as relative terms of status and value to construe and typify differences among students, not as younger and older, but as juniors and seniors.

On the day of the welcome function, there was excitement in my hallway. Bright and gaudy garments passed hands as my hostelmates tried on each other's clothes, hoping to strike the right combination. Sneakers were unpacked from dressers, sunglasses were shined, baseball hats, bracelets, and rings were mixed and matched. The welcome function was the first day in their college lives that these freshers were, within the strictures of ragging at least, officially allowed to ostentatiously ‘do *style*’ (*style paṉṟatu*), to put on their duds and strut their stuff. Today, their liminal status in the lifecycle as youth was replicated through this minor rite, which now inducted them as individuals capable of throwing off, or at least performing throwing off, the stifling rules of ragging and the larger institutional order of age (and class) hierarchy that ragging bracketed and figuratively reinscribed. They were now, in a sense, fully college youth.

Among all the signs of *style*, conspicuous on welcome day were the brand names and logos that adorned these young men’s bodies. The end of ragging was an opportunity to loudly display brands on their bodies, or at least things like brands. Indeed, the garments that adorned these young men’s bodies on this day and the days that followed were by and large not “originals.” They were “dummy pieces,” locally made, low-quality counterfeits, defect and surplus garments, brand pastiches, and other brand-inspired apparel, or what I call in this chapter “brand surfeits”: damaged Reebok polos, fake Diesel watches, misspelled “Pumaa” backpacks, and T-shirts with fictive brand names, nonsensical slogans (e.g., “Disquerd, Everinhu Canglong asiohdngy”), and seemingly unrelated designs (figure 3; also see figures 5–8 in chapter 3). While these young men were keen that such clothes have the trappings of brand apparel, they were outwardly indifferent to the particular brand identities displayed on their garments, as they were to their authenticity.

What are we to make of the uncanny brand surfeits adorning these young men’s bodies? Or of young men’s simultaneous desire for and indifference to the brands that embellished such garments? Or of their nonchalance about their authenticity? What made such fashion, stamped by

Figure 3. Two brand surfeits: left—a “Pumaa” bag (Chennai 2011); right—“Force” fictive brand shirt, with “Style Without Control” slogan (Madurai 2007)

mimicked marks of the global, objects to be policed during ragging and displayed with zeal after it? What made them *style*?

In this chapter, I explore the *style* of the brand and its relation to youth forms of status and sociality, focusing in particular on young men's clothing fashion.[5] Young men draw on branded forms to diagram and negotiate their relationships with adult respectability and masculinity, to manage their expectations and anxieties about future participation in the workforce, and most centrally, to do *style* in their peer groups. As I show, there is an ambivalence that underwrites and underplays young men's engagements with brand fashion, an ambivalence about the potential of the brand not simply to do *style* but to do too much *style*. This ambivalence manifests itself in acts of indifference to and outright disavowal of brand authenticity and value. It materializes as the very surfeits that adorn these young men's bodies. This ambivalence takes a positive form as what I call "an aesthetics of brandedness." This sartorial aesthetic revolves around the "*look*" of brand apparel, even as it problematizes the very question of what and when a brand *is*—a question I turn to at the end of chapter 3. The chapter then addresses the gendered nature of this aesthetic, discussing young men who draw on alternate masculinities that eschew branded forms, and *style* more generally, and college-going women, whose bodies are almost never visibly marked by branded forms. In concluding, I ask what kind of subject is presupposed and entailed by young men's fashion. I argue that it is a liminal, flirtatious subject, one that emerges out of a close distance with those other subjectivities that he invokes but keeps in quotes, reanimates but disavows, embraces but defers through his ambivalent reanimations of the brand. But first, I turn to a brief history of clothing in modern India to contextualize the terrain upon which college students encountered brand garments.

From Khadi to (Khadi) Brand

> The dhoti-kurta clad politician travelling in third class railway compartments is an image of the past. Today's rulers sport Gucci shoes, Cartier sunglasses and live five-star lifestyles. . . . The distance between Gandhi (Mahatma) and Gandhi (Rajiv) is a vast traverse in political ethic.
>
> —"THE NEW MAHARAJAHS," *SUNDAY*, APRIL 17–23, 1988, PP. 22, 26 (CITED IN FERNANDES 2006:36, CITING RUDOLPH 1989:2, NOTE 1)

The New Economic Policy (NEP) of 1991 is conventionally taken to mark a transition in Indian history. The NEP crystallized earlier gestures toward economic liberalization in the 1980s by Indira Gandhi and later by her son Rajiv Gandhi, inscribing a clear, if contested, break with the state-planned economic policies and "socialistic" vision associated with India's first prime minister, Indira Gandhi's father, Jawaharlal Nehru. The NEP responded to the fiscal crisis of 1991, instituting a number of structural reforms at the behest of the International Monetary Fund: liberalized industrial licensing, relaxed import quotas, reduced import tariffs, and increased allowances on foreign investment, among other changes (Jenkins 1999:12–41). In doing so, the Indian economy was opened to new commodities, labor relations, and global capital. Liberalization was, of course, not simply an issue of market economics but a shift in the political dispensation and ideological orientation of the nation-state (Mankekar 1999; Mazzarella 2003; Fernandes 2006; Srivastava 2007; Lukose 2009), a shift that has been felt in multiple domains, from higher education (chapter 1), language politics (chapter 4), and media entertainment (chapters 5–7) to, as I discuss in this chapter and the next, young men's fashion, among many others still.

To see this, one might track the modern history of cloth, clothing, and fashion in the subcontinent. As Giorgio Riello and Tirthankar Roy (2013[2009]b:6) put it, until the eighteenth century, "India clothed the world." It was this vibrant textile trade that in the seventeenth century attracted the East India Company, which bought low-cost, high-quality Indian cotton textiles for the consumer fashion market in England or for further trade in Southeast Asia. By the nineteenth century, English manufacturers had succeeded in mechanizing textile production. In the second half of the century, they were exporting their cheaper, industrially produced fabrics to the subcontinent, reversing earlier trade patterns and thus, as it came to be seen, decimating the Indian handicraft industry (Parthasarathi 2013[2009]; 2010).[6] In this same period, increasing colonial trade, governance, and Western education saw European dress styles of various sorts gain popularity among elite, educated Indian men (Cohn 1989:333ff.; Tarlo 1996:24, 320). By the end of the nineteenth century, Western cloth and clothing had come to represent the exploitative nature of colonialism to an emerging anticolonial sensibility. The response of the nascent nationalist movement, and that of the Mahatma Mohandas Gandhi in particular, took the form of traditionally hand-spun, handwoven Indian cotton. It took the form of khadi.

Mahatma Gandhi—one of those dapper, Western-dressed and Western-educated colonial subjects in his youth (Bean 1989; Tarlo 1996:64–69)—did the most to position and champion khadi dress as the answer to the political and economic subjugation of India under British colonialism (Trivedi 2007). For the nationalist movement, khadi emblematized *swadeshi* (literally, 'home country'): the boycott of foreign goods and the promotion of indigenous goods.[7] Gandhi advocated that every Indian exclusively wear khadi and, moreover, hand-spin their own yarn—a sacrifice of labor to uplift and free the to-be nation.[8] As Gandhi put it, "*Swadeshi* is the soul of *Swaraj* ('self-rule'), *Khadi* is the essence of *Swadeshi*" (quoted in Bean 1989:370). Locally produced, handmade, and worn in modest "traditional" "Indian" styles (Tarlo 1996), khadi dress—often all white and without any embellishment (the "dhoti-kurta" referred to above)—became a national symbol, or the "fabric of Indian independence," as Nehru put it (cited in Chakrabarthy 2001:28).

In the postindependence period, khadi came to stand in for the austere dispensation and aesthetic of Nehru's brand of nationalism, with its developmentalist emphasis on constrained consumption and import substitution production.[9] It is the breakdown of this nationalist dispensation and aesthetic that found political-economic expression in the policy shifts of the 1980s and 1990s. These shifts reconfigured the Indian economy—what one Gandhian dubbed, in the context of the textile industry, the government's "anti-khadi shift in policy" (Jain 1985:1121)—and ushered in a vigorous, if ambivalent, embrace of "global consumerism" (Mazzarella 2003:12).

Emblematic of this shift, I would suggest, was the multinational corporate brand. If hand-spun, hand-woven khadi stood as an indigenous, productivist emblem of the postindependence nation, the readymade, global brand garment now stood as a consumerist emblem for postliberalization India. Telling, perhaps, is that since liberalization, khadi cloth and clothing have been on the decline and thus subject to reinvigoration by brand marketing logics. In 2001, khadi was eponymously branded by the Khadi and Village Industries Commission and, ironically if not surprisingly, positioned as a fabric for high-end, elite fashion (Tarlo 2004; Mazzarella 2010).[10]

The increasingly visible presence of the global brand emblazoned on mass-produced, readymade garments evinced, then, that India had left behind the austerity of Nehruvian socialism and Gandhian-inflected moral consumerism, joined the global ecumene, and embraced "globalization," for better or for worse. A turn away from staid, state paternalism toward aspirational consumer choice, from a populist orientation of developmentalism for the uplift of the poor toward the mass-mediated, libidinal enjoyment for that chimerical segment, the "middle classes" (Mazzarella 2005; Fernandes 2006), the branded commodity—be it foreign or "world-class" Indian—appeared as a symptom and materialization of liberalization's promise, of India's long-anticipated arrival on the global stage (Mazzarella

2003:91, 250–63), one marked by the plenitude of consumption rather than the sacrificial deferral of abstention.

From Brand to Brandedness

My claim is not that brand clothing—even foreign brand clothing—wasn't available in the decades before liberalization, nor that after liberalization, only glitzy foreign brands have reigned.[11] Both claims would be false and would take the ideologies surrounding liberalization at face value. Rather, my claim is that liberalization entailed an altered vision of the relationship of the commodity to the nation that was mediated by the closer distance of the global brand, by fashionable brand consumption rather than selfless commodity production for the nation.

This ideological imaginary turned on the increased visibility and accessibility of branded commodities in the years following liberalization (Osella and Osella 1999; Rajagopal 1999; Fernandes 2006). Indeed, since liberalization, metropolitan Indian boutiques and high-end malls have mushroomed, teeming with global brand goods targeting the upper-middle classes, who have grown in size and wealth with the explosion of new investment and job opportunities. Such shifts in consumption have gone along with the expansion and privatization of mass-media platforms (Mankekar 1999; Page and Crawley 2001), themselves fueling and fueled by an explosion of advertising and brand marketing (Rajagopal 1999; Mazzarella 2003), as well as by increasingly stringent intellectual property law modeled on brand-protective American trademark law (Gangjee 2008) and by global shifts of commodity production to India (chapter 3).

Yet despite—or rather, precisely because of—this increasingly visible and hegemonic regime of brand value, more than the authorized brand, it is the brand's surfeits that permeate everyday life in India (Rajagopal 1999). Outside of the glitzy new malls and boutiques that cater to the upwardly mobile are the export surpluses, defects, duplicates, counterfeits, brand-inspired goods, and other brand mutations that spill out of local shops, bazaars, and roadside platforms (Sundaram 2013). In the penumbra of the brand, it is through such surfeit that the majority of Indians—otherwise excluded from consuming expensive brand commodities imported from or made for nations abroad—get a piece of the fruit that liberalization promised.[12] It is precisely such brand surfeits that young men like Nathan wore for fashion and *style*.

If we follow the brand's logic (or claim to being, its ontology), such forms are derivative. They are inauthentic, unauthorized, fake. They are excess, detritus, otherwise. If the brand represents the official face of liberalization, the surfeit is its unofficial Janus face—part of the shadow economy, illegal and illegitimate. This discourse of authenticity and identity, of the real and the fake, of the official and the illicit, is the ontological stake made in the name of the brand—an ideological and economic enclosure that aspires to contain all consumer commodity encounters within itself, either as authorized instances of it or as surfeit to it. This enclosure classifies the market, on the one hand, by distinct brand identities (Nike vs. Diesel vs. Armani vs. . . . , etc.) and, on the other hand, by the authenticity of their commodity instances (real Nike goods vs. fake Nike goods, real Diesel goods vs. fake Diesel goods, etc.).

The lower-middle-class and middle-class young men with whom I lived and worked could, and sometimes did, employ a version of this brand logic when it came to clothing, differentiating what they called "brand" (or "company") garments from "*local*" garments. "Brand" garments are made by a known, usually foreign, company that has a reputation and popular image in the market. They are high quality and expensive and are sold in "showrooms" and other elite stores. In this discourse, "brand" and "original" ('authentic good') are synonyms.[13] By contrast, "*local*" garments are cheap and badly made and are typically sold in nonelite shops and on roadside platforms. Denoting the low class and the low quality (as discussed more below), "*local*" here refers to unbranded garments, fictive or unknown brand garments, "duplicates" (i.e., goods that display the logo or name of a known company but are known not to be made by it), and in certain cases, Indian brands as such—a point I return to later in the chapter (cf. Vann 2006; Thomas 2013). By this logic, "brand" and "*local*" do not designate production locales per se. Indeed, many, if not most, of the global brand "originals" that circulate in domestic markets are manufactured in, and known to be manufactured in, India.[14] Rather, terms like "brand," "original," "*local*," and "duplicate" are defined by the question of *for whom* their commodity referents are made to be consumed (cf. Thomas 2013), offering a stark and telling contrast with the spatialized, productivist distinction of "foreign" and "swadeshi" articulated by the nationalist movement discussed above.

While young men, at times, evaluated garments based on the above distinctions, often they were indifferent to them. As noted at the outset of the chapter, these young men usually did not reckon apparel by questions of brand image or authenticity. Most didn't seem to care or (care to) know much about the brands on their bodies, sometimes not even caring if they were brands at all. In their indifference, they blurred the lines between unbranded and branded, real and fake, original and duplicate. When I asked

Stephen, my otherwise fashion-conscious and brand-knowledgeable Madurai hostelmate about the popularity of the Italian designer-brand Diesel (Stephen himself owned a "Diesel" canvas bag, pair of jeans, and T-shirt), he admitted ignorance: 'What is it? Is it a band or a brand?' Moreover, it wasn't branded forms with widespread recognition like Nike, Reebok, or Adidas (athletic brands that entered the market in the late 1980s and early 1990s and had ubiquitous advertisements, sports sponsorships, authorized retail stores, and priced-down products targeting middle-class young men) that were the most popular, as we might expect. Rather, it was brands like Diesel, Tommy Hilfiger, Ferrari, and Puma—brands that at the time lacked a significant authorized retail footprint in India—that proliferated in local markets and were the most worn by young college men. Diesel, the most ubiquitous brand name in youth fashion during my initial fieldwork (2007–2009), had absolutely no advertisements and no official retail market in India at all.[15] It only had factories in Tamil Nadu exporting commodities abroad. Whatever logic the consumption and circulation of Diesel and other branded garments were following (see chapter 3), it was not in any straightforward way that of the brand's official regimes of authenticity, identity, or provenance, those regimes that turned on consumers' familiarity with the brand's authorizing metadiscourses of marketing and intellectual property. As I show below, rather than as brands, young men evaluated the garments that they and their peers wore based on a different, but related, regime of value: that of brandedness, the quality of being *like* a branded garment (even if not one), of having the "*look*" of a brand commodity. Below I explore this disjunction between brand and brandedness and how it comes to be mediated by youth conceptions and practices of *style*, by desires and anxieties that turn on, and away from, the brand.[16]

Brand Desires

"*Brand illai ṇṇā style illa.*" ('If there's no brand, there's no style.')

—ZEISS BRAND EYEGLASSES ADVERTISEMENT (CHENNAI 2008)

I begin this section with a rather simple question that I frequently asked myself and my college friends: What about brands makes them *style* as such? What does *style* do such that a brand, or one of its citing surfeits, could be or do *style*?

As discussed in chapter 1, *style* is a shifting discourse and register of youth status, aesthetics, and value, typifying and collating a bewildering variety of objects and activities: whistling in theaters, smoking cigarettes at tea stalls, riding the bus on the "footboard," speaking English (chapter 4), wearing ripped jeans and many-pocketed cargo pants, using fist-bump handshakes, combing bangs out of one's face like the film "Superstar" Rajinikanth (chapter 6), teasing and flirting with girls on the college campus, romantic love itself, and more. But what did brands have to do with this potpourri of youth *style*?[17]

Visibility

Doing *style* is attention getting. As my friends would explain, "*Style ṇṇā taniyā teriyaṇum*" ('To be/do *style*, you have to be visible/individuated [from the crowd]'). Acts of *style* are public acts that scream "Look at me!" and, importantly, communicate that very desire to be seen. *Style* aims to attract others (*kavarkkiṟatu*)—in particular, as my hostelmates would note, the opposite sex (though in my experience, contrary to such discourse, *style* was mainly performed for one's same-sex peers). And it does so by flouting the norms of appropriate public self-presentation. As Melanie Dean (2013) and Sara Dickey (2013) have noted, in the Tamil context, to be seen and recognized in public presupposes some amount of respectability and social standing (Mines 1994). *Style* presumptuously presumes such standing, even if, or rather precisely because, youth don't command the necessary *mariyātai* ('respect') or *kauravam* ('prestige') to be so recognized.

Sartorially, *style*'s aesthetics are gaudy and flashy, indecent and irrational, akin to the loud and flamboyant fashion of the Malayali young men discussed by Caroline and Filippo Osella (1999; 2000b; 2007). Bright colors, (intentionally) ripped fabric, low-hanging jeans, shiny sunglasses, earrings, and superfluous pockets and zippers are all *style*. *Style*, like fashion more generally, lies in the realm of the nonfunctional (Simmel 1998[1904]:189–90; Sapir 1931b:140; Blumer 1969:286–87). It is, as it were, its own function. One student humorously but seriously explained this to me using the example of pants: 'Pants usually have four pockets. Typically, pants are tailored. That is normal, ordinary. So pants that have more pockets, pockets that are visible, are *style*. Pants that are readymade are *style*. At first, there was the "six pocket"—pants with six pockets. When that got ordinary, the fashion increased to twelve pockets—twelve pockets being more than six pockets, even more unnecessary. That was *style*. Then we came to know them as "cargoes." The more pockets, the more *style*.'

Style stretches the norm as far as possible, going to the edge of reason and verging on madness (*kiṟukku*). It attempts to make the non- and extranormative one's own. Under the metasign of *style*, deviation from normality is contained and made sensible. To own transgression, to co-opt the authority of something else where only nonsense and unintelligibility existed before, is *style.* All form, no substance, all surface, no meaning—such fashion was often seen as childish by adults (or conservative youth who disapproved of such excesses and opted for more staid clothing), as revealing an immaturity of judgment and a lack of self-discipline. As a Madurai college professor at the coeducational Hindu college bemoaned after scolding a fashionable middle-class student for entering his office with *stylish* ripped jeans, long hair, and an earring, 'Everything and anything today is *style.*' 'There is no rhyme or reason in it. Even a rip in a shirt is *style*!' he exclaimed with a laugh while gesturing to an imagined rip in his dress shirt's front pocket.

Nathan, the *stylish* middle-class youth whom we met above, explained this connection between the brand, *style,* and visibility while we *time pass*ed ('hung out') on the college campus of the Madurai college where I stayed. We sat on one of the many benches that lined the main walkways of the campus. Each bench was a vantage point in a public theater, offering a vista from which the young men sitting and standing around it would chat, people-watch, and comment on passersby (including their female peers, who guardedly and furtively moved through such spaces on their way to less visible indoor spaces). Prompted by my inquiries about *style,* Nathan pointed out examples in front of us, explaining that brands like Nike, Diesel, and Ferrari make people's heads turn. They attract attention because they are neither "ordinary" nor 'normal' ("*sātāraṇam*"). You want to look at them, you want to have them because they're beautiful, because they're "different," and wearing them shows your difference from the crowd (*vittiyāsam kāmikkiṟatu*). But different from what?

Difference

Clothing with brand names and logos stands in a set of differential relationships with other sartorial styles—most importantly here, those marked by particular age and class indexicalities. Echoing the longer history of clothing discussed above, for young men like Nathan, branded clothing, whether "original" or "duplicate," marked a difference from "traditional" adult clothing—in particular, the plain, unmarked, white cotton *vēṣṭi* (an unstitched cloth wrapped around the waist, also known as a *dhoti*) and the white, cotton, button-down, collared shirt. This "white on white" clothing style (figure 4) is associated with the *periya āḷ,* the 'big man' who embodies and displays *mariyātai* ('respect') and *kauravam* ('pres-

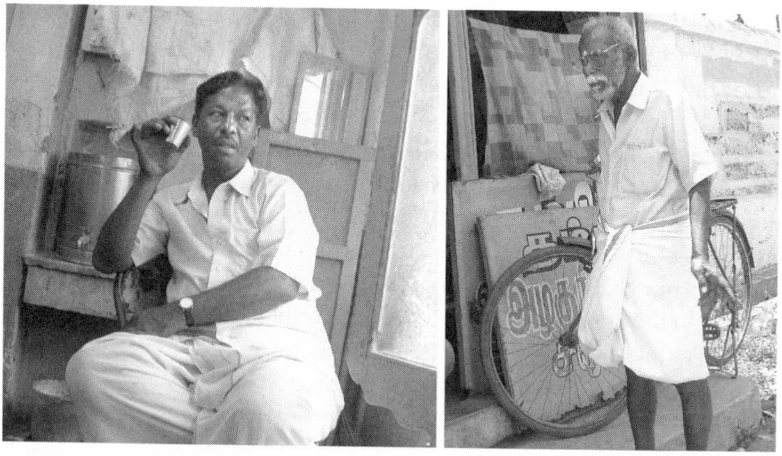

Figure 4. Two adult men wearing "traditional" white on white (photos by Nora Sweeney, used with permission)

tige,' 'honor') through his immaculate white dress (cf. Osella and Osella 1998:191; 1999:997). Such dress, while today naturalized as traditional, itself represents a tentative and hedged engagement with modernity, mixing the precolonial *vēṣṭi* with a tailored, European-style cotton shirt (Tarlo 1996:48–52).[18] Like Gandhian khadi styles (Chakravarthi 2001; Mazzarella 2010:13), such dress has come to serve as an emblem of the south Indian politician.[19]

As with other stereotyped forms of adult status—such as prominent mustaches (chapter 1), land, dependents (children and wives), and patronage relations (Mines 1994)—young men generally could not avail such sartorial styles, precisely because to do so would presuppose status that they did not, and could not, command at their age (cf. Osella and Osella 1999; 2000b). Indeed, young men generally only wore *vēṣṭi*s for special occasions (like the Tamil harvest-festival Pongal or marriages) or with a certain amount of discomfort or irony.

The branded garment, by contrast, presents a different scene: bright and colorful emblazoned logos, graphic designs (e.g., geometric figures, numbers, images), (quasi-)brand names in roman script (most often in English and never in Tamil; see chapters 3–4),[20] and loud, unconventional garment construction (e.g., extra straps, buttons, patches, zippers, pockets). These design elements are screen-printed, embroidered, and fastened on top of often multicolored fabric, added to the cloth as excessive supplements. Through such excess, these garments distinguish their wearers from an adult order of masculinity, with its blank, pure, white cotton weaves, and participate in a distinctly "modern" aesthetics and fashion associated specifically with college youth.

At the same time, the branded clothing that young men preferred was also different from what they called "formals," a term whose English origin indicates such clothing's association with nontraditional, Western fashion, its semantic meaning indicating such clothing's stereotyped formal contexts of use. By differentiating their branded garments from formals, students like Nathan indexed two class-linked personas and their sartorial styles. On the one hand, "formals" refers to unbranded, tailored slacks and shirts. Frequently cut from affordable, synthetic prints (often dark-colored checkered patterns or stripes) in recognizably standard shapes, such tailored clothing was considered "normal," worn by many students as well as by lower-middle-class and middle-class working adults. Because tailoring is cheap and easily available and has had a longstanding presence in India (becoming the urban norm for men postindependence; Tarlo 1996), tailored formals are unremarkable. They are, as Nathan put it, "ordinary" or "*sātāraṇam.*" By contrast, the readymade branded garments that many youth preferred—through their different stitching patterns (e.g., a T-shirt stitched on top of a cotton button-down shirt; see figure 3), different fabrics (e.g., knitwear for T-shirts or denim for jeans; neither fabric is regularly used for tailored clothing), and often looser fit (in particular for jeans and cargo pants)—marked themselves as *not* tailored and thus as neither ordinary nor normal.[21]

On the other hand, formals could carry another valence and invoke another persona. Formals also evoked the sartorial aesthetics associated with professional work contexts and, in particular, the postliberalization work opportunities that many of these young men, often ruefully, hoped to secure after college: employment in call centers, business processing outsourcing companies (BPOs), corporate human resources departments, or information technology (IT) companies. Such formals are readymades (and thus are unlike ordinary tailored formals), though unlike the brand surfeits that my hostelmates and friends preferred, they did not betray their brand status so brazenly. Their brand names and logos were inconspicuous, often hidden away behind the collar or on the corner of a pocket. Their prints were more muted, their design styles more conservative. The class distinction of such readymade formals from both ordinary tailored formals and the brand surfeits that youth wore was often clear from their fabric (high-quality cottons or cotton blends) and professional finishing. Such clothing would be worn with dress shoes and other signs of professionalism (e.g., watches, pens in the front shirt pocket) rather than with sneakers, sandals, or cheap bracelets. Like the *vēṣṭi* of the 'big man' (though of a much different inflection), such readymade clothing indexed a time when serious responsibilities were to begin, when one was to enter into the white-collar workforce and transition into adult status. And indeed, the students I knew voiced the expectation that they would likely wear traditional or professional dress styles (though most likely the latter) once they entered adulthood and their professional careers.[22]

In short, by contrast to formals, the loudness and prominence of brand(esque) designs on the *stylish* clothing preferred by my college friends distanced them from the *decent* sartorial codes of their future working selves. Their clothing played with and flouted expectations of future selfhood—inserting a gap between the here and now of college life, marked by aimless wandering (*ūr suṟṟatu*) and *jolly time pass* (Jeffrey 2010), and the then and there (and them) of postcollege working life and adulthood, marked by formality, responsibility, competition, and uncertainty—even as it figuratively brought that future that much closer through the surfeit of the global brand.

Exteriority

By being clearly differentiated from these figures of masculinity and status (the ordinary *local*, the white-collar professional, the respectable adult), eye-catching brand displays were also playfully hedged bids for youths' own modes of status and authority and were, to that extent, transgressive. *Stylish* brand clothing could be seen by authority figures as insolent, which was revealed both in Nathan's ragging and in the scolding students might have gotten for their in-your-face fashion from elder kin and professors, as we saw above. The college often attempted to police youth fashion by enforcing dress codes (and in some colleges, uniforms), not only under the aegis of training these young men how to dress as *decent* middle-class subjects, but also to discipline their excessive tendencies more generally.[23] *Style*, in its own way, presented a kind of challenge to adult authority, or at least it figurated such a challenge through cheeky fashion that played with adult aesthetics of respectability. In doing so, youth fashion articulated a hedged bid for its own regime of alternative value and authority.

Central to this was the double exteriority of the brand garment. On the one hand, beyond simply marking differences from other masculinities, *stylish* brand displays invoke and bring close a desired elsewhere exterior to both "society" and the peer group (Osella and Osella 1999:1010ff.): the "foreign." The foreign (synecdochically, the West and more specifically for many of these youth, the United States) denoted an imagined time-space filled with the moralities, fashions, forms of wealth and consumption, language (chapter 4), and personas—urban elites (including the white-collar professionals noted above), foreign returns, and foreigners of course—from the great beyond.[24] To invoke the foreign, drawing on Alexander Dent's discussion of cosmopolitanism in Brazilian country music (2009:212, citing Goodale 2006:641), is "to project a new world beyond the expected"—"expected" both in the mirative sense (the extra-"ordinary," as Nathan described *stylish* brand garments) and in the deontic sense of the weight of tradition. The foreign was a time-space without social demands, without the pressures to conform to family, kin, and caste. The foreign didn't abide by the rules of Tamil "society" and "culture." It was talked about, positively and negatively, as a space of individualism, freedom, equality, wealth, sexuality, and fashion—a fact reflected in the panoply of questions directed at me to confirm just those stereotypes that my presence curiously disrupted. After unpacking my clothes, my hostel roommates in Madurai and Chennai were especially shocked to see that I, an American, didn't have more brand clothing. And they found it especially perverse that I would go out of my way to take my loose-fitting readymades to local tailors to be recut and altered (Lukose 2009:77; Newell 2012:161).

The cosmopolitan exteriority invoked by the *stylish* branded garment was reflected in the quizzical laughs I would get by asking whether there were any Indian-brand garments, "original" or "duplicate," that were *style*. In the context of youth fashion, the phrase "Indian brand" is oxymoronic, explained Ranjith, a middle-class youth from Chennai. "Indian" means "*local*," he said. In contrast to both the regime of value anchored by *style* and the sociospatial imaginary invoked by the foreign, *local*, as noted above, denotes a cluster of unstatusful qualities (low-class, second-rate, old-fashioned, cheap) and, by extension, places and persons (the urban slum and its dwellers, the rural hinterlands and their hick residents [*paṭṭikkāṭṭānukaḷ*]). By contrast, Ranjith noted, "brand" means international (i.e., not Indian), *royal* ('rich'), expensive, of quality, and thus *style*. To combine "Indian" and "brand" together (at least in the context of youth fashion), he concluded, would be contradictory (cf. Halstead 2002; Vann 2005; Manning and Uplisashvili 2007). As a former music-television host quipped to me, "Charlie Nichols" sounds like a hip brand, but "Chandru Shekar"—no way!

On the other hand, the *style* of the brand garments that youth displayed also invoked another exterior regime of value and aesthetics, that of commercial Tamil cinema (cf. Osella and Osella 1998; 1999), that mass medium par excellence that has long been associated with indecency and transgression (chapter 6), flirtation with Western cultural forms (from romantic love to fashion), and flashy, subaltern masculinity (Dhareswhar and Niranjana 1996). Herein lies a complex citational entanglement (one that I touch on briefly in the next chapter and in chapters 6–7), for film fashion itself appropriates elements of global brand fashion (Srivastava 2007), which youth audiences themselves take up and cite, creating a mirroring feedback on both sides of the screen, a spiraling around the brand and its *stylish* aesthetics of exteriority. In particular, young men's donning of branded readymade apparel (ripped jeans, flashy T-shirts, multipocketed cargoes), among other *stylish* fashions (handkerchiefs wrapped around the hand, film-inspired haircuts, and the like), draws on the branded male body of the so-called mass hero and his alter, the villainous *rowdy* ('thug'). Like the foreigner and the urban cosmopolitan elite, the hero and the *rowdy* stand outside respectable "society." Invoking these exterior figures in its own alternate, local project of value and status (cf. Dent 2009:211–38), youth brand fashion appropriates to its performative aesthetics that which is disbarred within those economies of adult status from which youth themselves are excluded: the indecent, the foreign, the cinematic.

For all these reasons—their attention-demanding nature; their differentiations from the traditional, the formal, and the adult; their playful transgressions of respectability and *decency*; their invocations and appropriations of exteriority—loud and flashy brand displays do *style*. Like an ear-splitting whistle in public that turns heads, an English phrase that dazzles and confounds those who hear it (chapters 4–5), a peg of whisky at a local government bar that flaunts *decency*, a flirtatious encounter at a bus stand that transgresses patriarchal expectations of gender relations, or a "footboard *payaṇam*" (riding the bus while hanging outside of it) that defies good sense, brand displays garner social esteem from one's peers. They perform youth in the theater of the peer group. They do *style*.[25]

Brand Anxieties

To stand out, and thus to fit in, often required displaying signs of *style* like brands. And this made the brand not only an object of status-raising display and desire but also a site of peer pressure, conformity, and anxiety.

Kiran was a hip and smart young man from Madurai living in the same hostel as me in Chennai. He was from a middle-class background and had been educated in an elite private school in Madurai. When he first came to the fast-paced and cosmopolitan metropolis of Chennai, he saw that everyone at our elite college campus had Diesel bags. He had never heard of Diesel, but because of its visibility on campus, he figured that he too must get a Diesel bag, lest he be left out, lest he seem like a country bumpkin (*paṭṭikkāṭṭāṉ*) from backwater Madurai. Displaying brands, doing *style*, was part of fitting in. As another friend put it, citing a proverb, "*Ūrōṭu ottu vāḻ*" ('Live along with the village/place')—that is, whatever people around you do, you should also do.

But beyond the apprehension of not participating in brand fashion, of under *style* as we might say, there was another implicit anxiety surrounding brand displays: that they might be excessive, or "*over*," in their *style*, that they might come too close to those regimes of exteriority and social status that imbued them with social value. This was revealed to me by an encounter I witnessed between Sam, my upwardly mobile, middle-class hostel roommate in Chennai, and a pair of sneakers. Sam was an outgoing, convivial young man. He typically dressed in a *stylish* though not over-the-top fashion, wearing loose-fitting jeans and T-shirts featuring Western athletic and fashion brands. On that day, I came back to our Chennai hostel room to find Sam staring in awe at a pair of brand new Adidas sneakers that his father had bought him. It was his first pair. In Tamil and English (chapter 4), Sam said that he felt "*semma jolly, romba* happy" ('extremely excited/happy, so happy') to have an authentic pair of Adidas sneakers. He was giddy. 'I don't know why, but I feel like I accomplished something!' he exclaimed. Yet while he would wear these shoes out on occasion, with the sole example of this private confessional, to my knowledge, he never foregrounded the fact of their authenticity to others. Around his peers, he remained silent about these prized possessions. But if brands are *style*, and doing *style* is about ostentation and drawing attention, why keep quiet? If you've got 'em, flaunt 'em, right?

Acts of *style* are performatively unstable. While successful instances of *style* individuate and garner social esteem from one's peers, signs of *style* are always haunted by the risk that they might raise one's status and individuate too much. Felicitous brand displays navigate this fine line between acceptably deviating from adult norms of propriety while still conforming to the peer group's norms of appropriateness. There is such a thing as too much *style*, and the brand's tendencies toward *over*doing *style* always functioned implicitly as a source of anxiety for my friends and hostelmates.

This anxiety turned on the ways in which brand displays could disrupt the egalitarian ethos of the peer group by introducing forms of class distinction. As discussed in chapter 1, young men's sociality centers on common projects of transgression, on inversions and appropriations of adult norms of status, propriety, and the hierarchies and inequalities upon which they are based. Implicit as a condition of its status-raising performativity is the knowledge that *style* is founded not on institutional hierarchies of age, class, or caste (as is, say, *mariyātai*, 'respect,' or *mānam*, 'honor') but on a basic parity between peers. If *mariyātai* is a hierarchical boundary concept—separating and ranking the subject from others, often through recourse to relatively fixed statuses (Scherl 1996; Mines 2005:81–100)[26]—*style* is a relatively fluid and creative principle of foreground and background that, given its investment in parity, often self-consciously sits uncomfortably with hierarchy. Ultimately, it was this parity that a function like "fresher's day" celebrated, incorporating freshers through the cessation of ragging, suspending the norms of "society" (or at least figurating that suspension) while putting *style* in its place.

While the intimacy and solidarity afforded by the peer group provide the very theater for *style*, then, they also make its performance problematic. A tension underwrites *style*: to do *style* presupposes an equality between peers that the entailments of *style*—social difference and esteem—threaten to undermine.[27] There is a fundamental ambivalence, then, in every act of doing *style*. This ambivalence is inscribed in *style*'s citational form. By figurating social difference, by making a hedged gambit for social status in the peer group, playful acts of *style* always risk being taken too literally, taken not as jocular figurations of being cool but as implying the actual inferiority of one's peers. In the case of brand displays, given their association with global elite fashion, they may be seen as inscribing class difference. Acts of *style* thus always hazard being seen as what they cite, as literally performing what they otherwise disavow, pass over in silence, or profess indifference to. As I observed, brand displays could always be construed as arrogant (*bantā*), as uppity, as *over*.

One middle-class Madurai student, Ajith, illustrated this dynamic between *style* and *over style* to me while our group of friends hung out and waited for classes to begin just across the way from where Nathan and I sat months later. Drawing me near, he said, 'Look at my watch. It's nice, right? It's shiny. It's steel. It has the name of a brand on it. But look closer. It isn't running! It's broken. It's a fake. The watch is *style*, but it's *over*!' In this self-deprecating demonstration, Ajith first parodically performed a hypothetical presumption to brand authenticity. He then invited another point of view that, in revealing the fakeness of the watch (which, note, was still *style* despite, or rather because of, its inauthenticity), implicated the initial presumption as "*over*" ('excessive,' 'too much'). He deftly did this by attributing the charge of being *over* not to himself, the wearer, but to the watch. (In this is a contradiction, of course, for it was *his* hypothetical presumption to *style* that made the watch *over*, not the watch itself. How else, then, could he reframe the watch as a joke?) Yet this was no hypothetical: he *was* wearing the watch. In effect, through his joking explanation, Ajith preemptively status-leveled himself by explicitly pointing to the fakeness of his *stylish* watch. Indeed, his self-policing succeeded in drawing playful, if perhaps implicitly cautioning, laughs from his overhearing friends. To not do so would be to presume a level of class status that everyone in the peer group knew he didn't have—one with easy access to authentic, working brand commodities. It is this gap between the status Ajith could be seen as claiming and his self-presentation that potentially made his display presumptuous and absurd. But beyond ascribing a class position that he didn't have, more important was that such a display would presume class difference from his peers.

Whenever someone's brand displays were taken as serious expressions of social difference (as Ajith laughingly intimated that his might), that person would inevitably be disciplined or socially excluded in one way or another. Indeed, much of what went on in friends' circles like Ajith's was sitting around on the college benches, observing whose *style* was too much, derisively commenting on it, and teasing them about it. This potential to inscribe social difference made the (presumed-to-be) authentic brand a metonym for *over style* more generally. To parody and police those whose *style* was excessive, who were seen as arrogant (*talaikaṇam* or "head weight"), who showed off too much (*bantā kāmikkiṟatu*), who acted like they were of a higher status than they actually were or who implied the inferiority of others (*biku paṇṟatu*), young men might simply invoke their brand paraphernalia: 'Look at him showing off with all his brands!' Similarly, one might hear griping about overly brand-fashionable (and English-speaking) students who acted like they were born in London or America when everyone knew they were just local guys like everyone else (chapter 4). Commenting on another student's expensive, name-brand clothing, one friend exclaimed, 'Who does he think he is, some kind of big man ("*periya āḷ*") or something?!'

As these last two comments indicate, metadiscourses of *style* often rationalized who could and could not do *style* by appealing to some relatively fixed feature of the person (e.g., being from London or America) rather than as a differential relationship between persons or as an interactional achievement.[28] One such discourse was that "culture" or "native place" licensed *style*.[29] For example, my hip Madurai roommate Stephen came from Kodaikkanal, a hill station associated with Christian missionaries, colonial vacationers, and a famous American, English-medium convent school. Other students often explained Stephen's forays into sartorial *style* as being due to the fact that he was from Kodaikkanal.[30] *Style* was seen as being more natural for Stephen because it was part of his "culture," because it was "normal" for him, which is also to say that when Stephen sported a goatee (chapter 1), spoke in English (chapter 4), and wore loose-fitting pants or *stylish* T-shirts, he wasn't trying to show off per se.[31] That was just how people dressed where he was from. The converse assumption was that students from rural areas, whose "culture" was construed by default as traditional and thus not *stylish*, were less likely to be given the benefit of the doubt (cf. Tarlo 1996). For them, *style* was unnatural, an artifice, dissonant with their *local* background. (As we see below, some young men, like Stephen's and my roommate Sebastian, voiced this discourse to claim masculinities other than those performed by *style*.) Similarly, students from hipper and richer departments and colleges were assumed to be more *stylish*, just as those from less prestigious departments and colleges were assumed to be less predisposed to *style*.

Such metadiscourses attempt to fix and naturalize the unstable performativity and ambivalence of *style*—in particular, its relationship to class difference—by displacing *style* elsewhere (from class to "culture," from here to there, from us to them). Indeed, such discourse always pointed away from the here-and-now-and-us of the peer group. It was not a discourse that the *stylish* subject would voice about himself to ground his own *style*.[32] Stephen never explained his own dress by alluding to his being from Kodaikkanal, being from an elite English-medium school, being from a comfortable middle-class home, or being a student in the self-financing commerce department. This naturalizing metadiscourse of *style* only appeared at a remove from *style*, voiced in reference to some third person or some other place.

As with all performatives, the success or failure of doing *style* is interactionally emergent (even if the performative act ideologically presumes upon, for its felicity, its own fixity and stability), dependent on a range of acts gelling in some unfolding context. This is why, then, these ideologies of personhood or aesthetics fail to account for who actually did *style* (which they generally did, by my observations): not only do they presume that what is in flux is fixed, but such ideologies are, as part of the very unfolding negotiation of *style*, only one piece of a larger configuration of signs in fluid events of interaction between differentially positioned subjects. Such ideologies are themselves caught up in the unfolding interactional dynamics of *style* (they are one of its moving pieces among many kinds of citational bracketing), even as they reflexively reanalyze and partially efface such dynamics. These metadiscourses, I would suggest, then, are part of a more general interactional tendency to displace and disavow *style* in the here-and-now of the peer group precisely so that *style* can felicitously, if inoffensively, appear precisely where it and its potential entailments (i.e., invidious social difference) had just been denied as existing.

Hence, in talking about who does care about brands *as* brands, young men would inevitably point away from their own peer groups, denying that they were actually interested in brands (signs seemingly to the contrary notwithstanding). Through such disavowals—'No one here cares about brands'—such youth drew the boundaries of their peer groups, both temporally and by class (Bucholtz 2007). Young men pointed to working adults—notably, recent graduates in the white-collar private sector wearing authentic, expensive formals, as discussed above—as the ones who were really concerned with "original" brands. Similarly, nonelite students would inevitably point to those in richer, urban cliques (particularly in other departments or colleges) as being the ones who really cared about brands. In both cases, it was explained that this is because the working adult and the elite youth are more concerned with class distinction, "ego," and "prestige." By contrast, richer students pointed to poorer students as 'crazy' (*kiṟukku*) about brands without any actual knowledge of the "real" thing. They mimicked brand fashion and aped the rich in their desire to partake of elite consumption. By constantly pointing away from themselves, these various youth attempted to bracket the intra-peer-group status-differentiating potential of the brand, hedging its risky excess by displacing brand consciousness and concern outside of the group—hence, the implied corollary to the common refrain, 'No one *here* cares about brands': 'but *they* do *there*.'

Such displacements implicitly confront the specter that, indeed, there was class inequality between peers that potentially problematized the forms of sociality and intimacy that the peer group presumed upon. It is this haunting possibility that is the source of the brand's negative excess (and of *style*'s more generally). And it is this possibility that must be disavowed, silenced, rationalized, ignored.

This isn't to say that students of different classes didn't display brands differently or wear different types of branded clothing. They certainly did, as students were all too aware. As we might expect, as one went up the class hierarchy, one was likely to find higher-quality garments that more closely approximated the authorized, authentic brand and that followed global fashion trends more closely. Among the most elite students, for whom the expense of authorized brand commodities was not a big deal (a small minority in the colleges where I worked), surfeits were likely to be seen as indexes of bad taste or of low-class standing. The lexeme "style" even had a different meaning, being used in the British and American sense of self-expression and taste, as indexing individuality (rather than individuation) and distinction (rather than differentiation).

Most students didn't have easy financial access to authorized brand commodities, however. Yet, as I've been arguing, it ultimately wasn't their objective consumptive ability as individuals that mattered. Because brand displays are intersubjective communicative acts, what mattered was the consumption level of the peer group more generally (Nisbett 2007)—what Mary Douglas and Baron Isherwood (1996[1979]:90) have referred to as "consuming level." For example, one of my first-year Madurai roommates from the aided hostel, Yuvaraj, could buy authorized brand goods. His parents gave him a hefty monthly allowance. However, he preferred cheaper duplicate brand garments. As he said, 'If in the college no one cares about brands, why would I spend nine hundred Rupees [about $20 at the time] on one "company" piece of clothing when I can get three or four (fake) shirts? Among friends, everyone knows that no one has real brands.' More than a simple index of class position, brand displays diagram the relationships between individuals in their various reference groups. For Yuvaraj, fitting in meant consuming like his peers. Otherwise, it would be *over*. It would risk drawing charges of arrogance, of showing off too much (cf. Gell 1986).

When they did discuss "original" brands, youth like Yuvaraj talked about such goods not by their brand sign value or their commodity exchange value but by their material qualities: their utility, durability, and high quality.[33] By emphasizing the materiality of such goods—as Yuvaraj explained, 'They'll last you years rather than months' and 'The dye won't run the first time you wash it' (all true of course)—the potential of the brand garment to inscribe class position is suspended. Prefiguring and preempting possible peer censure, this discourse of quality serves the same role as the patent inauthenticity of the brand surfeit's material form. And like Sam's public silence about his beloved sneakers or Ajith's self-deprecating aside about his broken watch, this discourse marks a distance from the desires for and dangers of the authorized brand good. Such indifferences, hedges, disavowals, nervous laughs, and silences attempt to defang the authentic brand good and domesticate it for peer-group display, even as its potential indexical entailments hauntingly threaten to reappear as *style* that is *over*.

Crucial to understanding youths' indifference to authenticity and brand identity that I opened the chapter with, then, is not the question of whether these young men can or cannot tell the difference between the "real" and the "fake." They can, of course. And indeed, that is the point.[34] Underwriting young men's status negotiations is the bracketing of this regime of value as relevant for evaluating and using commodities in the peer group in the first place. Young men respond to the brand's disruptive powers by scrambling its very intelligibility and authenticity, for to display and evaluate branded garments in the peer group *as* authentic or inauthentic—that is, via their brand provenance, by their brand ontology—would problematically introduce class within a social context where such relatively perduring forms of status were supposed to be, but were never quite, suspended. This is precisely why brand displays in the college were citational: they reanimated that which they also had to disavow, presenting the brand even as they reflexively marked difference and distance from it, always keeping it at arm's length and in quotes.

The larger point is that the multiple mandates of the peer group require all signs of status to speak polyphonically, simultaneously indexing difference from adults and from one's peers, from the *local* and the foreign, from the traditional and the global, from the *jolly* present and the seriousness of the future workplace, all the while mitigating the very status that such attempts at differentiation figuratively presuppose and potentially literally, and infelicitously, entail. It is through this multivocality that the brand is refunctioned in the peer group, where animating that which is *like* comes to take on some, but not all, of the performative power of that which it is not and, more importantly, comes to enable performativities that are irreducible to that which is cited. Just as with the adult normativities they invert, by putting brands in quotes, the objective bases for brand value are denuded and reconverted as relative tropes: foreignness is converted into figurative reanimations of it, globally fungible exchange value into locally constituted symbolic value, brand identity and authenticity into brandedness and *style*. By representing the brand while simultaneously negating it—that is, by citing it—*local* "dummy pieces" can successfully do *style*, not despite, but because of their otherwise transparent inauthenticity.

It is from this point of view, then, that we can appreciate these young men's indifference to and disavowals of the brand *and* their keen interest in brandedness. In all these cases, brand garments, "fake" or "real," were not being reckoned as instances of brands as such. Rather, such displays figurate the brand; they cite and simulate the very idea of it. Only by both reanimating and suspending the brand, and the social imaginaries that it opens up, can the branded form, can brandedness, do *style*. Only by citing the brand can its absent presence be made a little less absent, a little more present. Only by putting one's own acts of *style* in quotes can *style* be felicitously performed.

This required that every potential instance of a brand be framed, at some level, as *not* a brand, neither real nor fake, but something else, something simply *like* a brand. This manifested not only in the materiality of the garments that so ubiquitously clothed young men's bodies (with their cheaper materials, misspelled names, etc.), nor in the ways that young men discursively framed their and others' brand fashion (their silences, indifference, disavowals, and rationalizations). It also manifested ontologically. Brandedness, in this case, implies a noncognizance of garments *being* or *not being* instances of brands as such. It requires garments to be something else, even as those very garments are in fact iconically tethered, sometimes hanging only by an indexical thread, to the brands they cite. This unresolved, ambivalent tension between brand and brandedness, identity and quality, means that while the brand and its surfeits are always materially and aesthetically related, they must never come too close. It also means that while they must be kept ontologically distant, they are never too distant. In young men's acts of balancing *style* and *over style*, the brands that they display are reflexively foregrounded as nonbrands in the here-ness of the peer group, even as those displays motion to an exteriority (and regime of class distinction) that exceeds, and must be kept distant from, the here-ness of the very act of display. Like its youth animators, the branded form must constantly be kept liminal, part tangled thread and part wax figure, clinging to its user's thin skin but also cooly detached from it, for to align too closely with the brand *as* brand is to, like Icarus in his skyward flight, risk coming too near to the sweating sun.

The Unbranded Body

Before concluding this chapter, I would like to turn to the unbranded body and its relation to the particular kind of masculinity enacted in and by *style*. Not all students partook in the aesthetics of brandedness that I discuss in this chapter. Some young men refrained from it. And almost all young women did not participate in it.

Hailing from a village near the small city of Tirunelveli, Sebastian, one of my roommates in Madurai, was considered a straight-laced and upright (even uptight) student. He inhabited something closer to the trappings of *decent* adult masculinity. I never knew him to go see films. He never drank or smoked. He sported a mustache that was always about to curl at its edges, though it never quite did. Sebastian eschewed the *style* of brand garments, opting for unostentatious tailored slacks, shirts, and sandals, though even he saved a pair of jeans, a polo shirt, sneakers, and a baseball hat for special occasions like the hostel's farewell day (chapter 5). This was because, as he put it when I asked him, he followed "*periyavaṅka* culture," the culture of adults (literally, the culture of 'big men'), and was from a village (i.e., he was "traditional" in his values). And while he was esteemed in the hostel for being upstanding and dependable and for never backing down from a challenge (reflected in his rigid posture and impressive physique), it was telling that his active disengagement from doing *style* also circumscribed his social circle. The crowd of guys with whom he socialized in the hostel were seen by other hostel students as a bunch of *cinna pasaṅka*, 'little boys' who avoided and feared getting in any trouble, who acted like immature children simply doing whatever adults (*periyavaṅka*) told them to. They, of course, saw it differently (chapter 1). For Sebastian and his friends, *style* and its trappings marked a boundary line through which they made their own, not uncontested, claims to identity, masculinity, and value, one based on notions of *decency*, control, and modesty.

While Sebastian's own self-conception of appropriate masculinity led him to abstain from brand fashion and *style*, young women's engagements with brandedness were largely experienced not as elective play but as serious prohibition.[35]

Young women's dress styles have historically more conservatively engaged with Western fashion (Tarlo 1996).[36] This reflects a longer-standing nationalist politics of gender that, as Partha Chatterjee (1993) has famously argued, relegates the middle-class Indian woman and her body to the interiority of the home, to the cultural and the traditional, insulating her as an emblem of the nation from the materialist realm of Western modernity. In Tamil Nadu, as elsewhere, this is inflected by a discourse of chastity (*kaṟpu*), in which the woman's body is taken as the site and sign of the honor (*mānam*) and respect (*mariyātai*) of the nested groups of men who contain her and her sexuality: the family, kin group, caste group, "Tamil culture" (Reynolds 1980; Anandhi 2005; Seizer 2005), and following Chatterjee, the Indian nation writ large (Niranjana 2001:48–55).

It is in this context that we can understand why most of the young women that I worked with did not visibly engage in a *stylish* aesthetics of brandedness or with stereotyped Western dress styles more generally (jeans, T-shirts, miniskirts, and the like), usually opting instead for north Indian dress styles, such as tailored chudhitars and salwar kameezs, which were seen as demurely modern and age appropriate for young college women (Lukose 2009).[37]

The *style* of the brand, as with *style* more generally, risked sexualizing women's bodies, for *style* turned precisely on its reflexive conspicuity, on the fact that it not only drew attention to one's embodied self but was taken to metacommunicate a desire to be seen. Such attention-demanding fashion, as I noted, is a hedged challenge to norms of respectable public propriety through flirtatious invocations of exterior imaginaries and social forms. While for young men, such transgression was tolerated and perhaps even expected (Jeffrey 2008 et al.), *stylish* fashion by a college woman keyed stereotypes of a selfish and arrogant (or "bold" and "independent," as young women positively put it) "modern" femininity that called into question the very basis of adult respectability: the control and containment of the young, female body.[38] Young men's *style* figurates adult masculinity through bracketing and transgressing it and thus is, in certain ways, continuous with it (e.g., given its emphasis on autonomy, boldness, and visibility). By contrast, young women's *style* presents a problematic discontinuity with adult femininity that manifests itself in the ways in which women's *stylish* fashion was deeply troubling to both young and adult men and women, though perhaps especially to men. Women's *stylish* fashion was conceited and snobbish, disgusting (*abāsam*) and immorally sexual and attractive (*glamour*).

The high stakes of women's fashion made it difficult for young women to citationally display brands on their bodies, for such *style*, even if in quotes, would always be (mis)read literally (also see chapter 6). Such *style* would inevitably be seen as *over* and be met with harsh forms of policing, from cruel gossip, teasing, and social ostracization by peers to explicit proscription from elder kin (not excluding physical violence) and the college administration.[39] When I asked a former student of a Madurai women's college about women's fashion, the topic came around to jeans. After noting that "society" thinks that women wearing jeans is bad, she said that of course women should wear what they like. She hedged with an addendum, however: as long as it didn't offend or "disturb" others. She continued, describing how when her college banned jeans, the principal burned a pair of jeans on campus to demonstrate the seriousness of the injunction. Only a few students protested, she said. We came to college in chudhitars.

Brand, Brandedness, and the Subject of Citation

In concluding this chapter I want to think with, and against, Jacques Derrida's (1988) and Judith Butler's (1993; 1997) discussions of citationality, performativity, and subjectivity to ask two intertwined questions: What does the act of citation *do* to its object? And what kind of empirical subject is presupposed and entailed through acts of citation?

Drawing on Jacques Derrida's (1988) critique of speech act theory,

Judith Butler (1993; 1997) has argued that performativity is made both possible and impossible by citationality, the way in which every act cites the "norm" that governs its identity and effectivity as such-and-such an act, repeating that norm anew while simultaneously opening up the gap of difference that such iteration "necessarily possibly" entails (Derrida 1988:15). On this line of argument, the capacity to reinscribe and break from the norm is a virtual possibility of all intelligible and repeatable acts, though it is most clearly manifested in particular types of acts, such as drag (Butler 1990:163–80; 1993:81–97, 169–85) and mimicry (Bhabha 2004[1993]:121–44). While most citations of the norm pass over this possibility in silence (this erasure being part of their naturalizing power to foreclose this potential/difference), acts such as drag and mimicry clearly inscribe their self-difference in their act of iteration and thus serve as an exception that reveals the rule. Through their iterability, then, citations entail their own potential performativity, their capacity to bracket, act on, deform, and render alter that which they repeat. They thus hold out the possibility of other forms of value, social relationality, aesthetics, and materiality, for other performative dispensations. It is in this possibility, in this gap between the norm and its citation, Butler (1997) suggests, that the subject dwells.

We might see these dynamics evinced in youth engagements with brand garments.[40] As we saw, in the hands of young Tamil men, branded garments (even the "real" ones) cease to be instances of brands as such. They are instances of brandedness, commodities that share the "*look*" of branded goods, even if they don't index any particular brand identity or image. They are of a different, if entangled, ontology. Youth citations elicit—or perhaps better, conjure—the qualities of brandedness out of the brand and its commodity instances, where the sharing of quality comes to take on performative force, even as, or precisely because, such citational forms are marked as not quite the same as either the brand or its material commodity instances.[41] This rendering of material indexes of multinational corporations (legally policed trademarks and other authorized indices of authenticity) into citations thereof is a creative, transformative act. It opens up something beyond the brand and its hierarchies of value (original/copy, real/fake, licit/illict, etc.). It opens up a space of youth sociality, a fashion aesthetic, and as I suggest below, a form of subjectivity.

Yet central here is the ambivalence, and the reflexivity to that ambivalence, that surrounds youths' fashion practices, the ways in which they are complex semiotic acts comprising moves and countermoves, embraces and repudiations, exuberant exclamations and mute silences that necessarily intertwine with each other. It is not, I would argue then, the "necessary possibility" of iteration that makes citations per se performative, that makes them open up alternate vistas of sociality, or that provides a space for the subject, as Butler and Derrida suggest. Rather, it is the actual *reflexivity* of citational acts that constitutes their performativity and enables their pragmatic entailments (if, and when, they indeed are performative and have such entailments). (This is why highly reflexive performances of drag and mimicry are not exceptions that prove the rule but stylized, genred instances of the rule itself.) More than iterability, what constitutes the citation's performativity is the achieved reflexive marking of its iterability, the *actuality* of the metacommunicative countergesture that registers and calls attention to the citation's difference from that which is putatively represenced in the act of citing (Nakassis 2013c). Acts that don't succeed in (being taken as) so marking themselves fail to cite. This is, of course, the problem of *over style* and the latent, negative performativity of the brand. Acts of displaying brands always threaten to simply be taken as *being* (or not being) brands rather than as citations of them. In failing to felicitously achieve citationality, such garments ontologically *become* real or fake. As citations, by contrast, they are neither real nor fake, but something else.

Youth don't simply display brands on their bodies, as if in mute, if altered, repetition of some global norm of fashion. They frame such displays, hedge on them, tentatively making claims through brands while avoiding being seen as making those very claims. They express indifference to, cultivate ignorance of, explicitly disavow, sometimes call attention to, or simply remain silent about the surfeit nature of their own consumption. Such indifference, ignorance, disavowal, confession, and silence have to be seen as quotation marks that steady the eruptive powers of the brand, readying it for display by containing and bracketing it. As Michael Taussig (1993) notes of the oscillation between sameness and difference in mimesis and as Georg Simmel (1998[1904]) notes of the simultaneity of both in fashion, citational acts are also forms of protection from what is cited, just as they are a way of yoking what is cited to the various social projects to which they are put.

Such suspensions produce experiences of liminality. Youths' citational engagements with brands register ambivalent experiences and expectations of trajectories of class- and age-inflected mobility. In particular, as we saw, the aesthetics of youth fashion turn on marking a distance from students' possible future workplace selves, from that step toward adulthood that is associated with authorized brand consumption. This distancing is accomplished precisely through the surfeit's loud and flashy design, its cheap materials, its conspicuously misspelled names and deformed logos, and its filmic quality. Such uncanny displays invoke and defer that future self through their deformative presencing of the brand. Such fashion inserts a liminal gap, invoking a possible future even as it brackets that future as just play.

This isn't a refusal of the future or a resistance to the adult social order that that future portends (Osella and Osella 1998; Newell 2012:238–39; cf. Hebdige 1979; Cosgrove 1984). Youths' citational practices are more complex and ambivalent. Even as their adult futures are constantly deferred in their transient, fashionable practice, youths' suspensions of their future selves implicitly voiced an equivocal and equivocating desire for that very future. We might follow James Ferguson (2002), then, and pose youth fashion practices, as well as youths' use of English (chapter 4) and other signs of cosmopolitanism, not as mimicry or resistance but as bids to attain a kind of global citizenship. Indeed, many of these young men did hope to become authenticated, credentialized consumer citizens working in multinational BPOs, IT centers, and the like for respectable salaries. *Just not on that day.*[42]

Youth fashion inserts into the here-and-now of its ambivalent desires a deferral, placeholding for that which may come to pass but cannot be embraced today. This deferral complicates the notion that youths' citations of brands are bids for global citizenship as such. Rather, such displays are citations of that very act of bidding. It is not simply that youth displays of brand commodities reanimate brands while disavowing them, invoking youths' future selves while holding them in abeyance; it is that in doing so, they also simultaneously hedge on their very disavowals, holding out for the object of desire that their act simultaneously denies in the here-and-now. It is this complex equivocation that puts youths' own citational practices, their own displays of branded forms, their own *style,* in fact, in quotes. By fixing and holding fixed this distant horizon for *style,* such acts open a space before the threshold, a space for other forms of sociality, intimacy, and status for those whom we might otherwise describe as in the waiting room of globalization (Weiss 2002; Liechty 2003:241; Luvaas 2009).

This suggests that the particular kind of empirical subjectivity presupposed and entailed by such citational practices is a liminal subject, not simply in the sense of being in between stages in the lifecycle or en route in some trajectory of class mobility (though these young men are both), but liminal in the sense of reflexively registering and managing multiple contradictory metapragmatic injunctions, in the sense of dwelling in the space created by experiences of being drawn and dispersed by multiple desires and anxieties at once. Liminality here denotes the possibilities opened up and actualized by deferring the threshold's presencing, the reflexively managed becoming of nonequivalence and self-difference, an excluded middle, a dynamic stasis of tension, contradiction, and ambivalence. This subject is located between a citing present and a cited future, between the subjectivity it tentatively performs (being a *stylish*, college youth) and those other subjectivities it ambivalently reanimates but claims not to *be* and thus is like (the 'big man,' the working professional, the urban cosmopolitan, the *local* hick, the cinema hero, the *rowdy*, etc.).

The pragmatics and metapragmatics of doing *style* simultaneously and gracefully hold together opposing tendencies and interests and, in doing so, enable a subject who, following Georg Simmel (1984[1909]), flirts—with the future, with adult masculinities of various sorts, with the "foreign," with the brand, and most important, with his peers. The flirt, Simmel tells us, refuses to decide, maintaining a coherent simultaneity of contradiction, cultivating the tension between the very opposites he declines to resolve. And in doing so, the flirt brackets flirtation's putative endgame, opening other pleasures and performativities that are irreducible to the less artful and more obvious desires that he puts into play as asymptotically (un)reachable horizons. The citing subject is not simply liminal and ambivalent, then, not simply the product of the gap between the self-same norm and its self-different repetition. He is a subject that flirts, that actively produces that very liminality and ambivalence in and through the reflexive act of doing *style*.

THREE

Brandedness and the Production of Surfeit

Introduction

A tightly packed grid of streets hemmed in by busy and noisy avenues, this "*tōṭṭam*" ('garden'), as the area was referred to, teemed with small textile production units, garment wholesalers, and a few retailers selling branded "export-surplus" jeans, shirts, and other accessories produced in India for consumption abroad. Hanging outside of the shops, sample wares flapped in the wind. Inside the production units, working-class boys and girls packaged and folded clothes, while owners—all older adult men—showed the latest wares to wholesalers and out-of-town retailers. I had been coming to this section of north Chennai for the past month to research the production and circulation of the brand-citing garments that were so popular among the college students discussed in the previous chapter.

North Chennai has a history of textile and garment production as old as the city of Madras itself, as Chennai was officially known before 1996. This particular *tōṭṭam* was only about three kilometers north of Peddanaickenpet, or Comerpet, as it used to be known, an area just outside of Fort St. George, the colonial center of the Madras Presidency. The first settlers of Madras's "Black Town," the neighborhoods outside of the Fort, were clothmakers brought to Comerpet from present-day Andhra Pradesh. They wove and dyed their wares by the Elambore River while merchants, traders, and

Figure 5. Ferrari brand shirt: A *local* "dummy piece" with the same font and typeface, name, and color scheme as an authorized Ferrari brand product

financiers in the cloth business settled close by (Muthiah 2004:33). This history is alive across contemporary north Chennai, with textile workshops and wholesalers scattered across its neighborhoods, tucked away in narrow lanes, and encroaching on congested roadsides, here and there and huddled together in areas like the one I was visiting.

Unlike the export-surplus brand garments in the retail shops—largely made in industrial towns and cities like Tiruppur, Erode, Ludhiana, Bangalore, and Bombay for foreign markets in the United States, Europe, and elsewhere—the wares manufactured in this *tōṭṭam* were generally of comparatively low quality. Made for the domestic market, such clothing also featured brand names and logos, often citationally copied (or "pirated") from the export surplus sold by neighboring retailers. These garments exhibited a range of fidelity toward the brands they reanimated, though ultimately, most all of these garments conspicuously betrayed their difference from the "originals" upon which they were based. Cheaply made shirts and hats with names like "Ferrari" (figure 5), "Reebok," or both (figure 6); brand-inspired apparel that animated brand names in novel typefaces and designs (figure 7); and shirts that had the look of branded garments but

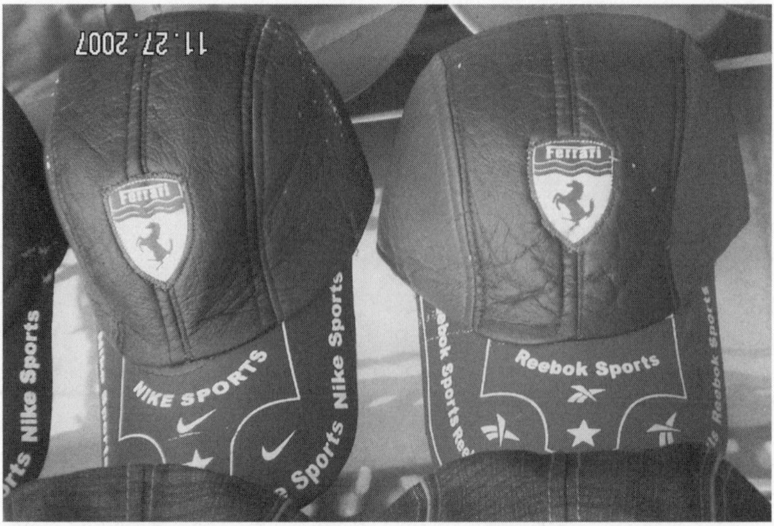

Figure 6. Ferrari-Nike and Ferrari-Reebok brand hybrids: three brands sutured together in two commodities

Figure 7. Levi's referencing brand surfeit: only the lexical form of the brand name ("Levi's") is retained, while the brand's typeface, logo, and design are discarded.

Figure 8. "Us 395" fictive brand name and logo paired with roman script design

with unrecognizable names and logos (figure 8)—such surfeits circulated in local markets and were produced in areas like this one in Chennai, Tiruppur, and other Indian cities.

Today I was chatting with a small-scale producer of Bermuda shorts about the "Columbian" brand shorts that he was selling. These shorts utilized the same logo, font and typeface, and name of the Columbia Sportswear Company, with the supplement of an "n" at the end of "Columbia" hanging on as an altering afterthought. I was trying to understand how and why he had decided on this design and on this brand. How did this winter apparel brand make its way from the blustery ski slopes of Oregon, USA, to the blistering heat of the local Chennai market? If, as we saw in the previous chapter, lower-middle-class and middle-class young men—this producer's ostensible target market—were ambivalently indifferent to, and even ignorant of, particular brands, then why was he making Columbia(n) shorts at all? Why Columbia? If there is no demand for particular brands as such, then why did producers like this one provide such a steady supply of brand-inspired and brandesque garments to local markets? If, as this producer himself noted, 'No one cares about brands' (a claim that harbors much ambivalence, as we saw from the last chapter), then why even creatively copy particular brands at all?

In this chapter, I focus on the design, manufacture, and circulation of the garments whose citational use I discussed in chapter 2, detailing the linkages that, on the one hand, connected the global circulation of brands to local markets and, on the other hand, entangled local producers of brandesque garments with the young men who bought and displayed them.[1] Building on chapter 2, this chapter looks at how youths' aesthetic of brandedness—that is, the quality of looking *like* a global brand garment without necessarily *being* one and the reflexive marking of that fact—materializes brand surfeits of various types, mediating the design, manufacture, and circulation (i.e., the supply) of such garments in Tamil Nadu. I show how the entanglement, and in certain cases, disconnection, of youths' citational practices with processes of garment design, manufacture, and circulation work to bracket and undermine what I have called in chapter 2 the "brand ontology"—that is, the reckoning of commodities, or elements of them, by their ability to authoritatively differentiate themselves from other commodities, or elements of them, through rigid indexes of (putative) origin of production (such as trademarks) and, by virtue of such differentiation and indexing, invoke a unique and authentic brand identity and "image" (as managed by marketing practice and policed by intellectual property law).[2]

What is at issue for this chapter, then, is the relationship between these two related but distinct modes of reckoning commodities—brand and brandedness—as they come to be mediated by the circulation and manufacture of the apparel that youth display to do *style*. While in chapter 2, I pointed to the tensions between brand and brandedness in the context of the youth peer group, we should note that these modes are not in inherent tension. As is the case in contexts in which brand intelligibility and authority is hegemonic, these two modes of construing commodities may work in lockstep, mutually implying and propping each other up. Any particular brand, and any brand ontology, necessarily presupposes and implies some aesthetics of brandedness, those qualities that characterize its look (or feel, etc.) over and above its policed signs of identity and image (Nakassis 2013e). Yet while every brand ontology and every particular brand necessarily presupposes and implies some such aesthetics (which is to say that the qualities of brandedness are always immanent to the brand and its token instances), these two modes of commodity intelligibility are disarticulatable from each other. There will always be more qualities of brandedness than those that authorize the inclusion of any brand instance *as* a brand instance, which is to say that the iconic qualities of any unitary identity exceed those select few that are taken to, and are made to, constitute that identity. Something can always look like a brand, even if it is not a brand. There is, then, always a latent, productive tension and gap between brand and brandedness. There is a tension and gap between any brand token (or instance) and the type (or identity) to which it belongs and hence between both token and type and the very ontology that such types stand under (Nakassis 2012b). As I showed in the previous chapter, these two modes of commodity reckoning may not always sit comfortably together.[3] In this chapter, I explore this relationship and tension between quality and identity, brandedness and brand, and the ways in which this tension can be played upon and amplified by various social actors to various ends.

It is important to note that the tension between brand and brandedness is not simply a function of differing commodity aesthetics or classification. It is not a simple matter of interpretation or social meaning, wherein some "see" brands while others only "see" brandedness. Rather, this tension is, as I show, underwritten by particular institutional and economic conditions that mediate the circulation and materialization of the very garments in question, even as these conditions are themselves mediated by these distinct commodity ontologies. The ambivalence that inheres in youth peer groups finds an analogous, if distinct, ambivalence in the very conditions of garment design, manufacture, and circulation. It is in the relationship between these ambivalences, I argue in this chapter, that we must site brand and brandedness, and the effectivity and materiality of *style* in Tamil youth fashion.

In what follows, I show how global capital that is attuned to markets outside of India but locates manufacture within India enables the circulation of branded garments in Tamil Nadu in two ways: by generating surplus brand commodities that circulate and are bought in local markets and, as a result of this, by providing the design templates and raw materials for local garment design and manufacture. In both cases, the paths by which branded forms reach local markets dismantle the classificatory logic of such clothing as instances of particular brands, thereby short-circuiting the semiotics of authorization and authenticity upon which the brand ontology stakes its claims. At the same time, by being mediated by the export-oriented textile industry (itself mediated by global brand logics), the local production and circulation of branded garments reproduce particular formal and aesthetic aspects of the brand, as well as fractions of particular brands (names, logos, slogans, labels, tags). All this results in an uncanny brand landscape that is often criminalized under labels such as "counterfeit" and "piracy" (Nakassis 2012a:715–18; Sundaram 2013). As I suggest, the entanglements that constitute this complex assemblage are citational in form, and it is such citational linkages, and their absence in certain cases, that conspire to materialize an aesthetics of brandedness.

In the conclusions of the chapter, I address the question of when a brand "is." I argue that rather than being peripheral to a theory of the brand, a focus on the surfeit and, more important, on the alternative aesthetics, regimes of value, and social relations that are opened through brand surfeits (here, brandedness and *style*) elucidate key issues that any theory of the brand must be able to account for. I suggest that to theorize the brand, we must proceed from an investigation of those excesses of value, meaning, and relationality that cannot be easily reduced back to the brand, as well as of those material forms that realize and produce such excesses. From the perspective of surfeit and brandedness, we can see that at the heart of the brand is already a tendency toward excess, a structural fragility that various social actors—local garment manufacturers and college youth, as well as global brand marketers and corporations—exploit for profit and performative effect. This excess, I argue, cannot always be easily recouped by the brand ontology precisely because the citational liability that looms around and in that very ontology always threatens to—and in the case discussed here, does—suspend the brand's being. This presents a productive problem, not only for intellectual property owners concerned with "piracy," but also for those who are interested in theorizing the brand as such.

Export Surplus and the Circulation of Surfeit

In addition to the opening up of consumer markets, the liberalization of the Indian economy in the 1980s and 1990s made it increasingly possible for foreign apparel companies to outsource their manufacture to India, enabling a boom in the Indian textile industry's export production.[4] Beginning in the 1980s, an increasing number of textile units modernized their productive capacities, orienting themselves to multinational corporations that were looking to produce garments in labor-cheap India for export to lucrative non-Indian markets (Chari 2000).[5] As Sharad Chari (2004:80ff.) indicates, this boom also entailed a shift in the industry's focus from cheaper textiles to higher-end, readymade fashion garments. When the Uruguay round of the Global Agreement on Tariffs and Trade agreed to end the Multifiber Agreement and its successor, the Agreement on Textiles and Clothing, in 2005 (agreements that imposed quotas on the amounts of textiles that developing countries could export to developed countries), many Indian manufacturers shifted to producing value-added fashion apparel for European and American markets so that they wouldn't face stiffer competition from China, Bangladesh, and Pakistan on low-end garments. The result has been the, perhaps ironic, return of India (and Asia more generally) as a production center of high-quality, low-price textiles for the rest of the world (cf. Riello and Roy 2013[2009]b).

Such export-oriented manufacture is consequential for the social lives of brand and brand-citing garments in contemporary, local Tamil markets for at least two reasons: First, export-oriented textile manufacture circulates global branded forms in local Tamil markets through the surplus, or "overage," that it creates. Second, such production provides "models," as local producers put it, for the design and manufacture of garments for domestic markets, whether they be knockoffs or brand-inspired pieces (cf. Crăciun 2009; Thomas 2013).[6]

Below I focus on both processes, drawing on research with export-oriented manufacturers in Tiruppur and Erode and with locally oriented producers in Chennai, as well as with individuals involved in the wholesaling, (re)distribution, and retail of such apparel in Tiruppur, Erode, Chennai, and Madurai. Tiruppur and Erode are small industrial cities located in northwestern Tamil Nadu (also called Kongunadu) with approximately 440,000 and 150,000 residents, with greater metropolitan areas of about one million and 500,000, respectively. Both cities are important centers of cotton textile production and garment manufacture for domestic and export markets (Tiruppur for knitwear and Erode for woven cotton), as well as for the distribution of export surplus and other surfeits in India and abroad. Industrialized textile production in Kongunadu grew out the region's agrarian economy in first half of the twentieth century (Baker 1984:267–74; Chari 2004:143–81) clustering in emerging urban centers like Coimbatore, Tiruppur, and Erode. By contrast to this region's relatively recent shift to the textile industry, Chennai (or Madras) has been a center for textile production, commercial trade, and export since the colonial origins of the city in the seventeenth century, as noted at the chapter's outset.[7]

The production units in Tiruppur and Erode that I discuss in this chapter range from large, all-inclusive factories to small workshops networked together in decentralized outsourcing relations (Chari 2004). Such units produce relatively large quantities of high-quality brand garments for export to the United States, Europe, and other wealthy consumer markets. By contrast, the local production units in Chennai that I discuss are very small, typically only having a handful of workers and producing limited amounts of relatively cheap, low-quality garments intended for the domestic market, and for lower-middle-class consumers in particular (figure 3 and figures 5–8). It is important to note that the units I discuss are not intended to be representative of the range of producers or goods made in these cities. Many more types of textiles are manufactured in these cities: from children's clothes to kitchen towels, from women's undergarments to *vēṣṭis* and *baniyans* ('undershirts'). I came to the producers that I discuss in this chapter by following the circulation of the garments that were popular on college campuses, from young men's bodies to the retailers who clothed them, from those retailers to their distributors and wholesalers, and finally, from these middlemen to those who designed and manufactured such garments.[8]

As noted, the centrality of export-oriented textile production for local markets lies in its regular and planned-for excess (Chari 2004; Norris 2010). The export-oriented manufacturer's contractual payment with the buyer—a brand company or a proxy thereof—includes within its calculation this "overage," a small percentage of the production run estimated to be slightly above the production process's margin of error. What is supposed to happen to that overage depends on the contract with the brand company (or their buying house). Some require the destruction of the surplus. Some allow it to circulate freely if marked as defective (e.g., with a crossed-out or ripped tag). Others allow it to circulate only within India (along with a bill of certification that deauthorizes the good while authorizing its circulation *as* defective/surplus). Whether in accordance with contract or not, however, a considerable amount of surplus and defective garments inevitably find their way to local markets.

From sites of manufacture, the distribution of such surplus and defective garments is often brokered by "seconds agents." Seconds agents collect the goods of many manufacturers and then sell them to wholesalers (who then deliver them to retail outlets) or to other producers who use such goods to create wares of their own. This latter case applies mainly to intermediate goods used to make garments like cloth, zippers, labels, and the like. From wholesalers, finished brand surfeits then move within India to showrooms, clothing shops, traveling bazaars, and platform merchants. They circulate either as what distributors and shop owners called "stock lots" (a hodgepodge of garments that are unsorted by design and brand) or as "fresh stock" (garments of a single design). In the stores I visited, "stock lot" was the most common way that garments came to them (figure 9), largely because of the incredibly cheap prices at which the stores and wholesalers were able to acquire such goods.[9]

The important point here is that, as excess, the afterlife of these surfeits in brand-peripheral local markets doesn't feed back into their production and, in this sense, is asymmetrically calibrated to the logic of nonlocal brand design and demand. The circulation of such garments is beholden to a local market whose demand doesn't control the production of its supply, and thus it circulates for much less than what can be extracted from the foreign target markets that drive the production and supply of these garments in the first place.

But why are such goods so cheap? First, manufacturers may not have independent access to a market where they can sell them. Even if they do

Figure 9. Stock lot of export surplus (Erode 2008): left—large bundles of stock lot garments outside an export-surplus retail store; right—inside of one such stock lot. The goods are sorted by garment type (here, button-down shirts) but unsorted by size, design, or brand.

have access, often the local market cannot bear the full cost of the good, so items are sold for whatever local distributors and wholesalers can pay, which is often less than manufacturing costs. Second, export overruns often lack the sufficient quantity or "spread"[10] required by wholesalers, giving factory or workshop owners little flexibility in dictating prices. Third, export-oriented manufacturers have already been paid for the excess through their contracts with the brand companies; thus the profits (and risks) reaped by selling such goods are over and above their bottom lines. And because the amounts of export surplus are relatively small compared to the total sizes of the contracts, and because the relative effort and risk of moving them on their own is relatively high for manufacturers (compounded since such reselling may be a breach of contract with the buying house), domestic buyers of export-surplus goods (seconds agents, wholesalers, local producers) are in a position to ask for relatively low prices. Finally, given the relative structural weakness of these manufacturers vis-à-vis the brand companies for whom they manufacture (on which, see Chari 2004:80–84), the brand company or its proxy has the right to refuse a shipment if it is late (which is likely, given the last-minute temporality of season-driven fashion markets), if the quality of the good is not up to standard, or if the brand company goes bankrupt and cannot pay for the goods.[11] Such rejected products end up getting resold to other companies, either for export (e.g., by simply attaching a new label and repackaging the good) or for sale in the domestic market. In both cases, the goods are often sold at a low price and at a heavy loss to the manufacturers.

In short, because such garments sell at incredibly low prices and often circulate in unsorted "stock lots," they largely make it into local stores independently of their brand identity. As retailers in Madurai and Chennai explained to me, given such low prices, there is little risk to the indiscriminate retailing of branded forms, especially because youth consumers, so they said, are indiscriminate regarding brand identity (see chapter 2). The result is that almost any and every brand made in India for export ends up in local markets for cheap.

Note how the logic of export-oriented manufacture simultaneously makes authorized brand goods prohibitively expensive for most south Indian consumers, and thus not widely circulated, while making deauthorized versions of those same goods cheap, and thus widely circulated. This is inherent in the asymmetry at the core of this late-capitalist logic: by being calibrated to markets with much higher buying power—the reason manufacture is in relatively labor-cheap India in the first place—the circulation of authorized brand goods becomes highly circumscribed just as alternate paths of circulation of nonauthorized brand surfeits are opened up. While it is ultimately the social life of the brand in non-Indian markets that brings branded forms to local Indian markets, the logic of local circulation systematically brackets the classificatory logic of such garments as instances of particular brand identities. That is, export-surplus branded clothes circulate in local markets, but such circulation is insensitive to any specific local demand for brands of such-and-such a type, whether or not it exists. While the logic of why brands come to be made in India would seem highly rational from the point of view of the supply and demand of brands in the global economy, that same logic introduces modes of circulation in local markets that appear highly ad hoc vis-à-vis those very same brands. From different vantages and in different sites, brand commodities stand under different citational regimes, tightly linked to brand identity at certain sites, while only loosely linked at others.

In addition to circulating export-surplus branded garments, export-oriented textile production is also central to the circulation of branded forms in two other ways. First, as I noted, export surplus includes not only finished apparel products but also components of such products. One can buy export-surplus yarn, T-shirt material, buttons, zippers, logos, collar tags, price tags, and so on. These are, like finished export-surplus goods, incredibly cheap, and they form an important source of raw (and symbolic) materials for local producers in whatever they make. By providing high-quality but low-priced materials, such excess makes low-level local production economically viable, especially given the incredibly small profit margin at which most producers operate (Norris 2010).

Second, circulating export-surplus brand garments provide the templates or "models," as local producers put it, from which most producers design their wares. When I asked such producers about their production process, many noted that the main source of their designs is export-surplus brand clothing. This is not, of course, to say that other modes of circulation do not bring brand templates to local producers; television, print and billboard advertisements, websites, trade fairs, authorized showrooms in high-end malls, and especially film all provide fodder for local production (as they did for youth *style* as well; see chapters 2, 4, and 6–7). However, among the local producers that I spoke with, following what was circulating in the local market and attending to export-surplus designs were the primary ways that they came into contact with new brand designs. Such producers may attempt stitch-for-stitch knockoffs or, just as commonly, use export-surplus garments as inspiration for their own designs. Below I focus on the latter, not only because such creatively altered branded forms were the most common among young men during my time in the field, but also because their design and production process illuminate how the logic of export surplus enables, yet is exceeded by, the aesthetics of brandedness that underwrites the local design, manufacture, purchase, and use of *stylish* garments.

Producing Brandedness

For local producers, the primary principle of design is that the brand garment made for export *is* fashion. Such brand garments are seen as exemplars of good design, as self-evidently attractive objects. As producers explained to me, brand garments—and their logos and names in particular—are beautiful, bright, colorful, attention grabbing, and interesting to look at. Voicing their target market (primarily, lower-middle-class young men), these producers repeatedly emphasized that brands are *style*. In our discussions, the invocation of this aesthetico-performative principle, *style*, justified their use of export-surplus branded forms as inspiration for their own designs, over and above such surplus forms' status as this or that particular brand. As one graphic designer put it, 'The question isn't the (particular) brand but whether the design looks good and has *style*' ("*Look-ā irukkā? Style-ā irukkā?*"). Brand garments made for foreign markets do have that *look* and *style*, they suggested, regardless of their origin or brand identity. For this reason, the brand—as an aesthetic principle—was a citational touchstone for locally oriented design.

It is important to note that the kind of low-level production that I am discussing here is not based on any kind of organized research by producers about their youth consumers. Rather, producers 'watch the market,' as they put it, following their own sales and the activities of their competitors, altering their production and designs accordingly (cf. Jain 2007:54; Thomas 2013). Producers' discourse about watching the market reveals a dual anxiety not dissimilar to youths' own fashion anxieties: the anxiety of being left behind regarding what is "moving" (i.e., 'selling well') in the market and the anxiety of one's goods not being differentiated enough from other producers' goods. This Simmelian dynamic results in both the compulsive copying of designs already circulating in the market and their continual alteration, elaboration, and hybridization. Once a brand design becomes popular—as those of Ferrari and Diesel had in 2007—there is a production frenzy to duplicate that brand design with minor alterations to differentiate one's wares from one's neighbors' (e.g., in the typeface, fonts, colors, spelling, logos, or accompanying designs). This continues until that design's citational cachet on the local market fades, as had that of Nike (an early entrant to the postliberalization Indian market that many of my friends now saw as old hat) by the mid-to-late 2000s and that of Ferrari by 2008, for example.

Without any systematic research, producers' imaginations of what their youth consumers are like are paramount. Here again, export surplus is central. Young men, producers explained, find brands and commodities (made for those) from abroad to be aesthetically pleasing. The brand garment produced for export is, by virtue of that very fact, a reasonable guarantee that an inspired version of it can be sold for profit. This faith in the export is grounded in a particular assumption about the political economy of consumption in India. Echoing Thorstein Veblen's (1899), Herbert Spencer's (1900), and Georg Simmel's (1998[1904]) turn-of-the-twentieth-century reflections on fashion (to say nothing of turn-of-the-twenty-first-century media objects such as *The Devil Wears Prada*), local Chennai producers self-evidently and, as this and the last chapter suggest, not quite correctly explained that the lower and middle classes emulate the rich, and the rich emulate the West.[12] Thus if you duplicate brands made for export (specifically, for the West), you will make sales in local markets.

In short, this belief that brands guarantee profits isn't held because producers see demand for such-and-such brands among young, lower-middle-class and middle-class men. Nor is it held because producers closely follow the sales of such-and-such brands in the West or among the Indian elite. Rather, this belief is grounded in an aesthetic that producers believe they share with their nonelite, youth consumers—that is, the branded form has that *look* and *style* that is performative of statusful modes of youth masculinity. Hence *stylish*ly brand-adorned forms will sell, while "plain" designs without brandesque names and designs won't. Again, this is independent of questions of brand identity or authenticity as such. As producers often justified the liberties that they would take with the branded form, 'The customer doesn't know the difference, and if they do, they don't care.'

And as I found out, often producers themselves didn't know about the brands that they were citing except that they were brands, and sometimes they didn't even (care to) know that. As one producer noted, 'We don't care what the brands are. We make them because they move on the market. There is no need to know the brands because consumers don't even know the brands.' The refashioning of branded forms happens, then, through an aesthetics shared, at least partially, with youth, or imagination thereof, which is to say that local garment producers' and youths' practices are calibrated to each other vis-à-vis their mutual orientation to brand(-citing) forms as performatively *stylish* aesthetic objects. This refashioning of branded forms also works through producers' and youths' common indifference to brands qua brands (producers' indifference, of course, being reflexively contingent on their consumers' indifference)—that is, through their mutual nonorientation, or discalibration, from the brand ontology. Through these aesthetico-economic (non)linkages, the logic of the youth peer group and its dynamics of *style* entangle local garment design and manufacture, orienting local producers' practices in ways that prefigure youths' citational practices in the very material and semiotic form of what local producers design and manufacture.

As a result, a dizzying number of brand garments produced for export are being duplicated, refashioned, and hybridized by local producers. Producers get a hold of branded forms and use them as the bases from which they make their own wares, whether they be faithful to the brand "originals" or ultimately novel in their designs. Indeed, because such capricious and capacious appropriation of branded forms is tangential to the image, target market, and product ranges of any so-appropriated brand, nearly any brand can be pulled into the cauldron of garment production. It is this dynamic of attraction and indifference to the brand that links the brand to and delinks it from brandedness, that conjures the qualities of brandedness from brand commodities in and by the very act of their alterating citation.

The contingencies involved here are important to emphasize. Consider the producer of Columbian Bermuda shorts that I began the chapter with. As he explained to me, he chose Columbia not because he knew anything about the brand (he didn't) but because he was able to acquire an incredibly large amount of Columbia-brand cardboard price tags for close to nothing. It was this windfall of export-surplus price tags that triggered his production of Columbia*n* shorts. While not all brand surfeits were designed with respect to such contingencies, the larger point is that the logics governing which brands were cited in the acts of design and manufacture were indifferent to the role of brand identity (and the demand for it) in local (or global) markets, even as they responded to the vagaries of global brand economies. Indeed, such production was only contingent relative to the brand and its metadiscourses of identity and image. It was inevitable, however, relative to how outsourced commodity manufacture works with respect to local markets (i.e., inevitable given the necessary excess that export-oriented manufacture generates and circulates at a low cost). By being circulated and reanimated in this way, the very logic of brand is bracketed, simulated by and rerendered as an aesthetics of brandedness. Below I look more closely at this aesthetics of brandedness and how it draws on the design form of brand commodities and their metamarks of identity while, at the same time, erasing those marks' ability to reliably index brand origin, identity, and image.

Brandedness and the Diversification of Surfeit

While some producers do attempt high-fidelity knockoffs of branded items, a large amount of what circulates and is made locally deviates from export-surplus models. Why?

First, there are particular exigencies of budget and manufacture. Fabric, threads, dyes, or other materials necessary to duplicate some brand garment may not be available, or they may be too expensive. Similarly, the stitches and cut of a design may be too difficult or time intensive relative to the budget, profit margin, or technology available to the producer. Beginning production of new garment types takes time and money, and thus there tends to be conservatism regarding taking up new processes of garment construction. Only elements of the garment that are seen as constitutive of its *look* are replicated by producers in their production process (to whatever ability they can). While this might include a new way of stitching a sleeve or pocket, for example, more often than not, the design elements taken up by producers in their own designs are widely recognized, citational fractions of the brand: the brand name, logo, slogan, or label. Such brand fractions are highly localizable, discretely bounded, visually foregrounded, consistent across different designs from the same brand, and easily transportable into other commodity forms (all of which, of course, are features of trademark design more generally). Furthermore, they are often already available to producers in the local market as export-surplus or export-inspired commodities themselves, as we saw with the Columbia tags discussed above. In short, even as the circulation and production of brand surfeits systematically compromise brand fidelity and suspend brand ontology, brand fractions tend to be conserved as building blocks for local production practices.

Second, as we've seen, producers imagine their youth consumers to be indifferent toward brand identity as such, even as they were keenly aware that those same youth were concerned with brandedness. One producer, for example, explained why he designed his shirts with one brand name on the pocket, another on the collar label, and a third on the cardboard tag attached to the garment. He noted that without the label, without the tag, without the visible marker of the brand on the pocket, the shirt would look 'bad' and 'ugly' ("*asiṅkam*"), it would look "cheap." But putting these brand names and logos in these strategic locations would make the shirt look more "*royal*" and attractive ("*look-ā irukku*"). The overall combination of these various brand fractions elevates the garment by figuratively participating in and aestheticizing an imagined elite fashion, by beautifying and making the garment eye-catching for a youth market that was believed to desire such a fashion aesthetic. The logic revealed here is that it isn't coherence of indexed brand identity that matters but that branded forms have a particular formal structure, of which the label and tag (among other elements) are a crucial part. Customers expect this structure, producers explained, though not the brand consistency of the subparts. In talking about a garment that had Adidas's three-stripe logo paired with the Fila brand name, one producer noted that he often combined different brand names, logos, and "wordings" (slogans or other supplementary text that he poached indiscriminately from English newspaper headlines). As long as the design elements are visually pleasing, separately and together, he said, there was never a problem with such mishmashes. The same producer emphasized that his wares—whether they be hybridizations between existing brands or original designs that utilized made-up brand names—always follow the proper name/noun plus logo/design formula, with "wordings" being optional. It is this aestheticized organization that is important, he explained, and not the pointing to actual brands through signs of brand fidelity. And indeed, his garments, like those of other producers, laid out their brand fractions in ways that calqued off of the formal structure of authorized brand garments: name and logo in close proximity, organized vertically with respect to each other, and foregrounded on the top left or center of the front of the garment (and sometimes across the back). The wordings on the garment were less prominent, often appearing under the name-logo pair or on the back of the garment. Finally, he would always package his clothes like an authorized brand commodity: labels on the collar and price tags attached to the final product. Here we see how an aesthetics of brandedness includes not simply those source-indexing fractions of the brand (name and logo) but a more general mode of design and presentation associated with high-end readymade apparel.

Third, anxieties about the legal status of citing a brand impinge on how local Chennai producers design their garments. When I began my research in this *tōṭṭam* of north Chennai, there was some amount of suspicion that I was an agent of a brand company out to get counterfeit producers (cf. Crăciun 2008). After producers realized I wasn't, I was told that big companies that had, or were coming to have, a substantial stake in retail in India—for example, athletic brands like Nike, Adidas, and Reebok—were exerting pressure on producers to cease their "counterfeit" productions. Regarding their designs, this meant that they either switched to brands that were not as policed (such as Diesel)[13] or increasingly altered the logos and names of the brand "models" they were citing in order to make them different enough to not count as counterfeit. To their mind, only producing an exact replica would constitute breaking the law.[14] But to treat such brand designs as aesthetic objects, freely able to be borrowed and cited the same way one might use a color palette or geometric shape, would be unproblematic (Nakassis 2013e). One simply had to alter the form slightly or recombine it in a novel design. One had to reflexively iterate a design, not simply replicate it. One had to put it in quotes.

The brand here is a template, a complex aesthetic whole whose subparts can be disassembled and reassembled with other brand fractions or with other design elements. Thus, as the producer of Columbian shorts explained, he changed Columbia to Columbian out of the fear of intellectual property rightsholders potentially coming down on him. But he didn't only make Columbian shorts. He also got requests from wholesalers for other brand names, like Fila and Adidas. Such shorts would keep the same stitching, overall layout of design elements, logo, and tags as his Columbian shorts, resulting in a kind of Frankenstein brand-monster: an Adidas or Fila brand name embroidered alongside a Columbia brand logo, topped off with an export-surplus Columbia-brand cardboard tag.

Note again the productive tension between brand and brandedness. Above I showed how the economic logic that articulates and disarticulates foreign brand demand and local markets encourages the local replication *and* diversification of brand designs. Here, local producers' fears surrounding the enforcement of intellectual property rights by their holders also functions to encourage the innovative, citational elaboration of branded forms in local markets in such a way that they only ever problematically index the brand types from which they derive inspiration.

While local garment production depends on tokens of the brand as material and aesthetic inputs, for all the reasons discussed above—aesthetic, economic, and legal—brand surfeits in local markets transgress and problematize that very brand ontology, in effect, reclassifying brand commodities (or fractions of them) by an aesthetics of brandedness that differently reckons the sameness/difference and value of circulating commodities, not based on authenticity or identity, but on the *look*, the *style*—that is, on the aesthetic qualities and performative pragmatics—of the garment in question. These qualities are abstracted, that is, conjured out of the brand and its commodity tokens. Here, brand dissolves into brandedness, identity into quality, indexicality into iconicity (Nakassis 2013e).

But the fact of this bracketing of the brand is also the reason this is an aesthetics of *brand*edness and not something else, why such frayed iterations remain tied, if only ever loosely, to the brand. Brand garments and fractions of them are reanalyzed and simulated by local producers as instances of *style*—as vague allusions to foreign lands and the fashion sensibilities of those who inhabit them. Under this aesthetics, local producers inevitably take up branded forms as building blocks and design templates from which to make *stylish* garments, duplicating them, hybridizing them, and refashioning them as parts of their strategic gambits to entail consumption in their target markets, which is to say, to entail their citational uptake by youth. Such local designs replicate (material) fractions of the brand (a name, a logo, a tag) *and*, at the same time, formal qualities of branded apparel. And in replicating both less than and more than the brand, the brand surfeits that circulate in local Tamil markets excise the heart of the brand ontology: the capacity of commodity tokens (or fractions thereof) to index brand identities and origins in the attempt to create consumer trust, recognition, loyalty, and thereby profits. In short, this complex assemblage of circulation and production rearticulates the citational semiotics of brand (Nakassis 2012b), a semiotics now routed through rematerialized qualities that, while immanent in brand commodities, are now marked as not quite of the brand, as different from and indifferent to it. They are marked as citations of it.

When Is a Brand?

In this chapter and the last, I have detailed the ways in which the brand comes to be reanimated and undone: through the logics that govern citations of the brand in young Tamil men's peer groups, through the logics that govern the circulation and production of branded garments in and for local markets, and most importantly, through the relationship between the two. I have shown how such logics and the relationships between them conspire to reconfigure the relations of difference and sameness upon which brands are founded, bracketing brand identity and authenticity and making indistinct what brand regimes attempt to keep apart: the "real" from the "fake," the "original" from the "copy," brand *X* from brand *Y*, and brand from nonbrand.

While in chapter 2, I argued that this suspension of the brand follows from the multiple mandates of the peer group—namely, to do *style* without under or *over*doing *style*—in this chapter, I showed how this suspension of the brand results from particular movements of global capital utilizing the cheap labor of the Indian textile industry; the resultant material excess of such manufacture; the loose calibration between export-oriented and locally oriented garment manufacture; local producers' reflexive attunement to, and (imagined-to-be) shared aesthetics of, youth *style*; and the seemingly ad hoc logic of local markets vis-à-vis the brand ontology. As I have argued, however, local markets seem ad hoc and blind as to what particular brands are or mean because what these low-level producers are making and what wholesalers are distributing aren't quite brands or instances of them, but instances of brandedness: the quality of *style* woven in fabric.

In the space opened by these entanglements, then, brands circulate, but not *as* brands. They circulate as something else still. They stand under a different ontology, a different formulation of what exists and what that existence entails, which is also to say, a different regime of citation that construes and materializes commodities by a different logic of identity (cf. Vann 2006; Norris 2010:141–74). The brand is cited out of being, cited into something else, something that is not unrelated to the brand (for it emerges through it) but not the brand nonetheless (as it cannot be reduced back to it). As I have argued, even if authentic instances of the brand and felicitous instances of brandedness share aesthetic form and material substance, by falling under different regimes of citation, they become ontologically distinct, their semiotic and material being alter to each other.[15] From this point of view, brandedness isn't simply a different way of reckoning commodities but a whole economy and infrastructure of citationality, modes of connection and calibration and disconnection and discalibration, market relations and social relations (and relations between those relations) that, through their articulation, manifest in aesthetic sensibilities, social acts, modes of sociality, profits, and material garments.

This raises a methodological point and a theoretical point. The methodological point is that the study of surfeit—and more to the point, what lies beyond and besides surfeit (in this case, brandedness and *style*)—is key to any study of the brand. The brand is naturalized when we take it at face value as stable and coherent, as already having been achieved, as simply existing. The study of brand, then, must also be a study of its excesses and undoings, which is also to say, of its continual becoming and contingent achievement. Such a study, however, is not simply to be done in peripheral sites like dusty Chennai bazaars or breezy Madurai colleges. It is also to be done in brand heartlands, by detailing the ways in which the brand—as defined by intellectual property law and contemporary marketing discourse, for example—already presupposes and produces such excesses and undoings in its very ontology and in its material realizations, an argument I have pursued in detail elsewhere (Nakassis 2012b; 2013a; 2013c; 2013e; in press).[16]

The theoretical point follows from this methodological point: brand and surfeit, brand and brandedness, resist and need each other. Even as youths' citations of brands, and local producers' citations of them, undermine and stand beyond and beside the brand, those citations emerge through it, always carrying over a remainder of that which they bracket, repeating something of that which they put in quotes. There is no surfeit, no brandedness, without the brand. But more importantly, there is no brand without those excesses of quality, materiality, meaning, and ontology that emerge from the brand but cannot be necessarily reduced, or recouped, back to it. Examples of this, as I have shown, are present in Tamil Nadu, as they are all over the world, and they challenge us to rethink the excesses of the brand without simply taking the brand ontology for granted (Nakassis 2013a).[17] They challenge us to rethink the whats and whens of the brand.

Let me suggest one important way in which this is so by returning to the notion of calibration. On analogy with so-called new media, Celia Lury (2004) has discussed the contemporary brand as an "interface": a mediating technology that coordinates feedback loops that link consumer engagements with brands to processes of brand design, manufacture, and marketing, and back again (Manovich 2001; Arvidsson 2005; see chapter 8). Brands, marketing theorists tell us today, do or do not succeed based on the ways in which consumers' citational engagements with them—what consumers creatively do with brands in forging selves through, social relations with, and communities around them (Fournier 1998; Muniz and O'Guinn 2001; Prahalad and Ramaswamy 2004)—can be recouped back into brand image and as commodity profits (Foster 2007; 2008; Jenkins, Ford, and Green 2013). The interface of the brand, then, functions as a mechanism to reincorporate and encompass the brand's own exteriorities and the value and meanings generated therein. Such an interface requires infrastructure, of course, most notably in the form of increasingly brand-protective intellectual property law, which polices "illegitimate" citations of the brand (be it as "piracy" or as "diluting" or "tarnishing" consumer appropriations; Coombe 1998:41–87, 130–65; Jenkins 2006; Nakassis 2012a:715–18), and in the form of market research—for instance, "brandthropological thick description" (Sherry 2005:40; Fournier 1998:344), informatized consumer feedback (Hardt 1999; Arvidsson 2005; Manovich 2008), event sponsorship (McAlexander and Schouten 1998; Moor 2003), trend hunting, and other reflexive marketing practices that attempt to fold the positive excesses of brand citation back into brand design and production.

What the Tamil case shows is that this "interface" and its infrastructures—those modes of calibration and discalibration that make the brand intelligible and performative for some dispersed, yet entangled, social domain of individuals—are extremely fragile and unstable. They are continually undercut by those gaps in the brand form, gaps between the qualities of brand commodities and the brand identities they instantiate and between the those identities (and commodities) and the very idea of the brand. The brand is always liable to, and *is*, being "pirated," having its look cited, and even having its very *being* simulated. While such gaps constitute the brand's semiotic innards, its vitality and profitability, they are also the sites of its fragility and undoing. Citations of the brand—be it of particular commodity tokens, brand types, or even the very ontology of the brand (as with brandedness)—expose and exploit such gaps to various ends. The consumption and production of branded forms, as detailed in this chapter and the last, show what happens when brand identity and image are unmoored from the commercial and legal interests that are invested in keeping commodity form (and other brand instances), brand identity, and brand ontology in lockstep.[18]

The whats and whens of brand, from this point of view, depend on how and to what extent brand instances like commodities, brand names, trademarks, and the like are capable of regularly indexing and iconically presencing particular brand identities and images, to say nothing of the more general category of brand. To speak of the brand, then, is to speak of the stability of this iconic indexicality across contexts of social interaction wherein the fact of being a brand is pragmatically consequential—that is, wherein there is a sufficiently tight calibration, or interdiscursivity (Silverstein 2005), between mutually entangled moments of "consumption," "circulation," and "production" *as* moments of engaging with brands as such.[19] The achievement of the brand as a stable and coherent identity and ontology presupposes that what designers are designing, producers producing, lawyers protecting, marketers marketing, consumers consuming, ad jammers jamming, brandthropologists researching, and the like are all mutually and reflexively, if only ever partially, oriented to the "same" thing: the brand. It is this by-degrees co-orientation, this calibration across social sites, that gives the brand and its ontology intelligible coherence (to whatever extent it is, in fact, coherent) and in turn contributes to the materialization of those commodities and other brand fractions that then circulate and entangle those social actors whose variegated practices are thereby co-oriented and mediated by the brand.

Of course, this sameness is never guaranteed within or across such sites. If ever, it is always a temporary and partial achievement. Part of Lury's point, of course, is that the contemporary brand as "interface" bridges the aforementioned gaps and recoups the differences across these sites by virtue of its very reflexive marketing form—that is, the contemporary brand presupposes these gaps and differences and anticipates them, thereby suturing those gaps in its gambit for profit. What I would emphasize, however, is the tenuousness and speculative nature of this anticipation, its aspirational and ideological nature (a fact that marketers, of course, recognize quite clearly). This interface itself has to be achieved, for without the successful and steady regimenting of these interdiscursive links (i.e., what the "interface" of the brand articulates and mediates), the ability of the brand to reproduce itself as a material and intelligible form in and out of the economy dissolves, its performativity defeased.

To speak of the being of brands, then, is to speak of the stability of these linkages, of the mutual, if partial, orientation and entanglement of those who are so linked vis-à-vis particular brands and of the materialization of such linkages and social relations across social space and time in commoditized forms taken *as* instances of those very brands. Without such stabilization, citations increasingly float away from what they cite. The inherent gaps between commodity and brand, quality and identity, are widened. The flood of excess and surfeit overwhelm the brand as new vistas of materiality, meaning, and being open in the wake of its erasure. The Tamil case offers such a counterpoint—a different set of regular and coherent calibrations across social sites, a different indexicality, a different materiality, and a different ontology that turns less on brand image than on *look* and *style*, less on identity than on citation thereof. Tamil youths' aesthetics of brandedness is undergirded by its own "interface" and infrastructures (themselves enmeshed with those of the brand, of course), by entanglements and calibrations (and discalibrations) wherein the ambivalent *style* of brandedness becomes consequential and thus manifested in material form. This counterpoint shows us what and when a brand is: the temporary overcoming of its tendency to exceed itself, to devolve into that which it is not.

My point, then, is not that the meanings or images of various brands are always resignifiable (by consumers or other producers), that different social or cultural groups impute different local meanings to global brands (i.e., brands for some and brandedness for others), for this would already grant the brand a fixity and coherence that I hope to have shown is deeply problematic. Rather, it is that the brand ontology, the very cultural institution of the brand, is itself a site of instability and fragility. To see why and how this is the case, to answer the question of what or when a brand is, requires that we trace out the ways in which the brand and its excesses are constituted by a complex assemblage of interdiscursive linkages between moments of "production" as they are calibrated and discalibrated to moments of "consumption." Such complex citational relations quite literally materialize in and as garments. Their weaves congeal these relations, registering past citational relations and prefiguring and anticipating future ones. To answer the question, what or when is a brand?—and just as importantly, to ask and answer the question, what or when is Tamil youths' aesthetics of brandedness and *style*?—requires that we see the brand, and youths' aesthetics of brandedness, as that which stabilizes and is stabilized by, if only temporarily and contingently, these fragile and tenuous interdiscursivities. Only by identifying and empirically locating such configurations and their sites of fragility, and thus their alternate configurations, can we begin to adequately situate our theories of the brand in ways that do not reify and naturalize the brand ontology and its claims to intelligibility, authenticity, and authority. To simply assume the stability and intelligibility of brands is to elide this complexity and its fragility. It is to elide the fact that the stability and intelligibility of brands must be continually achieved, and thus, that the brand is always under threat of being defeased, suspended, and undone by citation. It is to elide the fact that this imminent threat is not exterior to the brand's being but is, in fact, immanent to its palpitating, quivering heart.

PART II

Language

FOUR

Style and the Threshold of English

White Tamil

Sweating out the late summer months early on in my fieldwork in Madurai, I lay staring at the ceiling fan turning slowly above my metal cot. I started to complain to my roommates about the fan's insufficient speed but hesitated. Which word should I use? "*Minvisiṟi*" ('electric fan') or "fan"? Which one was the "normal" word they would use in their spoken Tamil? An artifact of the longstanding contact between English and Tamil, colloquial Tamil is littered with words of English origin. Was "fan" such a word? Was it part of the everyday Tamil of the college? And if it was, then what of "*minvisiṟi*"? Not totally unexpectedly (my linguistic mishaps being a common occurrence in the hostel), my roommates Sebastian and Stephen chuckled when I finally complained about the "*minvisiṟi*." It sounded funny. It was odd, old-fashioned. It wasn't like their speech.

But my (mis)use of words like *minvisiṟi* also did something else. It elicited pride (*perumai*) and happiness (*santōṣam*) from my Tamil friends. Even on my first trips to Tamil Nadu, when I could barely string together sentences, my interactions with Tamil speakers would almost obligatorily contain statements from them like, 'You speak Tamil better than we do!' 'Your Tamil is so pure, so beautiful,' and 'It's so innocent, like a child.'

It wasn't my Tamil, of course. It was the odd conjunction that I presented (Woolard 1989:73–76; Heller 1994:2): a (seemingly) white foreigner who spoke somewhat disfluent, but relatively unmixed, high-register Tamil and could also speak English natively (which, when I did, they often found wondrously incomprehensible and *stylish*). It was this conjunction that, over the course of the academic year in Madurai, earned me the affectionate, joking nickname of "*veḷḷai Tamiḻan*," the 'white Tamil,' in the aided hostel where I stayed (see chapter 5).

My linguistic presence in the college—an institution that my primarily Tamil-speaking friends availed with hedged hopes of accessing the English-dominated, global economy—also revealed an insecurity and an ambivalence, as keyed by the languages used to articulate such pride, amusement, and wonder. It wasn't uncommon for my Tamil friends to insist on speaking as much English as possible while we praised the Tamil language together. Equally common would be for the very same youth to lament, in Tamil, that they don't actually know Tamil anymore, that everyone only speaks in English. The mouth was moving in English but praising Tamil or was moving in Tamil while lamenting its absence. It was as if my presence reflected back to these youth something of their own linguistic predicament of liminality, of their own aspirations and anxieties, giving voice to those systematic and telling absences and silences in their own speech, to certain desires of their own that often seemed just out of reach. In their speech, this manifested as a flirtatious and tentative tacking between English and Tamil. This chapter and the next discuss these tensions between and ambivalences about English and Tamil as they play out in youths' linguistic practices. In order to do this, I first briefly outline the historical relations between these two languages and the sociopolitical linguistic regimes within which they stand.

Language Contact in South India

English has a long history in the subcontinent, functioning as a language of commerce, missionizing, governance, and education, substantively beginning with British contact through the East India Company in the seventeenth century (Kachru 1983; 1994:500ff.; Cohn 1996; Hickey 2004). Central to this history of contact have been institutions of education (Seth 2007), especially since nineteenth-century attacks on Orientalist approaches to governance and education by what Thomas Trautmann (1997) has called Victorian "Indophobia." Rather than promoting the learning and use of indigenous knowledges and languages in governance, law, commerce, education, and scholarly inquiry, as had been the policy until then, in the first half of the nineteenth century, it was increasingly argued that through education, the crown's elite and masses-mediating colonial subjects should be anglicized, made to be "a class of persons Indian in blood and color, but English in taste, in opinions, in morals, and in intellect," as Thomas Babington Macaulay put it in his now infamous 1835 minute on Indian education (see Basu 1991; Kachru 1994:500–508; Trautmann 1997:111; Seth 2007). Caught up in colonial relations of power; emerging class, caste, and sexual formations; and scales of civilization, English language and personhood—a whole social imaginary of English, in fact (Chandra 2012)—was to be promulgated to Indian elites through English-medium education.[1]

In south India, the institutional and ideological forces pushing for anglicization were coeval with philological and missionary activity that, in time, would give rise to various forms of regional ethnolinguistic consciousness. South Indian colonial projects of research and governance (e.g., the work of scholars such as Francis Ellis, Alexander Campbell, and later Reverend Robert Caldwell) promoted, praised, and championed the antiquity and sophistication of languages like Telugu and Tamil against north Indian languages of antiquity like Sanskrit and, by proxy, those northern Orientalists in Calcutta who studied them. The eighteenth and nineteenth centuries saw the academic "discovery" and anthologizing of ancient Tamil literatures, the print production of Tamil dictionaries and grammars,[2] and perhaps most important, the "proof" of the relatedness of the "Dravidian" languages of the south and their unrelatedness to the Indo-Aryan languages of the north (Ellis 1849[1816]; Caldwell 1856; see Blackburn 2003; Trautmann 2006; Mitchell 2009). By the next century, this linguistic renaissance was taken up by an emergent indigenous, and eventually populist, regional politics: the non-Brahmin Dravidian movement (Ramaswamy 1997; Pandian 2007). This movement, in reanimating this colonial discourse, rejected the subordination of the Tamil language community to north Indian languages, Aryan peoples (and by extension Tamil Brahmins), and metonymically, the nationalist Congress party.[3] By the early twentieth century, this language politics, refracted into a number of social projects, as Sumathi Ramaswamy (1997) has detailed, came to largely, though not exclusively, vest its attention on the need to abject "foreign" elements of the language—in particular, Sanskritic roots—so as to restore a "pure," uncontaminated Tamil language and polity. As a result, then and now, the antiquity and purity of Tamil (as an interior language of culture and tradition) has been intimately, if ambivalently, linked to the modernity of English (as an exterior language of commerce and mobility; cf. Chatterjee 1993). Sometimes figured as a threat to Tamil (as is often expressed today), English has also been figured as an alternative to and ally against the hegemony of Hindi (an Indo-Aryan language that is the most widely spoken language in India), as in the student agitations of the late 1930s and mid-1960s that protested proposed changes to make Hindi, rather than English, the primary official language of the nation-state, the civil service, and its exams (Ramaswamy 1997; Annamalai 2011). To date, this language politics has been relatively successful in keeping Hindi out of Tamil Nadu, both as an official language of state and education and as a language of everyday use.

This plurilingual situation makes for complex linguistic possibilities in the contemporary moment, wherein the sociohistorically intertwined identities that are invokable through different varieties of English and Tamil are continually in dialogic relations with each other, echoing, embracing, and repudiating each other. The two most ideologically marked, and prestigious, poles of this plurilingual space are pure Tamil (*sen Tamiḻ*) and proper English—be it American, British, or (Anglo-)Indian English (Kachru 1975; 1983; 1994; Hickey 2004).

Pure Tamil, as Bernard Bate (2009) has discussed, is a particular register of Tamil marked by the absence of words of non-Tamil origin as well as its literary quality, its elaborate grammatical constructions (many of which are not used in colloquial Tamil), its archaic(ized) lexicon,[4] and its "clear" and emphatic noncontracted pronunciation (Schiffman 1999). Stereotypically used by *periya āḷuṅka* ('big men') in public discourse, political oratory, and literary composition (Mines 1994; Bate 2009), this register is associated with (and hence performable of) pride in the antiquity, culturedness, and beauty of the language; a commitment to its protection; and, in certain measure, the language politics of the Dravidian movement. Few (can) speak such Tamil, its performative force directly tied to its distance from everyday life and speech.

Equally out of reach for most of the populace, and just as invested with social status, is fluent English. By contrast to pure Tamil, fluent English (of whatever regional variety) is stereotypically seen as a language of development and modernity, of (state) authority and (national) governance, and most saliently for college students, of education, global mobility, and *style* (Annamalai 2004; Jeffrey 2010; LaDousa 2014; Proctor 2014; cf. Basu 1991; Seth 2007). Such language is associated with white foreigners, Anglo-Indians, nonresident Indians, and English-educated urban elites.

These two prestige varieties organize much of the indexical field of linguistic interaction in Tamil Nadu. As I suggested above and discuss in more detail below, the youth with whom I worked were located between, and through, these two regimes, though in a complex and not completely intuitive way. While pure Tamil and fluent, proper English functioned in other contexts and for other speakers as prestige registers, among such youth, the use of these registers took on inverted, performative value. Given its associations with the archaic past, high literature, regional politics, and 'big men,' the use of pure Tamil in the peer group, no matter the amount, often had negative, if potentially comic, associations. It was absurd. It made one sound like a language fanatic, a lunatic (*kiṟukkan*), or like one had stepped out of a time warp. On the other hand, speaking, or trying to speak, in English could make one sound like a pretentious snob or a poseur, which would equally lead to teasing and other forms of censure.[5]

The youth with whom I worked and lived used neither proper English nor pure Tamil but what they called 'ordinary' (*sātāraṇam*), spoken Tamil (*pēccu Tamiḻ*). While *pēccu Tamiḻ* invokes a catch-all colloquial standard, what passes for it includes a great deal of sociolinguistic variation by region, caste, and class. Yet, even as youths' spoken Tamil at times betrayed and strategically deployed such variation, what they referred to as their normal speech generally avoided getting too closely aligned with the shibboleths of recognizable variants of such sociolinguistic diversity (as was considered appropriate for aspiring middle-class college students), or what was often labeled for lower-caste, lower-class, and rural speech forms as "*indecent*" or "*local*" speech. College students' speech, just as it avoided the pure and the proper, also avoided being too ordinary or too *local*, which is to say, too emplaced by region, social class, or caste. That isn't to say that students—and young men in particular—didn't use or draw on speech forms or discourse styles that were seen as *local* but that, in general, the forms and styles that they did use with frequency (e.g., expletives; symmetrical, nonhonorific second-person pronouns and address terms), rather than instating an uneducated, *local* identity per se, cited the *local*—in the expansive sense discussed in this chapter—so as to carve out intersubjective pockets of youth sociality by transgressing the norms of *decent*, respectable speech (chapter 1).

In short, college youths' speech struck a complex balance, tending toward unmarked registers of standard spoken Tamil, incorporating some amount of *local* speech and some amount of English, much of the latter comprising highly normalized lexical borrowings, like "fan," as we saw above.[6] To say that the everyday Tamil of the college domesticated some amount of English within it *as* Tamil, however, isn't to say that youth couldn't provide English etymologies for such normalized borrowings. They often did. Many who would consider words like "bus," "coffee," "tea," or "fan" as part of everyday spoken Tamil would also point out their English origins.[7] Yet, as they would insist, that's just how Tamils speak today. Nobody uses the "pure" Tamil equivalents (namely, *pēruntu, koṭṭai vaṭi nīr*, *ilai vaṭi nīr, minvisiṟi*). While often this was expressed ruefully ('No one today knows *either* Tamil or English correctly' being a common, if exaggerated, refrain), it was also accepted as an unavoidable fact of modern life. There was a tension, a sense that English and Tamil were separate languages that should be, yet could not be, kept separate.

But more important than their contact, than the unavoidable presence of English in Tamil, was the ambiguity of where exactly English stopped and Tamil began. The lines that divide these two languages (and in particular, their lexicons), and thus the social meanings that can be invoked through them, are shifty. The normalization of English forms in spoken Tamil is highly relative, as are the colloquialness of *local* Tamil and the purity of pure Tamil. Not all linguistic forms are equally normalized or standardized for all speakers (Myers-Scotton 1993:131–32; Meeuwis and Blommaert 1998). To that extent, there is always a certain amount of indeterminacy surrounding the usage of English and Tamil linguistic forms, an ambiguity and epistemic gap between their status as "normal" or not, between their status as prestigious (i.e., pure and proper, educated and elite) or stigmatized (i.e., rural or uneducated, absurd or show-offy).

It is in this indeterminacy, in this linguistic liminality between languages—or rather, between ideologically invested registers that are often taken to stand in for the named languages "Tamil" and "English" (namely, pure Tamil, standard spoken Tamil, or proper English)—that *style* is located. If "normal," everyday youth speech in the college is already constituted by a complex balance, youths' linguistic acts of *style* tentatively attempt to tip that balance through ambivalent acts of citing English that constantly push on, and consequently blur, the line between "Tamil" (of whatever variety) and (nonnormalized) "English," even as they thereby draw on that very boundary. The issue raised in this chapter, then, is less the differences between languages than the spaces and thresholds opened up between varieties of them. As I show below, navigating the pure, the proper, and the *local* results in a complex form of linguistic practice, a seeming criss-"crossing" (Rampton 1995) of linguistic boundaries. Exemplifying what Kathryn Woolard (1998) has called the "simultaneity" of speech—the concurrent animation of multiple social "voices" (Bakhtin 1982) without completely inhabiting any of them—these registers of linguistic (dis)value are continually alluded to, but obliquely, and not without their simultaneous disavowal (Hill 1995[1985]; Bucholtz 2011). Although I could exist (if oddly) in the space opened between these registers, these youth avoided their use, even as they practiced their mention.[8]

As we will see, the display of English and Tamil walks a fine line between *style* and its lack and between *style* and its excess, an unstable balancing act that manifests in complex citational forms. While the necessity for such balancing confronts all Tamil speakers to various degrees and in various ways, it was rendered particularly acute in the college, both as a preparatory space for *decent* middle-class speech (construed either as respectable, educated standard spoken Tamil *or* as fluent English) and mobility in the neoliberal global economy, and as a youth space that deferred and played with those very futures—a theme I elaborated in chapter 2.[9] In this chapter, I show how my college friends voiced English but kept it at arm's length, always figuring it as not their own. In doing this, these college students negotiated and pushed the boundary between Tamil and English by creatively using elements from both. As with youth engagements with brands and Tamil film, this citationality emerges out of and produces the particular kind of liminality experienced by these youth. And, as in those chapters, we see that such citationality and the liminalities it presupposes and entails require us to think critically about the very ontology of that which is cited—in this case, linguistic codes—and thus what it might mean to "mix" or "switch" codes.

English for Hire

While there is continuity and similarity between colonial and postcolonial attitudes toward Tamil and English (in particular, the association of English with social mobility and the job market; see Seth 2007), college students today are linguistically positioned in ways that are particular to the contemporary, postliberalization milieu and the opportunities, aspirations, and anxieties represented therein. If, in the past, higher education was seen as providing access to coveted public-sector employment, today colleges are promising entry to the burgeoning private sector through the access to and command over English they (aim to) provide. As discussed in chapter 1, the liberalization of the Indian economy in the 1980s and 1990s brought a whole host of changes to higher education, primary of which was its increasing privatization. This privatization of higher education has gone hand in hand with an intensified urgency for learning English as a path to postcollege neoliberal employment (for which the college is increasingly figured as a vocational training ground) for an increasingly linguistically diverse student body. English-educated urban elites, children of the middle-class intelligentsia, and lower-middle-class students from Tamil-medium schools (many of whom were first-generation college goers from rural areas or small towns), not to mention students from other linguistic communities, states, and even countries, all lived and studied together in the predominantly English-medium colleges where I worked (in particular, in the autonomous colleges). The result was a complex range of linguistic capabilities in both Tamil and English (among other languages), with some students more or less comfortable and competent in these languages.

Most all students felt, however, that their English left much to be desired. They felt highly anxious about their future chances in the job market, given what they saw as their insufficient command over English.[10] They explained that today it doesn't matter what one does or learns in college; the only thing that matters is "communication skills," the ability to speak in English. It was the skill of English, perhaps more than anything else, that they hoped to get out of the college and that the college hoped to get out of them. College administrators in all the colleges where I worked allocated increasing curricular energy toward (remedial) English teaching. Spoken-English classes had become mandatory for all incoming students, which one English professor at a Madurai college suggested, in effect, converted her English Literature Department into a spoken-English training center. The Madurai hostels that I lived in provided extra English tutorials after classes, and many students were encouraged to go to the proliferating private English institutes outside of the college on top of whatever other English training the college provided them (figure 10).[11]

The aided hostel that I lived in mandated that two hours of each day be reserved for English-language television programming, subject to fines of 25 Rupees (approximately $0.56 USD at the time) for putting on Tamil stations during the allotted time. Students were greeted daily with English words and quotations posted on the hostel whiteboard as they walked out of or into the hostel. There were only English newspapers on campus.

In these ways, English was presented to these youth as a language of authority, a language they often experienced passively (from teachers, from television, from newspapers). The (collegial) authority of English, of course, didn't go without pushback. As one of my Madurai roommates Sebastian said in Tamil in annoyance regarding the obligatory extracurricular English classes and the nonavailability of Tamil newspapers in the hostel, 'They are trying to stuff (*tiṇi*) English down our throats!' Explaining this resistance to English, one warden of a Madurai hostel lamented in English, "They [the students] are too much allergic to English." He elaborated, saying that most of students wouldn't go to the extra classes, watch television programming in English, read the English newspapers, or bother trying to speak in much English at all. The students even rejected his attempts to reorganize the hostel linguistically. At one point, this warden created an English-only "block" of the hostel where only students who were

Figure 10. Easy English Academy (Madurai 2008); Tamil ad copy, bottom photograph: *+2 māṇavarkaḷukku maṭṭum. Kālēj pōkum mun saraḷamāka Iṅkilīṣ eḻuta, pēsa kaṟṟuk koḷḷuṅkaḷ. Nāṅkaḷ uṅkaḷai nicciyam Iṅkilīṣla pēsa vaippōm.* ('For twelfth grade students only. Before you go to college, learn how to fluently speak and read in English. We will definitely make you speak in English.')

strong in English would be assigned rooms. This was not only to increase a critical density of English usage within the hostel (to overcome some of the peer-group dynamics discussed below) but also to increase the desire of those excluded from it. The students, however, joined together to reject this, as it was seen as creating divisions that broke apart the hostel's student solidarity, organizing students according to a principle of linguistic, and ultimately class, difference. There was not only a desire for and anxiety surrounding English, then, but also a refusal of what English represented and promised/menaced: adult authority, uncertain future participation in the job market, and class distinction. This made English a site of ambivalence and potential performative instability, even as it made it usable to do *style*.

Stylish English, *Local* Tamil

The urgency for learning English that students felt, or were made to feel, often registered as a palpable claustrophobia. 'With only Tamil, you can't *go* anywhere,' was a common refrain. 'You can't leave the state, you can't leave the country.' This was partly an implicit lament that the Dravidian movement's gains in keeping Hindi out of the state and maintaining English as an official language ironically marginalized Tamil speakers from the rest of the country (where Hindi was imagined to be the vernacular lingua franca), even as it presumably allowed Tamils to more equally vie for historically coveted government jobs. But this claustrophobia was felt not just as a sense of national marginalization but also as a global exclusion, for in this postliberalization moment, it was not the state that students primarily hoped to access but the global economy. As was repeatedly emphasized to me, English is a "universal language," a language to which people will listen. Hence English makes one audible and visible (usually, but not always, in a good way). It allows one to move and to access those on the move. As three middle-class first-year students in my self-financed Madurai hostel, Sunil (Su), Senthil (Se), and Manish (M), explained to me (CN),[12]

Su:	*Ellāttukkum //āsai irukku.//*	**Su:**	Everyone //has a desire// (for English).
M, Se:	*//āsai tān//*	**M, Se:**	//has a desire//
CN:	*Ēn?*	**CN:**	Why?
Se:	*Āmā, ippōtikki Āṅkilam illāme oṇṇum paṇṇamuṭiyātu.=*	**Se:**	Of course, these days, you can't do anything without English.=
Su, M:	*=Oṇṇum paṇṇamuṭiyātu.=*	**Su, M:**	=You can't do anything.=
Se:	=Job opportunities, *oru* business *toṭaṅka ṇṇā . . . English illai ṇṇā oṇṇum paṇṇamuṭiyātu. Kaṇṭippā English tēvaippaṭutu.*	**Se:**	=Job opportunities, if you want to start a business, . . . without English you can't do anything. You definitely need English.

M:	*State viṭṭu state pōnālē avvaḷavu tān.*	**M:**	If you go from state to state, that's it.
Se:	*English tēvaippaṭutu.=*	**Se:**	English is necessary.=
Su:	*=Anta mānilattu mol̲i teriyaṇum. Illai ṇṇā English tān.*	**Su:**	=You have to know that state's language. Otherwise (you have to know) English.
M, Se:	*English tān.*	**M, Se:**	(you have to know) English.
Su:	*English teriñcā ulakam eṅkanālum pōyiṭalāmē. Appaṭi ṇṇā English kattukkaraṇum ṇṇu tānē ārvam ellārukkum irukku innikki.*	**Su:**	If you know English, you can go wherever you want in the world. When it's like that, everyone today has the interest to learn English.

The necessity of and desire for English was more than simply a question of economic and spatial mobility. Without English, one is stuck, not just in a place, but in the restrictive, parochial Tamil "culture" and "tradition" of that place. English was a way out. Consider my upwardly mobile and hip Chennai roommate Sam, a Catholic Veerakodi Vellalar (an upper, non-Brahmin caste) from the small city of Salem in northwest Tamil Nadu. While explaining how many in today's generation don't see Tamil as a language of "status," Sam talks about English as a useful "tool" to bracket issues of caste and regional identity (Kachru 1983; Annamalai 2011):

Sam:	*Ippō, ippō vantu nān vantu ennōṭa caste kāraṅka ṇṇu vaccukkōṅka. Ennōṭa* region *ellāmē vēr̲a. Ippō ennōṭa anta* identity-*e nān* break *paṇṇi ippō nān veḷiyē varaṇum ṇṇā English tān enakku* tool-*ā irukku.*	**Sam:**	Now, now take the people from my caste. My region(al identity) is totally different. Now, if I want to break that identity, if I want to come outside of it, then English is a tool for me (to do that).
CN:	*Appaṭiyā?*	**CN:**	Really?
Sam:	*Āmā.*	**Sam:**	Yeah.
CN:	*Eppaṭi?*	**CN:**	How's that?
Sam:	*Ēnnā ippō vantuṭṭu sila pēru avaṅkaḷōṭa Tamil̲* slang *mūlamāvē avaṅka enta area, avaṅka-* <makes a clicking sound with his mouth>, *anta mātiri atu, uh, itu paṇṇuvāṅka. Enna sol̲ratu?* Regionalize *paṇṇiruvāṅka.*	**Sam:**	Because now with some people, you can tell their area through their Tamil slang, their- <makes a clicking sound with his mouth>, like that, uh, they do this. What to say? They'll regionalize (you).

CN:	*Mmm*	**CN:**	Mmm
Sam:	*Sila pēru caste motaṟ koṇṭu kaṇṭupiṭicciruvāṅka.* So, I mean, *inta problem enakku nān sollale. But ituvum* one of the problems *atule.*	**Sam:**	Some people will figure out your caste (from your language). So, I mean, that's not a problem I have. But it is also one of the problems in this.
CN:	*Mmm*	**CN:**	Mmm
Sam:	*So avanōṭa* identity break *paṇṇi veḷiye varatukku English oru* tool-*ā irukku. Nīṅka English pēsum pōtu uṅkaḷōṭa* background *yārum pākkuṟatille.*	**Sam:**	So to come out and break one's identity, English is a tool. When you speak in English, no one pays attention to your background.

As Sam indicates, English allows one to make an end run around those traditional hierarchies and ascriptive identities tethered to one's regional background, as always potentially revealed by one's Tamil (which he explicitly disavowed as a problem of his own; indeed, note his shift from the first person to the third person and then to the second person in his last two turns of the transcript).[13] Later in our conversation, Sam contrasted the power of English to "break" regional and caste identities with the insular mind-set of (the cultural politics of pure) Tamil, which, from his point of view, doesn't let people develop themselves or, as another friend from Madurai put it, get out of that "(traditional) culture." Voicing this mindset as hypothetical, represented speech and then describing it from his own point of view, Sam said,

Sam:	(Suppose) *enakku anta* language *mēle enakku romba* interest *irukku. Enakku ippō atellām paṇṇaṇum ṇṇu āsai.* *Ānā "Nān vantu Tamiḻan.* <gives more emphasis to and more clearly pronounces "*Tamiḻan*"—in particular, the retroflex continuant *ḻ* (see below)> *Nān Tamiḻan.* Language *viṭṭukkoṭukka kūṭātu. So itai vantu viṭaṇum ṇṇu avasiyam illai."*	**Sam:**	(Suppose that) I have a lot of interest (to learn) that language [Spanish]. I really want to do that. But 'I'm a *Tamiḻan* ('Tamilian'). <gives more emphasis to and more clearly pronounces "*Tamiḻan*"—in particular, the retroflex continuant *ḻ* (see below)> I'm a *Tamiḻan.* I shouldn't give space for other languages. So I shouldn't have to give up my language.'

	Okay tān. But enakku itu vantu puṭikkale. Ippō nān, nān vēṟa itukku pōṟēn, appaṭi ṇṇā kūṭa iṅkē atai vantu romba-, enna solla, avamatippā iṅkē vantu pākkuṟāṅka. Atuvē atukku oru negative-*ā āki pōccu.*	Okay, fine. But I don't like that. If I'm going toward something else, here it's really-, what to say, people here see it negatively. It's become really negative.
CN:	*Mmm*	Mmm
Sam:	I mean, *ippō uṅkaḷaiyum, ennaiyum kaṭṭuppaṭuttuṟa oru itukkuḷḷa pōvīṅkaḷā? Illai oraḷavukku* free-*ā irukkuṟa* atmosphere *pōvīṅkaḷā?*	I mean, will you go into something that constricts you and me? Or will you go somewhere where the atmosphere is relatively more free?
	So obvious-*āvē atukku Tamiḻukku romba ippaṭi oru anta oru neruṭal paṇṟa mātiri viṣayam niṟaiya irukku. So atanāleyē enakku atu mēle periya uṭanbāṭullām etuvum kiṭaiyātu.*	So obviously there are all these issues linked to Tamil that are really irritating. So I don't have any kind of big attachment to it.

Sam's negative perception of what he saw as narrow-minded Tamil attachment wasn't shared by all Tamil students. For many, if not most, the Tamil language and its literary history was a source of intense pride. My Madurai roommate Sebastian, for example, agreed with students like Sam that English was the language of mobility and opportunity, or what is often called "exposure" ('economic opportunity,' 'social/cultural capital,' but also the knowledge necessary to be keyed into the wider global world).[14] But instead of seeing Tamil conservativism as insular and provincial, he saw it positively, as linked to "culture" (*kalāccāram*) and "society" (*samūkam, samutāyam*) and to traditional notions of respectability (*mariyātai*), honor (*mānam*), and prestige (*kauravam*). For Sebastian, speaking pure Tamil (*sen Tamiḻ*) commanded respect and gave respect to others and to the language itself. Such Tamil was *aḻaku* ('beautiful'), *inimai* ('sweet'), and *rammiyam* ('beautiful,' 'satisfying'), qualities that no student I knew would ever use to describe English or youths' everyday speech. Yet, as noted above, higher registers of Tamil were almost never used by these young men to command status. Like other signs of *mariyātai* that youth avoided trafficking in, such Tamil was generally not spoken or even borrowed from by young people (except perhaps, in jest).

By contrast to Tamil, English was *style*.[15] English opened up a space and time exterior to that which was invoked and instated by respectable pure Tamil. Speaking in English projects a time-space linked not only to post-collegial work life and these youths' potential future selves ("job opportunities," as Senthil put it above) but also to a more general cosmopolitanism (or "exposure," as Sebastian put it). English affords access to a world that is "modern" and "developed," as Sam expressed in a different conversation. Like the authorized brands discussed in chapter 2, the *style* of English indexes an elite lifestyle and aesthetics associated with white-collar jobs in multinational corporations, easy relations with the opposite sex, "love marriages" (i.e., marriages that are not arranged by one's elders), foreign "pubs" and "discos," and the like.

In contrast to *mariyātai*, *style* was a regime of value that youth could linguistically access in their peer groups. *Style* was, however, as always, only ever problematically inhabited. Much like pure Tamil, fluent English was also out of reach for these youth. But not totally. English-medium educational institutions like colleges, as I pointed out, have increasingly become technologies for being socialized to English. This meant that however excluded students felt from the cosmopolitanism associated with fluent English, they all had, and were expected to show, some familiarity with it. It is this partial inclusion that made English a site both of urgent desire and *style* and of extreme ambivalence and intense anxiety. Every context in which full-on English had to be used risked humiliation, be it in the classroom or in the peer group, for it might reveal the extent of one's lack of English competence. In the college especially, but more generally as well, being unable to appropriately command English, however construed, was embarrassing. To not know it as well as the situation demanded was "*asiṅkam*" ('ugly,' 'embarrassing,' 'shameful'), "*indecent,*" and low class. It meant one was uneducated, poor, or a hick (*paṭṭikkāṭṭān*)—in a word, *local* (chapter 2). Students were quite explicit about this. 'If you don't know English, even a dog won't turn to look at you,' explained one middle-class Madurai friend ("*English teriyale ṇṇā nāy kūṭa tirumbi pākkātu*"; Rogers 2008; Lukose 2009:163–99; Proctor 2014:307).

By contrast, as two middle-class friends from the Catholic college in Chennai, Raj and Ralph, explained, if one has command of English, one can speak "confidently." This is because English is *style*, it is *gettu* ('prestige,' dominance'; here, 'bad ass'), it has "status." In comparison, they said, 'When we speak in Tamil, whatever we say, it won't have that effect' ("*Tamiḻle pēsinākkā nāma enna tān pēsinālum anta aḷavukku eṭupaṭātu*"). Drawing on and complicating the kinds of sartorial distinctions discussed in chapter 2, Raj and Ralph made the following comparison to highlight the power of English to transform the perceptions of others:

Raj:	*Inta mātiri romba cheap-ā* dress *paṇṇikkiṭṭiruntēn ṇṇu vaccukkōṅkaḷēn. Nān Tamiḻ pēsinā vēṟa mātiri pāppāṅka. Nān itai viṭa maṭṭamā* dress *paṇṇiruntā kūṭa English-le pēsinā* "<makes a clicking sound with his mouth> *Paravāyillai ivan romba simple pōla irukku" appaṭi ṇṇu ninaippāṅka.*	**Raj:**	Suppose I'm dressed right now in really cheap dress like this. If I speak in Tamil, people will look at me funny. If I'm wearing even crappier dress than this, if I speak in English, '<makes a clicking sound with his mouth> Not bad. It seems that he's so simple (i.e., humble, modest).' They'll think like that.
CN:	<laughs> *Appaṭiyā?*	**CN:**	<laughs> Really?
Raj:	*Appaṭi tān. "Ivan simple" appaṭi mbāṅka. Nānē Tamiḻle pōyi inta dress pōṭṭu pēsinā=*	**Raj:**	Just like that. 'He's so simple,' they'll say. If I put on this dress, and I go and speak in Tamil=
Ralph:	*=piccaikkāran mbān.*	**Ralph:**	=he'll say he's a beggar.
Raj:	*Piccaikkāra solluvān.*	**Raj:**	He'll say I'm a beggar.
CN:	*Local-ā iruppān.*	**CN:**	(He'll say) he's *local*.
Raj:	*Āmā. English pēsinākkā "Ivan simple." Oru itule māṟirutu pāttīṅkaḷā?*	**Raj:**	Yeah. (But) if I speak in English, 'He's simple.' See how much it's changed because of this one thing?
CN:	*Mmm*	**CN:**	Mmm
Raj:	Language. *Enna paṇṟatu? Nammakkulām itu* <laughs> *varale.*	**Raj:**	Language. What to do? We all don't have it [English]. <laughs>

Here we see how sartorial and linguistic modalities of self-presentation intersect, tropically amplifying and reversing each other—a dynamic that I return to in chapter 7 in discussing the overblown on-screen *style* and extremely humble off-screen image of film heroes. As this quote and the next show, not just one's mastery of English as a denotational and grammatical code, how one dressed one's speech was also of critical importance, for it could reveal one's social fluency (or lack thereof). Consider how Sam put it:

Sam:	*Illai, nīṅka ippō English-le pēsuṟīṅka. Ippō itē nān pēsuṟa English-le vantu*	**Sam:**	No, (it's like,) you're speaking English now(, right?). Now if I say the same thing in English like this,

	<in an exaggerated accent, slightly louder, more animated> "Hey Costas-*u*::, what [vɐʈ'] are you doing-*u*::?" *Appaṭi nān pēsinēn ṇṇā atu eppaṭi irukku? Illai ṇṇā,* <unmarked Indian English accent, normal volume> "Hey Costas, what are you doing?" *ṇṇā atu eppaṭi irukku?*	<in an exaggerated accent, slightly louder, more animated> "Hey Costas-*u*::, what [vɐʈ'] are you doing-*u*::?" If I say it like that, how is it? How about if I say, <unmarked Indian English accent, normal volume> "Hey Costas, what are you doing?" How is that?
CN:	*Mmm*	Mmm
Sam:	*Itu tān* difference. *English pēsuṟatu matter illai. Atai nīṅka eppaṭi* deliver *paṇṟīṅka. Enna mātiri* words *use paṇṟīṅka ṇṇu irukku, le?*	That's the difference. It's not a big deal to speak in English. It's how you deliver it. It's also what kinds of words you use, right?
CN:	*Mmm*	Mmm
Sam:	*Atuvē uṅkaḷai innum romba itu paṇṇum. Sila pēr English pēsuṟatu vantu bayaṅkara comedy ākkiṟum atu . . . .* *Comedy ākiṟum atu. Anta mātiri ippō nān pēsuṟatu vantu ennai oru* comedy person-*ā yārum pākka kūṭātu. Eppaṭi ṇṟa oru viṣayam atu. Ennai oru* funny-*ā yārum pākka kūṭātu appaṭi ṇṇuṭṭu.*	It'll do even more than that to you. Some people speaking English is such a comedy/joke. . . . It becomes a comedy. When I am speaking, no one should look at me like I am a comedy person. That's the issue. People shouldn't look at me in a funny way (because of my English).

In Sam's parodic example, "Hey Costas-*u*::, what [vɐʈ'] are you doing-*u*::?" the exaggerated, lengthened epenthetic -*u* [ɯ], the nondistinction of /v/ and /w/, the hyperbolic, ejective retroflex stop [ʈ'], and a louder, animated speech style all function as signs of a gauche Tamil speech style, of the wannabe whose attempts at speaking English inevitably fail (cf. Alvarez-Caccamo 1990; Bucholtz 2011).[16] They paint a portrait of a speaker whose English isn't quite up to the mark (and not for reasons of grammatical well-formedness) and thus is a "comedy person," a joker. This isn't who Sam wanted to be—at least, not unless it was on purpose. Indeed, parodically performing this persona by speaking mock, broken English with infelicitously exaggerated accents (Tamilized or anglicized) was a common form of humor among both students who felt comfortable with English and those who didn't (also see Rampton 1995:52–53; Woolard 1998; Park 2009:204–9). By parodying the inability to correctly speak in English, mock English figured such speech as not one's own (Goffman 1974:534–37; 1981:3; Tetreault 2009; Bucholtz 2011), distancing such youth both from the figure of the "comedy person" who can't quite get it right and, I would suggest, from English itself, from the anxiety that in another's eyes, they might actually be that person.

The *Over Style* of English and the *Peter*

Despite students' obsession with learning and speaking English and despite their admiration of its *style*, its economic potential, its universal intelligibility, and its indexing of elite status and education, besides joking around and words and phrases here and there, the students with whom I lived and worked didn't really speak much English in their peer groups. It wasn't for want of trying or even of capability. Indeed, having an American in the hostel only brought out the intense desire to learn some more English words or to practice what one already knew. I was constantly being cornered by students, individually or in small groups, to give pronunciation tips, to answer questions about word definitions, or just to help them practice some conversation. Inevitably, however, a third party would overhear, start laughing and sniggering, or offer explicit statements like "*Scene pōṭātē, nammai viṭa avarukku nalla Tamiḻ teriyum*," 'Stop putting on a (film) scene, he [Costas] knows better Tamil than we do.' Or "A, B, C, D, E, F, G . . . *eṅkaḷukkum English teriyum*," 'A, B, C, D, E, F, G . . . we also know our English (lessons).' In a word, shut up.

This censure was internalized by many youth as a paralyzing fear of speaking English incorrectly: of mispronunciation (as Sam elaborated above), of making a grammatical mistake, or of using a word with the wrong meaning. These youth found themselves often unable to utter any sound in English for fear of embarrassment (cf. Proctor 2014:302), a sentiment that advertisements for private English institutes capitalized on (figure 11).

In the first advertisement in figure 11, this anxious desire for English is picturized by a mouth zipped shut, sound unable to escape its lips. In the next advertisement, this silence is given written, linguistic form: "NEED FLUENCY." This bare verb phrase is not presented as a whole speech act but is disassembled across two persons sitting (or standing?) back-to-back, seemingly tied together in captivity. Each mouth is taped over by a single

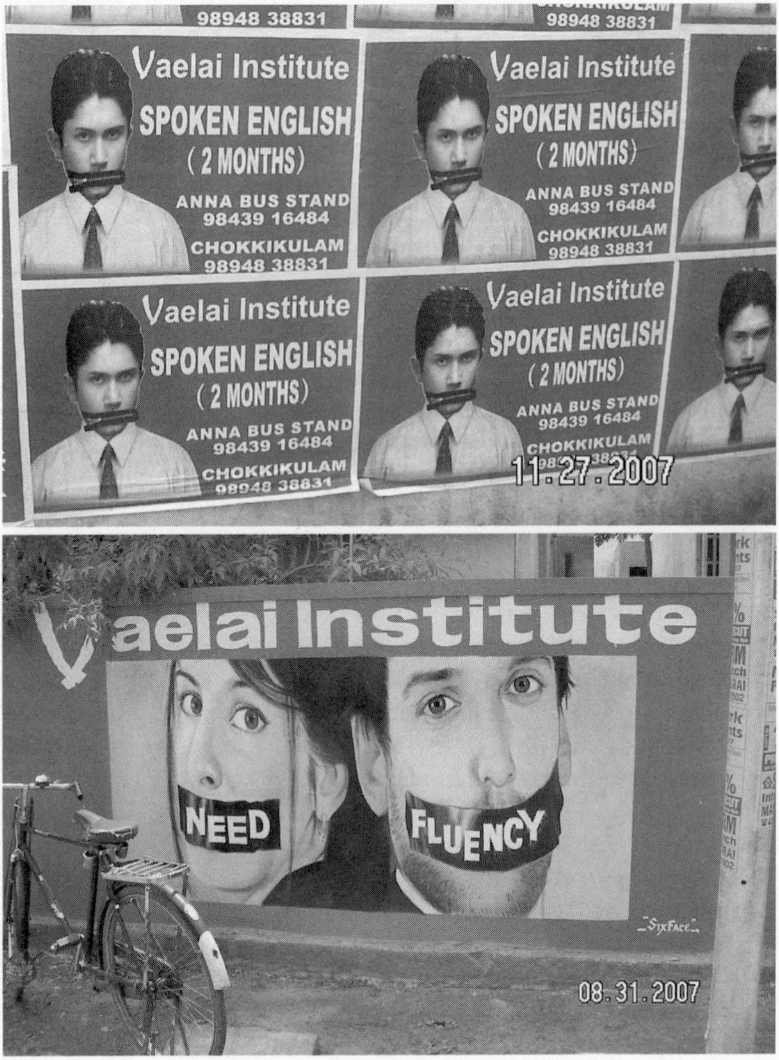

Figure 11. Two advertisements for Vaelai Institute (literally, 'Work Institute'; Madurai 2007)

word, as if one word was all that either could manage. Even taken together, the phrase lacks an explicit subject, an ellipsis of agency figurating youth feelings of being unable to competently speak or understand English. This suggestively disfluent phrase invites multiple readings. It ambiguously floats between an imperative diagnosis ("You need fluency!"), a plea ("I/we need fluency!"), and an interrogative ("Need fluency?").[17]

Sunil, Manish, and Senthil, the first years whom we met above, explained these inhibitions in the following way:

Su:	*Ellārum pēsa viruppa paṭuṟāṅka, ānā=*	**Su:**	Everyone has the desire to speak (English), but=
M:	*=viruppa paṭuṟāṅka ānā oruttan-ukkum oru tayakkam=*	**M:**	=has the desire, but everyone has a hesitation=
Su:	*=tayakkam, tayakkam.*	**Su:**	=hesitation, hesitation.
M:	*Oru nāppatu pēr irukkāṅka. Mutalē appaṭi ṇṇu-*	**M:**	There are forty people (in the class). (If you speak) like this in the beginning-
Su:	((*???*)) *tappā pēsiṭṭā sirippāṅka ṇṇu nakkal paṇṇuvāṅka, atu oru* shy-*yā irukkum.*	**Su:**	((???)) if you make a mistake speaking, they laugh, they'll make fun of you, you'll feel shy (to speak again).
CN:	*Ēn nakkal paṇṇuvāṅka?*	**CN:**	Why will they make fun of you?
Se:	*Tappā pēsi-, yārukkum oṇṇum teriyātu, atu oru viṣayam. Ellārumē muṭṭāḷ* ((*???*)) *tān.* <laughing> *Ēnnannā ippō, etō koñcam pēsiṭṭōm, takṇu ellārum ṣiriccāṅka ṇṇā ellārum enne sirikka ārambiccu, nāṅka pēsāme-. Appaṭi, appaṭi itu varaikkum appaṭi tān vantirukku.*	**Se:**	Making a mistake speaking-, no one knows anything, that's one thing. We're all idiots. <laughing> Because, now, we say something, if immediately everyone laughs, (if) everyone starts laughing at me, we'll become silent. Like that, like that, it's gone on like this.

While feeling uncomfortable speaking a language that one isn't fluent in is quite common (I continually felt that way with my Tamil), Sunil, Manish, and Senthil expressed a more particular anxiety linked with *style*: being the center of attention, being individuated and visible but in that moment failing, making a mistake and being humiliated by censorious laughs from the crowd. But as they made clear, the issue isn't simply in failing to speak English well enough. Senthil continued:

Se:	*Oru māsam pasaṅkaḷukkuḷḷē pēsiṭṭu paḻakiṭṭu iruntu ṇṇā* easy-*ā vantu-rum.*	**Se:**	If we spent time speaking (English) with the guys for a month, it'd come easily (to us).
Su:	<to Se> Easy *tān ṭā. Romba kaṣṭam illa. Veḷi irukkuṟavaṅka* ((*???*))-	**Su:**	<to Se> It's really easy, man. It isn't hard. People from the outside ((???))-

	<to CN> *Ippa nāṅka mūṇu pērumē muṭivu eṭuttu English-le pēsaṇum ṇṇu solliṭṭu, nāṅka veḷiyē pōkum pōtu "Enna ṭā periyappu"-*	<to CN> If all three of us made a decision right now to only speak in English, when we go outside, (they'll say,) 'What's this man, some big guys'-
M:	*Ah, ah.*	Yeah, yeah.
Se:	*Atāvatu, kīḻ eṟakkiṟāṅka ellārum.*	I mean, everyone is pulling you down.
	"Enna periya ivanuṅkaḷā ivaṅka, pēsiṭṭē irukkāṅka?"	'What, are they big shots (literally, 'big men'), continuously speaking (in English)?'
	"O::::ver-ā kāṭṭātīṅka." Anta mātiri solluvāṅka.	'Don't show off so much!' They'll say things like that.
M:	*"Paṭatte pōṭātīṅka" ṇṇu solluvāṅka.*	They'll say, 'Don't put on a movie' (i.e., show off).
Su:	*Vaḷara viṭamāṭṭāṅka iṅkē.*	They won't let you develop yourself here.
M:	*Poṟāmai anta mātiri tān varum.*	Their jealousies come out like that.
Su:	*Poṟāmaiye viṭa enna ivaṅka maṭṭum komāḷittanamā paṇṟāṅka ṇṇu neneppāṅka.*	More than jealousy, they'll think that you're acting like a clown.

The anxiety surrounding English use is not only about not being good enough, then; it is also about speaking English *too well*. (As Sunil, Manish, and Senthil optimistically, and perhaps wishfully, note, if they were allowed to, they could easily learn fluent English in a month's time.) Speaking in English is *style*, but too much English is *over style* ('excessive style'). It is uppity and arrogant. And note how the hypothetical criticisms that Sunil, Senthil, and Manish animated are articulated through the idiom of acting like a 'big man' (while actually being a 'clown') as well as through the idiom of cinema ("*Paṭatte pōṭātīṅka*," 'Don't put on a movie!'), a connection I return to in chapters 6 and 7. In short, the potential excess of English makes getting too close to it risky. One hazards laughs, teasing, and criticism (cf. Fanon 2008[1952]:8ff.; Park 2009), but also more. One might catch a blow, for example.

About three months into my fieldwork, on one autumn evening at around midnight, I was interviewing three of my self-financing Madurai hostelmates. In the middle of our interview, we heard a commotion next door. Rushing over, it turned out that two first-year students, Venkatesh and Bradley, had gotten into a fistfight. Earlier that day, there had been a cricket match among the third years. Back at the hostel, exercising their rights as seniors, the third years told these juniors to put away the equipment. Bradley, an upper-middle-class, urban student, told Venkatesh, a working-class, rural student, to put it away. Venkatesh, in turn, told Bradley to do it. As students of the same year, there was no institutional principle (e.g., age, year, caste, class) to decide who should do what, and a verbal fight of the "You-do-it-No-you-do-it" variety ensued. The skirmish escalated to physical confrontation, such that it had to be broken up, only after Bradley began speaking in proficient, unmixed English. Bradley's use of English was a direct insult, its implication being that Venkatesh was an ignorant bumpkin who was unable to speak in or understand English. Countering Bradley's linguistic jab, Venkatesh physically attacked Bradley, literally bringing him down a notch by hitting him with a mirror, drawing blood as Bradley parried the blow and the glass broke. Bradley's fluency with English exposed the class difference that both knew existed between them.[18] As Bradley later told me in an e-mail, writing from Chennai, "He always hated me i guess . . . the reasons may be, cos i used to talk in English, and may be he wasnt used to ppl [people] like me. . . . he thought I was a snob or something i guess. . . . People there believe that if someone talks in English he is a show off" (original formatting). Bradley schematizes social difference here through contrasting third-person expressions ("people like me" vs. "people there"), implicitly mapping such linguistic difference (English vs. Tamil) onto regional and class difference (cosmopolitan Chennai vs. backwater Madurai). Bradley, who many took issue with for his excessive English, generally had social problems in our hostel until he found a group of friends with similar English fluency and class standing. This example illustrates the fine-tuning that has to go on in peer groups in order to avoid the invidious differences inscribable by the deficiency or excess of English and thus the way in which the, here intentional, disruption of such fine-tuning can performatively wreak havoc.

Such snobbish *over style* is personified in the parodied figure of the "*Peter*" (or for a young woman, "*Peter akkā*," 'older sister *Peter*').[19] Someone who speaks too much English is said to "*Peter (v)uṯṟatu*" ('be a *Peter*'). Here the Christian name "Peter" stands in derisively for the persona of someone who unabashedly attempts to inhabit the space of cosmopolitan globalism through his or her use of English.[20] A *Peter* is someone who acts like he or she was born or lived abroad when everyone knows this isn't the case. A *Peter* speaks English when it isn't necessary. A *Peter* speaks like he doesn't know Tamil when he does and speaks English when he knows that the person he is speaking to speaks Tamil just fine.

To be a *Peter* wasn't simply an issue of English usage, however, though this was the most salient feature of this derided persona. It was a whole congeries of *style* that went too far. In fact, "*Peter (v)uṭṟatu*" can also be used as a synonym for showing off in general (cf. the leakage of the filmic idiom noted above). A group of my male friends described the *Peter* by saying he would have lots of flashy brands (see chapter 2), have long hair (or a buzz cut), and be clean-shaven ("*mīsai* like *paṇṇamāṭṭāru*," 'he won't like mustaches,' that stereotyped sign of traditional rural masculinity; see chapter 1).[21] The *Peter* acts like he doesn't want to be in Tamil Nadu, but somewhere else. He desires 'foreign culture' ("*anniyan kalāccāram*").

Linguistically, the *Peter* is emblematized through his or her anglicized pronunciation and affected, disfluent Tamil. The relevant phonological site is the retroflex frictionless continuant ழ் (*l̲* [ɻ]), a sound that many Tamils believe to be unique to Tamil. (It isn't part of the neighboring Dravidian languages' phonological repertoires.) As Harold Schiffman notes (1999:7–8), the sound is often replaced in colloquial Tamil by the retroflex lateral ள் (*ḷ* [ɭ]). Mispronunciation of this phoneme is often taken as an example of linguistic shift away from 'correct' Tamil, as the marker between good and bad speakers, native speakers and foreigners.[22] The emblematic lexical environment for this shibboleth is the name of the language itself, *Tamil̲* (தமிழ் [t̪ɐmɪɻ]). A *Peter*, it was said, thought it was "modern" to disclaim his or her ability to speak Tamil correctly (cf. Park 2009). Youth often parodied the figure of the *Peter* by voicing him or her through the mispronounced sentence,

Enkku	*Ṭamil*	*ṭeriyāṭu.*	←	"*Peter*" pronunciation
jɛnkkʉ	tæmɪl	tæɹija:du		
Enakku	*Tamil̲*	*teriyātu.*	←	"Correct" pronunciation
jenəkkʉ	t̪ɐmɪɻ	t̪əɾɪja:ðʉ		
I-OBL.DAT.	Tamil	know-FUT.NEG.NEUT.		

'I don't know Tamil.'

Here the dative first-person subject "*Enakku*" is shortened to "*Enkku*." The pronunciation of "*Tamil̲*" is rendered as "*Ṭamil*" (டமில் [tæmɪl]): the initial dental [t̪] is turned into a postalveolar/retroflex [t], and the retroflex frictionless continuent ழ் (*l̲* [ɻ]) is replaced not by the retroflex lateral ள் (*ḷ* [ɭ]) but by the dental lateral ல் (*l* [l]), in effect, turning the name of the language backward in one's mouth. The *a* in the *Peter*'s "*Ṭamil*" and the *e* in his "*ṭeriyāṭu*" are fronted and near-open [æ]; the *i* in "*ṭeriyāṭu*" is fronted and raised [i]; the tapped *r* is rendered an approximant [ɹ]; and the final *u* is raised and slightly rounded [ʉ]. This exaggerated performance of not knowing Tamil *in* English-pronounced Tamil diagrams and encapsulates the *Peter*, for the problem with the *Peter* isn't his or her inability to speak Tamil. Rather, it is the *choice* to anglicize his or her speech when he or she could in fact presumably speak Tamil without such affectation.

The *Peter* personifies the excess of *style*. But this excess is not simply a function of absolute ability or fluency in English or Tamil. Rather, similar to youths' brand displays discussed in chapter 2, it is about the differential relationship that such affected speech diagrams between a speaker and his or her interlocutors. In youth peer groups, the charge of "*Peter (v)uṯratu*" was relative to at least two factors: the fluency of the people who were nearby and the perceived status and fluency of the speaker (cf. chapter 2 on metadiscourses on the naturalness of certain persons' *stylish* fashion). Consider a conversation between myself, Sam, and his classmate Aravind. Aravind had gone to an international American school and spoke Indian English as his first language. He only spoke Tamil semifluently (though his ethnolinguistic background was Tamil). In discussing the *Peter*, Sam, a native Tamil speaker who was relatively proficient but not fluent in English, explained why Aravind couldn't be considered a *Peter* but he (Sam) could be:

Sam: *Ivan ivanōṭa* normal thing-*ē atu tān ṇṇu teriyum. Ippō vantu nīṅka English-le pēsuṅka. Avaṅka vantu kiṇṭal paṇṇamāṭṭāṅka.* <laughs> *Anta mātiri ivan English-le pēsinā yārum kiṇṭal paṇṇamāṭṭāṅka. . . .* I guess most likely, people know who is *Peter* and who speaks good English. *Ippō, ippō vantu nān eṅka ūrle nān pōyi English pēsinēn ṇṇu vaccukkōṅkaḷēn.* People who are not used to my English, they, they think that I'm this *Peter* fellow. But mostly *anta mātiri nān etaiyum* use *paṇṇamāṭṭēn*, but *nān solṟēn. Atu avaṅkaḷōṭa-, ippō Aravind avaṅka pāttatule iruntē, avan English-le pēsi avaṅkaḷukku paḻakkam ākiṟuccu. Ānā ippa nān vantu Tamiḻle aṭikkaṭi pēsuvēn. English-leyum pēsuṟatanāle ippō nān English-le full-ā pēsiṇēn ṇṇā ennai vantu Peter ṇṇuvāṅka.*

Sam: We know that speaking English is normal for him [Aravind]. Now you [Costas] speak English. No one will make fun of you. <laughs> Like that, if he speaks in English, no one will make fun of him. . . . I guess most likely, people know who is *Peter* and who speaks good English. Now, now, suppose that I went to my hometown and spoke in English. People who are not used to my English, they, they think that I'm this *Peter* fellow. But mostly, I won't ever speak like that (there), but I'm just saying. That's their-, now (with) Aravind, they've never seen him, but they'll get used to him speaking in English. But I speak in Tamil often. Because I'm also speaking in English, if I fully speak in English now, they'll say that I am a *Peter*.

As Sam indicates, the *Peter* is a shifter. In contexts in which no one speaks any English or one is known as a Tamil speaker (as is Sam in his hometown), speaking any amount of English might count as *Peter (v)uṯṟatu*. In contexts in which everyone is relatively fluent in English or one is known as a fluent English speaker (like Aravind), being a *Peter* requires an over-the-top performance—usually a put-on American or British accent (i.e., one that goes beyond standard Indian English "delivery" of the kind Sam earlier contrasted to the "comedy person" wannabe).

What this discussion shows is that any usage of English that deviates from the linguistic norms of one's reference group—not speaking English well enough or speaking it too well—risks a kind of negative performativity, tipping either into the *local* and uneducated (under *style*, as it were) or into being *over style* and arrogant. In the college, the peer group acted to even out differences in linguistic capability, either by excluding those who spoke English better or worse than others or by obliging those who could speak in English not to (cf. "consuming level" discussed in chapter 2). My Madurai roommate Stephen, for example, was relatively English fluent. And yet, with the exception of speaking with me and a few other English-fluent, non-Tamil students, he would rarely speak in full English in the hostel. Similarly, Gina, a hip female student from Chennai studying in Madurai, was, as she described it, unable to make any friends in her Madurai college until she changed her speech and dress. People kept her at arm's length, she told me, until she opted for more "homely" chudhitars instead of jeans and blouses and started speaking in Tamil instead of full-on English.

Not all students were so easily cowed. A friend, Kavitha, explained to me in an SMS how her English got so good. She wrote, "I made it a point to talk to them [my friends] in eng[lish] most of the time. That helped me a lot. There were people (in the college) who criticized sayin it was bandha ('showing off'), but I just neglected it. . . . theyll say she is showing off, cant she speak in tamil(?)" (original formatting with my additions in square brackets and parentheses). Kavitha's choice wasn't without its consequences. When I met her, she was in a master's program at the coeducational Hindu college in Madurai where I worked. Relative to the semielite Madurai women's college where she received her bachelor of arts and where I also conducted research, this college had a preponderance of monolingual Tamil students who commuted from surrounding peri-urban and rural areas. By contrast to her undergraduate experience, because of her English competence, she was generally isolated from classmates in her English master's program, suffering the stereotype of a stuck-up girl who thought she was better than everyone else.

Gender is important here. While it wasn't the case in my experience that young women used English any more than young men, the stereotype among students was that it was young women who mainly used English to show off, who put on airs so as to put others down. While voiced by both young men and women, this discourse was, by my observation, more frequently articulated by linguistically insecure young men (chapter 5). As discussed in chapter 2, for young women to do *style* was almost always to be *over*, though here we can note a difference between using brands and English to do *style*. As opposed to sexualizing her by drawing attention to her body, in Kavitha's case, her English simply socially isolated her, earning her a reputation as being aloof rather than morally compromised or challenging to patriarchy per se (cf. chapter 6).[23]

While Kavitha, Gina, and Stephen were on one end of the spectrum—students who felt pressure to tone down their English use—on the other end of the spectrum were youth who were so insecure about their English that they opted for total silence rather than the embarrassment their speech might cause them (cf. Bourdieu 1991:55, 71, 81, 83). Pandiraja, for example, was a third-year Tamil-medium student from a relatively poor background who attended the coeducational Catholic college in Chennai where I worked. His anxieties about revealing his English disfluency to his richer, English-fluent classmates isolated him during his first year. As his classmates put it, he would never "mingle" with them, keeping to himself and often not speaking at all, in or out of the classroom. Indeed, it took Pandiraja two full years to overcome this linguistic insecurity, and only in his third and final year did he begin to socialize with his classmates. Even then, it was only with a limited number of male students who tended to also be from Tamil-medium schools and who were from lower-middle-class backgrounds. Pandiraja still avoided his female classmates—especially the English-fluent, affluent ones—for fear of the embarrassment of having his English inability publicly exposed by them. As he and other young men explained, there is nothing worse than being embarrassed by young-women in public, a patriarchal insecurity here manifested by silence.

Bracketing Denotation

There is a redoubled tension that runs through youths' talk about language and, as a function of such talk, its use in the college peer group. On the one hand, while speaking in colloquial Tamil is appropriately "normal," too much Tamil, or the wrong kind of Tamil, is either *local* or absurd. On the other hand, while some English is appropriately *style*, too much

English *over*does it. As we saw with brands in chapter 2, *stylish* English always risks becoming that which it disavows: an act that hierarchically ranks the speaking subject and his interlocutors by their educational and class difference. The double mandate of the peer group, then, was to be neither under nor *over style*, to speak English and do *style* without speaking too much English and *over*doing *style*. It was to distinguish oneself simultaneously from the *local* bumpkin and from the global cosmopolitan, from the low-class slum dweller and from the elite urbanite, from the respectable 'big man' and from the *decent* white-collar professional (and thus from the college itself). It was to be somewhere in the middle.

Students' linguistic practice did just that, diagramming and navigating this tension through a careful balancing act—on the one hand, through phonologically straddling the threshold between excessively anglicized and gauche *local* pronunciation in both their Tamil and English and, on the other hand, through a finely tuned, if unstable, alchemy of nonnormalized, *stylish* English and normal, colloquial Tamil linguistic forms.[24] Tentatively using *stylish* English in their Tamil speech, these youth constantly pushed on the boundary of what constituted "normal" speech. At the same time, their linguistic practice managed the inherent riskiness of English: its power to entangle interlocutors in hierarchies of sociolinguistic difference.

To accomplish this balancing act, youths' linguistic practice reflexively sketched the very tension from which it emerged. This was materialized in the asymmetries of how English and Tamil were used by youth. Youths' speech refunctioned English, converting it from its status as a denotational code—for it is largely the use of English as a denotational code that triggered dispute and anxiety in the peer group (as we saw with Bradley and Venkatesh)—to a kind of interactional accoutrement, much as educated Americans are perhaps wont to do with Frenchisms (cf. Hill 1995[1985]). There is a tendency to bracket the denotational capabilities of English, to negate English as a code, even as it is yoked for its indexical associations. There is a tendency to put English as a language in quotes.[25]

Hence, for example, the youth with whom I worked often felt that the safest strategy to show *style* and to avoid being seen as *local* was to simply sprinkle certain important English "vocabularies" into their Tamil. As my lower-middle-class friend Amal put it, demonstrating the kind of garnishing that he was talking about,

Amal: *Sila nēraṅkaḷ-le namma Tamiḻlām pēsavē kūṭātu. Koñcam English kalantu pēsaṇum. . . .*	**Amal:** Sometimes we really shouldn't speak all that Tamil of ours. We have to speak with some English mixed in. . . .

Avaṅka nammaḷa local-ā	They shouldn't think of us as
neneccirukka kūṭātu.	*local.*
Appaṭi-ṅkuṟatukkāka sila	For that, we need some special
mukkiyamāna vocabularies. . . .	"vocabularies." . . .
Appaṭiyē eṭuttu Tamiḻōṭa kalantu	Just like that, we speak English
English-aiyum pēsuvōm.	by mixing it in with our Tamil.

The limits of such prophylactic English usage, however, often ended with the sentence. After having been slammed for trying to speak too much English with me, one of my hostelmates noted in Tamil:

> There isn't anything wrong with the sentence "Scissors-*e koṭu.* Paper cut *paṇṇaṇum*" ('Give the scissors. I want to cut paper'). It conveys some knowledge of English and is *style.* And it won't exclude anyone. But saying "Give the scissors. I want to cut paper" will cause teasing because it's show-offy ("*bantā*"), because it's trying to show that you are the big man ("*periya āḷ*").

As this student implied, even if everyone understands the English sentence, it is always safer to avoid clause- and sentence-level constructions. Indeed, there was a tendency to avoid full English clauses and sentences and a preference for simply inserting English words ("vocabularies") into Tamil grammatical constructions, thereby enveloping English and subordinating it to Tamil so as to offset its disruptive powers, to frame it not as too much but as just right.

Further, in such youth speech, words that are totally unfamiliar to one's peers (or what peers assume to be the expected linguistic knowledge of their social circle) tend to be avoided. The result is a push toward using English words that are just on the limits of intelligibility and familiarity, on the vanguard of lexical fashion. Words known and used by all are "normal" and cease to have *style*; words known by none invite censure as *over*doing *style*, as trying too hard, as showing off.

These youth tread lightly around the denotational and referential powers of English to inscribe differences in comprehension as differences in status. Instead, English was often simply used for routinized, interactional moves and phatic communications. Greetings and departures like "Hi," "What's up?," "How are you?," "Good morning," and "Bye"; phatic communications like "yeah" and "isn't it?"; discourse markers like "but," "suppose," "I mean," and "so"; and address terms like "dude," "buddy," and "bro"—all such linguistic garnishes display English without necessarily excluding anyone. The denotational content of these words and phrases is minimal, and often their basic interactional function is inferable from context without any knowledge of English. They are often highly routinized and formulaic as well. Indeed, they are by and large overdetermined by the genre of interaction (as with greetings and departures), by intonation and pauses (as with phatic communications and tag questions), or by the surrounding Tamil propositional content (as with discourse markers). Such usages manage the double bind to status-raise by speaking English but not status-raise too much by speaking too much English. And they do so by inhabiting the interstices of speech, occurring between interactions (greetings, departures), turns of talk (phatic communications), and sentences (discourse markers).

A further strategy is glossing between the two languages (also see Canagarajah 1995:12; cf. Gumperz 1982:78–79; Sankoff et al. 1990:92–93; Heller 1994:197), as if to prefigure and defuse censure by mirroring English with Tamil. Below is an example from my Madurai roommate Sebastian. Hanging out in 2011, his first year in the job market after finishing his master's degree in computer science, he, along with his roommates, reflected on their college days. In particular, he discussed how, in college at least, he learned a little bit of English every day, which was not the case now that he had graduated and was unemployed. (Contrast this with his frustration in 2007, while in college, at how the administration was trying to 'stuff' English down students' throats.) In the following transcription's interlinear gloss, I have underlined the English words that Sebastian glosses in his Tamil:

Appōv-	*āvatu*	at least	*oru* word-*āvatu*	*kattuṭṭu*	*iruppōm*	*paṭikkiṟappō.*
Then-	at least	at least	one word-at least	learn-COMPL.AVP.	be-FUT.1pers.pl.	study-PRES.-when
Kālaile	at least	at least	one word-*āvatu*		try *paṇṇuvōm.*	
Morning	at least	at least	one word-at least		try do-FUT.1pers.pl.	

'At least then, when we were studying, we would have learned at least one word. At least every morning we would try at least one word.'

In this tight poetic couplet, through glossing and parallelism, Sebastian diagrams the necessity to speak both English and Tamil at the same time without speaking either language alone (cf. Heller 1994:167; Woolard 1998).

Such linguistic practices ambivalently navigate a number of fine lines, articulating a desire for cosmopolitan exteriority and *style*; a distance from the rural, the uneducated, and the *local*; and a disregard for adult concepts of respect and seriousness, purity and propriety, all of which youth feel themselves to be, in one way or another, excluded from and exterior to. At the same time, youths' enveloping of English within their Tamil keeps its excesses and dangers in check, attempting to mitigate the potential divisiveness of English by bracketing its denotationality, just as it keeps in abeyance the anxieties that upon leaving the college and entering the hierarchical workforce, one *must* speak in proper English or flounder. While a bit of English "vocabularies" keeps the menace of the *local* at bay and brings the global a bit closer, colloquial Tamil keeps those hierarchies of class indexed by English at bay. In effect, one must speak English while disavowing that fact and speak Tamil while marking that one is not speaking only it. As we saw, this requires a complex citational play between these two languages and their associated imaginaries, each functioning as the other's citational quotation marks. It requires one's speech to stand ambivalently before a shifty threshold, neither here nor there, but in both places at once, and yet not quite in either. It requires one to speak from a liminal space beyond, or beside, both languages—a space in the interstices of the *local* and global, present and future, childhood and adulthood.

Aesthetics of English

Before concluding this chapter, I would like to note one other manifestation, and medium, of the denotational bracketing of English: the usage of English—or more accurately, roman script—in youth's brand fashion. (By being in roman script, brand names, slogans, and other "wordings" were seen by youth as being in English.) While in chapters 2 and 3, I argued that brand(esque) names are *style* for their aesthetic of brandedness, here I expand that discussion to what we might call an aesthetics of Englishness: the quality of being like English, even if not quite. Some youth fashion was denotationally reflexive about this aesthetic function of English, as was the case with a shirt I saw on a bus whose fictive brand name was simply "LETTERING." Similarly, consider the T-shirt design in figure 12 below.

Most of the *stylish* designs worn by Tamil young men, however, materialized this aesthetics not by reflexive denotational explicitness but by stretching the limits of denotational intelligibility and morphological and orthographic coherence (cf. Tarlo 1996:242–43). It wasn't uncommon to find nonsensical English splattered on garments, from letter sequences that roughly followed rules of English morphology ("Disquerd," "Everinhu Canglong") to those that completely transgressed them ("asiohdngy"). Or

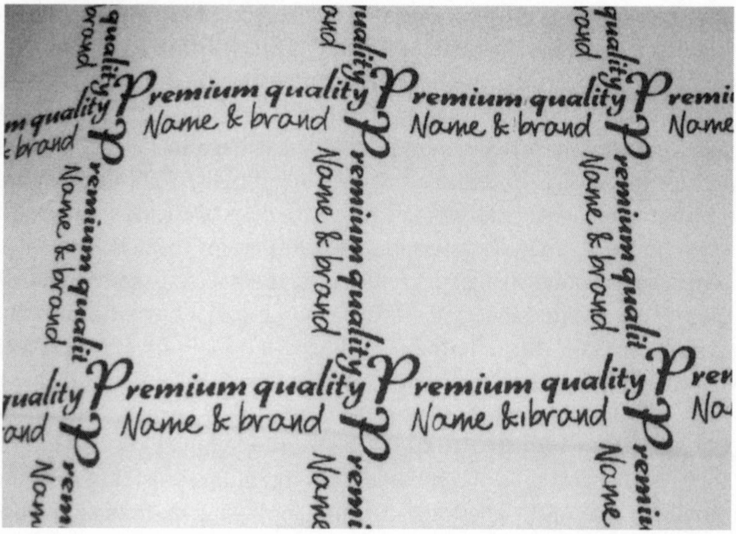

Figure 12. "Premium quality: Name & brand" as design element

consider figure 8 from chapter 3, where the shirt's design is a series of English words ("fresh," "with," "mine," "so," "BOY"), quasi-words ("frood," "chun," toybar," "de"), and strings of letters, punctuation marks, and numbers ("c,21," "u&s, "cotalll"), along with the fictive brand name "Us 395."

In such garments, English is displaced as a linguistic code and instead is presented as mere script, a simulacrum of denotational language.[26] The semantic vacuousness and, in certain cases, the inscrutability of such uses of "English" were, in fact, what made English(esque) forms safely able to be availed as *style* (also see chapter 5 on this point). As the local Chennai producers of such types of clothing (discussed in chapter 3) explained to me, the nondenotationality of English(esque) forms made them useful in garment design in a way that Tamil never could be. As one producer noted, if a shirt has Tamil on it, it has to have a meaning ("*Arttam irukkaṇum*"). The words have to be spelled correctly, the sentences grammatical (cf. Thomas 2009). This is because it addresses people. People won't just see it; they'll read it. By contrast, English letter sequences on apparel, whether they form morphologically or semantically coherent strings or not, have no such requirements. 'No one cares what it means,' was a refrain I heard from both producers of such garments and their youth consumers. Rather, like a curve, a square, a curlicue, or a swoosh, roman graphemes and English words, phrases, and (brand) names are mere design elements that make garments more attractive and *stylish*.

It might be argued whether such fashion is comparable to the kinds of spoken uses of English I've discussed in this chapter. As I noted, it often wasn't clear if the "English" on these garments was governed by any notion of a grammatical or morphological code and thus if it was, in that sense, linguistic at all. Further, the youth who wore such clothing were neither the authors nor the animators of the inscriptions on their bodies, unlike, presumably, the words out of their mouths. Such graphemes, words, and phrases were written by someone else, produced somewhere else. Moreover, unlike spoken language, the "English" on such clothing didn't interpellate others as addressees. It simply offered itself up to be seen at the leisure of those who so chose. Such clothing broadcasted English(ness) indiscriminately. Coming not out of the mouth but off of fabric (sometimes even from parts of the body that wearers themselves couldn't see, like their backs), such surfeit English didn't entangle those who apprehended it in the same way that spoken utterances always risked.

Yet, as I've been arguing, this is exactly what youths' speech attempts to do to/in English. Youth fashion literalizes and materializes the ways in which youth speech attempts to defuse the divisive powers of English's denotationality, albeit in another medium. Youth speech and fashion both accessorize English, turning it into a fashion accessory by citing it, by reducing it to the mere quality of being English-like. Both spoken and worn English display English while disclaiming and deforming it as one's own, attempting to render such linguistic forms into aesthetic objects denuded of denotation and addressivity, allowing such language to *stylish*ly adorn the subject without seeming to make any of the claims that such adornment always seems to (otherwise) make.

What Is a Code Such That It Can Be Mixed?

In this chapter, I have shown how youth language is mediated by multiple linguistic regimes: prestige registers of pure Tamil and fluent, proper English, and colloquial varieties of ordinary, *local* Tamil. The multiple mandates to transgress each of these through a careful linguistic alchemy creates complex and partial reanimations of these registers. Youth distance themselves from various social voices (of the politician, the purist, the traditionalist, the villager, the urban elite, the college professor/administrator, the white-collar working adult, the *Peter*) by toying with and disavowing both English and Tamil.[27] In doing so, they straddle the threshold between these languages, between the "foreign" and its domestication, carving out a space and time that resists resolving the ambivalences and tensions that make youths' linguistic practice intelligible and efficacious. This space created at the mouth of the threshold is where *style* is produced and where risks of under and *over style* continually menace. It is in this sliver of the linguistically transgressive—that which goes beyond the "normal"—where youth subjectivity is constituted and performed, flirted with and practiced (chapter 2).

We might follow Ben Rampton (1995) and call such linguistic practice "crossing," the movement across cultural and linguistic boundaries by speaking the language of another. Yet the forays of the Tamil youth I discuss in this chapter never quite cross over (or at least, not felicitously). Entry into the (imagined) world of English-speaking others is always hedged on by these youth, always marked and managed as not quite what it otherwise seems to be. Much as we saw with the display of brand surfeits in chapter 2, to sprinkle one's speech with English in the peer group was not to (try to) become (like) an authentic(ated) English speaker but to become *like* someone who performs being like an English speaker (cf. Heller 1984; Bucholtz 2003; 2011; Tetreault 2009:209). Youth speech hesitated when it got to the gates of English, veering away at the last minute. At the same time as speaking in English without being seen as claiming to *be* an English speaker as such, one also had to speak in Tamil without being seen as *only* a Tamil speaker. This is a complex form of polyvocality, for youths' ambivalent uses of Tamil and English are redoubled in their double-voicedness; both languages are embraced and disavowed at the same time through the tangling of particular registers of them. Not just the "simultaneity" of voices (Woolard 1998; also see Franceschini 1998:64), these youths' linguistic practices reflexively comment on that very simultaneity.[28]

The reflexivity involved in such practices problematizes labeling them "code mixing" or "code switching." This is because such practices trouble the very notion of "code" and hence the clarity of the boundary between linguistic codes such that it could be crossed or the codes mixed or switched.

Foundational work on code switching started from the assumption that any piece of language is governed by one discrete and coherent denotational/grammatical code. From this point of view, a "switch" in codes is a meaningful deviation from the implicitly monolingual norm. To such deviations, the linguist asks, Why here? Why now? And what is the function and meaning of such alternations? Work in recent decades has questioned this research program for a number of reasons. Most important is the assumption that what counts as a code can be unproblematically determined independently of participants' own construals (Heller 1988; Alvarez-Caccamo 1990; 1998; Swigart 1992; Urciuoli 1995; Auer 1998; Franceschini 1998; Meeuwis and Blommaert 1998; Woolard 1998; Agha 2009; Paz 2010). It has thus been argued that the question of code, and thus of code switches and mixes, has to be approached from the perspective of participants' reflexive models of language. Do participants construe code switching and code mixing as linguists tend to do: as discrete, autonomous denotational/grammatical codes that alternate in real-time discourse? Or do they attend to different linguistic levels or units? Or do they not even perceive such linguistic difference at all? On this line of thinking, in order to explain the meaningfulness of code switching and code mixing, we first have to determine the emic codes that are in play for participants. Having ethnographically grounded our units and the boundaries between them, linguistic analysis can then begin (proceeding, as it often turns out, much as it would have before).

This intervention is undoubtedly correct. Yet it risks assuming that the interpretive frames that participants bring to bear on any stretch of interaction are unproblematic and clear-cut for participants themselves. However, shifts or switches in interactional frames or "codes" are not always discrete or determinate for participants. They are often, in fact, the issue under interactional negotiation (Agha 2009). As we saw for the non-elite, college-going Tamil youth that I lived and worked with, it is the indeterminacy of and ambivalence about the ambiguous boundary between such frames where social meaning, identity, and performative force were generated (also see Heller 1984; 1994:167ff.; Woolard 1988; 1998; Meeuwis and Blommaert 1998; Bucholtz 2011; Hall and Nilep 2015). Doing *style* turned on pushing the line between normalized and excessive English, on constantly moving and playing with thresholds of indexical potency, tip-toeing the line of linguistic appropriation and (in)appropriateness. Beyond simply asking, then, if various discrete codes are recognized by participants, we might also ask *how* the/an ontology of code is itself reflexively figurated by those participants as a site of (in)difference, if indeed it is. Or put another way, in addition to determining the socially relevant linguistic differences that must be recognized for switching or mixing to be possible (be they differences in denotational/grammatical codes, dialects, lexical registers, repertoires, or social styles), we should also ask how it is that meaningfulness and difference are themselves constituted, or not, around the very question of code (or dialect, register, repertoire, or style; Irvine 2002). As we saw, for example, the issue of *style* was less about *what* the relevant codes were than of how variants, or fractions, of particular codes—or more precisely, particular lexical registers of English or Tamil as they stood under various ideologies of standard language (pure Tamil, *decent* spoken Tamil, *local* Tamil, proper English, etc.)—opened up a risky and potent threshold of linguistic performativity that had to be negotiated just so. Doing *style* was about expanding and playing with the unstable space in between these language varieties and the regimes that stood behind them. Within that linguistic liminality, youths' linguistic practices turned on bracketing the denotationality of English, on sidestepping the problematic indexicalities of *local* Tamil, and thus on finding a *stylish* balancing point between under and *over style* that constantly pushed the boundaries of each of these languages/registers into each other, and thus into productive ambiguity.

But more than simply undermining the particular linguistic codes or registers involved by rendering their boundaries unclear, the citationality of Tamil youths' linguistic practice troubles the notion of code in another way. Such citational practices point up that the stability of the form or intelligibility of ethnolinguistic categories of linguistic difference cannot be guaranteed across or within interactions. Any stable linguistic formation or formulation (a repertoire, a style, a register, a language) outlines its own exteriority, an anticipation of destabilization that we find continually actualized in tropes, ironizations, and citations of those very formations/formulations in interaction.[29] However, such tropes not only depend on and "deviate" from the norms and ontologies that they play off of but also potentially, and often actually, act back on them, bracketing, undermining, and decentering them, sometimes even generating new linguistic norms and ontologies—variously called in the linguistics literature "monolectal codes" (Meeuwis and Blommaert 1998), "mixed codes" (Auer 1998), or "registers" (Paz 2010)—and thus new tropic possibilities (e.g., of "layered code-mixing"; Meeuwis and Blommaert 1998).

Tamil youths' *stylish* linguistic practice situates itself precisely in this gap between norm and trope (Nakassis 2014), exploiting the immanent exteriority of those linguistic forms that it appropriates, using them even as it brackets them. It is this dialectic, this constant spilling out of the norm through the norm, that is key. It is why simply specifying the relevant codes (or registers or styles) fails to account for the ways in which *style* is performatively generated—that is, how *style* keeps in play and in abeyance the very notion of code itself. In being situated in this fuzzy, liminal space between under and *over style*, between *style* and its own reversals, youth speech doesn't just move "between" codes (however construed); it implicitly comments on its near but not-quite crossings. To capture this requires theorizing not just the "mix" or the "switch" but the reflexive management of the thresholds and intensities of linguistic normativities, of the ways in which code itself comes to be played with, decentered, rendered fuzzy, and reinscribed through semiotic practice.

For all these reasons, the Tamil youths' linguistic practices (spoken or sartorial) that I describe in this chapter are citational, for as previous chapters have shown, it is precisely the (meta)semiotics of citation that gives such liminality—with its contradictions and tensions—material form, that makes intelligible and palpable the excluded middle wherein youth practice sites itself. Youth linguistic practices put English and Tamil in quotes, reanimating, echoing, and embracing the voices invokable through them, even as those voices are hedged upon, disavowed, bracketed, and deformed. Such linguistic practices balance sameness with and difference from ideologically invested registers like pure (*sen*) Tamil, *local* colloquial Tamil, and proper English while commenting on, and tentatively tipping, that very balance. To bring English close but not too close, to keep Tamil far but not too far, requires a reflexive diagramming of the very fact of these languages' simultaneity. It requires making language itself liminal, ambivalent, indeterminate. It is precisely this ability to cite English and Tamil, and all that they stand in for, that makes them usable to perform *style*, to navigate the complexities of the peer group, to suture together the multiple spaces and times of exclusion in which youth subjectivity cannot be but flits through and flirts with. It is this reflexivity that partially undoes English and Tamil through (citations of) English and Tamil, enabling novel, if provisional, social possibilities, performative values, modes of sociality and youth being, and linguistic practices and forms.

FIVE

Bringing the Distant Voice Close

Introduction

I'm sitting in a cramped, ice-cold, air-conditioned control room with Arun, a television producer for the music-television station Southern Spice Music (or SS Music for short). We're in the middle of shooting one of the station's call-in shows, *Just Connect*, hosted by VJ Paloma. In the studio next door, technicians chat in Tamil as they prepare for the next shot while the phone operator is in the back of the room, fielding callers who are hoping to get a chance to talk to Paloma and dedicate a song on the air.

Paloma is touching up her makeup and adjusting her outfit. She's wearing pumps, knee-high socks, and a flowing blue blouse over a tight black miniskirt. She has kept her dark hair down, her makeup tasteful and sexy. In her early twenties, with light skin and fluent English, she looks and sounds like she could be a television host in any number of places across the globe.

Just Connect's theme is digital technology: in addition to telephone callers, the show features fan e-mails fielded on Paloma's laptop and video conferencing with viewers. The set reflects this theme. It is bright, youthful, and modern, even futuristic. Like Paloma's look, it is devoid of signs of locality. It has an aesthetic that seems to place it nowhere in particular (figure 13).

The clean lines of the set, its cool air, its soundproofed silence, and its modern design are all in stark contrast to the

Figure 13. VJ Paloma hosting *Just Connect* on SS Music (2008)

disarray, heat, and noise that lie buffered outside. The studio is on the fourth floor of a tall, gray building that looks down on the main road of the bustling neighborhood of Triplicane, one of the oldest and most crowded areas of Chennai. Just outside the studio, families sleep on the sidewalk, people loiter and chat on the corner, and bicycles, motorcycles, and cars all jostle to get ahead of each other, the heat of their exhaust mingling with the oppressive summer sun radiating off the asphalt and concrete.

As the producer calls the short break to an end, everyone gets ready to shoot the next "link," or caller segment. The operator takes the caller off hold, and the crackle of the open phone line is greeted by Paloma with a bubbly "Hallo:::w." Her affected pronunciation is met with an excited "Hi!" from the caller. Paloma asks, "Do you want to speak in English or Tamil?" The caller equivocates, and Paloma playfully suggests a little bit of both. It quickly becomes apparent, however, that the caller isn't quite comfortable in English.[1] An awkward "Huh?" following Paloma's lighthearted question about the caller's hobbies is quickly repaired by Paloma. She repeats the question in colloquial Tamil. What follows next is a two-minute back-and-forth dance between English and Tamil, both languages oscillating as VJ and caller attempt to manage having a conversation.

On-air exchanges like this were common on the station. These metalinguistic encounters negotiated an entanglement between two speaking subjects on opposite sides of the phone line and television screen. On one end were youth callers, who were not always fluent in English but whose speech was *stylish*ly peppered with it. On the other end were VJs like Paloma, native English speakers from non-Tamil Indian backgrounds who were not quite fluent in Tamil and who, to various degrees depending on the caller, incorporated and adopted colloquial Tamil into their speech. Such phone calls were a contact zone where youth callers and VJs, often from rather different class backgrounds and speaking out of quite distinct linguistic regimes, came into a kind of close distance. Drawing on ethnographic research at SS Music conducted between June 2008 and January 2009 (with periodic follow-ups until 2011) and research with my college friends who watched the channel over the course of my fieldwork, in this chapter I examine some of these on-air encounters. I show how changes in market viability, institutional organization, and target audience at the station lead to this particular linguistic configuration of close distance. I focus on how the mediatization of language at SS Music made possible and problematic a particular kind of citational linguistic practice, as well as certain attendant desires and ambivalences. This configuration, I suggest, is inflected by the fact that, on the one hand, VJs and their callers and audiences come from (and are understood to come from) different class and linguistic backgrounds and that, on the other hand, they are brought together and yet kept apart by the phone line and the television screen. Important to this latter distance is, as I discuss, a particular media ideology (Gershon 2010) about what kind of speech and comportment are appropriate to speaking on-screen. As I show, these social and medial distances make it so that VJs' on-air linguistic practices mirror but also invert the dynamics of linguistic practice in youths' peer groups. In chapter 4, I showed how the college youth with whom I worked brought themselves close to and distanced themselves from English through English, garnishing their Tamil with English words and phrases, in effect, putting their English in quotes. By contrast, as I show in this chapter, VJs at SS Music bring themselves closer to and distance themselves from Tamil through their Tamil. They inhabit non-Tamilness by putting the Tamil that they do use in quotes, enveloping it with English so as to frame it as not quite their own speech. As I argue, this inversion contributes to making these VJs appealing sites of English-language desire for the very same youth who struggled to speak English in their peer groups. Between the face-to-face conversation and the mass broadcast, for viewers (if not always for callers, as we see below) these call-in shows were occasions during which *stylish* English (and Tamil) could be safely touched on its thither side, where one could glimpse, and hear, beyond the threshold of youth *style* and *over style* without, to again invoke the cautionary tale of Icarus, melting one's wings in the heat of the burning sun.

Southern Spice Music

One of the major transformations inaugurated by the opening up of the Indian economy in the 1980s and 1990s was the spread and availability of television hardware and software. While since the 1960s, the Indian state had heavily invested in the expansion of television use as part of its development-oriented, modernization projects (as well as for purposes of political mobilization), it wasn't until the late 1980s and early 1990s that the widespread availability of television was possible (Farmer 2003).

It wasn't simply that before liberalization television sets were too expensive for most of the population or that the necessary infrastructure was nonexistent or patchy. It was also that until liberalization, the government maintained a monopoly on television, eschewing advertisement-driven, entertainment programming in favor of developmentally oriented programming designed to "uplift" and modernize the nation (Chatterji 1987; Pendakur 1991; Mankekar 1999; Rajagopal 2001). With liberalization, this Nehruvian "socialistic pattern of society" was displaced by a glitzier vision of a global India addressed to the (upper-)middle classes, focusing less on uplift of the poor than on a "consumer citizenship" (Lukose 2009) that emphasized access to global commodities and brands, international fashion, and entertainment, as discussed in chapters 1 and 2.

The expansion, and privatization, of television was part of this shift in imagining the nation. The decades after liberalization saw a proliferation of private and state television stations operating at the regional, state, national, and international level. Distributed through satellite and cable services, these stations dispersed the audience, addressing niche audiences—by language, region, age, class, and interest—and delivering them to advertisers in ways that the nationally focused state broadcast media, up to that point, had not (Juluri 2003; Kumar 2013).

It is in this context that Southern Spice Music was founded. A television station based out of Chennai, SS Music was started in 2001 by a lottery company that used the station to broadcast its live lottery results. To fill the rest of the airtime, the station's owner brought in a group of recent Visual Communications graduates from the elite Catholic college in Chennai where I worked. Largely Anglo-Indian[2] and upper-middle class, these cosmopolitan, English-fluent youth seized the opportunity to create, as they put it, a south Indian version of MTV.[3] As VJ Craig, the longest-standing and most popular VJ on the channel when I was there, explained,

It [SS Music] was (south India's MTV). It was south India's *answer* to MTV. Because what we look at-, at that point of time, the stuff that was-, that MTV and Channel V[4] and everybody were doing would *never* come to south India. Never. A-, a-, if they had to touch something, they would touch Bangalore. Nobody touched Kerala, nobody touched Chennai, nobody touched uh, anywhere in Hyderabad or Andhra Pradesh or anything, because they were all forgotten states. . . . And it was thought to be rural: "Why would I go to a village like Chennai? Why would I go to a village like-?" That was what (SS Music's founding producers and creative heads) and everybody-, our plan was "Why, in your face MTV!" you know, and we did it, and we kicked MTV's ass for the longest time here in south India, and Channel V as well.

Their ambition to be a south Indian MTV didn't go unnoticed. In 2004, Viacom—the owner of MTV—attempted, ultimately unsuccessfully (apparently due to disputes over Viacom's controlling stake, the price, and the desire of SS Music's owners to maintain their lottery broadcasts), to acquire SS Music as part of a strategic move to enter the south Indian television market (Srinivasan 2005).

From the outset, SS Music mainly played music videos—Western pop music, regional south Indian film songs, and Hindi film songs—most often through call-in show formats like the one discussed above. In addition, the station featured lifestyle shows (e.g., about elite pubs, discos, and restaurants in south Indian cities; regional travel shows; shows about romantic love), reality game shows of various kinds (e.g., *Voice Hunt*, an *American Idol*–type show; *VJ Factor*, a show to find new VJs modeled off of MTV India's *VJ Hunt*), shows reviewing Western films (*Cinema Central*), shows offering glimpses into regional film production (*First Frame*), and shows that visited and showcased Indian colleges (*College Da*). These shows aimed to provide "international"-quality programming—that is, programs whose production quality, content, and genre mirrored what one might find on MTV USA or MTV India[5]—while inflecting such "international" formulae with regional, south Indian (pop) culture (i.e., "southern spice"). I put "international" here in quotes, for much of what was seen as international at SS Music included programming—such as that of MTV India—whose content and form was itself already localized for an urban, elite, Hindi-speaking audience (cf. Kumar 2013:261). "International," then, is less a designator of place than an aesthetic imaginary that SS Music producers citationally modeled their programming on (cf. youths' conceptions of "brand" and "foreign" discussed in chapter 2).

By producing "international" content with "southern spice," the channel targeted, and provided to advertisers, (upper-)middle-class, English-familiar (if not fluent) youth in the metropolitan cities of south India—

that is, youth from the so-called A and A+ classes in places like Chennai, Bangalore, Cochin, and Hyderabad. These were elite children of liberalization, rooted in Dravidian vernaculars but cosmopolitan in outlook. They were viewers who, up until that point, had never been directly addressed by national broadcast media *as* south Indians, who were ignored as "villagers" in "forgotten states," as Craig put it above. SS Music, while positioning itself within a global imaginary, then, was also entangled with a long-standing south Indian imaginary of the nation within which the South is subordinate to the North (chapter 4), as well as with a local exceptionalist discourse that south India—given its distinct cultures—requires its own particular content. Ironically, then, SS Music projected a global aesthetic, even as what they produced was a localized format (at the regional level) of an already localized format (at the national level).

From its inception, SS Music faced the complex task of carving out an audience—affluent English-speaking youth living in the south Indian "metros"—from an increasingly crowded and competitive television market. As the founders of the station variously reminisced in conversations with me, when they began SS Music, television in India was composed of either boring, run-of-the-mill, "mass"-oriented Indian stations ("mass" in the sense that they addressed a wide, nondifferentiated class-spectrum) or "international" stations like Star TV, whose English-only programming was not specifically tailored for the Indian audience as such. Those stations that were doing innovative, urban, youth-oriented television for Indians—SS Music's desired niche—were largely in Hindi or English (e.g., Channel V, MTV India). None were in south Indian Dravidian languages or, as noted above, oriented to their speakers. SS Music aimed to fill, or rather create, that space.

What set SS Music apart from, on the one hand, regional music-television stations (e.g., the Tamil station SCV and later, as it was renamed, Sun Music) and, on the other hand, national and "international" music-television stations (e.g., Channel V, MTV India, and later VH1) was how it blended, balanced, and inflected different social imaginaries. Particularly important to its *masala* was its use of multiple languages. Alongside flashy and intricate graphics, rapid-fire editing, focus on Western music and global pop culture, and VJs' performances of youthful, elite, hip cosmopolitanism (all of this in stark contrast to the comparatively austere aesthetics of regional and national "mass" channels), SS Music stood apart from regional stations because of its VJs' fluent English. At the same time, it differentiated itself from global English and hip, national Hindi stations like VH1, MTV India, and Channel V based on its use of regional south Indian languages and its general orientation to south Indian popular culture.

Amazingly, SS Music started off by using the four major Dravidian languages—Tamil, Telugu, Malayalam, and Kannada—in addition to English and some Hindi (cf. Spitulnik 1996). Not only playing songs from the Malayalam, Telugu, Kannada, and Tamil film industries, the VJs of the station would speak, with varying degrees of fluency, in these different languages. This multilingual format was particularly important for their call-in shows. VJs, it was said, would speak to callers in any language in which callers felt at ease. As VJ Craig, who was known for his facility in moving between different languages, put it in English with some Tamil thrown in,

> We could speak in the other languages if you saw fit to speak (them) with us. Like if you call[ed] from an *ūr pakkattule* ('place close to') to *māpl-*, Madurai, I would be able to converse with you. If you called from Andhra Pradesh, I would understand you and be able to speak to you with Hindi because that's another (language spoken there). If you call[ed] from Karnataka, I knew Kannada. I used to speak Kannada very fluently because I'm from Bangalore, so that could happen. And if you called from Kerala, I could make fun-, because-, of you and chat with you (in Malayalam).

This polyglossia made SS Music popular with the college youth I lived with. As one Madurai hostelmate of mine explained, you could call in to the station and talk in any language you wanted, and even if it wasn't the VJ's language, or even if it wasn't your language (i.e., English), they'd talk to you and make you feel comfortable.[6]

Ultimately, English made this multilingual format possible. As we see below, English functioned as a framing language within which all other programming segments—songs, interviews, caller interactions, "intros," and "wind ups"—could be couched and thus sutured together. But more than functioning as a linking language between distinct regional audiences and languages, English was the "class" of the station, as producers put it. The term "class" here plays on the ambiguous senses of high social class and classiness, standing in opposition to its equally ambiguous antonyms "*local*" and "mass." English, as embodied by the figure of the hip and fluent VJ, gave SS Music its cosmopolitan credentials. It made the station cool and stand apart in an increasingly globalized and localized television market. And, as I suggest, ultimately it functioned to bracket the regional languages that VJs spoke, putting them in quotes so as to instate VJs' (and the station's) distance from the *local*ity of those very languages.

The Pedagogy and *Style* of English

While the station was founded on a multilingual south Indian format, when I came to conduct research as a production intern at the station in 2008, its orientation to language and audience had changed. From being a pan-south Indian station, it had shifted almost exclusively toward focusing on and using Tamil and English.[7] The reasons for this shift were multiple. Over the years, it became increasingly difficult for the station to maintain distribution in multiple television markets, a fact compounded by the explosion of vernacular music-television stations across different regional distribution networks (Kumar 2013). In addition, by 2008, the station's creative personnel and management had changed, as members of the "core (production) team" had gone on to new projects. These English-speaking cosmopolitans were largely, though not exclusively, replaced by monolingual Tamil speakers whose interest and expertise were in Tamil popular culture, and Tamil film in particular.

Rather than spread itself thin across different markets, the station chose to double down on its Tamil audience while still maintaining its "class" image. The result was a shift in target audience, from a pan-south Indian urban elite to a cross-class youth demographic located solely within Tamil Nadu. SS Music both narrowed (by region and language) and expanded (by class) its audience, curiously becoming even more of a niche station by becoming more of a "mass" station. This audience included a predominance of English-desiring, though not English-fluent, Tamil youth in smaller cities and towns (like Madurai, Coimbatore, Salem, Trichy, etc.) who were upwardly mobile, though decidedly not elite (the so-called B and C classes)—in short, youth like my hostelmates and college friends. This significantly changed the grounds of identification and relationality between the VJs—who were still expected to uphold the English "class" of the station, if encouraged to use more Tamil on-air—and their audience. From being relatively similar in linguistic and class background, now there was a stark gap between VJs and most of their audience. Rather than unifying them, English now divided the audience just as it divided large sections of the audience from VJs.

During my time at the station, this linguistic reorientation created a great deal of frustration among producers and VJs. It was often bemoaned that the earlier golden days of the station were over. Laments about the shift in language were often merged with complaints that production quality had gone downhill, that the station now lacked creative innovation and was simply aping itself. Among the VJs—almost all of whom predated the shift—the change was described as an "identity crisis," as a massification of the channel, a dumbing down and blunting of its competitive and creative edge.[8] One female VJ, describing how she initially felt when they switched linguistic formats, said,

That [changing to Tamil] was probably the biggest change. Once that changes, everything changes. You know, when you basically cater to a different audience with a different mind-set everything changes. . . . Before you were catering to people like, well, like me. Now it's-, now you gotta dumb it down a little bit. So you know. . . . So what would I say (to callers)? Would I say it the same way? Would I even be talking about the same things? Not really, no. So it's a small ((tweak)) on that level, but it actually changes, like everything.[9]

Shifting language, as this VJ put it, was seen as a shift in audience sophistication, interest, lifestyle orientation, and social class. And given that the management wanted the station to maintain its English and its cosmopolitan image, this created a tension in the station's addressivity. As this VJ put it, "So what would I say (to callers)? Would I say it the same way?" This was more than a question of language, of course. It was a change in "mind-set," in "everything." By this, this VJ was also motioning to the cultural politics that VJs, and female VJs like her in particular, were now entangled by. Indeed, female VJs' screen presence—their *stylish*, Western dress and jovial English—was now, more than ever, likely to be found immodest by conservative individuals that, in the earlier format, would have largely been excluded from SS Music's imagined audience. While critiques were occasionally levied against both male and female VJs that they were "disrespectful" to "Tamil culture"—given their orientation to a global, English imaginary and aesthetics of personhood (and dress) rather than a traditionally Tamil one—it was female VJs who were more likely to be singled out and criticized (chapter 2). This didn't significantly alter how female VJs used English, or how much they used, relative to male VJs (cf. chapter 4). But it did seem to inhibit female VJs from forging the kinds of informal, joking relations that male VJs more easily cultivated with callers,[10] as well as impacting some audience members' evaluations of VJs' on-air speech, a point I return to later in the chapter.

Linguistically, the challenge for the station was addressing an audience that included large sections that were not comfortable with the signature linguistic feature of the station: its fluent English. During my time at the station, one of the heads of creative programming, who was also a founding member of the graphics department, referred to this large audience segment as "the beginners," viewers whom he had to "teach" the finer points of global Western pop culture and language.

Okay, uh, uh, the spoken language for Southern Spice Music is English, which is not comfortable by, uh, yeah, not very comfortable by, uh, uh, south Indian people,

> except (in) Bangalore, (in) metro cities. If you take rural areas, people are not comfortable (with English) at all. So what we did is, we brought in a layman term. . . . Layman term is basically like, okay a rickshaw wallah ('driver') can understand what we speak. We don't complicate the language. . . . I always place myself on the layman term, and say, "Okay boss, I don't want a dictionary!" People are very simple, okay, people have to understand us. . . . whenever the person can't speak at all, okay, we ask them to like, to-, "No problem, you speak, okay? Don't worry about that, okay?" . . . Like how the child, uh, learns, uh, the first language from the parents. . . . Okay, so that is the way we spoon-feed it (to them)! . . . We make them feel comfortable in whatever they speak. We correct them in such a way that they don't feel hurt. We don't say, "Okay boss, you have done something wrong here." We'll say, "Okay, if you use this word here, it'll look-, (be) sounding better."

While this creative head exaggerated the extent to which English was simplified on the station, the quote is indicative of the ways in which producers and VJs were attentive to the linguistic differences between them and their audience and to the need to make sure that their language was not too unintelligible to their audience.

This pedagogical mandate wasn't simply a discourse of producers. It was also a discourse that the youth with whom I lived and worked in Madurai and Chennai also voiced. Not simply making the channel distinctive and fun to watch, VJs' fluent English made SS Music useful. One could watch SS Music to learn "practical," "conversational" English. One could get "exposure" and develop one's "soft skills" and "communication" (chapter 4). And this was because the English on SS Music wasn't like the formal, "proper" English that one might hear or read in the news, that one would learn in the classroom or read in a dictionary or grammar textbook. It was colloquial, down to earth, and hip. It was how college youth aspired to speak: fluent, *jolly*, and *stylish*.

The conversational style of SS Music was, indeed, different from other stations. VJs spoke with callers in ways that were transgressive of typical norms of on-air formality and politeness, though typical of youth peer-group interaction—for example, using fictive affinal kinterms like *macci* or *māpḷe* and other informal, nonhonorificating address terms such as *ṭā*, "dude," or "bro" (chapter 1; Nakassis 2014).[11] In asking a local Madurai television "compere"[12] if he could, like Craig and other SS Music VJs, ever use terms like *macci* or *māpḷe* with callers on-air, he was aghast. 'You never know who is on the end of the line!' he exclaimed. 'They could be older than you, a woman, or someone really conservative.' If you spoke like that, he explained, you were likely to end up offending someone. The fact that

VJs like Craig could liberally use such terms, then, was a way not simply of talking like youth and creating solidarity with them but also of *stylish*ly and playfully transgressing norms of propriety in public speech.

Style is the key word here. *Style* was consistently how the language on SS Music was described by my college friends and hostelmates, who often spontaneously proffered SS Music VJs as exemplars of *stylish* speech.[13] What is important here is that by addressing the so-called B- and C-class audiences, VJs were now in the orbit of the youth peer group, beholden to its multiple mandates and to its dynamics of *style* and *over style*; or, as VJ Craig put it, VJs now had to deal with youths' linguistic "complex": their ambivalent desire for and anxiety and insecurity about English (chapter 4). This "complex" was especially important for VJs' linguistic practices, given that much of the linguistic work on the channel occurred on call-in shows where VJs directly addressed particular individuals who would then have to speak back. This mass-mediated, yet direct, addressivity necessitated an on-air mélange of English and colloquial Tamil. One had to entice and entertain with *stylish* English while indexing solidarity and communicating with colloquial Tamil. Otherwise, the line might simply stay silent, as we see below.

In short, tensions between distribution access and cost, market competition, and station image necessitated SS Music's ambivalent shift in target audience. This, in turn, necessitated new modes of linguistic practice and addressivity. SS Music came to be caught in a linguistic liminality similar to that of the youth whom they addressed—indeed, *because* they addressed them. The language of the station became, in a very real sense, subject to the dynamics that governed how lower-middle-class and middle-class Tamil youth themselves engaged with English and Tamil. Below I look in detail at some examples of the on-air use of English and Tamil in call-in shows. I examine the ways in which Tamil is deployed, enveloped, and cited by VJs in their on-air performances. As I show, the citationality of VJs' speech takes an inverted form in relation to youths' citational speech. Rather than Tamil with sprinklings of English, VJs' speech largely comprised English with Tamil blended or thrown in, what is sometimes referred to among urban elites as "Tanglish." Such inverted, citational linguistic practice struck a balance: on the one hand, for VJs, it was a kind of prophylaxis against coming too close to the audience, a distancing from the youth subjectivities of those whom they addressed and cited; on the other hand, it was a mode of deference to and solidarity with the audience, a way to bring them close. This was a complex conjunction that reflexively managed the line between VJs' "normal" (English) speech and the *local* (Tamil) speech they cited. In this way, VJs stood on the opposite, mirror side of the threshold that youth stood before, between their "normal" (Tamil) speech and the *stylish* (English) speech that they cited. This inverting conjunction made SS Music a site of linguistic desire and interpellation as well as a source and site for the shifting and emergent texture of youth language.

Style On-Air

Call-in shows were particularly popular among youth audiences for the linguistic pleasures they afforded. Shows like *Reach Out* (hosted by VJ Craig), *PCO* (hosted by VJ Pooja), and *Just Connect* (hosted by VJ Paloma) allowed viewers to call in, chitchat with VJs (typically for thirty seconds to a couple of minutes), and then dedicate a song. These shows were taped, edited, and then aired later in the week. While the balancing of English and Tamil on these shows ranged from English-only conversations to conversations that were mainly in Tamil with some English thrown in, English was always the VJs' default language. But more than this, VJs' use of English framed Tamil. It enveloped it at the level of individual sentences, conversational sequences, and even in the way whole shows were organized. Such framing, I suggest, hierarchically ordered Tamil and English, diagramming the asymmetric relationship of VJs to their Tamil callers and audience as well as VJs' and the channel's ambivalent relationship to Tamil and the *local* more generally.

The call-in shows that I look at below had the following general format (table 1), with slight variations depending on the show's focus and length (45–60 minutes).

"Intros," "break links," and "windups" to these shows were almost always in full English, with Tamil used sparingly and always sandwiched by English. By contrast, caller interactions—which were framed by these

Table 1. Call-in show format on SS Music

VJ's "intro"	30–60 seconds
"Link"—Conversation with caller (telephone call, occasionally videoconferencing) or reading fan mail (six in total, each link comprising one to two segments/calls)	1.5–3 minutes
Song (six in total)	
"Break link" (three to four in total)	10–60 seconds
. . . Link, (break link,) song, (commercial,) . . .	
VJ's "windup"	30–120 seconds

English-dominant segments—were often conducted with a significant amount of Tamil; how much depended on the caller's (lack of) comfort with English. Even though calls were relatively ritualized and repetitive, they were often fraught with linguistic misunderstandings: the callers didn't understand the VJs' English, or less often, the VJs didn't understand the callers' Tamil. As we saw at the outset of the chapter, much of the talk in such encounters was about establishing the very basics of the conversation, feeling out which language would work best so as to move the conversation along toward its conclusion. To stave off these awkward breakdowns and misfires, VJs were quite sensitive to the caller's linguistic comfort zone and tended to mirror the speech style of the caller, though they always skewed toward a preference for English.

With speakers who were English fluent, Tamil was often simply used as an interactional garnish. For example, the VJ might throw in a Tamil response cry like *ayyō* ('gosh'; e.g., VJ Paloma: "*Ayyō!* So tell me what made you take physics?" *Just Connect*, episode 12), an address particle like *ṭā* ('man'), or youth-slang address terms like *maccā(n)* or *māpḷe*, as discussed above (e.g., VJ Craig: "Okay, *maccā*, you got it. You take care of yourself, and don't work too hard," *Reach Out*, episode 731). Similar to youths' usages of English in their speech to pepper their Tamil, such interjections of Tamil were almost purely indexical, simply linked to modes of stance-taking and identity work—in these cases, so as to align the VJ with his or her caller as youthful, hip south Indians. Using such garnishes was a way of speaking as/like a Tamil without having to speak the language.

With callers who were not comfortable with English, the conversation might quickly move into Tamil. Rather than as an indexical device to create interactional alignment between otherwise English-comfortable interlocutors, in such conversations Tamil functioned as the main language, creating denotational alignment—that is, having a conversation—between interlocutors from very different linguistic backgrounds. Consider the following interaction from *Reach Out* (episode 731) with VJ Craig. (See the front matter for symbols and abbreviations used in the transcripts that follow.) Here we see examples of Craig (Cr) using just English, using English to frame Tamil, and using just Tamil with a caller named Shanmugavalli (Sh):

01	**Cr:** Hello? (0.5)	
02		**Sh:** Hello↑=
03	**Cr:** =HI!↑ (1)	
04		**Sh:** Hi↑

05 **Cr:** Hi, what's your name? (0.7)

06 **Sh:** Shanmugavalli.

07 **Cr:** SHANMUGAVALLI!

08 **Sh:** Uh.

09 **Cr:** *Nalla pēru.* (0.5) *Atōṭa arttam enna ṇṇu sollamuṭiyumā uṅkaḷālē?* (1.5)
'Nice name. Can you [HON.] say what its meaning is?'

10 **Sh:** Don't know.

11 **Cr:** Don't know. You don't know the meaning of your name.

12 **Sh:** No.

13 **Cr:** Okay cool. So Shanmugavalli, (.) tell me more about yourself. What do you do? Where are you calling up from? (1)

14 **Sh:** I'm calling from Chennai.

15 **Cr:** From Chennai. (0.2) And you're a very shy girl. (.)

16 **Sh:** Yeah.=

17 **Cr:** =*Enkiṭṭe pēsuṟatu romba bayam.* (1)
'You are really afraid to speak with me.'

18 **Sh:** Yes.

19 **Cr:** Why are you *bayappaṭutt*ifying?=
'Why are you fearing me?'

20 **Cr:** =Is my *muñci* looking like a *pisāsi*? (.)
'Is my face looking like a demon?'

21 **Sh:** No, no.

22 **Cr:** Is it looking like a *āvi*?
'Is it looking like a ghost?'

23 **Sh:** No, no. <slight laugh>

24 **Cr:** Then↑ (.) *etukku bayappaṭuṟīṅka*?
'Then what are you [HON.] afraid of?'

25 **Sh:** <line noise (2.3)>

26 **Cr:** *Summā, oru veḷḷaikkāra paiyan kiṭṭe nīṅka itukku munnāṭi pēsuṟatukku kiṭaiyātā*? (0.5)
'Just joking around. Have you [HON.] never spoken to a white guy before?'

27 **Sh:** No.

28 **Cr:** <laughs> All right, do you want to dedicate a song to anybody? (.)

29		**Sh:** Ah, my parents↑=
30	**Cr:** =Ah, okay↑=	
31		=and my brother↑=
32	**Cr:** =Ah↑ (.)	
33	**Cr:** //Ah-//	and all my friends//, teachers.
34	**Cr:** Ah=all your friends and teachers↑	
35		**Sh:** Ah.
36	**Cr:** All right, all the best, okay?	
37		**Sh:** Ah, thank you.
38	**Cr:** Bye! . . .	

In this exchange, Craig moves from English (lines 1, 3, and 5, and then lines 11, 13, and 15) into Tamil (line 9 and then again in line 17) so as to try to get his interlocutor, the "very shy" Shanmugavalli, to engage with him. When she doesn't—preferring terse English answers instead of the Tamil that Craig assumes she is more fluent in[14]—he begins to joke with her. First he playfully uses the Tanglish construction *bayappaṭutt*ify ('to fear'; line 19), appending the English verbalizer "-ify" to a Tamil adverbial participle to create an English verb.[15] He then substitutes the English nouns for 'face,' 'demon' (line 20), and 'ghost' (line 22) with their Tamil equivalents, *muñci*, *pisāsu* (disfluently pronounced as *pisāsi*), and *āvi*, respectively. His playful and capricious Tamil insertions, part of his joking diagnoses for why she is so shy, attempt to bring Shanmugavalli out of her shell. As they continue to fail (note her consistently long pauses, including the excruciating two plus–second silence in line 25), he persistently uses more and more Tamil, attempting to get her to say something more than simply "yes" or "no." Eventually, Shanmugavalli's silence ends up becoming the very topic of the conversation, a joke in full-on Tamil about how Shanmugavalli is afraid of Craig because she's never spoken with a 'white guy' (line 26), a fact seemingly affirmed by her reticent "No" in line 27 and his tired laugh and "All right" in line 28. Faced with yet another failure, Craig returns to English for the ritual climax of this call-in genre, the dedication (lines 28–35), to which Shanmugavalli eagerly responds by rapidly giving a list of (probably preplanned) dedications.

In this interaction, we see a range of Tamil usage, from playful garnish to main denotational code. While Tamil functions both as a linguistic concession to the caller (lines 9, 17, 24, 26) and as a play on linguistic concession (lines 19, 20, 22), in both cases Craig's Tamil is framed by English and, in addition, as caused by Shanmugavalli's lack of speech (which Craig, in turn, jokingly attributes to the fact of his whiteness).[16] Shanmugavalli never speaks in Tamil, of course, but Craig's Tamil says it all. The cumulative effect is a metonymic chaining that differentiates (passive) silence from (agentive) speech, Tamil from English, Tamil from Anglo (or 'white'), caller from VJ, and Shanmugavalli from Craig. It is only at the request for a dedication that Shanmugavalli truly speaks. Shanmugavalli quickly snatches up this low-hanging cherry on the cake, a return to speech that also thereby confirms this emergent set of oppositions.[17] Not simply code mixing and code switching between Tamil and English, Craig's speech playfully pushes the threshold between these languages, reflexively fine-tuning his usage to what Shanmugavalli's might be (though he never seems to succeed), not in the interest of *style* per se, but in finding that liminal space wherein a conversation might be had.

What I would underscore is that while it wasn't uncommon for VJs to use Tamil to varying degrees and to various ends, Tamil was in one way or another framed as distant from the VJ. Consider the following interaction from *Just Connect* (episode 65) in which Paloma is talking with Gomathy, a Tamil-fluent caller. The interaction is mainly in Tamil with some English interspersed. The conversation has three main topics: first, how Gomathy finds Paloma's Tamil beautiful (*a̠laku*) and encourages her to keep speaking in Tamil (despite, and in response to, Paloma's playful disbelief that she speaks Tamil well: 'It doesn't make you laugh when you hear it?' "*Sirippu varaleyā kēṭkum pōtu*?"); second, Gomathy's sheer happiness and excitement to finally be speaking with Paloma; and third, Paloma's comments and queries about the speed and excitement of Gomathy's speech (what Paloma typifies early in the conversation as "*Kaṭakaṭalubalubalabalaba pēsu̠rīṅka nīṅka*," 'You're [HON.] speaking *kaṭakaṭalubalubalabalaba*'). At the end of the conversation, when Gomathy rattles off her list of friends to be dedicated to in rapid succession, Paloma iterates her earlier reanimation of the qualia of Gomathy's speech and asks her, in Tamil, if all her friends speak so "*kaṭakaṭakaṭa ṇṇu*," reducing the earlier onomatopoeia to a standard, if expanded, quotative adverbial for fast, flowing speech (*kaṭakaṭaven̠ru*). Are they a "*kaṭakaṭa* gang?" Paloma then asks in Tamil, now iterating the quotative adverb as an adjective. Gomathy laughs and answers in the affirmative. In Gomathy's final turn in the interaction, she says "Thanks-(*a*)*kkā*" ('Thanks, older sister').

What unfolds next is a complex split and shift in address by Paloma as she wraps up the call. Its net effect, as I show below, is an exclusion of Gomathy from what comes into visibility as a "modern" English-speaking audience. Paloma's address of and alignment to this audience distances her from the very Tamil language (and identity) in which she conducts the conversation with Gomathy. This is achieved through a complex citationality comprising language, gesture, and bodily hexis. (In the transcript below, I indicate address by a subscript to the right of the utterance: G for Gomathy, A for television audience, P for Paloma;? indicates ambiguity in address, ¬X indicates 'X not addressed.')

1 **G:** Thanks-(*a*)*kkā*!$_{\text{P}}$
'older sister'

2 **P:** See you!$_{\text{G}}$ *Ayyō*!$_{\text{G?, A?}}$ <light laugh> Bye!$_{\text{G}, \neg\text{A}}$
'Gosh!'

3 *"Akkā"*↑ *ṇṇu kūppiṭṭāṅka*::↑ $_{\neg\text{G, P, A}}$
'She called me older sister.'

4 Okay, it's time for you to check out this track.$_{\text{G?, A}}$

5 That was *kaṭakaṭa* Gomathi. $_{\neg\text{G, A}}$

6 Hope you like it. $_{\neg\text{G, A}}$

Following Gomathy's "Thanks-(*a*)*kkā*" ('Thanks, older sister') in line 1, Paloma, who is in a sitting position with her hands clasped on her crossed legs, says in line 2, "See you!" She then exclaims, "*Ayyō*!" ('Gosh!'), flashing her eyebrows, quickly shaking her head in mock surprise, and raising her right palm upward. Lightly chuckling, she says, "Bye!" as her right hand returns to rest on top of her left hand. While "See you!" and "Bye!" address Gomathy so as to mark the end of the conversation, the intervening response cry, "*Ayyō*!" and its attendant gestures are ambiguous as to whom they are for. As line 3 suggests, however, the response cry and mock shock in line 2 are in reaction to Gomathy addressing Paloma in line 1 with "*akkā*," an honorific, here fictive, patrilineal kinterm for an elder woman of the same generation. "*Akkā*" is not an address term used between age-equal peers and, as indicated by Paloma's response, presents something of a rupture by a more "traditional" and hierarchical kinship register into what Paloma thereby figures as the show's "modern" and laid-back egalitarian atmosphere (cf. men's fictive use of affinal kinterms, chapter 1).[18] Paloma's response cry registers this rupture as a self-interruption of her leave-taking, literally coming in between "See you!" and "Bye." Paloma's next utterance in line 3 is in Tamil, echoing her Tamil response cry in line 2 and Gomathy's infelicitous utterance in line 1. Continuing the utterance initiated with her response cry, Paloma repeats what Gomathy said to Paloma to prompt the self-interruption in a reported speech construction. With a lower pitch and volume, she says,

"Akkā"↑	*ṉṉu*	*kūppiṭṭāṅka*::↑
older sister	COMP.	call-PST.3pers.pl.

'She (HON.) called (me) "older sister."'

As she says this, her right hand raises up, palm perpendicular to the ground, and waves away from her body, twisting up and out. Her hand returns to her body at the end of the utterance, punctuating it with a clap on the open palm of her left hand. This utterance is a kind of stage aside. It is not addressed to Gomathy but refers to her as a (respectfully distant) third person. With this utterance, we begin to see that the *"Ayyō!"* in line 2 was already acting to winkingly include the audience in the show's putative space of modern sociality as implicitly addressed bystanders. Importantly, Paloma's delivery of this aside in line 3 is evocative of the Tamil film comedian Vadivelu, who often expresses himself in embarrassing situations with this same cadence and intonation (as also metacommunicated by Paloma's hand gesture). This implicit filmic citation resounds Gomathy but in the Tamil voice of a film buffoon. It serves not simply to playfully index that Paloma takes the address term *"akkā"* to be inappropriate but also, I would suggest, to distance and remove Paloma from the interaction itself. Here Paloma's Tamil and Tamil pop culture voicings, through their ironical address to a knowing audience, place Gomathy (we might even say *local*ize her) at a remove from Paloma and thus from the audience as well.

In line 4, Paloma then emphatically blinks, crisply raises her eyebrows, and leans back as she says, in English, "Okay, it is time for you to check out this track." Here Paloma's marked change in bodily hexis, pitch and stress (she increases her volume and stresses the second syllable of "okay"), and her use of English, while possibly addressed to Gomathy, more clearly addresses the audience. Paloma then captions the entire previous Tamil-language interaction in a way that is unambiguously for the audience and not for Gomathy by saying, "That was *kaṭakaṭa* Gomathi," the quotative Tamil onomatopoeia discussed above now iterated *as* Gomathy's (im)proper (nick)name. As Paloma says *"kaṭakaṭa,"* her left eye slowly winks, and she flashes her eyebrows twice while saying, "Gomathy." The overenthusiastic and chatty Tamil-speaking Gomathy is here embedded within an English sentence addressed to what is thereby constituted as an English-speaking (while still Tamil-pop-culture-savvy) audience, one that explicitly does not include her. Finishing off the call, Paloma says to the audience, "Hope you like it," pointing at the camera with her right hand.

At multiply embedded levels, here every instance of Tamil is kept in quotes, contained by English and distanced from the VJ. This distance is created not only by the patterning of English and Tamil (where English captions and finishes off the otherwise Tamil call) but also by the split address of Paloma's speech between the television audience and Gomathy. This split address is accomplished both verbally and through gesture, bodily hexis, and facial expression, which phone callers like Gomathy cannot attend to during the actual telephone conversation because the show is pretaped. While such bodily reactions might be read as proleptically addressed to the caller (through an erasure of the temporal disjuncture so as to simulate a live conversation), such visual cues in conjunction with the use of English, the use of demonstratives and personal pronouns, and the topics of conversation (e.g., the fact that they are about Gomathy) all serve to address the audience in an ironical metacommentary about the conversation itself. We can see how these visual and linguistic cues conspire to align Paloma with her television audience while distancing her and the audience from Gomathy, to whom Paloma speaks in Tamil simply because *she* (Gomathy) is comfortable in Tamil. This framing of Tamil as concession, in turn, confirms and reiterates Paloma's identity as not Tamil. The only Tamil that is used to address the audience here is joking, parodic, and playfully critical of Gomathy's earnest and respectful language. This split in addressivity materializes, and recoups in linguistic form, VJs' ambivalence toward the channel's shift in linguistic format, Paloma's anonymous address to the television audience in English here wishfully figuring the wider viewership as English-fluent, even as particular individual callers are, only out of necessity, addressed in Tamil.

But such distancing effects didn't only happen through the use of English and its associated paralanguage. I would also suggest that *within* uses of Tamil, there was an indexical trace that distanced VJs from Tamil. We saw this with Paloma's reanimation of the Tamil film comedian Vadivelu. But more generally, VJs' Tamil was riddled with mispronunciations, missing case markers, aberrant agreement, stuttering, and long, contemplative silences to find the right Tamil words. Such (mis)usages of Tamil distanced the VJ from the Tamil words they uttered—in effect, disavowing them as their own words. Such disfluencies were themselves often marked and brought to the audience's attention by VJs through cocked eyebrows and other gestures of confusion and surrender, creating multiply embedded citations and disavowals (cf. Goffman 1981:197–327).

Consider, for example, a call between VJ Craig and Santhosh during which Craig struggles to speak Tamil fluently and plays it up (*Reach Out*, episode 741). The conversation begins in English but quickly moves into Tamil. Responding to Santhosh's query of how Craig is doing, Craig goes into a description of the weather. (Craig's gaze and facial expressions are in <brackets> above his speech, their onset aligned with that of his speech. Disfluencies are marked with an *asterisk.)

<looking at camera>				<closes eyes, winces, looks up and right>	<opens eyes>	<looks back at camera>
Innikki	*vantu*:	weather	*romba*	slee:py-*ā:na*:: (.)	mood uh (.)	**koṭukkiṟatukku*.
today	come-AVP.		really	sleepy-ADJ.		give-PRES.NOM.DAT.

'Today the weather is, uh, giving a really sleepy mood.'

This malformed sentence, literally glossable as 'Today the weather is for giving a really sleepy mood,' is delivered slowly and unsurely. Craig closes his eyes and scrunches his face as his vowels elongate with the word "sleepy-*āna*," looking away from the camera as if struggling to finish the sentence. His gaze returns to the camera as he completes the utterance with a nominalization of the verb 'to give,' modified by the dative case: "*koṭukkiṟatukku*." Craig's infelicity is reflected in Santhosh's confused response: "*Ennaṅka*?" ('What's that [HON.]?') Craig shakes his head, telling Santhosh not to pay attention to it ("*Kaṇṭukkātīṅka Santhosh*!"). Craig then tries to query Santhosh about the weather where he is:

Nīṅka	*solluṅka,*	*eppaṭi*	**irukkāṅka?*	Weather	*vantu*	*eppaṭi*	*irukku?*
you-pl.	tell-IMP.pl.	how	be-PRES.3pers.pl.	weather	come-AVP.	how	be-PRES.NEUT.

'You tell me, how are they? How's the weather?'

Craig infelicitously conjugates the first question in the third-person human plural ("*irukkāṅka*"). His next utterance repairs this mistake by introducing the neuter singular subject 'weather' in agreement with the verb 'to be' ("*irukku*"). Craig and Santhosh then manage to complete a turn without grammatical infelicity, Santhosh telling Craig that it is really hot where he is. Craig repeats it back to him as a question, and then says,

<looking at camera>				<starting to look down>	<looking down and to the left>
Okay, super, super.	So uh	hot-*ā*	*irukkiṟatanāle*	*nīṅka*	*vantu*:: (.5)
		hot-ADV.	be-PRES.NOM.INST.	you-pl.	come-AVP.

<looks back at camera>	
indoors-*le(ru)ntu*	phone *paṇṟīṅkaḷā*?
indoors-ABL.	phone do-PRES.2pers.pl.INT.

'Okay, super, super. So, uh, because it's hot, you're calling from indoors?'

In the half-second pause after trailing off with the Tamil filler word "*vantu*," Craig's eyes look down to his left, as if searching for what he wants to say. His gaze returns back to the camera, and he continues, "indoors-*le(ru)ntu* phone *paṇṟīṅkaḷā*?" ('You're calling from indoors?'). Immediately after saying this, Craig makes a face and gestures as if exasperated (figure 14).

While Craig's utterance in this last turn is unproblematic (though he hesitates to find the Tamil word for "indoors," settling for the English word instead), through his wincing expression and gesture, he metacommunicates his frustration with his handling of the interaction, most immediately with his inane question about calling from indoors but also more generally, I would suggest, with his command of Tamil as such. The effect is to distance Craig from both the interaction and the Tamil he speaks.

The point here isn't that VJs like Craig were nonnative speakers of Tamil and that it sometimes showed, but that when they used Tamil, such disfluencies were often reflexively marked and foregrounded *as* disfluencies and, moreover, something humorous or expected (cf. Paloma's playful query to Gomathy about whether her Tamil makes her laugh). These disfluencies were performances of nonnativeness that distanced the VJ from the very Tamil that was also necessary to forge alignments between VJs and their

Figure 14. VJ Craig wincing at his Tamil on *Reach Out* (2008)

viewers, a complex kind of Goffmanian (1981:278ff.) "role distance." Consider the following segment from a "break link," in which Craig is trying to gloss in Tamil what he said in English (*Reach Out*, episode 741). (Gesture and gaze are notated in the left-hand column, their onset roughly corresponding with the beginning of the line in the right-hand column and their conclusion corresponding with the next annotation in the left-hand column; "-h" signifies an in-breath.)

1	<looking at camera>	Remember, for those of you who didn't watch *Crazy Craig in Your Colony* on Sunday, you can watch it on Thursday -h
2		It's coming again on Thursday, (.)
3		*vara* Thursday -h at five in the evening. 'coming Thursday at five in the evening.'
4	<looks down as if thinking>	Uh:::
5	<looks up, smiling off-camera at the technicians>	*Viyāḷa kiḷamaiyā, (illai)yā enna?* 'Thursday, right?'
6		*Viyāḷa kiḷamai!* 'Thursday!'
7	<slaps back of left hand on right palm, smiling at camera>	ENAKKU ÑĀBAKAM IRUKKU! -h 'I remember(ed)!'
8	<extended/emphatic blink (0.2)>	(0.2)
9		*Koñcam* and only. 'A little and only.'
10		Okay, we're going to go and take a break now. We'll see you soon. Stay tuned.

Craig first glosses "It's coming again on Thursday" (line 2) with the Tamil "*vara* Thursday" ('coming Thursday') in line 3. He then tries to gloss "Thursday" with the Tamil equivalent. He thinks about it, looking down and away from the camera (line 4), and then comes up with his best guess (line 5). He pronounces it as "*Viyāḷa kiḷamai*" instead of "*Viyāl̲a kil̲amai*," converting the Tamil shibboleth, the retroflex frictionless continuant *l̲*, to the retroflex lateral *ḷ* (see chapter 4). He checks his guess with the off-camera monolingual Tamil technicians, asking for confirmation that he remembered the Tamil word correctly ("*[illai]yā enna*?" 'right?'). When they answer in the affirmative off-camera, he claps his hands in success and repeats in Tamil "*Viyāḷa kiḷamai*" (line 6) and then yells in triumph: "ENAKKU ÑĀBAKAM IRUKKU!" ('I remembered!'; line 7). After a short pause accompanied by a slightly exaggerated blink (line 8), he qualifies his remembrance with the creatively odd conjunction, "*Koñcam* and only" (literally, 'a little and only'; line 9), typifying and diagramming his semifluency in Tamil with a humorous Tanglish flourish. Craig finally finishes the segment in fluent English, leading into the commercial break (line 10).

It is important to emphasize that in saying that VJs distanced themselves from Tamil through making fun of their own disfluencies, I am not ascribing to VJs an intention to speak badly. Nor am I saying that, overall, their Tamil was deficient or substandard. VJs like Craig, Pooja, and Paloma, in my experience, were sincere in their intent to speak Tamil well, even if they were highly ambivalent about the shift in the station's focus away from its English-dominant, multilingual format. Rather, what I am suggesting is that given their social and linguistic distance from many of their Tamil viewers, the ambivalent linguistic image of the station, and the entrenched indexical values that both English and Tamil invoked in this mass-mediated context (English as *stylish* and cosmopolitan, Tamil as *local* and traditional), there was a systematic way in which Tamil came to be citationally framed. This framing insisted on, and thereby created, distance between VJs and the Tamil they spoke, between VJs and their Tamil audience and callers.

In all these ways, language use on SS Music diagrammed a hierarchical relationship between English and Tamil. Every instance of VJs' Tamil, in one way or other, was bracketed and put in quotation marks through VJs' discourse. In this sense, VJs' language mirrored the very dynamics of the peer group, performing linguistic identities that their speech disavowed through citations of those very identities. Such VJs spoke and acted in ways construable by youth audiences as *like* young, nonelite Tamil speakers—their speech style was colloquial, informal, and used shibboleths of Tamil youth slang—even while marking the fact that they were not. VJs' citational framing of Tamil simultaneously functioned to bring the audience close while holding them at arm's length.

This was also a kind of deference. It was a "strategy of condescension" to the audience, as Pierre Bourdieu (1991:68–69) would put it: an attempt to convert the *local*, indexical connotations of Tamil into something hip and cosmopolitan, speaking in another's lower-status voice in order to create value and, in this case, playful entertainment. But it did so ambivalently. If youths' linguistic practice pushed the boundary between English and Tamil in their attempts to do *style*, VJs' uses of Tamil, straddling the other side of the threshold (here, the threshold of the *local*), always insisted that there was indeed a boundary, even as they too toyed with and troubled it. Such linguistic practice was a complex performance of differentiation and identification, an ambivalence about the social differences and samenesses that entangled these VJs and their audiences.

Bringing the Distant Voice Close

I have suggested that the (meta)discourse of a youth-targeting station like SS Music turns on a play of distance and closeness, of differentiation and identification. Further, I have suggested that this play and the tensions it generates manifest as and are dealt with through the citationality of VJs' linguistic practice. This linguistic practice was partially a result of institutional and market constraints on the station's addressivity. Just as important, however, were the demands made by the audience on VJs' on-air language, those demands themselves a function of the station's shift in focus and address. As a result of such shifts, VJs' speech was entangled by the dynamics of the youth peer group and by their expectations of how media personalities on a station like SS Music should speak.

In my experience living with those youth whom SS Music's production team imagined themselves to be addressing (the English "wannabes" or, as one VJ at SS Music put it through another derogatory delocutive, "the 'I-got-to-be-jeans-pants' type of group"), such citational strategies of differentiation and identification were, on the whole, successful. VJs like Craig, Paloma, and Pooja were continually lauded by my hostelmates for their "*stylish*" and "*royal*" speech (i.e., for their English) *and* for speaking 'like us youth' (though see below). Such success in creating a space of aspirational identification—where youth could imagine that such English-fluent VJs were speaking like them—was in spite of, or rather precisely because of, the disfluent Tamil that VJs sprinkled in with their English.

What made such *style* not tip over into *over style* and what made VJs' Tamil disfluency endearing rather than irritating—in a word, what made them not *Peters*—was the presumed social distance between these VJs and their youth audiences. My hostelmates and friends assumed that VJs were educated and rich and thus that speaking English (and not Tamil) was part of their "culture" (cf. the discourse surrounding brand that I discussed in chapter 2 and Sam's discussion about Aravind in chapter 4). It was natural to them because they were not Tamils; they were Anglo-Indians or from other states. This cultural, class, and linguistic alterity from their audience gave these VJs license for *stylish* English. Hence it would be unfair to criticize them for being *Peter*s.

But more than social distance, it was the medial distance—the very fact that VJs were on television—that was crucial. For these youth, being on-screen, hosting a youthful entertainment television show—versus, say, the nightly news—meant that VJs *had* to speak *stylish*ly, which is also to say that they had to speak in English. This became apparent to me one day while my Madurai hostelmates and I were watching some television clips that I had put together for us to talk about. After having watched a link by a local Madurai music-television compere, one of my friends commented,

Pēccu romba ordinary-*ā irukku. Uh,* media-*ukku suit ākātu. Sātāraṇamā* ordinary-*ā pēsuṟa mātiri pēsuṟāru.* Media-*ṅkuṟa pōtu taniyā atukku ṇṇu oru* qualities expect *paṇṇa pō-*, people *vēṟu mātiri* expect *paṇṟāṅka. Oru* attraction-*ā, romba* body language *romba pēsuṟa mātiri romba* attraction-*ā irukkaṇum. Ānā anta aḷavukku avar pēsale.*

His speech is really ordinary. Uh, it doesn't suit being in the media. He speaks like he's speaking normally, ordinarily. When you're in the media, people expect certain qualities that are unique. People have different expectations. There has to be some attraction. You need a lot of body language. You need to speak in a way that is really attractive. But he doesn't speak to that level.

My friends went on to explain that in comparison to the SS Music segments that we had just seen, such local television hosts' "ordinary" speech wasn't simply due to a lack of enthusiasm, body language, or charisma (though it was also those things); it was also because it was all in Tamil. It lacked *style*. There was no English. And if such hosts did speak in any English, it would only be English words that everybody uses in their Tamil, like "bus." The implication here is that to speak extraordinarily, to create an "attraction" for youth, one would need to use English linguistic forms that the audience wouldn't use or perhaps didn't even know.[19] Indeed, when I asked whether they understood all the English on SS Music, my friends replied that of course they did not, and that was the point! SS Music is interesting, they explained, because they can't always understand what VJs say (compare this with what the creative head of the channel expressed as the "layman term" strategy of on-air linguistic practice), because VJs speak in a way that wouldn't fly in the peer group. As one hostelmate put it,

Atān atān correct. Teriyātate oṇṇu pēsum pōtu, nammakku teriyāme oṇṇu naṭakkum pōtu atu koñcam, something *koñcam oru itā irukkum. Vittiyāsamā irukkum. Nāma pāttu-* ((*enna solṟatu*)), *koñcam viyappaṭaiyaṇum. Vittiyāsamā irukkum.* Different-*ā irukkum. Nammakku teriyātate pēsum pōtu,* different-*ā irukkum pōtu, nallā irukkum.*

Just that, just that [using words we don't know] is right. When something we don't know is said, when something that we don't know happens, it's a little, there'll be something there. It'll be different. We see-, ((what to say)), it should surprise us a bit. It'll be different (*vittiyāsamā*). It'll be different. When they use words we don't know, when it's different, it's good.

Important to the performative *style* of the language of SS Music, then, was the very fact that it was at times unintelligible to the audience (cf. the aesthetics of Englishness in youth fashion discussed in chapter 4), that it exceeded the very norms of face-to-face communication in the peer group. In contrast to college youths' speech in the peer group, for those very same youth, VJs' speech *had* to be *over*done in order for it to do *style*.[20]

At this horizon point of social and medial distance, the power of (*over*) *style* to unravel the peer group seems to be negated. The excess of *style* can be appreciated rather than be offensive. (Instead, the risk was under-doing *style*.) And yet, the excess of *style* lingered as a ghostly possibility that recast VJs' linguistic alterity as concealed indigeneity. While music-television VJs' English was generally accepted as *style*, a counterdiscourse circulated that such VJs' speech was, in fact, *over*, that such VJs weren't actually who their speech indexed them to be. SS Music VJs, I was told by some students, knew Tamil just fine. This was because they were actually Tamils. Their disfluencies were simply pretense designed to show off, to "attract" viewers (cf. Juluri 2003:58–59). By imputing to VJs a shared linguistic background—'they are actually Tamils'—such discourse brought VJs' distant voices back to the peer group, retethering them to its communicative norms.

This discourse was often used, particularly by young men but also by young women, to complain about young female media personalities in general, women whom they felt spoke too much English or too much anglicized Tamil (chapter 4).[21] And while this discourse of concealed indigeneity (or counterfeit, or surfeit, foreignness, we might say with chapters 2–3) was more likely to be invoked in discussing Tamil-medium television than SS Music, when it was used in relation to SS Music's VJs, it was generally in relation to the station's female VJs. Here, patriarchal ideologies that align women as the protectors and emblems of "Tamil culture" and language (chapters 2 and 6) gender *style* such that female media personalities are more likely to be criticized for their English, taken down a notch for presuming a status that they are not seen as warranting. This discourse presupposes, of course, the Tamil identity of such women.

Yet the charge that SS Music VJs, male or female, were actually Tamils was incorrect. They were neither ethnically nor linguistically Tamil (at least not based on the criteria that the charge assumed). Still the charge was correct in a sense. It rightly diagnosed those hierarchies of linguistic value within which English and Tamil, and VJs and audiences, were entangled. It is in response to the anxieties and insecurities raised by such entanglements that this discourse speaks. This ambivalence reads into mass-mediated linguistic practice a trace of elite resistance to Tamil, a disavowal of Tamil while having to speak in Tamil, and it attempts to refute it. Through its exposé, it literalizes VJs' citational Tamil ('they actually are Tamil speakers') and thus renders their 'natural' English citational ('they're just pretending not to be Tamil'), recruiting VJs to the figure of the *Peter*, he or she who pretends not to speak Tamil as a sign of prestige. Such a counterdiscourse relocates and *local*izes these socially distant VJs as if to say, we know who you really are. You are just like us.

The Camera Obscura of the Screen

In this chapter, I have aimed to show how the very same forces that constitute the youth peer group exert a force on the language of mass media as well. Enabled by their social and medial distance, VJs' language on SS Music hypertrophies those forms of *style* that are highly problematic in face-to-face peer-group interaction, creating a linguistic space outside of, but contiguous with, the peer group—a space for youths' aesthetic appreciation, aspirational identification, and pedagogical improvement. This space exists on the horizon of the peer-group, exterior to it yet, at the same time, hemmed in and encompassed by it. That's what made SS Music interesting to watch.

The texture of such mass-mediated language is citational. VJs' speech cited Tamil, reanimating it even as they bracketed it. This is, I suggested, the result of the ways in which changing market conditions and a commitment to the station's "class" image conspired to bring VJs and audiences of different backgrounds into linguistic contact, entangling them through the phone line and the television screen. This mass mediation of language, then, is a function of two worlds coming to orient their divergent social projects to each other, which is to say that it is a function of the ways in which the dynamics of the youth peer group intersect with the stakes that producers and VJs at SS Music had in their own practices—namely, increasing the ratings of their shows, making a name for themselves in the industry and among audiences, distinguishing what they did from regional, national, and international television stations, and having entertaining conversations on-air. Through this complex mediation, the citationality that binds VJs and their audiences to each other exhibits a camera obscura effect, a linguistic inversion created by passing through the television camera and tube. The sonic substance of *style*, here, is stretched across the phone line and through the screen, materialized on each end as an inverting function of entanglements of/with the other side.

These inversions add another layer—or vector, we might say—to the liminal quality of youth language. In the conclusions to chapter 4, I argued that youth language turns on thresholds of *style*, on tipping points between the ordinary/*local* and *style* and between *style* and *over style*. I further suggested that, at least with respect to youths' linguistic practice, central to questions of what and when a code, style, register, or repertoire are, are questions of the intensity, ambiguity, and ambivalence of linguistic indexicality. As we've seen in this chapter, the liminalities and thresholds that keep English and Tamil apart *and* close are complexified by their mass mediation—that is, the very same linguistic politics that opens up the space of liminal possibility and performative force within youth peer groups also opens up a related but distinct field of linguistic practice for music-television VJs like those on SS Music. Further, the relationship between these two vectors of liminality (those coming from Tamil to English and those coming from English to Tamil) disperse the linguistic field, creating multiple ways—often operationalized based on class and "culture"—in which one can distinguish oneself from the proper and respectful ('pure' Tamil), the rural and *local* (colloquial Tamil), and the formal and foreign (proper English) while, at the same time, keeping that linguistic field, at some level or other, unified (i.e., as "youth" language).

We might see this dynamic, following Pierre Bourdieu (1991), as simply the effect of a particular postcolonial "linguistic market." Yet such an account of strategies of distinction and forms of linguistic capital, it seems to me, fails to capture the complexity of the interrelationships between VJs' and youths' linguistic predicaments and entanglements. This is not because VJs and young college students are not engaged in practices of distinction, for we can certainly see their practices as doing just that (though even here I hesitate for reasons outlined in chapter 2 and discussed below). Rather, it is because such a model assumes that linguistic practice tends toward definite linguistic ends (the "best," most "standard" linguistic forms, whatever they are taken to be) rather than, as we have seen here, caught in a force field of ambivalent linguistic value. (Indeed, more than mastering "correct" forms—as we might expect from ideologies of standard language—here we find disfluent production and reception of mediatized language as being central to practices and understandings of *style*.)

While it is the case that youth are in some ways trying to increase their "linguistic capital" and that VJs are attempting to distinguish themselves from other linguistic speakers in the "market," the various countervailing forces and interconnections opened up *between* these social projects (youths' and VJs') necessarily distribute and multiply the liminal possibilities that are enabled by those linguistic poles that, if we followed Bourdieu, we might privilege as the teloses of linguistic practice. As we saw, much of VJs' and their youth audiences' linguistic practices are strategies of distinction put in quotes. Too much distinction and too much distancing, just like too much condescension and too much linguistic identification, negates the very value that such practices attempt to generate: they may result in a punch in the face or a silent telephone line, a mocking laugh or a critical dismissal as "ordinary" or as a "*Peter*." And it is this liminality and the citationalities within and across linguistic interactions that emerge therein/thereby that materialize *as* a heterogenous field of youth language, a field populated by polyphonic forms that can be taken up and cited on both sides of the screen for various social effects. It is that liminality and its linguistic dispersion that give youth language its coherent, if constantly shifting and mosaic, ethnographic texture.

White Tamils

In concluding this chapter, I want to return to the kinds of social and linguistic distances and intimacies that I presenced in the hostel and in the television studio. As I suggested in the introduction to chapter 4, my relatively English-absent, high-register Tamil was a constant source of laudation, pride, and mirth for my hostelmates. As I noted, my speech even earned me the nickname "*veḷḷai Tamiḻan*," or 'the white Tamil,' in one of my Madurai hostels. This nickname was itself a citation. The epithet "*veḷḷai Tamiḻan*" was an allusion to the song "*Style*" from the 2007 blockbuster *Sivaji: The Boss*, starring the "King of *Style*," Rajinikanth. In this filmic song sequence, Rajini turns his own famously dark and stereotypically south Indian skin white in order to impress the heroine (see figure 27 in chapter 7). He proclaims himself a "*veḷḷai Tamiḻan*" in the song's lyrics, with the caveat that even though he is now a white Tamil, he is always a "*paccai Tamiḻan*," a 'pure, authentic Tamil.' (This itself is a winking, if anxious, allusion to the fact that Rajinikanth is not, in fact, ethnolinguistically Tamil but a Maharashtrian born in Karnataka, redoubling, of course, the joking parallel between Rajinikanth and myself.) In the song sequence, Rajini is shown appropriating various signs of Western modernity: white women (with whom he dances), brand-name clothing (which he wears), luxury commodities (he enters in a Mercedes Benz sedan), Western music and language (he raps in English), and of course, white skin. The trope here is one of depth. In the film, Rajini's whiteface is a cover for a fundamental Tamilness. Indeed, after the song, when he realizes the heroine didn't really want him to be lighter skinned, he simply washes away the white. The joke in calling me "*veḷḷai Tamiḻan*," then, was an implicit play on this song and thus on the very notion of *style*: even though I was an American English speaker from what, to my hostelmates, was a white ethnic background, I spoke Tamil. While Rajini's character cited the signs of Western modernity (chapter 7), I cited Tamil culture. My citational epithet, then, stood in an inverse relationship to the *style* that Rajini embodied.

Given my ethnic distance from and linguistic proximity to Tamil, I was also similar in certain ways to Anglo-Indian VJs like Craig and Paloma, whose use of Tamil for many callers was also endearing (remember Gomathy's excitement about and appreciation of the 'beauty' of Paloma's Tamil). Yet I also presented something of an inversion of such VJs, for my status as *like* a *veḷḷai Tamiḻan* (versus as *like* an Anglo-Indian) turned not on disfluent sprinklings of colloquial Tamil in my English but on the relative absence of English words from my heavily accented and often disfluent Tamil. It was this multiply displaced linguistic position—not speaking like a youth, not like a 'big man' (*periya āḷ*), not like an Anglo-Indian, not like an urban elite, and not like a typical foreigner—that located me within, and yet outside of, the linguistic regimes that underwrote youth speech. It was this oddity, this not quite being in its place, that made my speech novel and perhaps uncanny for my hostelmates.

This oddity elicited similar reactions from those I encountered in the television, radio, and film industries. During my fieldwork, I was continually being asked and maneuvered (often in exchange for ethnographic access) to participate in media programming by television and film producers and directors. I was invited to participate in reality-television contests, radio and television interviews (as host and interviewee), televised awards functions, documentaries, infomercials, and films. As one producer of an SS Music reality show that I participated in put it, an American who spoke Tamil was "exotic." It made for good television. My oddity and exoticism bisected, but also ran orthogonally through, both mass-media discourse and the everyday language of the college. And this made me a resource to be cited, displayed, and reanimated in the peer group, onstage, and onscreen.

This was evinced by the role I was assigned at the "farewell party" of my Madurai hostel. Taking place at the end of the academic year, the farewell party is a ritual that marks the end of the reign of the third-years and the passing of the baton to the second-years. While the hostel's "welcome party," as discussed in chapter 2, celebrated the entrance of freshers into college life, the farewell party marked the exit of seniors into postcollege life. As the inverted complement of the welcome party, the farewell party also involved ragging. This time, however, it was the third-year seniors who were ragged by their second-year juniors, thereby proleptically figuring the second-years' own dominance as the new seniors of the hostel (cf. Turner 1967:168ff.).

The bulk of this rite of passage was dedicated to this ragging (which spared no one, not even our rather short hostel warden, who was interpellated as the "Little Superstar," a citation of the film actor Simbu, himself citing Rajinikanth [see chapter 7]). Each of the seniors was individually called to the stage. He was escorted by one of the second-years who was seen as, in one way or another, similar to him: for example, the general secretary of the hostel was escorted by the future general secretary, the "gym body" of the third-years by an equally muscular second-year student, a blind third-year by a blind second-year student, and so on. Once onstage, each third-year was forced to do something embarrassing on the stage: sing and/or lewdly dance to a film song (often a folk-sounding *kuttu* song), improvise how they would act in awkward situations (e.g., proposing your love to the "sex-bomb" Namitha), and so on. This was the same kind of ragging that these seniors had suffered when they were freshers two years prior. Once ragged, the students of the hostel clapped for them in appreciation. Finally, the student was presented with a memento commemorating their time at the college: a glass plaque with the college name and insignia and hostel name framing a silhouette of five friends waving. Above this image was written, "Farewell but not goodbye," and below it, the student's name.

When it was my turn to take the stage, I was called alone. (There was no junior ethnographer waiting in the wings.) My ragging task was to speak Tamil and English together. Neither pure Tamil nor proper English alone—both of which would elicit anxiety and laughs if they had to speak them—would suffice as a playfully demeaning task for me. Instead, I had to upend my own idiolect for them by inhabiting—or rather, figurating the inhabitance of—the very liminal space of *their* day-to-day linguistic practice, splitting and doubling my own subjectivity, making me flirt with their flirtations (chapter 2). I obliged, hamming it up to laughs and claps by speaking hyperproper English interspersed with shibboleths of "pure" Tamil. And in swapping the expected places of pure Tamil and proper English, my ragging performed an inverted figure of *style*: *style* in which pure Tamil was the language of youth prestige, in which Tamil was avowingly sprinkled into English. Written on my plaque was "*veḷḷai Tamiḻan*."

What made my ragging funny was also what made my Tamil elicit pride in other contexts. The nickname *veḷḷai Tamiḻan*—and the baptismal ritual where it was officially given to me—spoke back to the "inferiority complex" (*tāḻvu manappāṉmai*; cf. Fanon 2008[1952]:1–23) that many of my Tamil friends invoked to explain why they were so hesitant to speak in English (chapter 4). I gave value to what they felt others—north Indians, the English-fluent rich, the media, and to a certain extent, the college itself—devalued through their avoidances and disavowals of Tamil. Statements like 'You speak better Tamil than we do!' ultimately, then, must be interpreted not simply as self-deprecations but as circuitous self-laudations that condemn a whole order of status that many felt entrapped by (given that their English was never felt to be quite good enough). In speaking Tamil, I was taken to reveal the "false prestige" of English, the erroneous idea that English was a better or more important language than Tamil, that speaking English was the end all and be all of social mobility, prestige, and *style*.[22] Not dissimilar to SS Music's VJs' socially distant English, my use of Tamil converted aspects of the language that are avoided by, and otherwise unavailable to, youth into social value that they could avail, into a sense of pride (*perumai*). To cite me was to install me in the place of what was otherwise, and at certain times, seen as a lack: the inability and undesirability of using pure Tamil, the lost prestige of Tamil, and perhaps the loss of Tamil itself. To cite me was to attempt to recover that which was so distant that it could only be brought close through surrogate representations. I validated what they could only mention but not use: the value, and perhaps even the *style*, of speaking Tamil.

PART III

Film

SIX

College Heroes and Film Stars

Introduction

The first night in the first Madurai hostel that I stayed in began and ended with film. Upon arriving in the hostel, within minutes of putting my bags down on my metal cot, the room filled up with students from nearby rooms, chatting and firing questions at me: Is it true that at age fifteen American kids are forced out of the house to support themselves? America is a developed country, so why would you ever come to India to do research? Is WWE professional wrestling real or fake? Are you in love? Is it true that everyone in the United States divorces? What do you think of "Tamil culture"?

The question that sparked the most excitement by far, however, was 'Who is your favorite film hero?' It was a semiserious, semijoking question that presumed that the students were fans (*rasikarkaḷ*) of different heroes and that fans and fan clubs of different heroes are antipathetic to each other. As a play on fan rivalry, the question also framed these students as not quite fans. Playing along, I answered as I would answer any such potentially risky and divisive question: I equivocated. I like lots of different heroes, I said. I like the "Ultimate Star" Ajith (known by his fans as *Tala*, 'Boss') for his acting and his cool gangster image. I like Vijay, or *Iḷaiya Taḷapati* ('the Young General'), for his dancing. I like Kamal Hassan, or *Ulaka Nayakan* ('Hero of the World'), for his ability to act as any and every possible character. And, of course, I like "Superstar" Rajinikanth, the "King of *Style*" (*Style Mannan*), for his, well, *style*. Upon hearing their favorite hero's name, students beamed. And they grimaced upon hearing the names of other heroes. In particular, fans of Ajith and Vijay—the newest generation of established film stars—took opposing stances to each other. Such mock antagonism broke into earnest debates over the merits of the different stars, about whose films had more narrative coherence and thus tested audiences' ability to suspend disbelief more or less, about whose films grossed more money, about which hero could dance or act better, and about who had more *style* and *gettu* ('dominance,' 'prestige')—that is, who was the 'big man' (*periya āḷ*) to whom other actors were just subordinate 'little boys' (*cinna pasaṅka*). They rattled off the names of their favorite films, even writing them down for me so that I wouldn't forget. As the conversation died down, my new roommates Sebastian and Stephen gave me a blanket, pillow, and sheet. The lights-out curfew had come, and everyone went off to their rooms for the night. I fell asleep to Stephen reading by a dim light and to the sensations and sounds of mosquitoes biting and buzzing around my body.

I woke up the next morning with a jolt, disoriented. Distorted film music was blasting from buzzing speakers. Songs from Rajinikanth's latest blockbuster film, *Sivaji: The Boss* (2007), were being played throughout the hostel, rattling through my ears as if inside my skull. As I found out, being told over the dint of the noise, the hostel had its own sound system: a power amplifier and speakers that they used for playing music and for public speaking at hostel functions. Today, it had been repurposed to get students out of their beds. It was a reminder that there were exams. Film music provided our wakeup call to get our bodies moving, coordinating our movements to its rhythms and melodies, the soundtrack for a new day.

Film didn't just frame this day, though. It framed every day. Fractions of commercial Tamil film suffused college life, providing an important, perhaps the single most important, reference point for these youths' modes of sociality and speech, entertainment and aesthetics, humor and romance, and of course, their *style* (cf. Osella and Osella 2004). In what follows, I focus on how young people reanimate fractions of films as part of the rhythms of college life. I give particular attention to the relationship between film and *style*, to the ways in which the liminality and citationality of youth practice—the dynamics of the peer group that have been at issue throughout this book—mediate how cinema comes to be entangled with and engaged by college youth.

In order to appreciate youths' engagements with commercial film to do *style*, however, it is necessary to have some familiarity with what the films that youth take up are like (their narratological organization, tropes, and conventions) as well as with the practices of film-watching that accompany them, even if, as I argue in this chapter and the next, youths' *stylish* engagements with Tamil film cannot be reduced to the film text as such or its associated modes of spectatorship. To give a sense of these films and their attendant viewing practices, below I give a description of the introductory sequence of one commercial film, *Pokkiri* ('The Ruffian,' 2007, directed by Prabhu Deva).[1] *Pokkiri* is a so-called mass film, a genre characterized by its "commercial elements" and stereotyped content, that *masala* mix of over-the-top action sequences, bombastic dialogues, double entendre humor, romance, sexy "item numbers" and folk-inspired *kuttu* songs, and formulaic plots that center on "building up" the image and status of the film's hero-star.[2] While college youth take up many kinds of films to various ends, I focus on *Pokkiri* for two reasons. First, it was hero-oriented mass films like *Pokkiri* that were widely cited in youth peer groups to do *style*. While *style* takes many forms in many media, its prototypic locus is the figure of the so-called mass hero, the hero of the mass film. To the question, 'What is *style*?' the youth with whom I worked were equally likely to point to *stylish* forms or acts (like brands, speaking English, etc.) as they were to particular film heroes—in particular, to Rajinikanth, that paragon of mass heroes (Gerritsen 2012:26).[3] As I suggest below and demonstrate in more detail in chapter 7, the film screen allows the mass hero's *style* to achieve a kind of visibility, clarity, and excess that makes it particularly useful to youth in their peer groups, even while, or precisely because, it is distinct from the kinds of *style* that can fly in those very peer groups (cf. chapter 5). Second, it is mass films like *Pokkiri* that have garnered much attention in the academic literature about south Indian cinema (on which, more below).

First Day, First Show

Watching a mass-hero film in Tamil Nadu—especially its first showing on its first day—might be compared to a cross between a religious ritual, a rock concert, a dance party, and a carnival (Dickey 1993b:40; Rogers 2011; Gerritsen 2012:61–62; Rajanayagam 2015; cf. Srinivas 1998; Srinivas 2009:36–38).[4] For my college-going friends, excitement for the film started before even arriving at the theater, the thrill of the event piqued by the transgressions necessary to even get there: cutting classes to catch a matinee or surreptitiously hopping over hostel walls after curfew to watch the "second show" (chapter 1; cf. Hughes 1996:253–54). Getting close to

Figure 15. Vijay poster for *Pokkiri* outside of the Devi film theater (Chennai 2007; photo by Naoko Ataka, used with permission)

the vicinity of the theater, the film experience is further anticipated by crowds of other filmgoers milling about, talking and smoking in the shadows of larger-than-life images of the film's hero (figure 15).

On opening days for hero-stars' films, the theater's ticket counter is mobbed (if fan clubs haven't already booked all the tickets), bodies upon bodies compressed into a line that threatens to erupt, its integrity held together by the concrete walls and metal bars that only allow a couple of individuals to squeeze in front of the counter at any particular time. Hands on top of hands wave money to buy tickets printed on cheap paper, customers yelling to get the attention of the cashier. Upon entering the actual theater, the atmosphere is charged, with groups of young men passing the time before the film starts by whistling and collectively chanting slogans such as "*Vijay vāḻka! Vijay vāḻka!*" ('Long live Vijay! Long live Vijay!'). When the film's government certificate lights up the screen, screams, cheers, and whistles fill the air, a buildup of energy and excitement that finds its release in a screen image that only promises another. Thank-yous, credits, and producers' banners run across the screen. "*Iḷaiya Taḷapati Vijay Naṭikkum*" ('Starring the Young General Vijay') suddenly flashes on-screen along with hazy stills of Vijay's face (figure 16), only then followed by the

Figure 16. Vijay's name and epithet—*Iḷaiya Taḷapati Vijay Naṭikkum* ('Starring the Young General Vijay')—put on-screen before *Pokkiri*'s (2007) title frame

film's title frame. With this first introduction, audiences for mass-hero films like this erupt; confetti is thrown in the air and ear-splitting whistles thunder throughout the hall. With this, the film proper begins with the hero's introductory sequence.

Introductory sequences are one of the most important parts of mass films. The introductory sequence hypes the already-hyped audience, announcing the official beginning of the film diegesis. Not just the beginning of the story, it is also a microcosm and preview of the film itself, a film already split between the narrative proper and the hero-star's "parallel text" (Mishra et al. 1989; Prasad 2014). It is a portrait, a "buildup" of the hero-star's image in an overblown display of machismo and cool—in a word, of his *style*. This is, however, a very particular portrait of *style*, bombastic and hypertrophied. It is excessive, verging on being *over* (as it would be, as we'll see, if it weren't being done by an actor already recognized as licensed to do *style* on-screen). This portrait deploys not just canonical signs of *style* but also explicit displays of hierarchical dominance and hypermasculine violence. Like the SS Music VJs from the previous chapter, here we see *style* seemingly unmoored from the peer group's centripetal leveling, a runaway flight that propels the hero beyond *style*'s horizon, thereby constituting that very horizon for others who might cite it or him to shine light on their own skyward flights.

Pokkiri opens with a montage of scenes depicting the criminal activities of Chennai's two major gangs. The montage is narrated by an intercut conversation between two police officers, one of whom is the new Chennai police commissioner. The film then cuts to a number of tough-looking *rowdies* ('thugs') smoking next to the train tracks. A man has come to speak with this group of thugs-for-hire to arrange an attack on "Korattur" Logo, a gangster from a rival gang. When he asks these mercenaries who's going to beat up Korattur Logo, music kicks in. "*Tamiḻ*, *Tamiḻ*, *Tamiḻ* . . ." echoes loudly as the camera cuts to a body leaping over a fire, filmed from below. *Tamiḻ* is the answer to the question. It is the name of the 'ruffian' (*pōkkiri*) who will beat up Korattur Logo, the name, we discover as the sequence progresses, of the film's hero (as we already know, played by Vijay). His name is the name of the language, region, and people for whom his image is soon to be presenced.

The camera cuts back to the train tracks. The hero's sidekick (played by Sriman) reassures their client: 'If he hits (Korattur Logo), it won't be blows; it'll be lightning that'll strike' ("*Avan aṭiccā aṭi viḻātu; iṭi viḻum*"). Cut to a city street. The camera is shaking as if lightning has struck, the tremble of the frame rhythmically paralleled by frenetic drumming. We now see the ruffian-hero from behind. He is running through the street, chased by ten men brandishing machetes. One of them pushes a cart filled with eggplants, chilies, lemons, and other vegetables to trip him up from behind. Still running, the ruffian-hero leaps into the air to avoid the cart.

These first images kindle our excitement, rousing our anticipation and impatience: When will we finally *see* the hero? When will we see Vijay? Up until this point, the shots are indirect. We see the ruffian-hero from below, from behind, from above. Yet, until this very moment, we haven't seen his face; we haven't seen *him* (Gerritsen 2012:59ff.). Flying through the air in slow motion, the camera captures the ruffian-hero's flight from multiple angles edited together through jump cuts. The vegetables from the cart orbit his body, as if he, Jupiter, keeps them in thrall, circling him but not touching him. The chilies and lemons that hover around him allude to Tamil beliefs about the power of vision (*tiruṣṭi*) to harm those individuals and objects worthy of envy. Chilies and lemons are used to ward off the desire that threatens to harm the apple of its evil eye (Dean 2013). The shot finally reveals Vijay to us (figure 17). He is wearing dark boot-cut jeans, black shoes, and a bright red shirt over a white, plaid shirt, his sleeves rolled up. The camera lingers on him, allowing us to take him in.

With this first revelation, the audience's screams, claps, and whistles will reach a fever pitch. Excited viewers might take off their shirts and twirl them above their heads, jumping up and down on their seats and in the aisles, celebrating the plenitude of Vijay's larger-than-life hero image presenced once again.

A fight scene with Korattur Logo's men ensues. Vijay leads the men with machetes to an empty warehouse. The camera pans up from Vijay's feet as he, with his back to the *rowdies*, deftly unwraps a handkerchief that

Figure 17. Vijay's revelation in *Pokkiri* (2007)

fashionably decorates his hand, a signature *style* of the film. Vijay jokingly taunts the villains by admiring the location. A cell phone *stylish*ly flies into his hand from out of nowhere, and Vijay continues to mock the *rowdies* while speaking to someone on the phone. He states that while he was only paid to beat up one guy, he'll gladly beat up ten. After Vijay delivers a couple of provoking, humorous barbs, the head of the *rowdies* slaps his chest in anger and replies incredulously, 'What, you're gonna beat me up?!' Vijay coolly replies, 'Well, I have committed myself.' A distorted rock guitar kicks in, synchronized with numerous jump cuts that splice together shots of Vijay's body: his upper body, shot from his left, then from below. Then two close-ups of half of his face: first the right side, then the left. Vijay then delivers the film's signature "punch dialogue," a *stylish* one-liner repeated at key moments throughout the film: "*Oru vāṭṭi muṭivu paṇṇiṭṭēn ṇṇā en pēccu nānē kēṭkamāṭṭēn*" ('Once I make a decision, even I won't listen to what I say').

Vijay goes on to beat up all the *rowdies* in an incredible pastiche of moves citationally culled from videogame-esque kung-fu films and professional wrestling. This is not just a fight; it's a demonstration: of Vijay's status and *style*, of his dominance—symbolic and literal—over any and all who dare step to him. It is important that the *rowdies* in such films are uncanny versions of the mass hero, their swagger and machismo reflecting him, but deficiently and often in caricature. They wrongly think themselves to be superior to the hero. Their bravado betrays ignorance. They simply don't know who they're dealing with. The fight sequence that follows is as much about putting the *rowdies* in their place as it is putting the hero in his, the very seat of seemingly unsurpassable *style* and power. Indeed, the fight sequence is shot and edited through various conventionalized tropes of status and power that emphasize the symbolic superiority of the hero: slow motion and freeze-frame shots, repeated jump cuts, and trick shots that multiply and amplify his body on the screen. The *rowdies*' bodies fly across the screen as Vijay rips them to shreds.

This "buildup" of the hero-star cannot be contained by the screen or the text. Vijay's awesome presence exceeds the diegesis, reaching out both to the audience and to other film texts. My use here of the actor's name, Vijay, and not his character's name, *Tamiḻ*, is intentional. The audience isn't just watching a character in a film but Vijay as a persona, across and outside of his film texts. The background music to the fight is a song about how the hero, the *pōkkiri* or 'ruffian,' will beat anyone who stands against him. It refers to this *pōkkiri* as *Taḷapati*, the shorthand for Vijay's epithet, *Iḷaiya Taḷapati* ('the Young General'). Moreover, the audience isn't just watching Vijay; they are being addressed by him. The introductory sequence is characterized by an aesthetic of frontality, with copious shots of Vijay looking directly into the camera (Kapur 1987; cf. Brecht 1964:92). Vijay even alludes to the time of the film's theatrical release and thus, for those in the theater during its opening weekend, the very moment of screening. *Pokkiri* opened on the Friday before Pongal, the four-day Tamil harvest holiday that began that Sunday. As Vijay says before the fight starts, "*Inta Poṅkal nammakku super* collection-*mā*!" ('Dear, this Pongal, is going to be a super collection for us!')—that is, 'This film that you're watching here and now, it's gonna make us a lot of money at the box office over the Pongal holiday!' The addressee-inclusive, first-person plural, dative pronoun *nammakku* and intimate vocative *-mā* interpellate and address the audience, directly aligning viewers with Vijay as shareholders to his success.[5]

After he has defeated all the *rowdies*, Vijay opens the warehouse door from which he entered. The camera shows us the door from the outside. As it opens, we hear the sounds of the film's first song sequence, "*Pokkiri Pongal*" ('Ruffian's *Pongal*'). Vijay is smiling. He twirls his hand, and the handkerchief wrapped around it unfurls in a blurry time-lapse effect. Vijay's body is multiplied on-screen and he walks out of the warehouse in triplicate. The camera cuts to a shot of Vijay's feet and pans up to show him from behind. He has walked out of the warehouse, not into the gray alley from which he came, but into a sunny carnival scene taking place in front of a temple. It isn't uncommon for enthusiastic audience members to dance along with this first song, singing and whistling and thrusting their hips as they bring the filmic world into the theater. After this song, the introductory sequence is over and the rest of the film begins. (While there isn't space in this chapter to detail the subsequent ups and downs of our hero, I encourage the interested reader to watch the film. As in many such films, he meets a girl with whom he falls in love, faces various obstacles in his confrontations with the villain—featuring a flashback and plot twist—and ultimately defeats the villain in a glorious climax that avenges the various injustices that have occurred along the way.)

Introductory sequences like *Pokkiri*'s key a number of issues important to this and the next chapter. First, as metonyms of the mass films that they kick off, such sequences show the centrality of the hero-star's hypertrophied and unabashed *style* and machismo to the narrative trajectory of the film as a whole and to the ways in which the hero relates to other characters. Second, this excessive portrait of *style* has a citational quality to it, citing other filmic figures (in this case, Vijay's off-screen/transtextual image) and itself being composed of elements that are immanently citable (dress, dialogue, gestures, etc.). Further, such introductory sequences, like the films of which they are a part more generally, actively and reflexively bind the extratextual to the already intertextually constituted film world. And finally, such introductory sequences show how events of viewing mass films tend, both as a cultural genre of spectatorship and as a matter of fact, toward the carnivalesque. Events of film watching prompt and provide young men with a venue for an excessive efflorescence and a practiced lack of control that transgresses middle-class adult norms of *decent* public behavior, such as public seminudity, screaming, whistling, dancing, and if the audience doesn't like what it sees, booing and yelling at the screen. Each of these features of mass films and their introductory sequences are important to youths' engagements with such films (and, importantly, their gendered inflections), to the ways in which college students cite them, or do not cite them, in contexts far removed from the theater, to ends far removed from the film text and its narrative.

Text–Fan–Politics

What are we to make of this introductory sequence and the myriad mass films with scenes just like it? What are we to make of its formulaic and "unrealistic" aesthetics, its schizophrenic cuts between outrageous dialogues and fantastical fight scenes, in which, with no seemingly explanation, a hero can fly through the air, and a temple dance sequence can erupt out of a dark, grimy warehouse showdown? What are we to make of its blurring of the cinematic and the noncinematic, its disregard for the so-called fourth wall, its lack of "shamefaced voyeurism" (Metz 1982; see Prasad 1998), and its incessant invitation of the audience to be complicit in all the above? Further, what are we to make of the fact that fractions of films like *Pokkiri* are everywhere one looks and listens in Tamil Nadu—from street-side flexboards (figure 18) to the backs of auto-rickshaws (Pandian 2005; Jacob 2009; Gerritsen 2012), blaring from tea-stall radios and on never-ending repeat on television sets, woven into young men's fashion

Figure 18. *Pokkiri* flexboard (Chennai 2007). Note the handkerchief *style* on Vijay's left hand (photo by Naoko Ataka, used by permission).

(figure 19) and into everyday conversation? What are we to make of the fact that such films refuse to be confined to the text or theater?

In lay discourses that circulate in Tamil Nadu, mass films are a cinematic specialty of south India, and Tamil Nadu in particular, a homegrown film genre whose anomalous aesthetics and reception practices require special explanation. This discourse of particularity is often inflected with elitist disdain or lament, even by nonelite filmgoers themselves (Dickey 1993b; 2001; Gerritsen 2012:47).[6] Even the name of this type of film—the "mass film"—links it to the low-class, lumpen "masses," a discursive figure that William Mazzarella (2013) has dubbed "the pissing men." In this discourse, such incontinent viewers are interpellated by a market logic that only appeals to their basest common denominator. Such mass-oriented "commercial films" contrast with "serious films" (also tellingly called "class films") that are "realistic" rather than "fantastical," that are character and plot centered rather than hero-star centered, and whose narratives are coherent and linear rather than stitched together by a seemingly random and nonsensical mix of "*masala*" elements (Nakassis and Dean 2007; Srinivas 2009:73–128).[7] In this discourse, these films are mindless, escapist, stunted in their cinematic growth, formulaic, repetitive, and

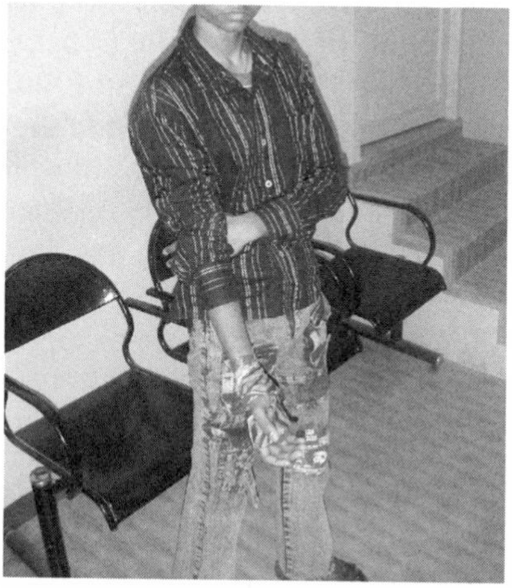

Figure 19. Handkerchief *style* from *Pokkiri* (2007) sported by a young man in Madurai (2008)

even dangerous to the viewer.[8] They are dangerous because such films foster "hero worship," an irrational, quasi-religious "devotion" by susceptible fans to their potentially demagogic heroes. Mass films blur the distinction between character and actor and position the male spectator to align himself with the hero-star by fostering a vicarious fantasy of transcending the mundanities of everyday life through identification with him (Hardgrave 1971; 1979; Pandian 1992; cf. Osella and Osella 2004; Srinivas 2009).

The fear from more rational and responsible sectors of society is that such films take advantage of those who can't distinguish real from reel, allowing hero-stars to segue into formal politics. Indeed, a favorite fact to be noted when it comes to Tamil politics is that every elected chief minister of the state since 1967 has been involved in film in one way or another and that the state's biggest politician of all time, M. G. Ramachandran (MGR), was also its biggest hero-star. We might find evidence for such political pretensions in Vijay's films—such as *Sura* (2010), originally titled *MGR*—that reference both MGR and Vijay's future political ambitions. And indeed, in recent years, both Vijay and his father, the director and producer Chandrasekhar, have publically intimated that Vijay's foray into electoral politics is imminent (Kolappan 2011).

Much academic work on south Indian film refutes the facile causal connections between film and politics that underwrite this elitist lay discourse, offering sophisticated and nuanced accounts of the filmic life of politics and the political life of films. For some authors, the question is how the representational organization of film, its narrative structure, its symbolic tropes or enunciative modalities, prefigure modes of political action and affiliation in the figure of the (subaltern-)hero-as-leader (Sivathambi 1981; Pandian 1992; Vaasanthi 2006; Krishnan 2009; Rajanayagam 2015). From the text, others turn to the figure of the spectator and his "reception" of film, to questions of why hero worship exists and what it means to those who "worship" or identify with the mass hero. To what psychological desires or real-world problems do these films speak (Dickey 1993b; 1995; Rajanayagam 2015)? And what do "adulation" or "devotion" do in the local life worlds of those fans cum cadres who engage with filmic representations (Dickey 1993a; 2001; Rogers 2009; 2011; Gerritsen 2012)? Most recently, Madhava Prasad (2014) has presented a subtle and complex argument that this nexus of cinema and politics, or "cinepolitics" as he puts it, turns on the way in which the mass hero represents—in the political sense—his subaltern fans, and by extension the ethnolinguistic community writ large, on and off the screen (also see Krishnan 2009; Srinivas 2009; 2013).[9] This relation of representation, one that appears more as a demand by fans than as an imposition by hero-stars or the film industry (Srinivas 2009), manifests in the textual, narrative form that congeals around and is taken to emanate from the mass hero, a figure who is himself emergent from that very textual form iterated over time (Prasad 2014:103).

Each of these different ways of approaching the mass hero and his films has something to commend it and captures something of their reality (a reality that is multiple, of course, given that these studies cover an extended historical period and multiple south Indian film industries). What I would point out is that a cluster of implicit assumptions consistently underwrites these diverse studies, assumptions about what such film *is* and for *whom* it is—namely, that (mass) films can be analytically, if not ontologically, treated as autonomous textual representations,[10] to which various empirical social practices (namely, "reception") come to stand as external phenomena; that to study such representations and their articulation to the social in south India is to primarily study fans (or the fan-hero relationship); and that such cinema is inherently, or at least most importantly, political in nature (see Srinivas 2012:83–84). These are the very bases of the elitist discourse that these various studies repudiate. And together with this elitist discourse, they form a discursive enclosure around the mass hero and his films.

My point, of course, is not that such films aren't, or can't be usefully seen as, forms of representational textuality (indeed, my description of *Pokkiri* above does this, as do examples discussed later in this and the next chapter), nor that fans and their relations to mass heroes aren't important to study, nor that mass films aren't political, as they certainly are. Rather, my point is that reduction of the cinematic to the representational text (which may be "read"), to the fan (whose "reception" may be ethnographically studied), or to the political (which may then be explained by recourse to the above) narrows the full range and complexity of the mass hero and his films. It occludes, as I explore in this chapter, the complex pragmatics of doing *style*, those citational practices that are enacted by youth who may not be fans in domains far removed from politics (narrowly or widely construed) and that turn less on "receiving" or making "meaning" with the film qua text than on reanimating fractions of films in performatively potent acts. As I argue in the chapter's conclusions, such practices problematize the very notion of "reception" in media studies precisely because they undermine the ontology of the autonomous representational text that the notion of reception implicitly, and ironically, presumes upon in its attempts to decenter the autonomy and authority of the text.

This reduction thereby also risks occluding one of the fundamental textual features of the mass-hero film (and film more generally perhaps): its citationality in the full sense developed in this book. As I show in the next chapter, the textuality of the mass-hero film is marked by, even as it thereby mediates, the dynamics of the peer group and the forms of citational practice that I discuss in this chapter. This is because mass heroes and their films are entangled by, even as they entangle, those who would cite them to do *style*. Such entanglement, I argue, entextualizes the mass-hero film as itself citational, making it incessantly intertextual and prefabricated for others' citation, its dispersion and dissemination beyond itself inscribed and anticipated in its semiotic form. The dynamics of *style* excise and perforate, and thus ultimately constitute, the film text's fragmented surfaces. Taken together, this and the next chapter show how the film text manifests as the medium and effect of various social projects as they come to be entangled with each other: those of youth in their peer groups, filmmakers in their film production, and actors in their image building. My argument, then, isn't that one can't approach such films as texts or that filmic textuality is irrelevant to youths' practices of *style* but rather that these practices require us to think differently about what a text is by showing us what it can be made to do as not quite a text.

Film in the College

As noted above, film permeated the life world of the Tamil youth with whom I worked and vice versa. Films about college life were a staple of the 1990s and 2000s (Nakassis and Dean 2007). By watching these films as kids, my friends and hostelmates learned what college was (supposed to be) all about—romance, drinking, fighting, goofing off with friends, and cutting class to watch films—even if it turned out that it wasn't quite. Film structured the rituals of the college: one was ragged by being made to sing and dance to film songs or by being forced to pretend to flirt with film heroines (chapter 2); "culturals" performances at departmental or hostel functions featured film mimicry, skits based on films, and dancing and singing to film songs (chapter 5). Film was often the topic of debate. It was a way by which to bring a point home: 'It's just like that film ________,' being a common phrase in relaying some happening or experience. Film was what people listened to, talked about, joked about, and wore. It was what students went to sleep to and what they woke up to. And going to watch films was, of course, one of the most common activities when going out with friends.

Before detailing the ways in which film provides a resource for youth practice, it is important to emphasize the transgressive, youthful quality of cinema in Tamil Nadu. Much of contemporary Tamil film depicts and targets a male youth demographic. But more than that, there is a resonance between youth as a life stage and cultural beliefs and stereotypes about film (on the screen and in the theater) and the cinema industry. As alluded to in describing the first show on the first day of a mass-hero film, neither are considered respectable or *decent*. Film's depictions of premarital romance, sexuality, violence, fashion, foreign locales and cultures, and the like have long ideologically placed the cinematic outside of the moral order of respectable "society" and "culture" (Sivathambi 1981; Dickey 1993b; Hughes 1996; Srinivas 2009:157–73; Mazzarella 2013). While this exteriority is often projected onto class difference, it also takes on age dimensions, both through the idiom of the childish impressionability of the masses and through the association of film as a prototypical youth activity. The young men with whom I worked often defined their experience of leaving childhood through the transgressions associated with film. It wasn't simply smoking one's first cigarette, drinking one's first alcoholic drink, or loving one's first girl that friends associated with the "maturity" of leaving childhood. It was also sneaking out to go to the movies with friends. It was losing control and letting loose at a first show on opening day. Not only did this association of film with youthful transgression make film a fun pastime for young men (and to some extent women); it also made it a potent resource for them in performing and negotiating youth itself, for doing and talking about *style*.

Citing Films

In the college, film was reanimated in a number of ways, both as the content (that is, the stuff that was talked about) and as the form (that is, the semiotic vestments) of interaction. Film was often an explicit topic of conversation: 'Did you see Suriya's latest film *Vel* ('Spear,' 2007)? It was great!' 'The theme of Jiiva's *Katrathu Tamil* ('Learned Tamil,' 2007) was really good, but the second half was boring!' Such invocations often were explicitly about film and its representational content. But not simply about film, such talk also served as the context for interaction more generally and the basis for the creation and maintenance of a common background between peers (Osella and Osella 2004). Thus, for example, when discussing one's romantic travails, it was common to draw parallels with commercial film.[11] Explaining the ups and downs of his love life, Naren, a lower-middle-class friend said, 'It's just like *Paruthiveeran*. That's my story. I loved a girl and was going to marry her, but before I could she died.' In such situations, poignant and aphoristic film dialogues might be cited, ready-at-hand captions to capture the cinematic quality of the everyday. To explain why he took up a smoking habit (as well as other destructive habits like burning himself with cigarettes and cutting himself with a razor), one heartbroken friend quoted the comedian Vivek's dialogue: "*Puṇ paṭṭa manatai, pukai viṭṭu āttu*" ('Heal the broken heart by blowing out smoke').

Film wasn't just good for conversation or for narrating one's own life. It was also good to tease friends, bestow nicknames (e.g., *veḷḷai Tamiḻan*, chapter 5), or get laughs. Students often made fun of each other by reanimating comedy dialogues from films, as in, for example, my Madurai aided hostel's "farewell party," where the emcee played audio recordings of comedy dialogues through his cell phone over the PA system (see chapter 5 for discussion of this function). Every time someone got onstage, before they got to the microphone, a film voice spoke for them: "*Ēy, enne veccu oṇṇum comedy kīmiṭi paṇṇaleyā?*" ('Hey, you aren't using me to make some kind of comedy, are you?'). By ventriloquating the buffoon Vadivelu from the film *Thalainagaram* (2006)—throwing his digitally mediated voice into the mouth of the lampooned peer—this student emcee succeeded in teasing his classmates. By commenting on the fact that they were about to get ragged onstage with some "*comedy kīmiṭi*," he humorously rubbed it in and thus ragged them.

Such film dialogues often became youth slang catchphrases (Spitulnik

1996). For example, one might exclaim "*Enna koṭumai Saravanan itu?!*" ('What horror, Saravanan, is this?!'), a dramatic line originally uttered by the actor Prabhu in Rajinikanth's *Chandiramukhi* (2005) but comically taken up by college youth to humorously exclaim about anything they found unjust or absurd. (The line was subsequently comically reanimated by Livingston in Rajinikanth's *Sivaji* [2007] as "*Enna koṭumai Saravanan sir?*" and by the comedian Premji in Venkat Prabhu's films *Chennai-600028* [2007], *Saroja* [2008], *Goa* [2010], and *Mankatha* [2011] as "*Enna koṭumai sir?*"[12])

But more than captioning a situation or creating referential or interpersonal alignments, such uses of film often aimed to frame and transform the very contexts of their utterance. While taking a stroll one evening through a local Madurai park, one of my hostelmates, P. J., broke into song, singing with a sideways glance to a group of young women sitting under a tree: "*Maccānai pāttīṅkaḷā malai vāḻai tōppukkuḷḷē?*" ('In the mountain banana grove, did you see *maccān*?'). "*Maccān*" refers, in female-to-male usage, to a marriageable cross cousin, here a euphemism for lover or future husband (Nakassis 2014). Reanimating a lyric from the classic film *Annakili* (1976), P. J. took the filmic sequence, a love song in a mountain banana grove, and projected it onto our own arboreal mise-en-scène, in effect flirting with the young women by using the alignment of hero with heroine as his opening gambit to initiate a "line," or romantic relationship. In fact, the voicing was more complex. In the original film sequence, it is the heroine who sings this line about the hero. P. J., then, was voicing her desire for *him* by singing the song for/as her, by hypothetically reanimating *her* as the desirous one and himself as the object of her desire.[13] His friends laughed as we strolled on, and the young women giggled in embarrassment.

Examples like this could be multiplied endlessly. In all such cases, filmic voices and scenarios are grafted onto the contexts of their reanimation, brought near and close for context-transforming, performative effect. As these brief examples show, whatever these youth thought about or felt regarding these films qua films—that is, however they "received" the films that they cited—their invocation of fractions of these films had pragmatic force. Such citations do something in, and to, the contexts (and interlocutors) of their reanimation, be it eliciting sympathy, justifying self-destructive behavior, romanticizing the quotidian, or doing *style*. And this is the point: whatever else it is, film is particularly good to do things with. Below I show how the dynamics of the peer group make film a useful resource for doing *style*. Such usage requires, however, a complex citational framing, an incorporation and repudiation, a simultaneous inhabitation and negation.

Style and Heroism

In the college, *style* was often used in the same breath as another related filmic term of youth masculinity and status: "heroism." In the context of film, this term refers to heroic things the protagonist does: saving the damsel in distress, fighting off droves of bad guys, combatting social injustice, and delivering grandiloquent monologues. When used in the college context, "heroism" invokes a register of *style* associated with film heroes (in particular, mass heroes), captioning those who dress and act like film heroes. The phrase "college hero" typifies that person who acts like, or is, the most *stylish*, important, and popular student in the college.

"Heroism" and "college hero" were also used derisively, of course. Like *style*, these terms are ambivalent. Acting like a hero is fraught precisely because the status it presupposes and potentially entails risks exceeding the centripetal normativity of the peer group. The excess involved in citing filmic *style* and acting like the hero is captured in phrases such as "*overacting*" and "*over*action," "*scene pōṭuṟatu*" ('to put on a scene' [from a film]), "*film kāṭṭuṟatu*" ('to show a film'), "*paṭam pōṭuṟatu*" ('to put on a film'), and "build up *paṇṟatu*" ('to build up [oneself]'). In addition to being used to describe a person who acts too much like a film hero or heroine, these phrases are also used more generally for those who show off too much in any modality, belying the degree to which cinema is central to understandings of youth status and its excesses more generally (cf. chapter 4 on the *Peter*). My friends often described youth whose displays of *style* were seen as arrogant or *over*done (often with respect to fashion), whether they were filmic citations or not, by exclaiming, 'Who does he think he is? Vijay?' or 'Look at her acting like some kind of Simran [a famous film heroine]!' Similar to the dynamics of *style* that we've seen in previous chapters, doing *style* by reanimating film (and the mass hero or heroine in particular) always hazards incurring the annoyance, anger, and censure of one's peers, where the "as if" may be taken as an "is," where the subject of *style* is seen as problematically assuming the status presupposed and figurated by the *stylish* act, as the act's origin and author and not its mere reanimator.

Prakash's Dance

Walking down the hallway of my Madurai self-financing hostel one evening in January 2008, I passed by the room of Prakash, a second-year student with whom I had become friendly. The hit song "*Pokkiri Pongal*" from

Figure 20. Dancing to "*Pokkiri Pongal*" at a department function (Madurai 2008)

Vijay's *Pokkiri*, described earlier in the chapter, was playing through his cell phone. Its heavy rhythms sounded tinny out of his phone's small speaker, echoing off the bare empty walls of his room. I peeked through the door and saw Prakash dancing to the song. He invited me in and explained that he was practicing a dance routine. He was going to perform a solo dance to the song the next day at his department's Pongal function. He invited me to the function, and I promised I would come to check it out.

The next day at the function, with a handkerchief wrapped around his left hand, a red shirt on top of a white T-shirt, a white pair of slacks, his best pair of leather sandals, and a silver chain, Prakash was dressed in a way that was reminiscent of Vijay's character in the film (figure 20).

He took the stage to a crowd of department majors and friends from other departments. The music started, and Prakash began the dance he had been practicing the night before. He selectively replicated dance steps from the choreography of *Pokkiri Pongal*—in particular, the most identifiable and recurrent steps of the song: those danced during its chorus. By reanimating Vijay's dance, Prakash captured something of Vijay's *style*, showing, in the process, his own prowess as a dancer (for Vijay is considered to excel at difficult dance steps) as well as differentiating himself from his peers and, given cinema's suspect status vis-à-vis middle-class adult propriety, the faculty in attendance. (Or at least, his performance playfully figurated that difference and transgressiveness, for such dances were commonplace on college campuses.) However, doing all this required that the *style* Prakash did be figured as not quite his own, as authorized by the absent figure of the mass hero. If Prakash was 'doing *style*' and 'showing heroism,' as his classmates put it, it was only by deferring to Vijay, only by maintaining a kind of plausible deniability to the status of the very act that Prakash was, in fact, performing.[14] Ironically perhaps, in the name of the hero-star, doing *style* could avoid the censuring claims of 'putting on a film scene' (*scene pōṭuṟatu*), of one's *style* being "*overacting*."

Yet Prakash only reanimated parts of *Pokkiri*'s choreography, intercalating Vijay's steps with some of his own. But if incarnating Vijay onstage could garner Prakash some esteem among his peers and perform youth, why not *only* dance the steps from the song? Why only dress *like* Vijay's character and not *as* him? Why was there a lingering difference, a recalcitrance of the "as if" in Prakash's performance? While with brands and English (chapters 2–5), the excess of *style* primarily risked presencing that which was cited—an authorized upper-class, English-speaking subject who could afford authentic brand commodities—in this case, the risk was differently inflected. Coming too close to Vijay was problematic not simply because it presumed a level of status that Prakash (and his peers) obviously didn't have (of being a celebrity, an elite film actor, a superheroic 'ruffian'). It was also problematic because the act of reanimation itself could be seen as low class and *local*, inverting Prakash's very pretension to status through the slippage of citation into mere repetition.

As Prakash explained, dancing Vijay's steps shouldn't be seen as imitation. For to imitate the hero-star is to fall into the stereotype of the fanatical fan: the youth who has gone 'crazy' (*kiṟukku*) about film and slavishly follows the hero-star and whatever he does. While some of these college youth may have counted themselves as fans of various hero-stars, to be an actual member of a fan club was seen in the college as something childish (Gerritsen 2012). It was something that they might have done when they were school kids. Indeed, many of my hostelmates and friends were former fan club members. They almost always spoke about such membership, however, as something they did when they weren't "mature" and didn't know any better. Or if their memberships were current, they played that fact down (Dickey 1993b).

Within the college peer groups that I socialized with, to act too much like a film hero, then, would be to risk figuring oneself as being, in some sense, controlled by that hero-star. It would be to signal allegiance through mimesis rather than agentively appropriating the hero's image. It would be to be one of those presumed dupes who fails to differentiate real from reel, who takes the representation for its referent. As Prakash noted, he didn't dress or dance exactly like Vijay because to do so would make him seem like a "*cinna paiyan*," a 'little boy.' The point of doing *style* was to individuate and show off his talents, not to dissolve into the hero-star's image by uncreatively aping him. This required putting filmic *style* in quotes, metacommunicating that inhabiting the hero was just for the stage, just for a moment, just for a step or two. To do *style*, the gap between the citing and cited event had to be reflexively maintained. To do *style*, its animator had to be liminal and split, located between the statusful mass hero and the fan, between he who, in being cited, authorizes others' acts of *style* and he who gives himself over totally to that authority.

At stake here, of course, is a politics of class, for Prakash's reauthoring (or coauthoring) of Vijay's dance didn't simply disavow the figures of the little boy and the fan. It also, through that detour, disavowed the figures of the slum dweller and the rural bumpkin, those of the "masses" presumed to be taken by mass films and their hero-stars. Being lower-middle class and with rural ties, Prakash's background placed him anxiously close to these subaltern figures, close enough to require putting a distance between himself and those specters by asserting his agency and thus his class and educational difference.

This distancing by Prakash was not confined to this dance performance. When taking the bus with him one day, we passed a roadside merchant selling T-shirts with film stars' faces and names on them. Remarking on it, I asked him why such shirts weren't popular on campus. Such shirts are widely available and affordable and abide by a *stylish* aesthetics of brandedness not dissimilar to the garments discussed in chapters 2 and 3. Yet they weren't considered *stylish* by young men like Prakash. Indeed, Prakash replied that such shirts are "*cillaṟattanam*" ('cheap,' 'worthless'). If a young man were to wear one, the "public," as he put it, would look at him funny, like he was uneducated. The wearer would get teased by his friends. It wouldn't be "nice," he said, simply concluding by naming those who wore such badges of allegiance—tellingly given in Tamil and then glossed in English (chapter 4)—"*kāṭṭāḷkaḷ* ('rough, rustic people'), village peoples, uneducated peoples."

In distancing themselves from film through film (and through English use), youth like Prakash asserted middle-class distinction, voicing the elitist discourse that disavowed cinema as debased, trashy popular culture made for the lowest common denominator (the "masses"), even as he himself, in other contexts and in other ways, embraced aspects of the filmic. (While academic scholarship has problematized this elitist discourse as an account of mass heroes and their films, here we can see the ethnographic importance of this elitist ideology as constituting the local metapragmatics for citational acts like Prakash's engagements with film.) Young men's reanimations of film strike a complex balance, then, of doing *style* without doing too much *style*, while also managing difference from the poor, the rural, and the uneducated—in a word, from the *local*. One had to individuate without inscribing invidious difference between one's self and one's peers, while at the same time inscribing that very difference with respect to *local* others (cf. Sam's discussion of the "comedy person" speaking English in chapter 4).

Interestingly, because this indexical association of cinema with the masses is so longstanding and widespread, this dynamic of distancing and disavowal is at play across nearly all class segments, making it a shifting discourse of differentiation (cf. Hughes 1996:222). No matter who a person is, as he or she looks down the social ladder, others' engagement with film always appears to be low class and *local*, and thus childish and fan-like. Thus, for upper-middle-class individuals, the middle classes and the poor unreflectively copy and imitate film and thus betray a kind of childishness; for middle-class individuals, the poor signal too much allegiance and thus are too fanatical when it comes to hero-stars;[15] and for elders, youth are always too taken with film. Yet examples of citing film in the ways discussed in this chapter can be found across classes, in both urban and rural locales, and among nonfans and fans, though they manifest themselves differently.[16] For youth like Prakash, explicit signs that invoked the hero-star—for instance, his name or face on a shirt—were *local*, but implicit reanimations that clearly alluded without directly pointing to the film character or star were fine. For (aspiring) upper-middle-class college students, by contrast, sartorial forms like a handkerchief wrapped around the hand would be excessive and gauche because they were identifiable with a *particular* hero-star (Vijay in *Pokkiri*), but dressing in flashy T-shirts and expensive brand-name jeans like a film star or hero would be fashionable (chapter 2). Here it isn't specific forms that are borrowed but instead a mode of fashion that is implicitly allusive of the film world, if also ambiguously associated with elite, urban youth fashion more generally. Similarly, as one moves up the class ladder, filmic reanimations tend to be bracketed out of the everyday and explicitly framed as exceptional—for example, as something one would only do onstage in a performance, in the context of being inside the theater (e.g., dancing to a song, singing its lyrics), or on the opening day of a hero-star's newest film (but not at every showing). Such bracketings serve to distance oneself from film while reanimating it; they stave off the interpretation of being taken by film, even as one takes it in and ambivalently reprojects it in, and as, one's own act of *style*.

We can note the class-inflected metadiscourse on brand discussed in chapter 2 as similar in semiotic form and function. As we saw there, talk about who 'really' cares about authentic brands always motioned to others, elsewhere, elsewhen, accompanied by the counterrefrain that 'no one here cares about brands.' This, I argued, acted to mitigate the potentially excessive performativity of the brand rebounding back on those very youth who did, in fact, display branded forms on their bodies. Similarly, filmic citations must be kept in brackets, suspended both in the material expression of one's own citational act and in the metadiscursive frames that rationalize others' citations (e.g., as identification, imitation). In the case of film citations, however, what we see with particular clarity is how this citationality is not simply in response to the potentially excessive performativity entailed by citing what is otherwise high status (the "foreign" brand, the hero-star). It is also motivated by the negative performativity that is entailed by too closely approaching the subject of failed citation—in this case, the *local* fan and his mimetic modes of subaltern film reception. While the *local* is often cited in youth practices of *style* (as noted in chapters 1 and 4), proximity to it brings its own risks of infelicity, of simultaneously being under (and thus also *over*) the mark. Not just the scorching sun, the heavy moisture of the churning dark-blue sea below also weighed on *style*, leaving youth to carefully travel between sea and sky.

Filmic reanimations, like their animators, then, are liminally suspended and suspending, their performativity caught between multiple ways of getting too close to the cinematic. And it is precisely these multiple ways of infelicitously reanimating filmic *style* that the citationality of such acts attempts to manage. This renders the status of the filmic fractions that are cited ambivalent. Film fractions are usable in the peer group because they manage the dual mandate to differentiate from *and* conform to the peer group. Reanimations of film fractions do *style* in the name of another, disavowing the status of the very acts they perform by citing the hero-star as the act's underwriting origin. At the same time, they disavow that they only do *style* in the name of the hero-star, holding out a space of agency that inserts a gap between themselves and the hero-star, his *local* fans, their former childish selves, their peers, and their elders. For these reasons, fractions of the mass hero can never be wholly integrated into one's presentation of self, even as they are compulsively put on as the semiotic vestments of a subject that produces himself only by flirting with what or who he is not and refuses to be (chapter 2).

Diya's Dance

The subject instated by citing film to do *style* is gendered. While for young men, this is largely unproblematic (given that both *style* and commercial Tamil cinema are masculinized in various ways), for young women, citing film to do *style*, and cinema more generally, are extremely fraught. Given the highly hero-centric organization of contemporary commercial Tamil cinema, the often racy dress of heroines on-screen, the intense problematics surrounding public visibility and norms of modesty for women (chapter 2), and the often raucous space of the theater, this gender asymmetry is not surprising (Srinivas 2012). It also doesn't help that young actresses are often considered by many to be no better than "prostitutes" and their characters no more than eye candy who are there to validate the hero's machismo and symbolic dominance in the narrative (Nakassis 2015).[17]

The young women with whom I did my research, then, had an understandably complex and ambivalent relationship to film, much as they had a complex and ambivalent relationship to *style* more generally. While they may have desired to go to the theater, to try out cinematic fashions, and the like, many young women were, at the same time, resigned to the fact that filmic *style* often couldn't be publicly availed by them, especially when such *style* focalized their bodies (chapter 2).[18] 'Heroines like Trisha look beautiful and fashionable, but we can never dress like that. Society won't let us,' was a lament that one might hear from female college students. 'We would be teased and stared at,' many young women said. 'We would feel uncomfortable in public.'

The "modern" and "glamorous" dress of film heroines often elicited both desire and disgust from my female friends, an appreciation of their aesthetic beauty tempered by the idea that such dress wasn't proper, or at least not for girls like them. Indeed, citing film to do *style* and even attending films (Srinivas 2012; cf. Hughes 1996:185) had moral implications for young women. As one middle-class female student somewhat exaggeratedly put it, 'What kind of girl would dress like *that*? A homely, traditional girl wouldn't dress or act like a film heroine. She wouldn't even go to the movies,' at least not without her family. By contrast, she continued, a "bold," "modern" girl, an independent girl who doesn't care or who doesn't have to care about what others think would (or rather could) dress and act like a film heroine.

"Homely" and "bold," "traditional" and "modern" here must be understood as ideological sites of tension and contradiction, intersection points of multiple desires that are not easily reconciled by these young women, coordinates of a gendered liminality that young women acutely experienced and routinely dealt with in their day-to-day lives (Dickey 1993:61ff.; Lukose 2009). This is not to say that young women do not cite films to crack jokes; to tease friends; to make a point; to flirt; to perform a skit, a song, or a dance; or to appropriate some fashion. They certainly do. Yet the intelligibility and the pragmatic force of such uses of film carry very different consequences for young women than they do for young men.

The example of one female Madurai student, Diya, is telling here, given its parallels with and differences from the case of Prakash discussed above (cf. Barucha 2000:135–43; Mazzarella 2013:186–88). Diya was not someone I knew well but someone about whom I knew from the college's gossip mill. Diya was a first-year student in the Madurai college where Prakash and I lived. She was from an upper-middle-class background and had early on received a bad reputation among some of the young men in the self-financing hostel that I stayed in. They claimed that after accepting a proposal of love from one of our hostelmates in the first semester, she dumped him a week later and started "loving" someone else. This earned her their disdain, confirming for them the stereotyped litany of patriarchal nostalgia that young men often voiced: today's "modern" girls aren't to be trusted, they aren't sincere in their love, they've become too independent and arrogant, they've lost their "Tamil culture."

After the hubbub of this episode died down and our hostelmate himself moved on to loving another girl, talk about Diya dissipated. Months later, she again became a topic of discussion in the aided hostel that I had since moved to. In the spring semester, one of the big events was the yearly college festival. The festival was a college-wide function that featured a "culturals" competition—onstage performances of dance, mimicry, oratory, skits, and singing—between various visiting colleges as well as noncompetitive performances by our own college's students. The atmosphere of this two-day festival was raucous, with young men whistling, dancing on their plastic chairs, throwing them up in the air, hooting, hollering, clapping, and mocking the teachers and administrators who tried to discipline them. The young women of the crowd, perhaps a fifth of the audience, sat in a separate section off to the left side of the stage. They were quiet and well behaved in stark contrast to their male classmates.

While most of the performers were young men, some women also performed. When they did perform, many did so timidly, displaying a reservation and tentativeness that seemed to put their own performances in quotes, disavowing their actual participation in what they were clearly doing: displaying their bodies and their talents onstage for (semi)public consumption (Weidman 2012).[19] Other young women, however, were not so timid and performed "boldly," with confidence, without hedging on their obvious skill and talent.

Diya was one of those young women. Wearing black pants with a blouse and glittery shawl, she performed a dance number that mixed film-inspired steps (though not of any particular filmic provenance that I or my friends recognized) with Western pop-music-inspired steps. To my eyes, the dance was not particularly racy, though in comparison to the other female dances, it was refreshingly surprising in its energy and enthusiasm. While Diya's dance, like Prakash's, was a gambit for *style* that mixed the borrowed and the self-authored, the discourse that construed it was radically different. Prakash's dance was an expected, even ordinary, performance. It showed him to be *stylish* but neither too ostentatious nor too *local*.

By contrast, for many, but not all, of my male friends and hostelmates, Diya's dance was "*scene*" ('showing off'). It was "*over*" ('excessive'). It was also highly sexualized and threatening to them. It angered them. Talk about the dance quickly devolved into statements that conflated her sexual desires and her arrogance (*timiru*). She was the kind of girl to pursue guys (*pinnāṭi alaikiṟatu*). She did the dance to show her *gettu* ('dominance,' 'prestige'), to show that she was better than the rest (i.e., her male classmates). It was claimed that, in general, she would tease guys, talk and laugh too much, and wander around town (*ūr suṟṟatu*). Her dance was proof of that, they said. It was "*glamour*" ('racy,' 'sexy'). She did it to get attention. My hostelmates gave explicit voice to what they saw at the dance's intention: "*Pasaṅka enne pākkaṇum*" ('Boys have to look at me'), "*Ellārum ennuṭaiya aḻaku pākkaṇum*" ('Everyone has to see my beauty'). She wasn't acting like a good Tamil girl: silent and calm (*amaiti*), "homely," modest.

Beyond this sexist slippage between status display, arrogance, and sexuality, however, what was so troubling to these young men about Diya and her dance, as one young man lucidly noted, was that she was acting *just like they were*. It was this transgression—a young woman showing off just like a young man—that so threatened my hostelmates, that threw out of whack the entire gender economy of *style*. Diya's performance questioned and confirmed the gendered foundation of *style* at once. Her dance cited that which was the purview of young men—*style* and its figurations of transgressing male adult normativity—and in doing so, undermined their masculinity. Her citational act subverted and decentered the hierarchical gender norms of the college, at least as these young men saw it (cf. Nakassis 2014).

Diya's dance shows how, in such cases, doing *style* for a young woman is almost always *over*, how the excessive negative performativity of her *style* is near indefeasible. As never simply play, as never quite bracketed enough, the citationality of *style*, when done by a young woman, cannot quite hold in abeyance the immanent excesses that always threaten to undermine the act itself (Fleming 2011; Nakassis 2013b). And this is because, in such situations, doing *style* can no longer figurate transgression. For young women like Diya, merely figurating transgression is itself an act of transgression. For some of my hostelmates, this required putting Diya in her place through gossip.

From Reception to Reanimation

In concluding this chapter, I ask what kinds of acts are these engagements with cinema and, in particular, are they acts of "reception"? In asking these questions, I want to problematize both the notion of reception and the semiotic ideologies that animate it.

If "reception" was one site where an emergent anthropology of media in the 1990s inserted itself into media studies (and in which it encountered its uncanny reflection), this has not been without anthropologists' ambivalence (Spitulnik 1993; 1996; 2002; Dickey 1997; Kulick and Willson 1997; Dornfeld 2002; Ginsburg et al 2002; Peterson 2005; Lukács 2010; Hughes 2011; Mazzarella 2013:2; also see Silverstone 1989; Ang 1991; Couldry and Hepp 2013). This ambivalence is part methodological (i.e., that "reception" is a shallow gloss of and entry into the complex social processes that ethnographic research evinces) and part analytic (i.e., that "reception" artificially segregates itself from, even as it thereby fails to fully grasp, other media processes—namely, "production" and "circulation").

Is reception, then, an inapt gloss for the sophisticated ways in which anthropologists approach media today? Haven't we moved beyond mere reception? And haven't the analytical challenges presented by so-called new media—media whose very technological form seems to blur processes and divisions of production, circulation, and reception—rendered the very conceit of reception out of date? Yet, perhaps precisely because this is the case, there is something still to be learned from a critique of the term from the vantage point of the ethnographic examples discussed in this chapter. As I show below, such a critique highlights the textualist ideology that unwittingly underwrites the academic discourse of reception (Peterson 2005), an ideology and ontology of the text (and medium) that, on the one hand, persists in framing how media studies approach their objects of study (this is particularly so for film studies), whether or not they are reception studies or use the term "reception," and, on the other hand, implicitly persists in framing the very distinction between so-called old and new media (an issue I return to in the concluding chapter of the book).

Anthropologists and other ethnographically oriented media scholars have long critically argued that much Euro-American media theory is oriented around a particular ideology of the text, one that treats the media text as transcendent and autonomous, as a semiotic form that presents itself to us to be "read" against the worlds or ideologies it purports to represent or "encode" (cf. Bakhtin 1982:273–74). In discussions of film, this often plays out through the deeply entrenched and implicitly normative distinction of "realism" versus "fantasy," the very coordinates by which the particularity and peculiarity of Tamil mass films and Tamil filmic culture are all too often evaluated and dismissed (Dickey 1993b; Nakassis and Dean 2007; Krishnan 2009:14–21). Within the anthropology of media, the movement to "reception"—that is, the focus on how actual empirical audiences watch, apprehend, and discourse about media texts—was precisely meant to intervene into the overly text-centric and formalist analyses of media like print, film, and television that characterized much of media studies of the time.[20] "Reception" was to move us outside the text, allowing us to break subjective, ethnocentric preconceptions that propped up academic analyses, opening the space for other voices and ways of understanding media. By eliciting audience discourse about media texts, one could situate those texts in the larger cultural contexts within which they were variably understood. One could show how the text didn't impose meaning on those who "received" and "decoded" it; rather, such audiences were "active," "making meaning" in ways that subverted or negotiated the text. (Here 1980s and 1990s media theory and marketing practice and theory converge [see chapter 3], both turning away from top-down models of mass communication and instead embracing the active, free subject of consumption.)

Within the study of Indian film, such a move allowed academics to make commercial films make sense by situating them in their authentic life worlds. In doing so, seemingly nonserious films could be commensurated with "serious" (i.e., Western or Western-like) cinema. Incoherent plots, campy comedy, unbelievable fight sequences, and sappy romance could be recouped as expressing understandable, even rational, audience desires or as conforming to local traditions, genres, or spectatorial practices. "Reception," then, would complete the text, fill in its gaps, as well as provide a check to the idiosyncrasies of analysts' methodologically individualist readings (Nakassis 2009).

It is ironic and telling, then, that in decentering and problematizing the text by making space for the autonomous audience, the very autonomy and self-identity of the text is retrenched. Reception needs the text. (Indeed, what does one "actively" "receive," if not the text?) It demands, at some level, its autonomous identity and ideality. (Otherwise, how could multiple meanings be made with "it"?) But if reception substantializes the text (and medium, we might also suggest) by conferring on it ontological stability and coherence (Agha 2011a), this is only achieved by an epistemic bracketing, deferral, and transposition—that is, it is only achieved by citing our informants. It requires projecting what is denied in our own practice onto those whose reception we elicit and record. The notion of reception clings to the text as an object to be thought about, interpreted ("read"), and made meaning of, not by us, of course, but by those we study. On this view, film is implicitly figured as a surrogate mental object (of another): something good to think with, to feel with, to sense with, and thus something one makes sense of, likes, identifies with, rejects, and the like. Hence the recurrent anxieties that always seem to hover over and haunt the film text, its fearsome capacity to "influence" and have "effects" on viewers' mental and affective states (and on those of fans in particular) or, alternatively, the need to compulsively deny those effects by pointing to "negotiated" readings and the ever-presence of "resistance" in viewers' reception, as in now-classic cultural studies work on media.

Social practices like Prakash's or Diya's dances are not easily analyzed by the psychologism and textualism of reception, reducible to the representational qualities or "meanings" of the film texts that they reanimate. These are not cases of "active audiences" "making meaning" with the "text." Neither Prakash nor Diya were audiences or viewers in any clear sense. And while certainly active and agentive, their agency was not grounded in interpreting or making meaning of the films they invoked but in performatively citing them through their bodily movements. Moreover, what they were citing was not the film "text." It was a series of steps, a look, a tableau of *style*. It was a surface on the screen, a selectively curated set of semiotic features reprojected from another's bodily performance of *style* (i.e., the actor's) that itself had less meaning than pragmatic force and performative potential.

This is why reanimating film was not so much an issue of what youth thought or said about films or even whether they "liked" or "identified" with the films they cited, their stories, or their protagonists. Indeed, they may have even disliked the filmic originators that their reanimations cited. Rather, what was relevant was that the filmic fractions that were reanimated had social currency—that is, that they could do *style* in the theater of the peer group (cf. Jain 2007:292 on "metapopularity"). Hence Prakash's usage of dance steps from Vijay's *Pokkiri* was an issue less of his relationship to *Pokkiri* or even to Vijay per se than of what his reanimation of a particular performance by Vijay could afford. Rather than being a function of his presumed proclivity to Vijay, this reanimation turned on Prakash's ability to skillfully appropriate and disavow Vijay's own pragmatic performance of *style*.

My point here, of course, is *not* that films are not texts, that they do not represent or are not taken to represent by viewers or audiences, or that film textuality is irrelevant to *stylish* acts of citation. Rather, my point is that approaching cinema by already prefiguring film *as* essentially textual representation (which we may "read" or whose "reception" or "production" we may study) effaces the fundamental citationality of cinema in Tamil Nadu and its complex pragmatics, as well as the ways in which both operate far beyond the text, the theater, and the audience.

To account for acts like Prakash's or Diya's dances requires us to attend to the performative economy of *style*, to its citational semiotics and its (meta)sociology. It requires us to think differently about textuality and reception *as* species of citationality. This is for at least two reasons. The first reason is that, as we saw with Prakash's dance, such citationality implicitly puts the very ontology of the representational text into play *and* into abeyance at once. Reflexively staying on the surface, performatives such as Prakash's dance, through their altering iterations of the hero-star and (fractions of) his films, disavow the modes of spectatorship and reception that lurk in the ambit of the representational text and its "effects"—namely, identification, devotion, imitation, and the like. Indeed, the immanent failure and thus potential felicity of doing *style* in Prakash's case was wrapped up precisely with identification and its repudiation (a fact that, again, complicates the notion that citation follows liking or identifying with a film or film hero in any straightforward way). The pragmatics of Prakash's dance turned on the shadow presence of that figure who "(mis)reads" and "(mis)receives" the film and star text, he who identifies with the hero-star by being taken in by the narrative's fantasy—namely, the *local* fan. To understand Prakash's dance, then, requires us to see how, through the figure of the fan, citational acts of *style* invoke and bracket the ontology of the representational text.

The second reason the citationality detailed in this chapter requires us to think differently about filmic textuality is that such citationality does something to the text; it perforates it, alters and deforms it, and as we will see in the next chapter, thereby lodges its complex and dispersed semiotics "in" it. This is because youth citational acts entangle the hero-star, projecting the liminal subjectivity that youth achieve through doing *style* onto, and in a sense *as*, the mass hero, he who, by being entangled by those who cite him, must in turn cite others.[21] For as I show in the next chapter, in that entanglement, he too risks melting his waxen wings in the blaze of the projector's lamplight.

SEVEN

Status through the Screen

Introduction

While riding the bus on the north side of Madurai one late afternoon in the winter of 2007, I started up a conversation with three middle-class students from an engineering college located outside of the city. They had come into town to pick up copies of a T-shirt that they had designed. The T-shirts were for a performance they were going to give on the Tamil television station Vijay TV as part of a program featuring college "culturals" (i.e., performances of dancing, singing, mimicry, etc.). They had planned on each wearing the shirt on the program, the idea being that such fashion coordination—a not uncommon practice on college campuses for special occasions—would create an eye-catching visual effect. It would do *style*.

On the front of the shirt was a check mark enclosed in a circle, around which was written, in roman script, "CORRECTED MACHI." On the back of the shirt was written,

Beware of the
B^3
Back Bench Boys

B^3 was the stylized acronym of their self-named college clique ("Back Bench Boys"). "Back Bench" here refers to the last row of seats in the classroom, and "back bench *pasaṅka*" or "back bench boys" is a slang phrase for students who goof off and get in trouble both in and out of the classroom.[1] This caption was meant to playfully convey their clique's *gettu*

Figure 21. "Corrected *macci*" stamp from the film *Manmadhan* (2004)

('dominance,' 'prestige'; here, being 'bad ass'), a playful voicing of *rowdy* machismo and violence. While I had never heard of their clique, I was already familiar with the design on the front of the T-shirt. It was appropriated, with typographical and design modification, from the 2004 youth hit film *Manmadhan*, starring Simbu, the self-anointed "Little Superstar."

Manmadhan is a noiresque, psychological thriller about a college youth bent on taking revenge on (who he sees as) loose women. He does this to avenge the death of his brother (also played by Simbu), who committed suicide after being cheated on by an unfaithful college classmate. Painting a patriarchal picture of "modern" women's loss of morality, the women the protagonist seduces and then kills dress in revealing Western clothes, speak in English, and hang out in expensive spaces of consumption like discothèques and coffee shops in high-end malls. For each such woman, at the moment of the hero/villain's seduction, a circular stamp appears on the screen. It is this stamp that the B^3 boys had appropriated in their T-shirt design.

Figure 21 is taken from one such episode. In this film still, we can see the hero's face kissing a girl whom he then goes on to kill. Like the Back Bench Boys' shirt, around the circumference of the stamp is written, "corrected *macci*," though *macci* appears in *Manmadhan* in Tamil script (மச்சி). "*Correct paṉṟatu*" is a youth slang phrase meaning 'to pick up (someone of the opposite sex)' or 'to charm or seduce.' In this context, "corrected" refers to the young woman in the film who has been seduced, or "corrected," by Simbu's character. "*Macci*" is a fictive kinterm used in address between young men—something like "dude" in American youth slang (chapters 1 and 5; Nakassis 2014). In this context, it addresses the male audience watching the film. In the middle of the circle are what look like a Nike swoosh and a Playboy bunny. ('Playboy' is roughly a gloss of the eponymous *Manmadhan*, the Hindu god of love. It is also a nod to the actor Simbu's reputation in the film industry as a lothario.)

In reanimating a fraction of Simbu's *Manmadhan*, but also in altering it (e.g., the Playboy logo is elided in the B³'s design, மச்சி is rendered in roman script as MACHI), these Back Bench Boys borrowed something of the *style* of the film. Of course, Simbu's on-screen *style* is itself equally citational, invoking and refunctioning the Nike and Playboy brands, binding the prowess of the hero/villain to "*correct*" girls with a *stylish* sign of global brandhood that, with its edges made slightly more angular, also looks like a check mark from a corrected college paper.

But things are more complex than this, for the "Little Superstar's" swooshesque design isn't simply a citation of the Nike brand. It is also interpretable as an implicit allusion to the *style* of the not-little "Superstar" of Tamil cinema, Rajinikanth, and more particularly, to his 1992 film *Pandiyan*. At different points in this film, the hero, Pandiyan (played by Rajinikanth), wears shirts featuring a check mark, or "tick," on them (figure 22).

One of Rajini's punch dialogues early in the film (reiterated again at the end of the film by his sister in reference to him and alluded to in the song "*Pandiyana Kokka Kokka*") is visually punctuated with a close-up of this tick design: 'This Pandiyan is right in everything, everywhere, always' ("*Inta Pandiyan eppōvum, eṅkēyum, etilum* right"). Hence his moniker of "Mr. Right" in the film and hence the "tick" check mark on his shirts. For some, mainly working-class men in their thirties and above, the Nike swoosh on apparel and vehicle stickers (and Simbu's "corrected *macci*" stamp as well, perhaps) was not primarily a brand logo at all. Rather, it was a sign that cited Rajini so as to say, 'Whatever I do is correct,' 'I know what I am doing.' One friend in his early thirties even misremembered that *Pandiyan* had introduced the Nike brand to Tamil audiences in the 1990s.[2] Here Nike and its logo, like Simbu's epithet, citationally stand under Rajinikanth's name and image as instances not simply of a brand but of Rajinikanth himself.[3]

Rajini's tick shirts (plus dialogue), Simbu's on-screen tick/swoosh stamp, the Back Bench Boys' tick/swoosh-stamp T-shirt—these representations are linked to each other by a series of relays and interdiscursive nods, by an aesthetics of *style* performed by borrowing and reanimating but also erasing certain qualities from what is cited. An older film star serves as a citational resource for the status work of younger film stars that in turn serves as a resource for youths', and others' (figure 23), own advertising work.[4]

In this chapter, I explore these citational linkages across the screen. I am particularly interested to show the ways in which such citational inter-

Figure 22. Three of Rajini's "tick" getups in *Pandiyan* (1992)

discursivities weave the texture of Tamil commercial film—that is, to cite Roland Barthes's (1977:146) felicitous dictum, to show how "the text is a tissue of quotations drawn from innumerable centres of culture." I describe how the discourses of those involved in filmmaking imagine and anticipate youths' citational practices, prefiguring such citationality in the textual forms that they have a hand in creating. Further, I show how such aspects of filmic entextualization abide by similar dynamics to those of young men's peer groups. Film heroes do *style* much like young men do (namely, citationally), though the mediation of the screen introduces differences that, not coincidentally, are what make film so useful for youths' *stylish* citation (cf. chapter 5). The screen allows for hypertrophied acts of *style* but only, as I suggest, through the alibi of the hero-star's off-screen image as humble and modest, as deferential to his reference groups and his publics. As shown in the other chapters of this book, this involves is a complex

Figure 23. "*IDEAL*© innerwear" sign board: Nike's swoosh as a "right" tick (Madurai 2009). Also note the similarities between the font and typeface of the word "*IDEAL*©" and those of Nike's typically italicized block letters.

balance of under and *over style* that is managed by *style*'s citational, double-voiced semiotics. In the conclusion of this chapter, I reflect on these ethnographic data as they speak to the question of what a film text is.

Prefiguring Reanimation

> People like Vijay or Simbu are constantly thinking about what we can do (to set a trend), because the person who started it was Rajini. . . . Now there's Simbu. (He) wants to do that. Now Vijay wants to do that as well. So they know that the only and easiest way to capture an audience is to either capture a step, a movement, a dance step; the kids like the step, they catch it. They like something the guy is wearing, so they want to wear (it) too. It's easy (for youth audiences) to relate to fashion or to your dance movements. So that's what Vijay, as well as Simbu, are trying to do. They've started trying to work hard on their dance skills, and on (fashion). Something (that) has never been worn and since he's wearing this all the-, (they) want to wear the same things, because they know that it's a fashion thing, and once they (do) this, they all feel cool.

Vasuki Bhaskar, a young film stylist and costume designer, and I are sitting in a crowded Café Coffee Day in Chennai in 2008, chatting in English about film fashion and the work of styling in film. As she notes in the quote above, fashion and dance are central to the how actors craft their image and attempt to "capture an audience." As she explained earlier in our conversation, a film stylist's job is to sartorially render the director's vision of the story. In addition, and at times in tension with this, one of the main parts of the job is addressing the hero's concern with his own image. This is so often the case that established big-name hero-stars often have their own personal stylist who works for them on all their films.

In explaining how a mass hero has to be dressed in his films, Vasuki noted that the hero's styling always has to be different and hip. He should stand out. This, as she self-evidently pointed out, is "because he's a hero," and "you have to do everything around him." As she put it,

> The thing is, when you are doing a sequence for . . . a big hero . . . , you know the things you'll need to cater (to). . . . (And) unless (the director) is clear in his head—"I don't want any of this. He's going to wear a costume that fits the character"—(and) if he convinced the hero like that, whoever it is, you know, (then it's different). But actually they [heroes], they wouldn't do that because they already, they already think, "They are against (it), they won't take it, and the movie might be a flop, so why risk it? My guys aren't gonna-, I mean, my audience, my fans are not going to accept it, you know, so I don't wanna do that."

Reanimating the hero-star's fears of alienating his audience and thus risking commercial failure, Vasuki notes, with some disapproval, that as far as fashion and styling goes, the hero-star's image transcends the demands of the character or script, and often even the director's desires. It's not just the hero character but the *star* who is styled. As Vasuki went on to say, "So if you are (styling) a mass hero, you need to give a new look of his hair, and a new look of accessory, and new outfit, a new style of clothing. All that is mandatory. . . . Something new, you know? It's not just the extension of the costume; it's also the extension-, it's also him [the actor], not just (the character)." At the same time, the hero-star's look has to be usable by others. As Vasuki pointed out above, "he needs to set a trend" among youth.

The "dance master" (choreographer) Kalyan echoed Vasuki, making similar points regarding the work of dance in film. As he explained to me over tea in his office in the summer of 2011, producers, directors, and heroes are often looking for a "signature step," a "catchy" dance step that comes throughout a song that everyone can do, like the steps that Prakash performed from the song "*Pokkiri Pongal*" described in chapter 6. Such steps are a must for the hero's opening song. As Kalyan put it, 'The audience expects (such steps). Definitely for Vijay's opening song, they'll be fervidly expecting it. Really-, if it's not good, they'll start screaming at the screen' ("Audience *vantu* expect *paṇṇum-, kaṇṭippā Vijay tān* opening song *ṇṇā bayaṅkaramā* expect *paṇṇiṭuvāṅka. Romba-, nallā illai ṇṇā kattiṭuvāṅka appuṟam*").

As Vasuki and Kalyan frame it, then, such elements of film are made to engage, satisfy, and be cited by an audience and wider public that are not always obedient (Srinivas 2009). Such elements of film thereby also have economic implications. The actor Sriman (Sri), the sidekick of Vijay in *Pokkiri* (2007) and the son of producer Prakash Reddy, put it to me in the following way when I interviewed him in his Chennai home in 2008:

Sri: Money plays a vital role. *Ippō oru anta* youth cover *paṇṟa samāsāraṅkaḷ itu ellāmē. Ānā avaṅka vantā tān film-uṭaiya anubavam vantu romba nāḷ irukkum. Ille ṇṇā paṭam ōṭātē.*

So avan uḷḷa, theater-ukkuḷḷa avuṅka varaṇum appaṭi ṇṇā nāma avuṅkaḷukku ennennellām tēvaiyō what all elements do they like? *Enna mātiri* scenes *varumpōtu* clap *paṇṟāṅka*?
Ate ate ellātteyum kuṭukka vēṇṭiyirukku. Atukkāka definite *sila dialogues vantu avuṅkaḷukku puṭiccatā varum.*

Sri: Money plays a vital role. Now, all this is just a business to attract the youth.
But only if they come will the film's experience last for a long time. If not, the film won't run (in the theaters).
So in order to get them into the theater, we (have to give) them whatever they want: What all elements do they like? What kinds of scenes do they clap for?

All those things have to be given. In order to do that, definitely some dialogues that they like will come.

Sriman's example of such a dialogue that they "like" is the "punch dialogue" that we saw in the introductory sequence of *Pokkiri*, discussed in chapter 6:

Sri: *Ippa Prabakara sārōṭa oru* particular *dialogue vantu romba* popular-*ā iruntatu, Pokkiri* release *uṭanē: "Oru vāṭṭi muṭivu paṇṇiṭṭēn ṇṇā en pēccai nānē kēṭkamāṭṭēn."*
Hero-, so atu vantu oru commercial word *mātiri. Ivuṅka veḷiyile pōnatukkappuṟam avan* friend *pōkaṇum ṇṇu neneppān.*
"Enna ṭā tiṭīrnu varale ṇṇu solliṭṭiyām."

"Āmā ṭā oru vāṭṭi muṭivu paṇṇiṭṭēn ṇṇā en pēccu nānē kēṭkamāṭṭēn. Varale ṭā."

Sri: Now, Prabhakaran sir's [the dialogue writer's] dialogue was really popular immediately after *Pokkiri*'s release: 'Once I make a decision, even I won't listen to what I say.'
Hero-, so that's like a commercial word. When they go out of (the theater), he'll think that his friend has to leave.
'Hey man, it seems like all of a sudden, you're saying you're not coming.'
'Yeah man, once I make a decision, even I won't listen to what I say. I'm not coming man.'

Itu vantu avuṅkaḷukkuḻḻa, they, they start using it. *Avuṅkaḷukku aṅkellām* suitable *irukkō atellām anta eṭatule use paṇṇa ārambicciṭuṟāṅka.*	So this is something among themselves, they, they start using it. Wherever they find it suitable, in that context, they start using all this.

Here Sriman imagines and reanimates youths' own reanimation of filmic dialogue, citing how youth appropriate and cite fractions of films that are designed precisely for this citability. The circulation of such filmic fractions boosts a film's public visibility and thus increases its chances of box-office success. As film producer T. Siva put it, such circulation is good "publicity" for the film.

While youth reanimations are not filmmakers' only, or even main, concern, the important point for my discussion here is that through the relationship between young people's filmic reanimation and filmmakers' imagination of such reanimation, the film text comes to presuppose and entail something of its own social life outside of the theater (and outside of its own textuality). Film texts anticipate, as Sriman noted, youth using filmic fractions "among themselves . . . wherever they find it suitable."

Actors Do *Style* like Youth Do

That filmmakers make films with their audiences and larger publics in mind is hardly surprising (Ganti 2002; Jenkins 2006; cf. Ang 1991). It would be surprising if they didn't. When it comes to mass-hero oriented films, however, this interdiscursive linkage is rather more extensive than simple acts of imagining the audience or giving them what they "want." As I argue below, to the extent that films prefigure youths' citational engagements, filmmakers and actors are subject to the centrifugal and centripetal push and pull of the youth peer group and its regimentation of *style*, creating a camera obscura effect not dissimilar to what we saw with music-television VJs in chapter 5. By being entangled by the peer group, this dynamic comes to be part and parcel of the decomposable, fractionated aesthetics of the so-called mass film.

When it comes to doing *style*, not all heroes are equally reanimatable. As I argued in chapter 6, college youths' filmic reanimations are not necessarily a function of liking or identifying with the actor, his image, or his character (though these aren't irrelevant either, as we see below). Rather, what is crucial is that the hero-star being cited is seen as being popular enough by a critical mass of one's peers to authorize one's own *style*—that is, that the hero-star's *style* is a public fact. While in chapter 6, I showed how reanimations of film fractions are acts of *style* negotiated with respect to one's peers, we see a parallel problem confronting the actor in his relationship to his audience and his reference groups: if young men ground their *style* in films, then how do actors do it? How does an actor become statusful enough to license his own on-screen *style*, not to mention the *style* of others?

The quotation from Vasuki Bhaskar with which I began the previous section gives a hint about how this works: film stars cite other film stars. As I show below, actors negotiate their public image in much the same way that young men do, and this is because audiences evaluate actors' performances of status on-screen by a similar logic to how they evaluate peers' performances of status in their peer groups. Just as youth *style* is mediated by the dynamics of the peer group, actors' *style* is as well.

In the Habit of *Style*

While doing my fieldwork, it quickly became clear to me that for my college friends, just as important to what was happening on-screen was how such filmic representations lined up against the persona and status of the actor off-screen *and* against his filmic image across his oeuvre. For these youth, the main question to evaluate on-screen performances, and thus to gauge an actor's citability, was whether he was an established star or a "new face." In the industry, is he a *periya āḷ* ('big man') or a *cinna paiyan* ('little boy')? This was explained in the following way by one of my middle-class Madurai roommates, Yuvaraj: 'If Rajini or Vijay lights a cigarette by shooting it with a gun or if they come back to life, people will clap and appreciate it. They will take it seriously. But if a new face does the exact same thing, they won't accept it. They will boo at the screen. They will laugh at it as ridiculous, absurd, and unrealistic. Who are such young actors to try to do all that heroism and *style*? They are just "*cinna pasaṅka*" ('little boys').' To applaud and reanimate such non-hero-stars is to act the buffoon, to align oneself with someone who no one takes seriously, as my friends often did for a laugh with certain yesteryear heroes whose on-screen antics now seemed silly.

Much of this discourse is wrapped up in the notion of *paḻakkam*, glossable as 'familiarity,' 'habit,' or 'acquaintance.' A "new face" is unknown. He is a stranger. By contrast, an established star like Rajinikanth or Vijay has made numerous hit films over many years and is recognized as someone who is widely popular. As someone we know, this familiarity, this trust, this *pa̲lakkam*, gives him the license to do *style* on-screen. As one lower-middle-class friend from rural Vizhuppuram explained, 'When a new face gives a punch dialogue or hits ten guys, we'll always be comparing him to Rajini. But we'll prefer Rajini because we've come to know him. First you have to get to know (*pa̲laku*) the actor before he can start flying.' My middle-class Madurai friend, Nathan, expanded on this, saying that watching a new face on-screen doing *style* is 'like if someone you don't know comes up to you and says, "Hi." How would you feel? You aren't familiar with him, so it's weird. In the same way, a new face can't be a mass hero. There has to be a familiarity. But with an established actor, we know him, so it's okay.'

The point here is that a condition on being taken seriously as a hero on-screen, and thus as a potential source for reanimation, depends on seeing through the screen to the actor's background and biographical history in the industry, as well as to the familiarity created by repeated mediatized encounters with him on (and off) the screen.

Consider how the up-and-coming hero Krishna Sekar explained it to me while we had tea at a roadside stall in July 2010. He noted, echoing this discourse of familiarity, that one crucial thing for any hero (and for him in particular as a relatively new face) was not to have long gaps in time between film releases. As he put it in English, "The more people see you, the more they start liking you. . . . See, if I see you five times, even if I don't like you, I'll be okay with you. . . . If I see you ten times, I'm your friend. If I see you twenty times, then you're my best friend. So the more people see me on-screen, the more they get used to my face, and the more I can (do on-screen)." While simplifying the complexity of (meta)popularity, Krishna points to the necessary, but not sufficient, link between repetition and the amassing of star image, to an infrastructure of recognizability and self-referentiality (here, the iterated visibility of his face) that interdiscursively conserves identity across films and thus makes familiarity, social status, and *style* possible in and out of the industry and thus on and off the screen.

For film producers, this *pa̲lakkam* is reflected in, and translates into, a guarantee of box-office success. To trust an actor to helm a big-budget mass-hero film means minimally, in box-office terms, that his image will be able to pack theaters—that is, draw in the "masses"—for the first three or four days. The "psychological" logic behind this economic guarantee is this discourse of *pa̲lakkam*. As the producer T. Siva (TS) explained to me (CN),

TS:	*Tamiḻ-(paṭattu)le atu paṇṇa-muṭiyātu. Enna kāraṇam ṇṇu kēṭṭīṅka ṇṇā eṭuttavuṭaneyē* action hero first *paṭattule* action hero *ākamuṭiyātu. Nīṅka* slow-*ā* release *paṇṇi* release *paṇṇi*. . . .	In Tamil films, you can't do that [have new faces in mass-hero roles]. The reason for that is because you can't become an action hero immediately in your first film. You have to slowly release (over many films). . . .
CN:	*Ēn appaṭi?*	Why is that?
TS:	*Nāma appaṭiyē paḻakiṭṭōm. Anta* image *vēṇṭiyirukku ellāttukkumē. Vijay, nallā āṭuvān, nallā* fight *paṇṇuvān, pōṟān. Mota paṭattule āṭunān ṇṇā,* "<makes a clicking sound with his mouth> *O::kay." Anta mātiri . . .* People are tuned that way. . . . Psychologically, *nāma koñca koñcamā pēsi* adjust *paṇṟappō, mota vāṭṭi pākkum pōtu,* "<makes a clicking sound with his mouth> *Unnai summārā puṭiccu irukku." Appuṟam pēsum pōtu, kammiyā puṭikkum. So, nāl añcu* meeting-*kku appuṟam,* "Hi Costas!" *appaṭi free-yā āyiṭum. Eppaṭi nāma* friendly-*ā paḻakuṟōm.* First meeting-*le appaṭiyē kaṭṭi puṭiccitamuṭiyātu, le?. . . Anta mātiri tān* audience *āyiṭṭāṅka. Enta naṭikarum* first *paṭattule* friend *ākuṟatulle.* Very rare.	We've become used to it (*paḻaku*) like that. You need that image for everything. Vijay, he dances well, he fights well. If he did all those things [i.e., heroism] in his first film, "<makes a clicking sound with his mouth> O::kay." It's like that . . . People are tuned that way. . . . Psychologically, after we've talked a little bit and adjusted with each other, the first time I see you, '<makes a clicking sound with his mouth> I don't really like you.' But when we speak, I'll like you a little. So after meeting four or five times, "Hi Costas!" like that, we'll become free with each other. Like how we're interacting (*paḻaku*) friendly with each other now. In our first meeting, we can't hug each other, can we? . . . The audience has become just like that. No actor becomes your friend in his first film. Very rare.

The hero's ability to performatively entail his status in on-screen performances of *style* requires, then, sanctioning by the audience, or as T. Siva figures them, the hero's "friends."[5] Because of this entanglement, and because this entanglement has economic consequences that condition how producers and directors cast their heroes, actors have to negotiate status with the audience *through* the characters that they play, even while such on-screen performances are being read against the actors' off-screen status (cf. Srinivas 2009; Lukács 2010)—hence the perforation of the film text by the very logic of the peer group. Audiences are not simply addressed, or even "targeted," by the film and its on-screen acts of *style*. They ratify and approve, and thus constitute, such acts *as* acts of *style*.

Take the hero-star Vijay, for example. Vijay's career was intentionally planned with these on-screen/off-screen dynamics in mind. With the aim of making him a "mass hero," Chandrasekhar, Vijay's father and a noted producer and director in his own right, produced and directed Vijay's first five films, none of which were financial successes.[6] He persisted, however, in order to get audiences familiar with his son *as* a hero. In our 2010 interview, Chandrasekhar noted that in introducing Vijay, he couldn't immediately show him doing "heroism," though he tried. As he explained in English,

> When I introduced Vijay, he was only eighteen. And he looked very young, so I couldn't do dynamic subjects (with him), fighting with ten persons. I can't do that kind of heroism because the audience won't accept it. He was just a young boy. What can he do? So when I directed Vijay, (I directed him as a) romantic hero. *Naalaiya Theerpu* (1992) was our first film. It was a college story with love, but I also showed Vijay doing some (social) reforms (in the film). . . . But nobody accepted it. . . . It was a failure because the audience couldn't digest Vijay doing heroism. . . . So second picture, immediately—"Okay, I have to think about our calculations. Why the picture has failed? This is the reason: the audience has not accepted Vijay as a mass hero." So next picture, immediately, next picture, I did (just a) romantic, love (subject) . . . First five pictures, I did like this. . . . Up to *Poove Unakkaga* (1996), Vijay was only doing love, love, love. . . . Then after fifteen pictures is over, after the public has accepted (him) as a hero, then we changed the pattern. . . . *Bhagavathi* (2002), that's the first movie we changed him to a mass hero. . . . (and the) audience, they accepted (him as a mass hero). That picture really ran (in the theaters).

Getting the audience used to Vijay as a hero meant repeated performances in quasi-realist roles in small-budget romance films. After fifteen films and ten years in the industry as a so-called soft hero, Vijay made the jump to bigger and bigger budget action films. Since then, and up until recently (see below), all his subsequent films have followed a mass-hero "formula," as his father put it.

Vijay's career history is not unique. Indeed, in surveying the biggest hero-stars of this and the last generation, none were able to inhabit the figure of the mass hero until gaining some popularity in smaller-budget, realistic films, often helmed by critically acclaimed directors (cf. Srinivas 2009:95). Some examples include Rajinikanth first appearing as a villainous character in K. Balachander's *Apoorva Raagangal* (1975) and Bharatiraja's *16 Vayathinile* (1977); Ajith in *Aasai* (1995), *Kaadhal Kottai* (1996), and *Vaali* (1999); Vikram in Bala's *Sethu* (1999; before which he had a dismal decade of flops as an action hero); Suriya in Bala's *Nandha* (2001) and *Pithamagan* (2003); Dhanush in his brother Selvaraghavan's *Thulluvadho Ilamai* (2002) and *Kaadhal Kondein* (2003); Suriya's younger brother Karthi in Ameer's *Paruthiveeran* (2007); Jiiva in Ameer's *Raam* (2005) and Ram's *Katrathu Tamil* (2007). All these actors depended on acting in a number of "good stories" directed by acclaimed directors, playing "realistic" and "natural" protagonists in "serious" films that were—and this is crucial—successes at the box office. Only given these character-based films in which they were seen as successful actors could these individuals begin their forays into heroism and thereby cultivate and increasingly "build up" a star image.[7]

More than simply being a robust pattern describing actors' trajectories, such "career graphs" are themselves reflexively understood by actors (and those who manage their careers) as part of how they must navigate and plan their careers, to the extent that they can. As the upcoming actors with whom I spoke explained, because they have no standing with audiences or with industry insiders, they are limited to films where the strength of the director's name and the film's story get people into the theaters. These aspiring hero-stars—such as Ashok, Krishna Sekar, and Vishnu Vishal—emphasized to me that their plan was to try to do as many *different* kinds of hero roles as possible.

When I spoke to him in July 2010, Vishnu Vishal was an upcoming actor who had received critical acclaim and box-office success in a small-budget realist film called *Vennila Kabadi Kuzhu* (2010). After six years of trying to get into cinema, he had finally gotten his break. As he said in English,

> After that, I realized I have to stand out from the competition because I see so many youngsters coming, so many youngsters going. . . . And you know, after that I got tense, you know. I've got to make a mark now. I've got a beginning, as I wanted, to occupy that position in everyone's heart. . . . Now I have to make a mark with that. . . . I thought, let me plan, let me try something which youngsters have not tried in the beginning. That is, one is, first four or five movies are different genres. Second, . . . (in) every movie, I should have a different hairstyle, look, body. Third is, different characterization. . . . These three things I've tried. So that, you know, when a movie does well, all is well. When a movie doesn't do well, a director watches

a movie from the industry, and he thinks, this boy has done some good. . . . Every movie they should look at me as a new character, not the same hero who did *Vennila* (*Kabadi Kuzhu*).

Vishnu's strategy to achieve his goal of becoming a mass hero was to first act in films in which his status as a new face could work to his advantage. In order to showcase his talent, he chose a range of films: light comedy, sentimental romance, and gritty realist action with a tentative dash of "heroism," each film highlighting a different talent of his. By doing this, Vishnu (Vi) hoped to get the audience's attention as well as industry insiders':

Vi: And I, I am somewhat confident that, *"Hey anta paiyan ellā paṇṟān" appaṭi ṇṇu oru itu. Appavē teriyutu. Ēnnā ippa irukkuṟa* competition *vantu itu maṭṭum tān atu maṭṭum tān pōka kūṭātu*. . . . If one director-, you know, if ten directors are having an action script, after seeing *Droghi, "Okay," pattu pērum, "Inta paiyan paṇṇuvān" appaṭi nenekkuvār*. If someone is having a comedy script, after watching *Kullanari Koottam, "Hey inta paiyan comedy paṇṇuvān." "Vennila Kabadi* already *appāviyā* emotional-*ā paṇṟān, anta oru itu." Bale Pandiya pākkum pōtu* "City-*um paṇṟān."* So what happens, the more directors think of me, the more opportunities I'm gonna get.

Vi: And I, I am somewhat confident that, 'Hey that kid's doing everything,' if they're saying like that, it's a thing. Then I understood. Because in the competition that there is now, I shouldn't be doing only this or that (type of film/hero-role). . . . If one director-, you know, if ten directors are having an action script, after seeing *Droghi*, 'Okay,' all ten people, 'This kid does (action),' he'll think like that. If someone is having a comedy script, after watching *Kullanari Koottam*, 'Hey that kid does comedy.' 'He's already done tragic emotional (roles) in *Vennila Kabadi (Kuzhu)*, so he's got that skill.' When (they) see *Bale Pandiya*, 'He also does city (roles).' So what happens, the more directors think of me, the more opportunities I'm gonna get.

As Vishnu emphasizes, by showing a range of acting skill, he aimed to maximize his chances of industry insiders thinking of him when developing a script or when casting new movies. The end goal is inhabiting the figure of the mass hero. As Vishnu said, "See, at the end of the day, everybody wants to be a-, see, why do we come into cinema? You want to be famous, right? Automatically, you get money, you get power, you get fame, whatever-, the biggest criteria is you want to be famous. Definitely, you know, everybody wants mass. . . . But I think it's a step-by-step process. Today, I can't think of that. It's too far from me." Within the scripts that Vishnu had picked at the time, interestingly, one of them, *Droghi*, was an action film. It wasn't, however, as he emphasized in describing it, a typical mass-hero role, again, because this would likely be rejected by the audience:

> So at the same time, the action should be in such a way that I'm not hitting ten to twenty people at a time, I'm hitting one or two-. (CN: Realistic.) Yeah, realistic kind of action. That's why I did *Droghi*. . . . So I planned it like that; I planned that I wouldn't go action overboard. At the same time, there is buildup; there is, you know, a, a slight, uh, heroism in the character. But at the same time, it isn't so big that people won't accept it.

As Vishnu indicates, his strategy was to tentatively introduce more and more "heroism" into the realist aesthetics of his films, to carve out an increasingly large space for the hero role while not *over*doing it. Here the narrative's and diegesis's independence from the hero's image, the enveloping of heroism within a larger aesthetics of realism, serve as a hedge on the very heroism depicted within the film. Such heroism is bracketed, contained, and kept in quotes. As conversation with the more established but still young film hero Karthi indicated, for a rising star, the emphasis on that bracketing comes to decrease with each subsequent film as the centrality of heroism to the narrative is increased to the point where, as we see in the following sections, it is the story that is bracketed by, and subservient to, the hero-star's mass image.

To sum up the discussion so far, in contrast to established hero-stars, for these up-and-coming film heroes, realist aesthetics, story, and character are techniques to insert themselves into the film industry, allowing them to negotiate their acceptability with audiences as a hero, with directors as appropriate to their films, and with producers as a good investment. This contrasts with the highly formulaic qualities of the mass hero, as Chandrasekhar put it, where filmic representation and box-office success depend less on story, character, or realist aesthetics than on star persona and off-screen status, a point I take up in more detail below. In short, film publics' evaluations of actors *through* the screen condition youths' reanimations of their film characters and personas, and this in turn conditions how various actors can enter the acting field, what kinds of roles they can take, and how much *style* and heroism they can do on-screen. This also conditions the generic and stylistic organization of Tamil cinema as well: realist films (*etārttamāna paṭaṅkaḷ*), family films (*kuṭumba paṭaṅkaḷ*), and offbeat comedies all rely on "new faces" and midlevel actors, while big-budget mass films are the purview of established actors, 'big men' who have established themselves in the industry.

The Texture of Filmic *Style*

As I have been arguing, the aesthetics and pragmatics of youth concepts of status condition not only how audiences evaluate film heroes' displays of *style* and heroism but also, as a function of this, what kinds of actors can act in what kinds of films and thus their overall career trajectories. But more than this, this dynamic also marks the narrative organization of mass films as well.[8] We saw this in chapter 6 through our discussion of the introductory sequence of Vijay's *Pokkiri* (2007), whose organization is oriented almost exclusively toward the "buildup" of Vijay's star persona, to the performative presencing of his status, his power and dominance, his hypermasculinity, his *style*. But extending beyond such introductions, I would suggest that mass-hero films narrativize the very dynamics of youth status more generally, distributing *style* and its excesses and deficiencies variously to different characters as part of the emplotment of the hero-star's image and status (Nakassis 2010:150–220).

To take one pattern (common in Rajinikanth's films in the 1990s but also in other hero-stars' films since), the hero is introduced as an average (if rough) "guy next door," his true status hidden under his ordinary, even humble, exterior. The hero tends not to boast or to attribute status to himself and instead is spoken for, heralded, or cited by others: most commonly by his comic sidekicks, whose comedy often simply turns on failed performances of heroism and *style*, or the heroine, whose attraction to the hero is often attributed to, and ratified by, his heroic *style* (Rajanayagam 2015). For example, in the *Pokkiri* introductory sequence, it is Vijay's sidekick, played by Sriman, who praises his fighting ability before we ever even see Vijay: 'If he hits, it won't be blows; it'll be lightning that'll strike' ("*Avan aṭiccā aṭi viḻātu, iṭi viḻum*"). Ultimately, however, through forces external to his own desire, the hero is forced to reveal what the audience already knows of him, and what is often hinted at, or in the case of *Pokkiri* simply shown, by the introductory sequence: he is a force to be reckoned with. Through various confrontations, often prompted by the need to protect the women under his stewardship (sisters, mothers, girlfriends; Prasad 2010:15), the hero reveals his status through acts of *style* and heroism: fashionable clothing, oratorically elaborate "punch dialogues," and acts of physical valor.[9]

His *style* is fully put on display in his confrontation with the often almost equally *stylish* villain and his henchmen (the head villain also commonly taking on the vestments of the 'big man'), with whom he engages in symbolic status negotiations. Such showdowns not only feature fisticuffs but also frequently feature rhetorical battles and competing displays of fashionable and expensive commodities. It is in such confrontations that the hero fully displays his *style* and heroism. Yet the justness and the agency of the unveiling of his *style* are always warranted through the narrative's machinations, by the arrogance of and injustices committed by the villains he encounters, and not by the hero's own desires to show off as such. Such revelations are disavowed by the narrative as solely originating from the hero character (even as that very *style* is presumed as, in fact, originating in the star actor). By contrast to the hero, the villain constantly boasts without restraint and without prompting. As my hostelmates explained in discussing the villain, the villain *has* to ooze arrogance so that it's that much sweeter when the hero puts him in his place. Tellingly, villains in such films are generally talked about not as evil per se but as arrogant. The plot culminates with the villain's subordination, his *style* (and status more generally) delegitimated and shown to be *over*.

At the end of this two to three hour process of revelation, order is restored, and inevitably the hero returns to his original state as a humble man of the people. Often he is portrayed as moving into adulthood, for example, by marrying the heroine. His heroism and *style* are put into abeyance by the story's resolution—that is, until the next film. At the narratological level, then, such films are as much about the genesis and negotiation of the hero's *style* and heroism (and the reconfirmation and revelation of the star's *style* and status) as they are about this *style* and heroism being temporarily suspended and contained.

Beyond the narrative arc, the tropes of heroism in such films take on the double-voicing of youth *style*, both individuating from and deferring to other characters in the diegesis, other actors in the industry, and ultimately, the audience. The hero's acts of on-screen ostentation are almost always tempered by co-occurring signs of simplicity, of being a normal guy like anyone else (Nakassis 2010; Rajanayagam 2015; also see Srinivas 2009:129–56). For example, Vijay in *Pokkiri* dresses like a cosmopolitan, upper-class youth, but his speech, mannerisms, and neighborhood mark him as relatively lower class. Rajinikanth's characters are often individuals from working-class professions (e.g., a milkman in *Annamalai* [1992], an autorickshaw driver in *Baasha* [1995]) but are decked out in name-brand clothing and fashionable haircuts.[10] Whether or not we read such co-occurring signs of low status as serving to align the hero-star with the "masses" as part of an attempt to create forms of populist political mobilization (Hardgrave 1971; 1979; Sivathambi 1981; Pandian 1992; Dickey 1993b; Vaasanthi 2006; Jacob 2009; Rajanayagam 2015) or as articulating models of subaltern political belonging and representation (Srinivas 2009; 2013; Prasad 2014), what I'd suggest is that such tropes are always already part of a performative economy in which multiple exteriorities (the elite and the subaltern, the foreign and the *local*) are continually being drawn on to do *style*. Within this economy, such leveling signs function as citational quotation marks that liminally situate the hero-star, partially negating/yoking the class-linked indexicalities of the exteriorities that he reanimates, thereby performatively entailing the disjunctive union of both as *style*. Such citational acts are simultaneously tropes of condescension and acts of status. They are balancing acts that navigate differentiation and deference. As I've argued throughout the book, *style* only emerges within quotation marks, hedged by its citationality. This is as true within film as it is outside of it.

But more important than the intratextual organization of any single film text is the coherent "buildup" of the hero-star persona over many such films, or what Mishra et al. (1989) have referred to as the hero-star's "parallel text." Becoming a mass hero—that is, a source of reanimation for others—is never a single-film affair. It requires many films, and not simply as an accumulation over time but as an intertextually organized whole that coherently, and insistently, "builds up" the mass image and identity of the hero-star. As I show in the next section, one of the most salient features of the mass-hero film is its dense intertextuality, its compulsive and obsessive citing of other actors and other films—in particular, those of the hero-star himself.

The Citationality of Heroism

Much of what goes on in Tamil commercial film is implicitly or explicitly citational, the texture of such films woven from gestures that link the film in question to some other social locale, discourse, text, or social persona. In particular, the buildup and *style* of any hero-star is largely constructed through the alignment of his film character, and transfilmic image more generally, to other more statusful individuals: historical figures, deities, and internationally famous politicians (figure 24), among others. Most commonly, however, it is more senior film stars who are cited.

Rajinikanth's 2007 blockbuster *Sivaji: The Boss*, for example, revolves

Figure 24. Poster for the Rajinikanth film *Arasan* (2009), a dubbed, recut, and partially reshot version of the 1991 Hindi film *Khoon Ka Karz*, starring Sanjay Dutt and Rajinikanth

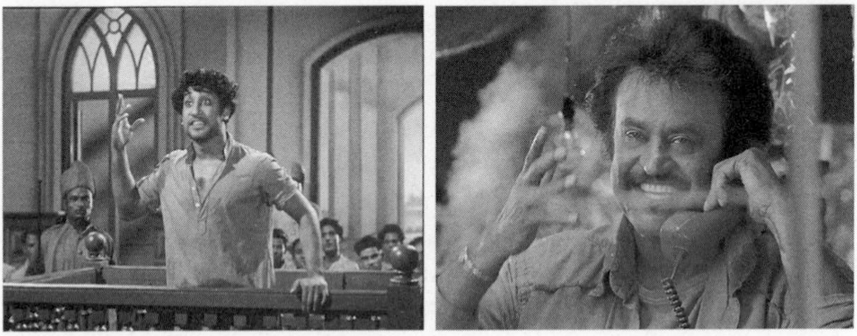

Figure 25. Rajinikanth citing Sivaji Ganesan: left—Sivaji **Ganesan** in *Parasakthi* (1952); right—Rajinikanth as Sivaji **Arumugam** in *Sivaji: The Boss* (2007), saying, *"Parasakthi hero ṭā! Pēre kēṭṭa uṭanē cummā atirutu, le?!"* ('I'm the hero of *Parasakthi*, man! Just hearing the name makes you tremble, doesn't it?!')

around his co-optation and reanimation of the two great actors of the previous generation: Sivaji Ganesan and M. G. Ramachandran (or Sivaji and MGR for short).[11] In the first half of the film, Rajini's character is named Sivaji Arumugam, known simply as "Sivaji." Here Rajini inhabits and pays homage to Sivaji Ganesan (figure 25).

Having called the villain to taunt him, Rajini is asked, 'Who are you?' He replies, 'The hero of *Parasakthi*, man,' identifying himself through allusion to Sivaji Ganesan's debut in this classic 1952 film. Rajini then appends his own signature "punch dialogue": "*Pēre kēṭṭa uṭanē cumma atirutu, le*?!" ('Just hearing the name makes you tremble, doesn't it?!') Later in the film, having made medical arrangements to be brought back to life, Rajini

Figure 26. Rajinikanth citing M. G. Ramachandran: above—M. G. **Ramachandran** in *Nadoodi Mannan* (1958); below—Rajinikanth as M. G. **Ravi**chandran in *Sivaji: The Boss* (2007)

allows himself to be 'killed' by the villain. He is reincarnated as M. G. Ravichandran, or "MGR" for short.[12] Here Rajini takes on not just the acronym of the late great M. G. Ramachandran but his signature mannerisms as well.[13] Having been asked by one of the villain's henchmen, 'Who are you?' Rajini answers, to a cheering crowd, "MGR," while performing MGR's patented gesture of flipping his fingers across his nose (figure 26).

At the same time, however, Rajini is marked as distinct from these two stars. His characters' names are Sivaji *Arumugam* and M. G. *Ravi*chandran. This difference is also evident in the unique Rajini *style*s that co-occur with his citational acts of naming himself: his *stylish* punch dialogue in the first example and his new, *stylish* "getup" in the second (bald head, sunglasses, diamond earrings, and well-manicured beard). Like Prakash's reanimation of Vijay in chapter 6, Rajini's reanimations re-present iconic film stars like MGR and Sivaji Ganesan while reflexively indexing difference from them.[14] There is also an element of autocitationality here as well, for the name of Rajini's first avatar, Sivaji, also gestures to Rajini's birth name, Sivaji Rao Gaekwad, creating an extratextual allusion to Rajini's own career trajectory, born as the normal Sivaji but reincarnated as the biggest star of Tamil cinema, Rajinikanth.[15]

Just as actors like Rajinikanth borrow status from the senior-most artists of yesteryear, current aspirants use Rajinikanth's image to playfully, but also seriously, do *style*. In *Pokkiri*, for example, Vijay, who has also been referred to as the "next Superstar" (Behindwoods 2014) and as "*cinna Rajini*" ('small Rajini'; see Rajanayagam 2002:308), is explicitly addressed by the female villain as "hero." She throws him a gun, which he catches and *stylish*ly twirls around his finger, popping the magazine and loading it back up. When she asks him in amazement how he is able to do that, he replies, 'How many Rajini films I must have seen' ("*Nān ettane Rajini paṭam pāttirukkēn*"). He then throws the gun up in the air and catches it behind his back with a flair reminiscent of Rajinikanth. Or again consider Simbu, whose 2008 film *Silambattam* features a quasi-comedic scene toward the end of the film wherein the hero and his sidekicks show up to meet some *rowdies*. Simbu and his sidekicks arrive dressed just like the "Ultimate Star," Ajith Kumar, and his henchmen in Ajith's 2007 smash-hit remake of the Rajinikanth classic *Billa* (1980).[16] When one of the villains asks the comic sidekick, Santhanam, 'So (are you) *kuruvi* ('the smuggler')?' (a reference to the Vijay film *Kuruvi* [2008]), he intones slowly, 'No, Billa' (a reference to the eponymous hero of the Ajith/Rajinikanth film). The scene cuts to a low shot of Simbu emerging out of a car and proceeds with a set of "buildup" shots of him along with the 2007 *Billa* theme music. Santhanam goes on to tell the *rowdy* that this isn't the 'big boss' (*periya tala*; literally, 'big head')—a reference to Ajith's nickname *Tala*—but 'our big boss's little boss' ("*Itu eṅka periya talaiyōṭa cinna tala*"). An extended punch dialogue, in both English and Tamil, follows in which Simbu reanimates the *stylish* mode of rhyming speech famously associated with his father and yesteryear hero, T. Rajendar (or TR for short).

By implicitly or explicitly reanimating more statusful others, film actors ground their own acts of *style*. While often such framing is playful, it is also serious (box-office) business as well as part of the sociological positioning of hero-stars within a citational filmic hierarchy of status. Simbu isn't simply playfully reanimating Ajith, he is praising him (and voicing himself as a fan of a sort), even as he attempts to carve out his own space as a mass hero.[17]

The regress of such intertextuality is the full-blown autocitationality of the established mass hero, the hero-star's constant, insistent referencing of himself (also see Srinivas 2009:94–107; 2013:184ff.). Mass-hero films are rampant with implicit allusions to and explicit reanimations of previous characters, the transtextual image of the hero-star, and the off-screen image of the actor himself. For example, Rajinikanth's signature *style*s from older films are compulsively repeated in his later films. In all his films, Rajini does the same *stylish* salute accompanied by the same sound effect, the same pushing back of his shirt to put his hands on his hips, and the same throwing of a cigar(ette)—or, more recently, a piece of gum—into his mouth. This goes along with the repetition of songs (e.g., the theme song of *Annamalai* [1992] is redeployed in *Baasha* [1995], the song "*Annamalai*

Annamalai" in *Pandiyan* [1992]), camera shots (e.g., *Sivaji* [2007] references *Baasha* [1995] through a similar shot of Rajini walking toward the camera with flames behind him), and even whole dialogues from previous films, as in *Sivaji* (2007) and *Lingaa* (2014), where Rajini and other characters re-enact dialogues from numerous of his past films. Often this takes the form of referring to, or addressing, the hero of the film with the names of past characters. For example, in the song "*Athiradi*" from *Sivaji* (2007), Rajini is referenced as "*Thalapathi*" (the name of his 1991 film), "*Billa*" (the name and character of his 1980 film), and "*Baasha*" (the name and character of his 1995 film). Similarly, the song "*Kaalai Kaalai*" from the film *Manithan* (1987) variously refers to Rajini's previous films *Murattu Kaalai* (1980), *Pokkiri Raja* (1982), *Paayum Puli* (1983), and *Nallavanukku Nallavan* (1984; see Rajanayagam 2015:144).

Even more explicitly, the mass hero is constantly referred to by the actor's epithet: Rajini as "Superstar," Vijay as "*Iḷaiya Taḷapati*" ('the Young General'), or Simbu as "Little Superstar." Rajini's films, since the mid-1990s, like Vijay's films from the late 1990s, begin with the display of the actor's name and epithet in bright letters (see chapter 6, figure 16). This acts to suture together all their roles as instances of "Superstar" or "*Iḷaiya Taḷapati*" films. Such references to the hero's transtextual persona don't simply frame the film; they abound *within* the films themselves: to take one of the many examples in *Sijvai* (2007), the song "*Style*" begins "Hero, Hero, you are the Hero. Staro, Staro, *nī* Superstaro" ('You are the hero! You are Superstar!')[18]

Besides simply referring, older roles are also reenacted in many films. Consider, for example, Rajinikanth's *Annamalai* (1992). During a song sequence, the hero and heroine look into a moving image-finder with eyeholes on either side, one for Rajini, the other for the heroine played by Khushboo. Peering into it, what do they see but a montage of shots of Rajini doing *style* in as many as twelve getups from other films! Later, a montage of Khushboo dancing in seven different getups is spliced together. The film characters are watching the actors who animate them acting in other films.[19] The song goes even further in its lyrics when it references Rajinikanth explicitly as "Rajini" and the heroine as "Khushboo." Similarly, in *Pokkiri* (2007), the hero from Vijay's previous blockbuster *Gilli* (2004) makes an appearance in the same exact outfit, singing the song "*Appadi Podu*" from *Gilli* to *Pokkiri*'s hero as he contemplates hugging the heroine in an elevator encounter.

Vijay's father, Chandrasekhar (Ch), explained such purposive intertextuality to me with regard to his son's films by saying,

Ch: Audience mind-*le iruntuṭṭē irukkaṇum*. Pictures they can't forget. . . . *Maṟakkamuṭiyātu, ovvoru naṭikanukkum. Vijay eṭuttuṭṭīṅka ṇṇā oru Rasigan, oru Poove Unakkaga, Kadhalukku Mariyadhai . . . , oru Gilli, . . . ellā* picture *vantu* super hit-*ānatu*, some mind response will be there. . . . *So vantu* audience *maṟakkamāṭṭāṅka . . . Tiruppi* remind *paṇṇaṇum*, remind *paṇṇum pōtu "Oh, okay, atu oru nalla paṭam atu," atāvatu itu tān solṟēn, itellām* extra, extra plus point. . . . *Oru* happiness, *oru* plus point will be there.

Ch: One has to be in the audience's mind constantly. Pictures they can't forget. . . . For every actor, (there are films) they can't forget. If you take Vijay, a *Rasigan*, a *Poove Unakkaga, Kadhalukku Mariyadhai* . . . , a *Gilli*, . . . all of these pictures are super hits, (so) some mind response will be there. . . . So the audience won't forget. You have to remind them again, and when you remind them, "Oh, okay, that's a good film that one," that is to say, this is what I am saying, all of this is an extra, extra plus point. . . . Some happiness, a plus point will be there.

This autocitationality, as Chandrasekhar explains, bootstraps status through "reminding" the audience, 'I did that, remember, and it was a hit!' As the actor Karthi put it, voicing the audience for whom such autocitational moments give pleasure, "They call it film history. You have a history of films. And that-, that works when you say a dialogue. When you say something, he, he [the viewer] imagines (all) the others characters (the actor has ever played) are all saying that line."

As Karthi and Chandrasekhar indicate, every film is implicitly or explicitly a citational composite of the hero's past films, a polyphonic, choral reiteration of all that came before (also see Srinivas 2009:117; 2013:184ff.). Yet, even as the mass hero thereby comes to seemingly play, and to retroactively have played, the same role in every film (namely, his transtextual persona), each next film also contains something different and something more. (Remember how Vasuki emphasized the constant need for something "new" in styling the hero.) Through such compulsive intertextuality, these films attempt to compile and conserve the hero's past filmic feats of *style*, thereby creating a transtextual launch pad for more and more extreme *style* with every subsequent film (cf. the performative "interface" of the brand discussed in chapter 3). It is at this stage in an actor's career—when his mass image and his status conspire to stabilize the dialectics of *style* and *over style*—that his transtextual image, or "film history," self-grounds his filmic acts. It is here that the hero-star's self-same image comes closest to that of a pure performative (Nakassis 2013c), every act of *style* entailing status precisely because it seems to indefeasibly instantiate, through its mere appearance on-screen, that which always already is: the hero-star's *style*. By successfully self-grounding his own performances of *style* through this compulsive autocitationality, the mass hero seemingly brings his own status as a mass hero into being, his on-screen acts no longer merely signs of his status but the very embodiment of his autopoetic essence as statusful. Here the hero-star appears as that very burning sun that illuminates a horizon of *style*, that celestial mass that bends all others' trajectories into orbit around him. Radioactive and iridescent, the mass hero presences as that putative source of all others' *style*, that mythic origin that all other citations harken back to (Žižek 1989; Butler 1997). This effect is generated by a performative intertextual loop that, while seemingly out of time, has emerged through it, through a history of films chained together by these intercalated reel-time acts of *style*. In this moment that is not a moment, the mass hero offers himself up for others to cite by seeming to solve for the performative contradiction of *style*, but only with the realization that looking too much like and coming too close to the sun can blind and burn.

Viewers expect this runaway, hypertrophied *style*, and they're often disappointed when hero-stars don't deliver on it. It is this "image trap," as M. S. S. Pandian (1992) put it, that constrains but enables the mass hero's range of cinematic possibility.[20] Discussing Ajith's fiftieth film, *Mankatha* (2011), the director of the film, Venkat Prabhu, discussed with me the balance he had to strike to insert his own mark on the film (e.g., his signature humor, flair, and Hollywoodesque realism) while making a film that would please the audience that watches for Ajith's *style* and mass image. As he said to me, because it is an Ajith film, he has to give "build-ups because his image is like that . . . a larger-than-life image, . . . a little bit beyond reality." If he didn't give such "buildups," the film would risk rejection by audiences, like with Ajith's 2007 film *Kireedam*, which broke with Ajith's "larger-than-life image" and fared poorly at the box office (cf. Pandian 1992:46; Krishnan 2009:202, 259; Srinivas 2009:64–67; Gerritsen 2012:75).[21] Like the SS Music VJ and her unintelligibly *stylish* English, the hero-star's *style* has to be *over* or else it risks underwhelming.

The flipside of this, as Venkat Prabhu hinted at, is that a hero-star often has trouble going back to doing "normal" realistic films once his image as a mass hero has been sedimented. Such attempts to return to realism often fail financially, are criticized by (nonelite) film publics, and thus are avoided by established mass heroes. As Chandrasekhar explained to me, realistic films are a practical impossibility for Vijay (a fact that has more recently presented its own problematics, as discussed in the chapter's post-script):

Ch: *Etārttam paṇṇamuṭiyātu. Pattu pēr sērntu Vijaye aṭikkiṟāṅka. Avaru uṇmaile paṇṇamuṭiyale. Appaṭi sollamuṭiyātu.*

Ch: (Vijay) can't do realism. (Imagine that) ten guys are beating up Vijay together. In real life, he can't do anything. But you can't say/show that.

CN: Fans *ottukkamāṭṭāṅka*?

CN: The fans won't accept it?

Ch: Fans-*um ille*. General-*āvē makkaḷ*. Not only fans. *Janaṅkaḷ*. *Oru* image *vanta piṟaku, koñcam kaṣṭam*. . . . *Sāka kūṭātu*, love failure *āka kūṭātu, itellām oru* accepted hero *uṇṭa ṇṇā (irukkamuṭiyātu)*.

Ch: Not only the fans. Generally, the people. Not only the fans. The public. Once you have an image, it's a little hard. . . . The hero shouldn't die, his love shouldn't fail, all these things can't happen to an accepted hero.

While young actors, then, are contained by the space of the story and its characters, and thus their on-screen actions are ultimately authorized from within the text (or by the director's name), mass heroes exist in a complementary space, elevated yet hemmed in by their own transtextual image and off-screen status as mass heroes, an image and a status that ground, and thus constitute, the text from its outside, that mark and re-mark the text with the hero-star's *style*.[22]

Real-Life Stars

Here we come to a curious but now understandable feature about south Indian mass heroes of this and the last generation: the bigger they get on-screen, the more humble and modest they get off-screen. It is this fact that the youth I worked with mentioned as much as the on-screen image of the hero-star. If they appreciated them, such youth appreciated hero-stars like Vijay, Ajith, and Rajinikanth because they are good people, they do social service, they are humble and modest, and they come from simple socioeconomic backgrounds (Dickey 2001:222ff.; Rajanayagam 2002:299; 2015:134ff.; Rogers 2011:46; Gerritsen 2012; cf. Osella and Osella 2004:235; Srinivas 2009:62, 86). As one Rajinikanth fan from Madurai explained to me,

'In contrast to other film actors . . . who act in real life and on-screen, Rajini doesn't act in real life. He is so simple. He doesn't wear makeup when you see him in real life or in television appearances. He comes as he is: balding, dark-skinned, unshaven, with white hair. If there is a function, he doesn't come late and make everyone wait.

Figure 27. Off-screen and on-screen Rajini: left—Rajinikanth at S. P. Muthuraman's Sankara Rathna award ceremony (2011; photo by A. S. Ganesh for the *New Indian Express*, used with permission); right—Rajinikanth as a *veḷḷai Tamiḻan* ('white Tamil'), from *Sivaji: The Boss* (2007)

Rather, he'll be the first one to come. He never acts like he is better than anyone else. He acts on-screen but not in real life.'

Indeed, this simplicity is part of Rajini's public self-presentation (figure 27). Consider, for example, a 2007 interview on the English news channel NDTV about the release of his film *Sivaji*.[23]

Interviewer: <To the camera> It's not every day that you get to meet and interview the god of Indian cinema. With me is the one and only Rajinikanth. <Turns to Rajini> Sir, thank you very much for talking to us. We know that you do not give interviews normally. There's a lot of expectation and hype around *Sivaji*. And people have been talking about the Rajinikanth *style*, the Rajinikanth *style*. Let's hear it from you. What is the Rajini *style*?

Rajinikanth: <Laughs embarrassedly; rubbing his neck; looking down> See, actually, it's only the media who have made it so big to be frank with you. Now they are comparing Rajinikanth with Amitabh Bachchan.[24] To be frank with you, in the cinema world, Rajinikanth is only a king, probably a king. But Amitabh Bachchan is an emperor.

Interviewer: Don't be very modest.

Rajinikanth: No, it's a fact. So don't compare emperor to a king, right? Ami-*jī* is my inspiration; he is my role model. Okay? And this hype, see whatever-, this is Shankar's [the director's] picture, AVM's [the producers'] (picture). Whole credit goes to Shankar. He's the master, master director. Hats off to him for everything. We should congratulate, we should appreciate everything to Shankar. I am only an actor, just like a puppet-

Interviewer: That is typical Rajini modesty. People say Rajinikanth doesn't do *stylish* stuff; what Rajini does becomes *style*.

Rajinikanth: Maybe. I don't know about that <laughs embarrassedly>. I don't know about that. Maybe. It's a god's grace.

Rajini's comportment in this interview ranges from the submissive to the embarrassed: his nervous laughter, his swaying back and forth, his compact posture, the nervous rubbing of his neck, his downward, avoidant eye gaze, and his quiet, timid voice. At every turn, he humbles himself and praises others: saying that Amitabh Bachchan—referred to intimately as "Ami" but with the honorific "*jī*"—is his superior and "role model" (also note Rajini's third-person self-reference in his first mention of Amitabh Bachchan); saying that the director, Shankar, is the "master"; attributing his success to "god's grace" or to media "hype." He even makes the hard-to-believe assertion that he is "only an actor, just like a puppet." He explicitly humbles himself to the point where the interviewer interrupts him by saying, "That is typical Rajini modesty," a dismissal of Rajini's self-effacing manner that ironically ratifies it through the very act of interruption. Even when Rajini self-attributes status, he hedges: "probably a king," "Maybe. I don't know about that."

This necessity to publicly perform modesty is practically de rigueur for contemporary film stars, manifested in their often quiet and shy public demeanors and their regular performances of public charity, as with Vijay's 2007 birthday, which he celebrated with poor, sick children (Indiaglitz 2007).[25] As the young but established actor Jiiva notes in this regard, "It's very clear, um, people are very emotional here (in Tamil Nadu). So they relate both things [on-screen and off-screen image]. So everything is in a package, everything comes for-, comes in a package. You're a good guy, okay, it's different. You, uh-. 'He has got a very good image, okay. This guy is very good. Come, let's go see this film.' It's like that. 'This guy has a very negative image, ah:::: . . .'." Narrating the "emotional" way in which people in Tamil Nadu think about the hero-star's on-screen and off-screen images as a single "package," Jiiva implies with his final ellipsis and elongated "ah:::: . . ." that to *not* perform acts of modesty off-screen is to risk peril at the hands of audiences at the box office. And indeed, film stars who do not humble themselves off-screen were generally seen by the youth with whom I worked and lived as immodest and arrogant. While everyone agreed, for example, that Simbu is talented, for many, his "head weight," his arrogance, and his off-screen "buildup" is a turnoff and thus a reason to dismiss his attempts at heroism on-screen. My Chennai roommate Sam explained why he didn't watch Simbu films by appealing to his conceitedness as an actor. As Sam elaborated, 'Even in his *first film*, he introduced himself as "Little Superstar" with the same lights as Rajinikanth. But how can he have a name already in his first film? And how can you name yourself that? That is something a director or producer gives you, someone else more senior in the industry gives you. You can't give it to yourself. That's just arrogant!' Here Sam articulates an account of the sociological felicity conditions of successful celebrity naming and the citational "abuse," in the Austinian (1962) sense, of autobaptism. What I would draw attention to is how the extratextual image of the film actor acts as a kind of alibi for the character's on-screen heroism, grounding it through self-effacement off-screen, or in the case of Simbu, as evidence damning the fates of his characters. While on-screen *style* must be *over* for it to be felicitous, this presencing of the mass hero simultaneously requires his off-screen self to perform a lack of *style*. The result is a complex balancing act that is distributed across the split subjectivity of the hero-star.

Filmic acts of *style*, like their reanimations in peer groups, are always multiply voiced, managing through their citational form the dual mandate to differentiate from and defer to one's peers/audience. By framing their filmic acts against their humble "real" selves, mass heroes' on-screen selves become bracketed, always in quotes, as if to equivocally say, "This is not *really* who I am; it's just a reanimation of me by me." Caught between and constituted by multiple mandates, the hero-star's image is split by the screen, each half the other's inverse, each implicitly invoking the other as its justification.[26] Just as young men's double-voiced acts of *style* hedge on their own performances by partially negating them, the hero-star's off-screen simplicity, his modesty, and his constant status-leveling all bracket his on-screen antics, serving as a disavowing caption of that which is, of course, being done by him in his own name.

Of course, self-effacement and condescension are themselves acts of status-raising, for only the person who has something to downplay can downplay it, and only one who is expected to act haughtily (a big-name celebrity) can be appreciated for not doing so (cf. chapter 5). Indeed, this is the dilemma of doing *style* for anyone whose status within his reference group is uncertain, be he a college youth or a young actor: one can't simply be *stylish*, and one can't simply be modest—one has to be both and neither. As one industry insider pointed out to me, if Rajinikanth walks into a director's office with plain dress and slippers, everyone will say how simple he is and praise him. But if a new face appears in the same way, he'll be dismissed out of hand and not taken seriously. (Compare this with Raj and Ralph's observations in chapter 4 regarding use of English, dress, and others' perceptions of the self.) On the other hand, trying to entail *style* without modesty and self-effacement is inherently risky, as the case of the "Little Superstar," Simbu, shows. It is the complex balance of both, this graceful union of opposites, that must be achieved. The citationality of the hero-star in his various cinematic manifestations attempts to manage this union. The total fact of the hero-star is this complex and persistent (inter)citationality: the dialectically reiterative calibration of his multiple images, projected within, across, and outside of his films as a play between over-the-top on-screen *style* and underwhelming off-screen humility.

These comparisons between young men and established hero-stars can only be pushed so far, however. This is because the dynamics of *style* upon which the comparison is drawn are asymmetrically crosscut by the technological mediation of the screen, to say nothing of the social distance between hero-stars and the youth who cite them. Young men in college peer groups primarily display, and hedge on, *style* in the copresence of peers. By contrast, to a degree unavailable to college youth, the hero-star has multiple surrogates circulating at any one time: his physical body, his manifold film characters, his transfilmic image, and the many metadiscursive representations of him (e.g., by fans, in gossip magazines, in newspapers, in television interviews, on Internet forums; cf. Mazumdar 2013).[27] While virtually united by his names and face, each of these surrogates is variously engaging in different acts: some displaying *stylish* fashion, some helping orphans, some flying through the air doing jump kicks, some meditating in the ashram, some rhyming insults at villains, some helping blind kids. Precisely because of the coeval multiplicity of these various images and their densely layered and entangled framings and citations of each other, the hero-star can tack between and unite these disparate images so as to project *both* equality *and* difference in ways that are difficult, if not impossible, in the peer group. This mediation by the screen and the multiplicity of interdiscursively linked avatars that it affords enable the hero-star to perform feats of *style* on-screen that cannot be done in the youth peer group. While youths' acts of *style*, then, tend toward hybridity—where signs of youth status simultaneously disavow themselves and metacommunicate sameness with the peer group—the hero-star's status expressions hypertrophically split themselves across the screen: on the one hand, his on-screen acts of *style* tend toward hyperbolic extremity (if still tempered in ways akin to youth *style*, as discussed above); on the other hand, his acts of humility and self-deprecation, equally hypertrophied, are ultimately deferred to his off-screen self, to other media, other times, and other spaces beyond and beside the filmic. And it is these extremities that makes the hero-star's *style* a site of pleasure and citational utility for his publics (cf. chapter 5's discussion of *stylish* speech on the television screen). What I would emphasize, then, is that youth and their peer groups and mass heroes and their media worlds are part of intersecting but distinct citational economies of *style*, their intersection the achievement of the very linkages and entanglements that *style*, as citational practice and semiotic form, demands and creates.

When Is a Film Text?

In this chapter and the last, I showed how the screen is not something that is projected onto but is a mediating link, something that is projected through. This analysis suggests that we see the textuality of contemporary Tamil commercial cinema—or at least those aspects discussed in these chapters—as the sedimentation of the interdiscursive linkages between the reanimations of film by youth and the reflexive apprehension of, and entanglement with, such reanimation by those involved in filmmaking. The result of such entanglements is a form of status negotiation across, within, and behind the screen as actors, filmmakers, and their audiences attempt to procure a *stylish* leg to stand on, replicating and altering the citational logics of the other side of the screen in the process.

Filmic *style* is inherently interdiscursive, always pointing to another *stylish* act. And it is reflexively so. *Style*, as I've argued, is always presenced in quotes. That which is cited is always marked in one way or another as not quite one's own, as a reanimation of some other act originating from another, more statusful subject or object. The performativity of film to do *style* is contingent on this citationality, the ability of the citation to figurate *this* performance here and now as an instance of *style* by virtue of its grounding in *another* cited performance, which, in being so cited, is figured as its originary moment. This originary moment, however, is not strictly localizable within or outside the film text. That fictive origin, rather, is distributed and dispersed—its performativity the result of an accumulation, a reflexively mediated sedimentation of citationality organized over time and space (Butler 1997).

It is important to see that this interdiscursivity is not simply each side of the screen reflecting, imagining, or imitating the other—that is, it is not the case that youth simply imitate film stars (as I argued in chapter 6) nor that filmmakers simply give youth what (they imagine) they want (as I have suggested in this chapter). Rather, this interdiscursivity is a function of the entanglement *between* these various parties as they engage in their own social projects of negotiating their reference groups through film, orienting and bending the other side of the screen to the dynamics that govern those negotiations in the process. It is a function of the fact that filmic performances of *style* are only ever such if they are entangled and ratified by social others who are themselves reanimators of such *style*.

Further, it is important to see that these are not simply semiotic relations but economic ones as well, that the political economy of film mediates these interdiscursivities, even as they in turn condition the commodity life of film. These entanglements make up what we might call the citational economy of film.

In short, the semiotics of *style*, the economics of the box office, and the various ideologies of the cinematic image that mediate how various publics engage with film materialize *as* film texts, film genres, and hero-stars' "parallel texts." Which is to say that the textuality of commercial Tamil film is mediated by these different logics and social entanglements, even as, of course, it mediates and calibrates them to each other in turn.

As I have argued, this citational economy enables, and in fact requires, filmic *style* to be decoupled from the film text and reanimatable in other contexts, by other film stars and by such films' wider publics. This citational economy requires that the text be perforated, fragmented, and dispersed in sites outside of the film proper. Textual features of mass-hero films such as punch dialogues, *stylish* fashion, "signature" dance steps, and other tropes of "heroism"; these films' intertextual references and compulsive reflexivity; their formulaic narrative arcs and character types—these are all defined by the fact of their repeatability, their citability, their potential to be detached and reanimated elsewhere (and thus, recalling the conclusions of chapter 6, not simply by their representationality). And it is these features that contribute to the distinctively fragmented textuality of commercial mass-hero films, a textuality that is so often interpreted as a sign of industry incompetence ("They don't know how to, or can't, make 'good' films") or audience crudity ("They don't know how to appreciate 'serious' cinema"). From the point of view I have developed in this chapter and the last, however, we can see such textual features as functions of the (meta)semiotic dynamics that govern the performative basis of filmic *style* within a more general economy of youth *style*.

One conclusion to draw from all this is that filmic textuality is, paradoxically, always already located beyond the text, to say nothing of the text's contexts of "production" and "reception." I don't mean this in the sense in which we say that a film text is shaped by its sociohistorical "context." Rather, this exteriority and self-difference of filmic textuality is inherent to the semiotic form and pragmatics of the text (or at least the textual features I have discussed in this chapter). Such films' textuality is woven out of citations that (pre)figure other citations elsewhere (Hanks 1989:113). The very textual form of such film is riddled with proleptic anticipations of other citing events, some filmic and some not. As we've seen, peer-group reanimations, filmmakers' imaginations of them, actors' on-screen and off-screen personas—these interdiscursivities, all projected through the screen, constantly exceed the film text by implicating and being taken up in social sites that are outside the text. Yet by being necessarily mediated by the screen, such interdiscursivities leave their material traces on its surface, not to be "read" or "received," however, but to be brought to life again and again (Peterson 2005).

In order to understand how *style* is woven through and weaves the texture of film, then, our analysis cannot simply be sited outside of the text in some putative "context" (e.g., in doing reception studies, in ethnographies of production, or in both). Rather, it has to be sited in that outside-of-the-text that is already within and across texts in social time and space. This requires us to see the film text as one part, or phase, in a larger semiotic process—an idea for which we can draw inspiration from Edward Sapir (1931a)—and not, as film theorist Christian Metz (1991:755) famously suggested, a one-sided semiotic, a "monodirectional" and "noninteractive" medium where "enunciator and addressee . . . do not exchange their marks along the way" (also see Metz 1982; Bazin 2005:95–124).[28] This complicates the classic film theory position that film is a medium defined by absence, where the desired encounter between the spectator and the profilmic reality behind the screen is always missed (Hansen 1991; Prasad 1998). Rather, we have to see the text as the mediator and outcome of multiple moments of interaction as they come to be mutually oriented to each other vis-à-vis that very text (an argument that I elaborate in the concluding chapter). We have to see the film text as a contact zone and space of encounter (cf. chapter 5 on the television screen).

Linguistic anthropologists have used the term "entextualization" to describe the process by which signs unfolding in space and time contingently come to form coherence as "text," bounded off from their contextual surroundings and hanging together as a construable unity (Silverstein and Urban 1996). Entextualization describes the semiotic movement between singular token signs and the more general semiotic type that they are contingently and emergently taken to constitute (that is, "text"). As Richard Bauman and Charles Briggs (1990; Briggs and Bauman 1992) have argued, constitutive of the very fact of that metasemiotic identity, such text can, and must, be de- and recontextualizable—that is, transported into new contexts and thus, as Jacques Derrida (1998) has argued, cited and altered, repeated and conserved. Text(uality), from this point of view, is a function of the reflexive or metadiscursive mediation of what Michael Silverstein (2005) calls interdiscursivity: the ways discursive events and the signs therein, by being indexically linked to each other, come to be related as part of an intelligible (self-iconic) whole. From this point of view, text(uality) names the entailments of those reflexive operations that construe and create relations between signs as belonging to some putatively unitary identity (Hanks 1989).

This study of Tamil film elucidates this process of entextualization as a process of mediation. It shows the ways in which interdiscursive entanglements between different social parties (e.g., between youth in their peer groups; among actors, filmmakers, stylists, and dance masters negotiating their own career trajectories; and between both) bring into being textual unities—hero-star images, mass-hero genres, particular films, and so on—which, in turn, coordinate those very entanglements, which serve as the point around which these dispersed and otherwise disparate parties orient themselves. And by mediating such entanglements, the textual precipitates of such variegated entanglements are themselves open to, and constituted by, intertextual and interdiscursive links to other so-constituted texts and discursive acts. Such entanglements and links comprise a complex assemblage of textual and nontextual interconnections that while centered around film also always radiate outward from the text in multiple directions. *Style* is the fraying and frayed thread through which such texts come to cohere and adhere. The citationality of doing *style* serves as the knot that tangles films to each other, audiences to filmmakers (and vice versa), actors to other actors, actors to characters to transtextual mass-hero images, the youth peer group to the film set, and so on. Here we see how entextualization is always already a reflexively—that is, citationally—mediated interdiscursive process of mediation and materialization, one that precipitates not simply text artifacts but also genres, aesthetic sensibilities, forms of embodied social practice, subjectivities, and social relations.

These entanglements that weave the (inter)texture of film are neither complete nor total, however. They are open ended, partial, shifting. As I've emphasized, there is always a gap, a difference between the film text, what it cites, and what cites it; between filmmakers' imaginations of their audiences and audiences' actual behaviors; between a hero-star's *style* and youths' citations of it; between a character and the hero-star's image; between that image and the actor's "real-life" self; and so on. The mass-hero film is especially interesting in this regard, for its texture is characterized, even defined, by those gaps—in particular, by the excesses introduced by the film's anticipation of future reanimations, by the impossibility of its self-contained coherence and autonomy. The mass-hero film is a text marked by rips, holes, and loose strands. These are not lacks or deficiencies, of course, but opportunities for engagement that open up out of the text, opportunities for the text to be transported and deployed elsewhere, to be used to other novel ends, to be cited.

In short, what defines the texture of the mass-hero film is that which defines textuality more generally: the ability to be decontextualized and recontextualized, to be cited and transported. In this sense, the mass-hero film distills and explicitly diagrams, even narrativizes, the constitutive tension at the heart of every text—that is, that the condition of possibility and impossibility of text is citationality. The mass-hero film genre manifests this tendency toward detextualization and dissemination as its definitive textual quality, calling attention to this constitutive fact about all texts. Rather than being peripheral to Euro-American film theory and "serious" cinema, does not the Tamil mass film, then, lay threadbare the very essence of filmic textuality itself? Is it, in its fractionated form, with its body riddled with gaps and holes, not textuality (re)incarnate?

Postscript: The Last Mass Hero?

While the mass hero has been one of the iconic figures of Tamil popular culture for the last half-century, actual mass heroes have faced increasing precariousness at the box office for more than the past decade. Even Rajinikanth, whose starring in a film used to be a literal promise of profit (to the point where if his films lost money, he was expected to personally recompense distributors), faced an unexpectedly poor box-office return for his 2002 film *Baba* (for which he did compensate distributors). While there are multiple reasons for the current precarity of mass-hero films, one factor has been the unfolding effects of the Indian economy's liberalization. While economic liberalization began in the mid-1980s and early 1990s, in certain ways its effects were only fully realized in the Tamil film industry in the late 1990s and early 2000s. With the rise in television use (in particular, satellite and cable television; chapter 5), technologies for home viewing (first VHS in the 1980s, then VCD and DVD technologies in the late 1990s and 2000s), and thus rampant piracy (Sundaram 2013), the circulation of film expanded without concomitant increases in producers' ability to reap profits from that circulation. The difficulties of the industry to make ticket sales transparent, to control piracy, to create a viable market for ancillary products, and to maximize profits from television rights, not to mention to fully capitalize on its diaspora market (Velayutham 2008) as "Bollywood" cinema did in the 1990s (Prasad 2003; Rajadhyaksha 2009; Srinivas 2009) have all meant increased risk for producing and distributing big-budget films. One veteran producer went so far as to characterize filmmaking since 2001 as simply a form of "gambling."[29] This has also been driven by ballooning production costs linked to increasing salary demands by major (and minor) stars, increased publicity and marketing costs, and directors' bigger and bigger ambitions in terms of scale and concomitant production quality, as enabled by developments in technology to realize such ambitions (e.g., newer cameras, digital sound, editing software, and more recently, computer graphics).[30] Crucial here have also been changing audience demographics (the decreasing importance of the "family audience" and the increasing importance of young male audiences since the 1990s) and changing audience tastes and sensibilities (e.g., the increased availability of films and television programming from abroad; Pendakur 2005[1996]:153; Nakassis and Dean 2007; Srinivas 2009; Kurai 2012). These sea changes in the film industry have necessitated new business models and new ways of marketing and raising capital, not to mention new genre types and modes of theatrical release and exhibition venues. Yet, as the arrival and quick departure of international production companies in the late 2000s attests, the viability of such new models is anything but set or guaranteed.

All of this has led to a situation in which we are perhaps seeing the last of the mass heroes.[31] Take Vijay, again, as an example. While Vijay weathered the 2000s well, his big-budget mass films in the late 2000s and early 2010s did not fare well at the box office, not to mention in the press and among general (i.e., nonfan) audiences. For many industry insiders with whom I spoke, these failures were symptomatic of the breakdown of the mass-hero "formula," a reflection of the inability of big hero-stars (and producers) to recognize that audiences don't just want "mindless" plots sprinkled with *masala* elements, elaborate fight sequences, high-energy dance songs, and catchy punch dialogues. Or, if they do recognize it, they haven't come up with viable alternatives. The problem, as was often lamented, was that hero-stars like Vijay were sticking to the formula but without any real content, without a good story that made sense and was emotionally gripping. Such actors were "trapped" by their own image, unable to break out of the set recipe that was suffocating them and the industry as a whole.

This is not a new lament, and it should be taken with a grain of salt. In recent years, however, this crisis of image and industry profits has seemingly registered with big hero-stars like Vijay, who have started to diversify the kinds of subjects, genres, film aesthetics, and characters of their films. Indeed, as Vijay's father, Chandrasekhar, explained in our 2010 interview, he was advising Vijay to expand the types of films he was doing. Vijay's fiftieth film, *Sura* (2010), was a flop. As he put it, "We are in the deepest block," a crisis that he thought required Vijay to start making "different movies," movies with nonformulaic but still entertainment-driven stories. And indeed, Vijay's releases in the years following *Sura* have included films erring on the side of relatively muted heroism (e.g., the romantic comedy *Kavalan* [2010] and the lighthearted, multistar film *Nanban* [2012], directed by the hugely popular Shankar) alongside otherwise typical action films (e.g., *Velayutham* [2011], *Thuppakki* [2012], *Thalaivaa* [2013], and most recently *Jilla* [2014]). These films have, overall, succeeded at the box office and with audiences.

But more telling than Vijay's recent film choices and his selective deviations from typical mass-hero fare are the relatively consistent successes of increasingly popular actors like Suriya, Dhanush, Karthi, and Jiiva who have oscillated between story-driven ("class") films and hero-driven ("mass") films, between being an "actor" and being a "star" (cf. Srinivas 2009:210–11). Such actors, at least at this stage in their careers, have consciously avoided doing mass-hero roles too often. Here heroism becomes simply one facet of the actor's oeuvre (and mass films one type of film that an actor acts in) rather than *the* element and telos that determines the actor's image work, his role selections, and his films' narrative forms as a whole.[32] As actors Karthi and Jiiva each explained to me, this oscillation attempts to prevent the star from becoming "trapped." It multiplies the possible textual vehicles for popularity and profits, allowing the actor to avoid being pigeonholed and stereotyped while maintaining a serious engagement with the craft of acting (something important to both Karthi and Jiiva).[33]

From this point of view, rather than being licensed only through the transtextual successes of previous films and the extratextual alibi of the humble real-life persona of the actor, being the mass hero on-screen also presupposes being able to inhabit the figure of the good actor, where doing *style* and heroism on-screen also turns on not *over*doing it by doing it too often, on having acted recently in other films as *not* a mass hero, as just a character in a story.[34] The open question for the future, then, is whether the figure of the mass hero instantiated by iconic hero-stars like M. G. Ramachandran, Rajinikanth, and for a time at least, Vijay is giving way, or has already given way, to forms of on-screen image work that require partially disavowing the figure of the mass hero, even as he is occasionally reanimated, as if to, in effect, envelop and suspend the mass hero in quotation marks as just for a moment, just for a film.

Conclusions

EIGHT

Media's Entanglements

Style's Entanglements

This book has offered an ethnographic account of a particular embodiment of multiplicity and ambivalence, of how a sociologically located experience of liminality manifests as particular semiotic forms that are construed, negotiated, and lived as the very category of youth. Through Tamil youths' own practices of and discourses about *style*, I have endeavored to show how their experiences of liminality come to be managed and produced through citational acts. Such acts harbor multiple voices and desires and manage multiple anxieties, and do so by reanimating objects and subjectivities from elsewhere while reflexively marking those objects and subjectivities as not quite themselves.

Situated by intersecting hierarchies of age and generation, class and caste, gender, language, and region, the college students with whom I worked experienced their positions in such hierarchies as both like and not quite the social coordinates that kept them liminal, excluded, and exterior. Neither a 'big man' nor a 'little boy' but like both, neither a *local* subaltern nor a cosmopolitan elite but like both, neither an English speaker nor just a Tamil speaker but like both, liminality for my friends and hostelmates was felt as a necessity to be more than one thing at once, a requirement to be self-different, to be not quite and not yet and yet alike and almost.

The colleges where I worked enabled and amplified this ambivalence and multiplicity by promising these youth access to middle-class, adult *decency* and social mobility in the liberalized economy, even as they kept the sites and futures of that promise in abeyance. The college brought close and kept distant those very hierarchies wherein youth experienced their own exclusion and in-betweenness, allowing for a moment to pause and play on those hierarchies by figuratively reanimating and deforming them. In the college, acts of *style* responded to but also transformed these experiences of liminality and hierarchy, opening up spaces for youth sociality, aesthetics, value, and subjectivity.

Framing liminality and youth in this way allows us to see that neither are static, structural relations nor stages of a teleological trajectory; instead, they are reflexively produced and performatively productive interdiscursive processes. Youths' acts of *style* offer an example of such dynamic processes and the entailments that follow in their wake.

Central to the pragmatics and metapragmatics of *style* are those mass-mediated forms and subjectivities that youth seize upon and cite in their peer groups: brands and elite consumers, swatches of English and music-television VJs, films and mass heroes. These forms and subjectivities are importantly, in one way or another, exterior to both an adult order of respectability and to these youths' peer groups. By bringing these exteriorities into the peer group by citing them, my college friends and hostelmates attempted to instate an alternative metric of status and value, *style*, inaugurating a space beyond and beside that also stood in the place of and thus partially conserved that which *style* attempted to suspend: those very hierarchies that situated these college students as youth.

The exteriority of such forms and subjectivities was critical to their utility for my college friends, for by always being also sited elsewhere—and thus by being partially untethered from the centripetal peer group—their *stylish* potency could be exaggerated and spectacularly built up, taking a naturalized and seemingly self-grounding, autopoetic form in that not-here-and-now. In their irreducible distance, that other side of the film screen, phone line, and commodity chain presented the promise of resolving and surpassing those tensions that demanded *style* in the peer group. Mass-hero films, music-television programming, and global brand fashions were all sites where my college friends could find something approximating a never-ending horizon of *style*, *style* without its hedging citational marks, *style* unconstrained by the peer group, *style* that was never *over*. It was this abundant excess—as presenced by the mass hero and his films, the music-television VJ and her English, and the elite cosmopolitan and his fashionable brands—that made these media subjects and their semiotic vestments so useful for my college friends to do *style* in their peer groups.

And so problematic. While the seemingly pure performativity of the *stylish* media object makes it immanently usable to do *style*, it also makes it necessary that youth put such forms in quotes, for what makes them desirable to use as *style* (their statusful distance, their seemingly unconstrained excess, etc.) also makes them impossible to use as such in the peer group. Acts of *style* replay and transduce youths' ambivalence about status hierarchies into the very medium that youth mobilize to suspend such hierarchies, doubling and reinscribing that ambivalence as *style*'s citational marks. All that was bracketed in the act of citing a film, a brand, or an English word—invidious difference, exclusion, the responsibility of the future, the stigma of the *local*—threatens to erupt out of its citational containment and dangerously return. This is because, as noted above, the forms through which such alternate sociality, value, and status are *stylish*ly produced already double, and thus conserve, such status hierarchies in the act of displacing them. This is why youths' acts of doing *style* always hedge on themselves, and hedge twice. Acts of *style* abjure forms of adult hierarchy through objects that simultaneously keep in play the very terms of the adult status economy that underwrite such suspended hierarchies (e.g., the 'big man' and the 'little boy' but also class distinctions and the like). This necessitates forestalling the very potential of these objects of *style* to become that which they reanimate (i.e., signs and acts of hierarchical ranking), continually requiring their bracketing and disavowal. This is a double displacement and a double citation, displacing an adult order of things by being like a 'big man' (and a 'little boy') through *stylish* forms that must, at the same time, be marked as not quite themselves, as surfeit, as altered and partial, as deformed. This complex embedding is why doing *style* manifests multiply as an embrace and repudiation, why *style* never simply presences what it reanimates without reflexively putting it in quotes. Otherwise, it would be *over*. The distance that makes brands, English, and mass-hero films *stylish*, then, requires another distance, a prophylactic suspension of the very forms that are represenced in the peer group.

At the same time, citing global brands, music-television VJs, and mass heroes brings them close, for only then can their performative potency be yoked and made usable in youths' own practices. Citing such objects and subjects draws them into the orbit of the peer group, tethering their fates to youths' ambivalent and liminal social worlds. As we have seen, music-television VJs, film heroes, and garment producers are entangled by youths' citational acts of *style*, required to pursue their own social projects (making a film, hosting a television show, designing and selling garments) by orienting and calibrating those projects to the very youth who would cite them. This calibration reiterates the dynamics of the youth peer group on the "production" side of the screen and commodity chain, a camera obscura that doubles youths' doubling, requiring film heroes, VJs, and garment producers to reflexively manage repetition of and difference from those social others with respect to which they themselves are liminal and entangled: bigger and smaller actors, international and regional VJs, foreign brand companies and local competitors, and most importantly, their youth publics, audiences, and target markets. This calibration renders the practices of film heroes, VJs, and garment producers, not unlike the youth who cite them, citational, both in the sense of citing those social others *and* in the sense of continually putting their own citational practices in quotation marks, be it by the humble off-screen persona of the actor hedging on his on-screen heroism, the disfluent Tamil of English-fluent VJs mitigating the *local*ness of their hybrid speech, or garment producers' surfeit designs circumventing the feared illegalities of copying. In this performative economy of *style*, citations entangle what and whom they cite, and thus they calibrate and co-orient the act and agent of citing and the cited, disseminating them through the interdiscursive linkages and loops that their entanglement constitutes.

Citation leaves its mark. Youths' citations of brands, English, and film stars; film actors' citations of other film actors and of their imagined youth publics; local garment producers' citations of global brands and their youth target markets and their aesthetics of brandedness; music-television producers' and VJs' citations of other stations and of the Tamil speech of their youth audiences—these acts are the very stuff of youth culture's mass mediation in Tamil Nadu. And the citationality of these acts—and the calibration of such citationalities to each other—materializes *as* the very media forms in question. They make the media object a contact zone between otherwise distant social parties that are, by the fact of their mass mediation, entangled, even intimate. Such media forms come to be reflexively marked by these entanglements, by the possibility, actuality, and necessity of being taken up elsewhere, altered and appropriated by others. Such media become citational and open to citation—or rather, as I suggest below, to the extent that they are media at all, they *are* citational and open to citation.

From this point of view, then, doing *style* denotes a process of mass mediation and materialization constituted by the fact of its multiply entangled citationalities. In concluding this book, I explore what *style*'s entanglements can tell us about mass mediation more generally and about the role of citationality in those entanglements that constitute and materialize media.

Media's Entanglements

In this book, I have approached *style*'s entanglements as a form of mediation, with media understood as the conditions of possibility and precipitates of such entanglements, as their beginning and end points. To function as a medium is to be materialized by and in the very events and relations that it makes possible, even as such media, manifested in particular media forms, exceed and resist being totalized by those events and relations.[1] This is a curious circularity—performative even. Even more curiously, as this book has shown, to study these entanglements requires bracketing the analytic and ontological primacy of the forms that such entanglements materialize, whether it be a brand, a linguistic code, or a film text or genre.

This simultaneous analytic bracketing and engagement is not dissimilar to the ways in which the Tamil youth that I have discussed in this book, through doing *style*, also problematize and suspend the ontologies that they reanimate in their peer groups, undermining the rigid indexicality of brands, the denotationality of English, and the representationality of film texts. Like them, we have to problematize the assumption that things like brands, linguistic codes, and film texts exist out there in the world as coherent, autonomous, and stable forms, pre- and postdating the relations they mediate. To study these entanglements, then, means having to account for, and put into question, what Valentin Voloshinov (1986:48) referred to as the all too ready-at-hand "inert crust" (in his case, grammatical structure) that is precipitated by creative events of semiosis over time and space. To do this means seeing such analytics and ontologies, the "inert crust" of our object of study, as achievements (Murphy 2015), as the outcomes of this curious circularity that is at the heart of mediation.

As this book suggests, one important way to study media is to study the entanglements that constitute them. How do such entanglements come to be, and how do they come to be with regularity? In particular, how do we account for those entanglements that are not face-to-face, where the parties involved are not always explicitly (or even knowingly) oriented to the other sides of the screen, line, or commodity chain, where the parties involved are also engaged in their own independent social projects that may ultimately have little to do with the media that they mobilize in those very projects? Making a film, reanimating filmic forms on the college stage, displaying a garment on campus, designing and manufacturing a shirt in a textile workshop, speaking English with friends in the hostel, and recording a television program in the studio are all complex events unto themselves with their own internal dynamics, concerns, and politics. And just as any media form harbors the multiple interests, values, and desires of the social actors whose projects materialize it, any one of those social projects itself radiates out in multiple directions, being entangled with other social projects still and thus materializing other media forms besides. Dancing to a Vijay song for a department function (chapter 6), for example, is not just about reanimating film to do *style*; it is also part of the constitution of the department and college space itself. And it participates in manifesting not only film texts and star images but other media forms as well, such as figure 20 in chapter 6 and even this book as a whole. Similarly, filming a movie is not simply about making a film; it is also caught up in investing money, expressing directors' artistic visions, and advancing individual actors', stylists', and dance masters' careers, among many other social projects and media (e.g., account books, screenplays, posters, press interviews). This is a complex terrain, for of all the possible entanglements mediated by a particular media form, not all are equally relevant to the pragmatics of its being/becoming, just as for each such social project, there are many more media at play besides the one that we may be provisionally focusing on.

How do we determine what the points of contact are, the sites of friction and collusion that are relevant to the constitution of any particular media form, to its contingent ontogenesis *as* a media form of such-and-such an identifiable type across social time and space? That is, how do we methodologically and analytically study how multiple social actors and their projects come to be calibrated to each other vis-à-vis the "same" media object, that object to which those very projects are mutually oriented to varying degrees and varying ends? And how does such partial, mutual orientation and engagement bring that form into being, sustaining it as the hinge or medium through which the complex relationship between these social actors and their projects is constituted, through which they act and interact?

These are empirical questions. There are many ways that social projects might be calibrated to each other vis-à-vis some media form or medium. Political economy names one familiar principle wherein media objects qua commodities come into being through the calibration of culture-industrial "production" and "consumption" (e.g., via market principles like supply and demand). Others include media and language ideologies (say, in evaluating speech on television); modes of spectatorship and genres (say, in appraising and reanimating a mass hero); aesthetic discourses (say, in determining what counts as a good "*look*" in fashion); intellectual property regimes; "audience measurement" and other "market feedback technologies" (Ang 1991; Hardt 1999; Lury 2004); and many others still. The list of such linkages is perhaps innumerable and, in any case, most are certainly larger than can be studied for any particular medium.

Some linkages, however, are more important than others from the vantage point of the pragmatics of the media form's or medium's becoming and being. And some are more illuminating in the contexts of certain arguments than others. This book, for example, has put much importance on the citationality of *style* as entangling various social actors, calibrating their projects and activities to each other, and thus iteratively materializing *as* the media form around which those citational entanglements, projects, and activities themselves dialectically pivot. Wrought by citation, this media form is rendered open to those who would come to be entangled by it, inviting them in turn to propel their practices and projects by reanimating and refashioning the media form—now altered, now conserved—once again. More generally, I would suggest that citationality is a central principle underwriting mass mediation. Any medium and any media object is already marked by its iterability, is already citational and constituted by citational acts, enabling it to entangle what or who is cited and to live through those entanglements as a dialectical unfolding of reflexively marked repetition and difference.

One way of framing this is to say that the study of mass mediation necessarily involves triangulating between "producers," "consumers," and the media forms to which producers and consumers are commonly oriented *as* producers or consumers, thereby detailing how production is calibrated to consumption, how consumption feeds back into production, and so on. In certain measure, this book has done just that. Yet such a formulation doesn't go far enough to realize its own critical interventions—namely, problematizing the parceling of mass mediation into discrete, autonomous, and linearly organized phases and sites by blurring and rendering them nondistinct and coterminous and, further, refusing to reduce the complex and mutually entangled social projects that are part and parcel of processes of mass mediation to simple glosses such as "production" or "consumption" (or "reception"; chapter 6).

These critical interventions have, in fact, already been made in the name of so-called new, or digital, media that have proliferated in the late twentieth and early twenty-first centuries. In contrast to "old" media (such as radio, film, and television), it has been argued that digital media, like videogames, websites, and the like, blur and collapse the traditional understanding of mass mediation as a top-down, linear process of distinct phases of production, circulation, and consumption (Jenkins, Ford, and Green 2013), prompting some authors to merge terms like "production" and "consumption" into portmanteau neologisms like "prosumption" (Manovich 2001; cf. Toffler 1980) or "produsage" (Bruns 2008).

Important to this argument is the so-called interactivity of such media: the ways in which new media objects like web 2.0 sites (Bruns 2008; Manovich 2008), open-source software (O'Reilly 2005), and even brands (Lury 2004; Arvidsson 2005; chapter 3) are able to incorporate, through their "interface" (Manovich 2001:63–115; Gane and Beer 2008:53–70), users' engagements with them.[2] These media objects are altered in and through their very use, their material and encoded textual form the palimpsest of so many actions and interactions by various social parties. Such media are thereby "underdetermined" (Poster 1999:16). They require users in order to be completed and hence are open to, and invite, appropriation and alteration. This interactivity is said to make such media "new," differentiating them from so-called old media that are relatively unreactive and fixed, whose very material form and textuality are supposedly autonomous from, and even indifferent to, their consumers and audiences.[3]

As those critical of the notion that new media are inherently interactive have argued, however, interactivity is as much ideological discourse, and salvific hope and fetish, as it is a technological or material property of new media.[4] Or, as I would emphasize, (non)interactivity, like citationality, is an achievement, an empirical, sociohistorical fact about how certain engagements with media forms (namely, "consumption" or "production," or "prosumption") come to be (made to be) regularly calibrated to past and future events of engagement, where mutually presupposing and entailing interdiscursive relationships between contextually particular moments of semiosis come to be institutionalized and thus materialized *as* the media form or medium in question (Rafaeli 1988).[5]

Interactivity, in this sense, is not unique to new media, as discussion of the interactive nature of surfeit brand garments, music-television programming and its mediatized youth slang, and film texts and hero-star images in this book have all showed. While digital media represent one highly salient site for reflecting on the interactive quality of media (precisely because such media presuppose, and reflexively focalize, this very quality in their design and normative functioning), this book's discussion of *style* has suggested that we can and must also locate and study such interactivity elsewhere as well, in places that we might otherwise not expect.

My point isn't to assert the sameness of so-called old and new media or to deny their very real differences. Rather, it is to elucidate what I see as one productive avenue for the study of media and mediation that cuts across such a distinction—namely, asking what are the (meta)semiotic processes that are at issue in the continual, ongoing achievement and constitution of various media. This is, I would suggest, the very question that interactivity poses to all media by the very fact of their mediating capacity. Citationality is one of its answers. From this point of view, the question isn't whether or not some media are interactive as such, but how, by what politics and in what kinds of political economies, and to what ends? How open are different media objects to alteration and replication, and what is the quality of that openness? (Indeed, "open" and "closed" seem too simple as glosses for the complex ways in which media entangle and are entangled.) To whom are they open or closed and to what degree? How are they made to be so open or closed? Through what complex interdiscursivities, infrastructures, and technologies and by and with respect to what social projects does interaction performatively happen or fail to happen? And at what level of generality (e.g., at the level of genres, of token artifacts) and by what temporality does interaction happen? While web 2.0 sites, presumably, are instantly alterable at the type level by users' real-time usage of token instances of them, a mass hero's image in Tamil cinema is a function of many films stretched over years and mediated by many points of contact (with the hero's audiences and larger publics, other actors, directors, producers, stylists, industry magazines, censors, fan clubs, etc.).

The achievement of this calibration, or interactivity, between those entangled by media is never perfect. It is riddled with gaps and differences between the social actors, events, and projects whose mutual orientation to the "same" media form materializes "it." This is, of course, implied by the very notion of interactivity, by the presumption that a medium is the outcome *and* precondition of particular social relations and practices (and thus stands apart from them, even as it cannot exist without them) and by the notion that interactivity and mediality are achievements (and thus are continually emergent and contingent). It is also implied by the citationality of the acts that forge (and undermine) such calibrations, of the gaps reflexively managed between the act of citing and that which it cites and of the instabilities of the media forms that are cited into and out of being. As this in turn implies, the ontologies of different media are variably (un)stable across time, space, and social domain. It is always an open, empirical question whether, across sites and relations of entanglement, we are dealing with the "same" media form or medium at all.

Such an approach to mass mediation, then, must also be about discalibration, about failure, friction, and the indifference and insensitivity of social parties to each other.[6] As the discussion of brand garments in chapters 2 and 3 showed, for example, the stabilization of a Tamil youth aesthetics of brandedness, materialized in and as a market of surfeits, is as much about the relations and mutual orientations between local producers and their youth target market as it is about the nonrelations and disorientations between global capital, brand production located in India for export, and production for the local market. It is this partial calibration that materializes the particular kinds of garments that one finds made for and taken up in nonelite youth Tamil fashion, that one finds mediating and mediated by youth sociality in the college. Similarly, chapters 4–7 showed how the close distance of the screen is founded on various distances and gaps—between VJs and youth callers and audiences (chapters 4–5) and between film heroes and their citing publics (chapters 6–7)—that, while partially sutured by citationality, necessarily remain. This dynamic close distance opens up a complex linguistic field of youth language on and off the screen, just as it constitutes the perforated and nonautonomous texture of the mass hero and his films.

Mass mediation, then, is a fragile achievement. But as I've suggested throughout the book, the gaps between parties entangled by and through media, their indifferences and resistances, their appropriations and misunderstandings, are not noise in the circuit or blockage in the channel but sites of becoming where new possibilities of use, meaning, and materiality are waiting in the wings. Again, as discussion of youth fashion in chapters 2 and 3 showed, gaps in the ontology of brand are precisely the sites from which an aesthetics of brandedness can come to be actualized in a surfeit materiality, where performativities of *style* and possibilities of aesthetic form and social relationality can emerge out of an ontology of brand that is cited, as it were, out of existence—and similarly for *stylish* linguistic forms (chapters 4–5) and film texts/genres and hero-star images (chapters 6–7).

Calibration is a relative notion. There are degrees of tightness in the linkages across the entangled social sites and events that materialize media. The smaller these gaps are kept and the more they tend to be ideologically glossed over, the more naturalized the media form becomes, the more it seems to determine its usages, and the more what it is made to do in particular contexts seems to be inherent in the form itself. The tighter these linkages and the more stably they are managed, the less we are able to imagine other uses and other horizons of possibility, and in certain cases, the less we are able to see them when they indeed exist. One task of this approach to mass mediation is to find those chinks, those sites of (dis)connection and (non)contact, of potential alteration and change, and to study how they are ideologically managed and mismanaged—that is, how those (dis)calibrations are made, maintained, changed, glossed over, or ignored—and thus how these media come into stabilized, if precarious and temporary, being.

If the notion of medium implies and presupposes a curious circularity, it is because the citationalities that constitute its material and intelligible form reach both forward and backward, invoking and conserving its pasts and anticipating and entailing its futures, its here-and-now and its elsewheres, and in doing so, dialectically unfold as the very medium in question. This requires an achievement of calibration, the articulation and coordination of social projects that, by all being oriented to that "same" thing, keep it in a stabilized yet dynamic state of becoming. The achievement of this performativity, this mass mediation, constitutes the particularity as well as the generality of any semistable media form, any semistable medium. This, we might say, catachrestically reanimating my young Tamil friends, is the doing *style* of mass mediation.

Notes

CHAPTER ONE

1. Herein lies a complex citational history, for mustaches such as Anthony's (*arivā mīsai*, 'machete mustache' in Tamil; also known as an "imperial" [partial beard] mustache in the United States and Britain) are enmeshed both with south Indian regional and caste styles and with colonial British military grooming styles. Among the British military, large, lustrous mustaches were prompted by nineteenth-century encounters with the mustachioed French military (whose mustaches were said to be "appurtenances of terror") and, importantly for us here, with the British's Indian subjects (Brendon 2007:127). In the first half of the nineteenth century, British soldiers were required to be clean-shaven, while the sepoys were allowed facial hair (Reynolds 1949:273). Given Indian associations of facial hair with virility and the shaven face with effeminacy, and an increasingly felt need by the British to assert racial and martial superiority, mustaches became compulsory for British soldiers in India from 1854 to 1916 (Brendon 2007:127–28). More generally, facial hair flourished on male British faces in the latter half of the nineteenth century with the so-called mustache movement.
2. Not all mustaches are linked to respectability, of course. The excessively large and thus aggressive mustache can also transgress the civility of *mariyātai*. There is a complex and historically deep semiotics and sociology of adult facial hair that can be elaborated here (in particular, as it interfaces with caste, as seen in various entries of Thurston and Rangachari 1909; Srinivas 1976:68, 152; Olivelle 1998; Osella and Osella 2006:12, 46, 209–10; Gorringe and Rafanell 2007:103). My interest, however, is in contextualizing how young men today

figure their own facial hair vis-à-vis their stereotypes of adult facial hair (which simplifies this complexity to a certain extent). On the cultural concept of *mariyātai*, see Mines 2005:81–100; on its linguistic manifestations, see Levinson 1977 and Scherl 1996. On 'big men' in Tamil Nadu, see Mines and Gourishankar 1990 and Mines 1994.

3. In Anthony's case, such an ample mustache indexed forms of masculinity at odds with the urbane, *decent* subject that was supposed to be cultivated in/by the college (cf. Jeffrey et al. 2008). Before they went on job interviews, many of these students would make sure to—among other things, like putting on a tie, getting a haircut, and wearing cologne—shave or trim their facial hair, conforming to their idea of what a young professional should look like.
4. Beards are highly meaningful in Tamil Nadu; they can index "love failure" (*kātal tōlvi*), or depression more generally, and are also associated with non-normative masculinities (cf. Srinivas 1976:152; Olivelle 1998)—from the *rowdy* to the mentally unstable and the mendicant—as well as, for certain beard styles, religious identity (orthodox Islam).
5. Suriya's mustache is also reminiscent of Kamal Hassan's famous *arivā mīsai* from the 1992 film *Thevar Magan*, where he plays the eponymous 'son of Thevar' (the name of a dominant, martial caste in the Madurai region), drawing on and reinforcing the stereotypical associations of this style of mustache (see notes 1 and 2 in this chapter).
6. Such ambivalent citational acts, as reanimations in Erving Goffman's (1981) sense of "animation," represence forms while reflexively marking particular stances toward what is being presenced. In this case, reanimating another's act marks differences in what Goffman terms the author (who composes the act's form), the principal (who is responsible for it, who stands by and behind it), and the animator (who materializes it), hence reanimation's complex (meta)semiotic form, as Goffman (1981:227ff.) notes in his discussion of the "embedding" of utterances (and the various footings implied therein). See the main text for more discussion.
7. We might compare *style* to Sanjay Srivastava's (2007:227ff.) discussion of what he calls "ishtyle" (utilizing the north Indian borrowing of the English word "style") and "fashion." In discussing Indian sex and health magazine advertisements, Srivastava analytically distinguishes "fashion," a cosmopolitan aesthetic of the upper-middle classes, from "ishtyle," an aesthetics of surface among the "non–middle classes" that stands in an "*excessive* relationship with fashion" (ibid.:228, original emphasis). Ishtyle "wants fashion" (ibid.), makes overtures to it, and thus is entangled by it. Taking up these terms in their discussion of Malayali youth dress, Caroline and Filippo Osella (2007) make a more stark differentiation: "ishtyle" denotes a working-class, vernacular, film-driven mode of status and aesthetics (what their informants called "*freak style*") as opposed to a middle-class focus on "fashion" and global trends (cf. Osella and Osella 1999). While there are resonances among my discussion, Srivastava's, and the Osellas's (cf. Nakassis 2010:295), there

are also some differences. First, while Srivastava notes that ishtyle (and here, *style*) is always already interlinked to questions of what he calls "fashion," I would also emphasize that *style*'s relationship to upper-middle-class modes of consumption (e.g., brands and English, as discussed in chapters 2 and 4) is not a straightforward one of "wanting" but is more ambivalent. Second, the students with whom I worked were liminally located between the two class segments that "ishtyle" and "fashion" index. Further, they were part of an institution—the college—that they hoped would move them across these segments. *Style* expresses and intervenes in that liminality (and thus mediates these two terms), problematizing any clear isomorphism between ishtyle or fashion and *style* (or for that matter, with what my young friends called "*fashion*," a word often used along with "*style*" to denote something trendy and new). A further complication is that Tamil film fashion (on and off the screen) is—as Srivastava notes in the north Indian case—wrapped up with, and disseminates, global fashion.

8. While both "*style*" and "*stylish*" are used in Tamil with roughly equivalent meanings (and both as nouns), "*style*" is more common and can be used in a wider number of constructions. In my own discussion, rather than write "*style*-ish" for the adjectival form of the Tamil word "*style*," I simply write "*stylish*."

9. In this book I interchangeably use the terms "media form" and "media object" for those mass-mediated artifacts, signs, texts, and genres (or fractions thereof) that youth reanimate in their peer groups. This is a heterogeneous set that includes, but also cuts across, how we typically unitize media (e.g., as entextualized commodity forms such as programs or films), comprising not only swatches of linguistic form, visual design elements, dance movements, and mustaches but also television programs, registers of language, film texts and genres, garments, and brands. These are not "objects" in the canonical way we figure things like, say, chairs (but neither perhaps are chairs). Rather, they are semiotic objects constituted and materialized by their metasemiotic objectification (cf. Silverstein and Urban 1996). Part material object, part culturally genred form, these fractions of mass mediation are united by the fact of being cited by Tamil youth to do *style*. (In these cases, it is the act of citation that objectifies them.) The terms "media form" and "media object," then, conflate distinctions of (material) token and (genred) type (following the fact that citational acts may reanimate either or both of them). While I often move between discussion of tokens and types of media objects/forms, my concerns lie mainly with types of media objects/forms. See the main text in this chapter and chapter 8 for more discussion.

10. "English-medium" and "Tamil-medium" refer to the English and Tamil languages, respectively, being used as the languages of instruction and examination. While all departments in the colleges where I worked (except literature departments) offered English-medium streams, only certain departments offered Tamil-medium streams. In addition to a bachelors in

Tamil literature, the government college in Chennai that I worked in also offered a Tamil-medium bachelor's degree in history, while the autonomous Madurai colleges that I worked in offered Tamil-medium bachelor's degrees in economics. Both courses of study were considered to be unprestigious and to have little "value" in the job market. The autonomous college in Chennai where I worked offered no Tamil-medium undergraduate degrees besides its bachelors in Tamil literature. Even in English-medium courses, however, teaching and classroom discussion was often conducted in Tamil. (Some classes were conducted almost entirely in Tamil, with only the "notes"—that is, the materials that would be tested on examinations—dictated in English.) The amount of Tamil depended on students' and professors' (lack of) comfort with English. As English competence was generally higher in the more prestigious, or more expensive, departments and colleges, instruction in those colleges and departments was more likely to be in English than Tamil. See following main text and note 19 in this chapter for more discussion.

11. Population data for cities in Tamil Nadu that are discussed in this book are taken from the 2011 census (accessed January 26, 2015, http://www.census.tn.nic.in).
12. By "elite" I mean colleges that have a national reputation for excellence and draw the most competitive students; by "semielite" I mean colleges that have a regional reputation for excellence, but are perceived as less prestigious and less competitive than elite colleges. The distinction also registers the different, if overlapping, economic, social, and cultural capital of colleges' student bodies. These terms are my own and are rough due to the fact that, as I discuss in the main text, student demographics and the perceived "value" of liberal arts education have been undergoing dramatic change in recent decades.
13. Colleges in India are affiliated with either government or private degree-granting universities. The colleges I worked in, whether they were autonomous or not, were all affiliated with government universities and received subsidies from the state, though to varying degrees.
14. All of the colleges I worked in were coeducational at the postgraduate level with the exception of the women's college. Note that saying that the elite Chennai college was Catholic or that the Madurai colleges were founded by Protestant missionaries does not imply that only Christian students attended. Students from every community attended these colleges (as per government reservations), though these colleges did have more Christian students than represented in the general population (given the administrations' discretion with their "management quota," which at the Catholic college's aided courses, for example, was 50 percent).
15. Here the noun "Orientalist" refers to a generation of scholar-administrators working in early British India. It is distinct from, though not completely unrelated to, Edward Said's (1977) use of the term "Orientalism" and its adjectival derivation "Orientalist." See Trautmann 1997:22ff. for discussion.

16. Female education has been an issue of reform in India since the nineteenth century, though its ends in the nineteenth and much of the twentieth century largely focused on uplift of the family and nation by producing a better wife and mother rather than gender equity per se. On this, see Chanana 1988; 1994; Jeffrey and Jeffrey 1994; Seymour 2002; Seth 2007; Chandra 2012.
17. Reservations are akin to American "affirmative action." The early adoption of reservation policies in higher education in the Madras Presidency, P. Radhakrishnan (1993) argues, were not simply due to the non-Brahmin politics of the Justice Party, but had a longer history linked to Britain's worry (and collection of statistics) about the dominance of, and thus dependence upon, Brahmins in colonial administration and higher education (also see Fuller and Narasimhan 2014:9–10, 61–89). The victory of the non-Brahmin Justice Party in the first direct election in 1920 saw the state government instate reservations in higher education to mitigate Brahmin dominance and to increase access for otherwise subordinate social groups.
18. Shah (2013[2005]) and Tilak (2013) note that in India, there were 3 universities and 27 colleges in 1857, 19 universities and 500 colleges in 1947, 320 universities and 16,000 colleges in 2005, with close to 634 universities and 33,000 colleges in 2013. Fuller and Narasimhan (2014:94) report that while between 1949 and 1950, only 5,500 engineering graduates were produced, by 1970, the output was around 20,000. In 1997, 65,000 graduates were produced, and in 2006, 220,000 were produced. Chanana (2013[2007]) notes that self-financing colleges in Tamil Nadu increased from 54 to 247 between 1993 and 2001 (while government arts and sciences colleges increased from 56 to 60, and aided colleges from 132 to 133), while self-financed engineering colleges increased from 71 to 212 between 1996 and 2001 (government and aided engineering colleges remained the same at 7 and 3, respectively; also see Fuller and Narasimhan 2014:95). As of 2014, there are more than 500 self-financed engineering colleges in Tamil Nadu. Enrollments in private colleges in Tamil Nadu from 1996 to 2001 increased from 20,250 to 55,500, and in 2010, 150,000 places were available.
19. Tamil-medium education is generally less prestigious and less expensive than its English-medium counterparts. This is an effect both of the Indian education system's colonial heritage and of the current global political economy. On vernacular-medium versus English-medium schooling in north India, see LaDousa 2014 and Proctor 2014; see Ramanathan 2005 for discussion in the college context; for general discussion of English-medium education in India, see Annamalai 1991; 2004.
20. On the complex and contentious debates surrounding inequality in contemporary higher education, see the essays in Tilak 2013.
21. This is complicated because the historical reputation of the government college where I did research is as a center of student politics, and thus as a tough and rowdy place. More than *style*, the keyword to denote youth status in this college was *gettu* (literally, 'prestige,' 'dominance'). Like *style*, *gettu* was used

in all the colleges I worked in. It was used for an overlapping set of practices and objects as *style* (though *gettu* could be used to talk about adults, while *style* almost never was), and often with a similar, if not the same sense (see Nakassis 2010:95–108). By contrast to *style* (as a mode of ego-focal individuation performed for an audience), *gettu* was often used to typify acts or objects that instated hierarchical ranking vis-à-vis social others. Hence, unlike *style*, its use was more often to outline relationships of dominance between groups (e.g., seniors vs. juniors, between cliques, or between colleges), or to describe particularly dominant individuals in the college (e.g., the head, or "*tala*," of a bus route, see Nakassis 2010:100; n.d.). *Gettu* is generally associated with a more rugged working-class masculinity (it was almost never used to typify women), a toughness that figurated, and sometimes instantiated, physical domination and violence. This was most stark in the comparisons made by the students at the two Chennai colleges where I worked. When typifying the other college, *gettu* and *style* took on class-inflected meanings, even if both terms were used at both colleges largely to denote the same objects and activities. While the government college was known as a *gettāna* college ('tough college'), the Catholic college was a *style-āna* college ('*stylish* college'). The terms were also used slightly differently in the two colleges. Students from the elite college (who were more affluent) used *gettu* and *style* with more overlap (thus eliding the class-linked indexicalities and semantics of these two terms and their extensions), while the government college students differentiated *style* and *gettu* to a greater extent. In general, it was the case that less affluent students were more likely to point to more affluent students as the ones who really do *style*, though as I suggest in this chapter and argue in chapter 2, this reveals a complex ambivalence toward class that the economy of *style* necessitates.

22. As Deborah Durham (2004) has argued, "youth" is akin to a linguistic shifter (also Bucholtz 2002:527–28), an indexical sign whose reference "shifts" based on who is animating it and in what context. As this implies, youth is not a homogeneous category of analysis or experience. As the history and anthropology of youth has demonstrated, the category is historically and culturally variable. Certainly, youth as it is currently imagined and experienced in South Asia is a relatively recent phenomenon (Nandy 2004[1987]; Saraswathi 1999; Liechty 2003; Lukose 2009), differentially experienced by age, class, caste, gender, and region—among other sociological and psychological variables (cf. Comaroff and Comaroff 2005; de Boeck and Honwana 2005; Cole and Durham 2008 and references therein). Indeed, for reasons linked to their quick integration into the workforce (especially for the working-class poor) or into the kin or community group (especially for those from highly orthodox families, and especially for young women), many young people in Tamil Nadu have little to no experience of the age-category youth as discussed in this book. For the students with whom I worked, however, youth was a salient framing of their social practices and modes of

sociality. And given explosions of youth-targeting media and marketing, the expansion of education institutions, and the steadily rising age of marriage, the experience of youth is important for an ever-increasing number of people in Tamil Nadu.

But more than its cultural and historical variability, saying that youth is a shifter implies that it is multiply realizable in and across events of interaction. Shifters like youth are ambivalent signs, their uses and meanings specific to their contexts, and yet simultaneously independent of them. If youth is a shifter, then what counts as youth depends on the pragmatics of the particular interactions in which the category itself is in play, on the social relations and contexts it presupposes and brings into being, and crucially, on how the category is cited or troped on in novel ways. To be a shifter means precisely being open to the proliferation of the not quite, to the porousness of normativity that gives the indexical category in question its performative potentiality. Hence when it comes to youth, "old" men can act *like* (or by being *like*, even *be*) youths, and "young" men can, depending on the context, not be considered youth at all (Meiu 2014). This is also why the demographic extension of youth is never sufficient to exhaust its social meanings, why its boundaries can never be completely shored up, and why it can never be completely fixed. It is why youth is always a gradient category, a composite effect, only ever inhabited in partial ways and only some of the time (Johnson-Hanks 2002). The important questions, then, are under what conditions and in what contexts is youth as a category intelligible, and to what effect? Through what kinds of performances is youth inhabited and made intelligible and palpable to others, its qualities of personhood performatively materialized in the world? In a word, how is youth and its semiotic vestments, as linguistic anthropologists would put it (Silverstein 2003; Agha 2007), enregistered?

23. Anthropologists have long approached youth and adolescence as a transitory stage between childhood and adulthood. As Mary Bucholtz (2002) has argued, this has conferred upon studies of youth an adult-centric point of view, treating youth as not quite adults, as unfinished and only partially socialized beings. The result has often been that youth culture is not treated as its own site of cultural creativity and autonomous normativity. While Bucholtz (2002) is correct in warning anthropologists not to reduce youth practices to a teleology of adulthood, *style* as youth practice and discourse cannot be understood except as that which animates and keeps in abeyance the adult (and the child). The issue, then, is not just an epistemological problem for anthropologists. It is also an issue for those with whom we work; Tamil youth reflexively figurate their experience as liminally between childhood and adulthood, a fact that must be taken into account in theorizing their social practices.

At the same time, as Deborah Durham (2008:166) has noted, by approaching youth through notions of the rite of passage (Van Gennep 1960) and ritual liminality (Turner 1967) anthropologists have tended to romanticize the figure of youth as the vanguard of change, social development, and resistance to the status quo. Often such studies analyze the ways in which youth cultural practices appropriate and recontextualize hegemonic, often global social forms (say, a brand, an English phrase, a mustache), doubling them in the act of defying them and, in doing so, opening up new social and political horizons (Willis 1977; Hebdige 1979; Comaroff and Comaroff 2005:27–29; de Boeck and Honwana 2005:10; Lukose 2009; Jeffrey 2010: 72–102). In this book I too highlight the liminality of youth and their creative appropriations, or as I prefer, citations. As I show, however, less a question of resistance or subversion, youths' *stylish* citations have everything to do with the politics of the peer group, with the necessity to manage intimacies and solidarities with peers while negotiating status through transgressions of adult normativity (Nakassis 2013d).

24. Many, if not all, youth cultures around the world are characterized by the dynamics of liminality that I discuss in this book (see, e.g., Willis 1977; Hebdige 1979; Cosgrove 1984; Rampton 1995; Gondola 1999; Osella and Osella 1999; 2000b; Bucholtz 2002; 2011; Weiss 2002; Lukose 2009; Tetreault 2009; Jeffrey 2010; Newell 2012). Though, in this, youth cultures are certainly not unique. Examples of this dynamic of liminality, ambivalence, and citationality can be found in writing about (post)coloniality (Fanon 2008[1952]; Bhabha 2004[1993]; Chatterjee 1993; Taussig 1993:176–92; Povinelli 2002; Blackburn 2003), fashion (Simmel 1998[1904]), flirtation (Simmel 1984[1909]), queer sexuality and gender (Newton 1972; Butler 1993; 1997; Harvey 2002; Hall 2005), the ("new") middle classes (Liechty 2003:61–86; Fernandes 2006; Dickey 2013), ritual (Turner 1967), performance (Brecht 1964; Turner 1982; Schechner 1985), and psychodynamics (Freud 1995[1915]; 1995[1925]; 1938; Bateson 1972).
25. For these youth, the discourse of "society" agentified a generalized experience of hierarchy and subordination, the real and imagined strictures and adult normativities of propriety and respectability that they felt their own practices to push up against. In my discussion, neither "adult" nor "society" should be taken as descriptions of how such entities exist in the world as such, but how they must be taken to exist by young people so that their own activities and experiences are intelligible to them and pragmatically efficacious in their peer groups. I do little to unpack what one could possibly mean by "society" as an analytical construct useful for describing social life. Instead I use it as a placeholder, as young people themselves use it, to explicate youth sociality.
26. On "maturity" and its connection with youth status and the lifecycle in the Kerala context, see Osella and Osella 2000b.
27. Such acts were not primarily addressed to, or designed for, adults. More than rebellion, youth fashion, slang, smoking, and the like were directed toward one's peers (Juluri 2003; Bucholtz 2011:12; cf. Willis 1977:12–13). When

statusful adults, especially elder kin, were present as possible addressees or bystanders of such acts, youth were likely to quickly put out their cigarettes, clean up their speech, and squash their *style*. My hostelmates often underwent a minor makeover before they went back home—cutting their hair, removing their earrings, and putting on staid, muted dress.

28. Cf. Schwartz and Merten's (1967:461ff.) discussion of the "hoody" and the "socie," Willis's (1977:13ff.) discussion of "lads" versus "ear'oles," and Eckert's (2000) discussion of "jocks" and "burnouts." All such categories divide youth based on alignment to adult authority. Jock/burnout and socie/hoody primarily vest such differences in class identities. By contrast, the opposition between the *cinna paiyan* and the *periya āḷ* figurates student difference through age categories (cf. Willis 1977:15 on the childishness of the "ear'oles").
29. This experimentation and freedom was experienced more as a form of leisure and play than anything else. In contrast to the Indian colleges that Craig Jeffrey (2010) and Ritty Lukose (2009) have written about, the student bodies of the colleges where I worked were relatively apolitical. This was partially due to the historical particularities of Tamil Nadu (compared with Uttar Pradesh and Kerala) and to the institutional particularities of the colleges where I worked. In the autonomous colleges where I worked, students largely had no formal rights to contest collegial decisions. The college administration reserved the right to expel students without appeal, effectively reducing any possible political power that students might have. Even in the government college in Chennai where I worked—a college famous for its political activism and for being a training ground for politicians—political activity was generally absent, the result of a concerted effort by the college administration in the 1990s to stamp out student politics in the name of "academic excellence" and "discipline" (Nakassis n.d.).
30. A common explanation for why my friends and hostelmates did something—like grow out their hair, pierce their ears, or grow their thumb or pinky nail—was simply that they could *not* do it at home or in school. College was figured by these students as a space of relative freedom in direct contrast to the stifling rules of the home or school. In general, my college friends made every effort to not seem like school students (Nakassis 2010:45).
31. During the time of my fieldwork, there were a number of caste conflicts between Dalit and Thevar students in the law college of Chennai, as well as at various government colleges in southern Tamil Nadu. Such conflicts, however, did not spill over into the colleges where I worked, though students were relatively sensitive about issues of caste, a fact registered by how they avoided the subject altogether. In this book, I am interested to highlight what kinds of sociality, subjectivity, aesthetics, and value emerge in the space of this ideological disavowal of caste and other forms of inequality. While there is more that could be explored as to how caste and community mediated the practices that I discuss in this book—for example, in spaces where

such disavowals were not operative or failed to hold—and how "caste feeling," as students sometimes put it (Nakassis 2014:183), may have persisted and insinuated itself within peer groups, I do not pursue such avenues of inquiry.

32. In distinction to the other colleges I worked at, where department affiliation was one of the key modes of student identity and peer-group organization, in the Chennai government college, for most day scholars, one's "bus route"—that organization and identity defined by the named city bus route that one took to the college—was a more important mode of peer-group organization and identity. On bus routes, see Nakassis 2010:72–75, 98–105; n.d.
33. For postgraduate students, year cohorts would be ranked as first-year MA students, second-year MA students, and M.Phil students, each more "senior" than the previous and to the undergraduates.
34. The term "mediatization" is also used by media and communication scholars, though with a different, if not totally unrelated, sense (see, e.g., Schulz 2004; Livingstone 2009; Lundby 2009; Couldry and Hepp 2013; Hjarvard and Peterson 2013). This large literature is primarily concerned with what happens to social forms ("culture" and "society") when they come into the technological and institutional ambit of particular media (cf. McLuhan 1964; Baudrillard 1994; Bolter and Grusin 1999). Like Agha (2011a; 2011b), this literature has tried to shift focus away from the typically narrow definitions of mass media and from concerns with media "effects." But rather than situating media within larger interdiscursive networks (of which their status as "mass media" is a particular phase), this literature attempts to understand how media institutions and technologies increasingly (often, in epochal terms) come to "mediatize" nonmediatized spaces and activities. In this book, my focus is not on what happens to putatively nonmediatized practices when they become mediatized. Such a formulation already presumes a distinct temporal boundary between the nonmediatized and the mediatized, as well as imputing an ontological autonomy and stability to "the media" (Deacon and Staneyer 2014). As I argue in this book, to study mass mediation is to fundamentally problematize and blur the coordinates by which we could even pose this formulation. This requires not focusing on "the media" or their "logics" as they mediatize social actors' practices and projects (which are thereby figured as external to such media), but on the relations and entanglements between such actors and their projects as they come to materialize *as* particular media and media objects. The question here, then, is how we are to account for how media objects come into being through interdiscursive linkages that continually, if tenuously, sustain such media objects as the site of coordination between such so-linked projects.
35. The converse methodological emphasis would focus primarily on a particular site of media production or a particular media form and trace out its entanglements with its multiple publics.
36. The temporalities and socioinfrastructural organization of so-called new me-

dia are certainly different from so-called old media, a fact that reflections on new media's novelty have pointed out. The socioinfrastructural organization of certain old (i.e., broadcast) media similarly, if inversely, motivate reanalyses of their functioning as top-down in nature and as involving a radical disconnect of producer, text, and audience. And yet, what such reanalyses of old media obscure is precisely what those of new media exaggerate. What differs between so-called old and new media are the scale and rate of spatiotemporal calibration (or "interactivity") between the multiple parties that are oriented to the media objects that their relationships materialize. This is, I would suggest, ultimately not a difference in kind. Rather, it is a difference in how different media reflexively prefigure particular ideologies of circulation and use in their very technomaterial form across a history of use, reanalysis, institutionalization, and reuse. See chapter 8 for more discussion.

CHAPTER TWO

1. The Oxford English Dictionary (3rd edition; 2008) has its first entry for "ragging" in 1788 Britain, in the sense of scolding or boisterously teasing (see Davis 1899:133–47 and Peck 1904:432–33 on ragging at Oxford in the late nineteenth century and 1840s, respectively). The sense of "ritually humiliating new army recruits or university students by physical or verbal bullying" is a later development, attributed by the OED to early twentieth-century Britain and South Asia. Today, the term "ragging" is predominantly used in South Asia, with specific reference to higher education.
2. This was ironic, since Sebastian also narrated to me how he refused to be ragged by his seniors, standing up to them and thus eliciting more ragging from them. Sebastian's steadfast courage in the face of ragging was one of the reasons his same-year hostelmates looked up to him, even if he refused to participate in the college's economy of *style*, as I describe later in the chapter.
3. This hierarchical intimacy was modeled by the fictive patrilineal kinterms used across years (Nakassis 2014): male seniors addressed their male juniors with "*tambi*" ('younger brother') and received "*aṇṇan*" ('older brother') in return. This relationship not only entailed juniors' subordination to seniors but also entailed seniors' responsibility to advise and help out their juniors. One mode of ragging that diagrams the ambivalence of this intimacy within hierarchy is the practice of seniors forcing freshers to take them out to the movies (moviegoing typically being an activity done with peers) while demanding that they pay for their tickets (a command entailing their juniors' subordination).
4. For some students, this reformulation of age and generational difference as year difference was upsetting. Arun was a second-year student when we lived in the same Madurai hostel. Before coming to Madurai, he had discontinued his studies at another college, making him one year older than his cohort members. Over the course of the next two years, he increasingly began to

withdraw from the social life of the hostel partly because his self-image was hurt by the fact that his same-year cohort members addressed and referred to him in ways that were dissonant with their age difference but consonant with their year equality. On top of that, his third-year seniors, who were the same age as he, addressed and referred to him with terms reserved for juniors, and thus, by implication, as being of lower status. While he found it upsetting, protestation was likely to fall on deaf ears since his hostelmates and department classmates would reject any appeals to age as a condition of how they should treat him.

5. My discussion here is particular to clothing and accessories. Other brand commodities, such as cell phones, operated by a different set of dynamics.
6. The actual effects of the rise of the British textile industry on the Indian textile industry were not uniform by market, region, or type of clothing. Bernard Cohn (1989:338–40) notes that Lancashire cloths mainly displaced mid- and low-grade Indian cotton textiles, while Indian fine textile industries remained less affected, in particular in the Madras Presidency (Baker 1984:338, 393; Parthasarathi 2013[2009]:432–33; on other regions, see Roy 2010:258–65). On a more general questioning, and complexifying, of the narrative of Indian decline and European ascendency, see the essays in Riello and Roy 2013[2009]a; on the south Indian context in particular, see Wendt 2013[2009].
7. The first swadeshi movement took place in Bengal in the first decade of the twentieth century. It was prompted by Lord Curzon's call to partition Bengal. It was the swadeshi movement's first expression of dissatisfaction with colonialism, expressed through cloth, among other things, that Gandhi scaled up to the national level in the 1920s (Cohn 1989:343–45; Tarlo 1996:23–61).
8. The meanings of "khadi" and "swadeshi" were contested and labile, of course, even in Gandhi's own discourse. For an early Gandhi, swadeshi cloth(ing) required indigenously grown fibers (preferably cotton), hand-spun and hand-woven by Indian subjects in India. Under critique, however, often by Gandhi's own industrialist supporters, swadeshi sometimes was expanded to include indigenously made industrial yarn and fabrics (Trivedi 2007).
9. In contrast to the rural self-sufficiency and nonindustrial technology embodied and emblematized by khadi, however, Nehru emphasized heavy industrialization as the route for national uplift and development. Textile policy in the decades after independence balanced concessions to handloom production (to protect it from competition with Indian mills and powerlooms, the latter of which were "officially unrecognized and illegal" [Roy 2010:271]) and protections for the industrial sector (to protect it from international competition). One ironic effect of this policy was the emergence of a more informal and decentralized powerloom industry in places like Tiruppur that took advantage of low-wage labor and the concessions reserved for handloom production (Roy 2010:271; also see Chari 2004). It is this section of the industry that boomed with the liberalization of the textile industry in

the 1980s, increasingly manufacturing global brand garments for export, as I discuss in chapter 3.

10. Here, khadi also evinces the postliberalization emergence of "ethnic chic" design (Tarlo 1996:284–317; Trivedi 2007:155; Kuldova 2013), itself an example of the utilization of "Indian tradition" as a source of "world-class" brand (or designer) value (Mazzarella 2003). As one might expect, the government's Khadi Brand is not the only brand of khadi, with Khaddar brand and Khaadi brand clothing on the market, to say nothing of other surfeits in circulation. Of course, khadi had long been branded. However, the point here is that since liberalization, khadi has come under the ambit of a brand metadiscourse that reckons its economic life not primarily in terms of its production origins (as did Gandhi's discourse on swadeshi and khadi) but instead in terms of its marketing, fashionability (Mazzarella 2010), and more recently, legal trademarkability (see, e.g., Khadi and Village Industries Commission, Standing Order No. 1724, February 19, 2014, accessed February 1, 2015, http://www.kvic.org.in/update/circulars/SO-1724-Final.pdf).
11. Indeed, swadeshi itself operated under the metasign of various brand names (e.g., in textile production) and engaged in rather modern marketing methods (Trivedi 2007; cf. Mazzarella 2010). Bernard Cohn (1989:327, 342) also points to the way in which the conspicuous display of textile trademarks on fabrics functioned as a mode of distinction among Indian subjects in the nineteenth century, indicating that an aesthetics of brandedness (of a different variety, of course) is not simply a postliberalization artifact.
12. Access to the brand through its surfeits is not particular to the postliberalization era (e.g., see Mazzarella 2003:258–63), even if the scale and visibility of brand logics (and their surfeits) have increased with liberalization. Consider a quote from a pirated 1928 edition of the book *Mathimosa Villakkam*, a book about fraud in Chennai:

    > Gandhi is the most venerated and respected of names among the present-day public. Therefore all kinds of stuff are being named for him. This is indeed highly disgusting. Gandhi hotel, Gandhi umbrella, Gandhi soda, Gandhi bidi, Gandhi cigarette, Gandhi balm, Gandhi vest, Gandhi & co., Gandhi saree, Gandhi buttons, Gandhi matches and other such unmentionable brands. Is Mahatma Gandhi manufacturing these? Does he smoke bidis and cigarettes? . . . Alas! Some are even selling toddy wearing a Gandhi cap! (cited in Venkatachalapathy 2004:25)

    Also see Trivedi (2007:51) on the problem of inauthentic khadi, and Parthasarathi (2010:567–68, 570) on the proliferation of European imitations of Indian textiles circulating in African, Asian, and European markets in the eighteenth century. The surfeit has always been at the heart of the brand (Nakassis 2013a).
13. "Brand" and "original," importantly, denote the good as such, and thus include export-surplus and grey-market goods.

14. Moreover, "duplicates" made in China are also "*local*," and hence aren't "foreign"; the term "foreign" is reserved for goods that come from the United States, Europe, Singapore, and other first-world locales.
15. Diesel opened official retail stores in India in 2010, and in Chennai in 2013 in the high-end mall Phoenix MarketCity.
16. The intersection of youth fashion aesthetics and concepts of status with brand commodities produces an ambivalent doubling. It is precisely because of this doubling that I use both the terms "surfeit" (a term that presumes upon the brand ontology as its origo) and "brandedness" (a term that motions beyond it), each term representing a complementary, if contradictory, face of the liminality created through youths' citational practices. Outlining this ambivalent relationship requires us to keep these two ontological relations—brand and brandedness, brand and surfeit—in a kind of stereoscopic double vision without falling to the illusion that two eyes truly see as one, or even see the same thing. Surfeit (an indexical notion that implies an excess beyond some identity to which it is anchored) is a term I use to discuss the pragmatics of transgressing the brand ontology. Brandedness (a relatively iconic notion that denotes qualities of similarity irrespective of questions of identity per se) is a term I use to indicate the space opened up through that transgression. This is an aesthetic space that has its own logics and pragmatics distinct from that of the brand and its hierarchies of value. Each term partakes of the other, mixing a play of indexicality and iconicity, difference and sameness that is constitutive of the citational act more generally, as discussion throughout the book highlights.
17. Caroline and Filippo Osella's (1999; 2000a; 2000b; 2007) and Ritty Lukose's (2009:66–71) discussions of youth fashion in the neighboring south Indian state of Kerala bear many resonances with my discussion of *style* here. The Osellas show how consumption in postliberalization Kerala mediates, and is mediated by, aspirational projects of self and group transformation and mobility as they come to be traversed by and projected across hierarchies of caste, class, and age. Particularly useful is how they point out the homologies of age and class/caste hierarchy as they come to be expressed in youth and subaltern fashion, both of which are transient, flashy, and bodily oriented. Where my analysis diverges, however, is in my insistence on framing questions of youth fashion and hierarchy from the reflexive vantage of youth themselves rather than from the viewpoint of the normative telos of this lifecycle and class hierarchy: the landed, economically secure, high-caste male adult. In this way I follow the Osellas's (1998) work on friendship, intimacy, and romance, where they show how, from youths' liminal viewpoint, age and gender hierarchies appear rather differently. The question I ask, then, is if the brand ontology delineates its own hierarchy of value—original/copy, real/fake, licit/illicit—which, within young Tamil men's peer groups, are linked to local class and age hierarchies, then what does this hierarchy look like from their viewpoints? Besides and beyond the telos, what others social

forms and experiences emerge from an experience of hierarchy that cannot be reduced back to the terms of that hierarchy?

I also hesitate to reduce *style* to a form of "commodified masculinity" (Lukose 2009:66) or to a mode of consumption or fashion-consciousness per se. While it is the case that *style* involves the conspicuous consumption of fashionable commoditized signs (e.g., brands and English), it also includes a range of social practices, such as whistling in the theatre, riding the "footboard" of the bus, romance, and wearing the same shirt at the same time as your friends. These are all *style* because they index exteriority, individuate and foreground their user(s), and are transgressive of adult propriety. And while consuming some commodities can perform this function, they are not the only way that such interactional work can be done.

18. The shirt worn with a *vēṣṭi* might also be stitched from a cotton blend or synthetic fabric. On more formal occasions the shirt and *vēṣṭi* might be made from silk. An older, precolonial dress style involved a *vēṣṭi* with an unstitched cloth, made of cotton or on formal occasions silk, which would cover the upper body. Sometimes collarless tunics are worn with *vēṣṭi*s. Despite these variations, in its most stereotyped and common contemporary form this dress style involves white cotton *vēṣṭi*s and white button-down collared shirts.
19. The emblematic sartorial style associated with the Dravidian party politician involves this "white on white" dress along with a *tuṇṭu*, a small, white cotton cloth worn on the shoulder, with the bottom edges of the *vēṣṭi* and *tuṇṭu* adorned with the party's colors. Hence "*tuṇṭukkāraṅka*" (literally, 'towel people') is one term for DMK (Dravida Munnetra Kazhagam, or 'Dravidian Progress Federation') party men (E. Annamalai, personal communication, August 22, 2014).
20. On a trip in 2014, I came across a Chennai brand of T-shirts, "Dude தமிழா" (Dude *Tamiḻā*) in a high-end mall (note the linguistic diagram of cosmopolitan/vernacular youth cool; see chapter 4). Such shirts used Tamil script to hiply (meta)communicate fashion (Parthasarathy 2014). I didn't observe such use of Tamil script in fashion during my fieldwork period and I wonder if—with the exception of the students of the elite Catholic college in Chennai perhaps—such shirts would have been popular among students (see chapter 4 on the aesthetics of Englishness).
21. Tailored garments weren't necessarily non*stylish*, though to the extent that they were they often partook of the aesthetics of the *stylish* readymade. Indeed, one Chennai tailor noted to me that much of his business involved making tailored clothing look and fit like readymades. Alternatively, formals might be worn in way that did *style*—for example, rolling up the sleeves, unbuttoning the top buttons, or (un)tucking the shirt in a particular way.
22. This isn't to say that students' dress drastically and immediately changed after college, though sometimes it did. Rather, it is to say that the indexicality of such dress turned on students' understandings of age, the lifecycle, and

the informality of their time as undergraduates (as is evinced by the staid, formal dress of many postgraduate students who, as undergraduates, used to dress *stylish*ly).

23. A common point of view of college administrators was that students need rules and discipline to be controlled. Without discipline, they would go "berserk," one hostel warden explained—smoking cigarettes until their lungs burst, drinking alcohol until they poisoned themselves, watching cinema until they went blind, and beating each other in fights until thoroughly black and blue. At the same time, by naturalizing such male youth excess, this discourse expected and enabled it. Further, the colleges where I lived and worked were (positively) considered to give relatively more "freedom" than other colleges, resulting in an ambivalent stance to student discipline that often turned a blind eye to students' (minor) transgressions (chapter 1).
24. On similar associations of the foreign in other contexts, see Tarlo 1996:23–61; Weiss 2002; Vann 2006; Yurchak 2006:156–206; Luvaas 2009; Manning 2009; Newell 2012.
25. Tamil youths' *style* recalls, if with important differences, the dynamics of other youth cultures and their use of clothing, such as migrant youth in Kerala (Osella and Osella 1999), punks, mods, and rastas in post–World War II Britain (Hebdige 1979), zoot-suiters in the United States (Cosgrove 1984), *saga* boys or dudes in Trinidad (Miller 1995), *sapeur*s in Congo and France (Gondola 1999), and *bluffeur*s in Cote d'Ivoire (Newell 2012).
26. Here I say "relatively" because, in contrast to the ethnometapragmatic presupposition that *mariyātai* merely reflects fixed social rank, *mariyātai* is of course also made and unmade through emergent interaction, as Diane Mines (2005:81–100) has argued. The converse, of course, is that *style* presupposes a fluidity that itself glosses over the ways in which doing *style* may come to be experienced and rationalized as relatively rigid and fixed vis-à-vis particular social types of people, as discussion later in this chapter shows (also see chapter 5).
27. Herein lies a conundrum, of course, one that plagues many such performative acts (Butler 1993). For if to do *style* presumes that one has the requisite status to back it up (i.e., has fulfilled the relevant Austinian felicity conditions), how does one get that status if not through doing *style*? This conundrum is the product of the fact that *style* is interactionally emergent and negotiated—that is, it is a relatively entailing form of status, rather than an institutionally backed, relatively presupposing form of status (though see note 26 in this chapter). It is precisely the citationality of *style* that, through its simultaneous assertion and disavowal, attempts to tentatively entail the status that doing *style* itself seems to presuppose (cf. Nakassis 2013b). See the main text in this chapter and chapter 7 for more discussion.
28. In addition to claims about personhood, metadiscourse about *style* often took the form of aesthetic claims; for example, a student with a tough-looking face might be able to pull off certain kinds of *style* (e.g., an earring),

while someone with a baby face might not. Or just the opposite, as Sam noted explaining why he, with his hairless face, wore an earring. It made him look older and tougher.

29. This discourse that "culture" or "native place" differentially licenses *style* turned on an interlinked and nested set of spatialized hierarchies regarding the naturalness (and quantity/intensity) of *style*: Western countries > other foreign countries > India; north India > other south Indian states > Tamil Nadu; Chennai > other cities in Tamil Nadu > rural Tamil Nadu.
30. While Stephan's ethnolinguistic background was Malayali, this fact was not part of his peers' justifications of his *style*, though such an appeal would generally fall in line with the kind of rationalizations that I describe in the main text (also see note 29 in this chapter).
31. Similarly, many of my sartorial deviations from the norm were rendered intelligible by the idea that people in the United States naturally did *style*. Most confusing for youth, in fact, was why I didn't do more *style* (cf. Lukose 2009:77).
32. One can compare the third-person focality of this discourse on *style* to invocations of the relatively more status-presupposing concept of *mariyātai*, which can be commanded precisely by explicitly appealing to the hierarchical principle that grounds the social difference between the subject and those from whom he demands respect (though also see notes 26 and 27 in this chapter).
33. See Barthes 1983[1967]:267–68 on such rationalizations of quality as a "rhetoric" of fashion (also Douglas and Isherwood 1996[1979]:85).
34. At the same time, to say that these young men know the difference between the "real" and the "fake" but take up a stance of indifference isn't to say that lower-middle- and middle-class young men are secretly doing brand calculations even as they feign disregard for brand authenticity and authorization—which is to say that Yuvaraj's disavowals and Sam's silences are not of a fundamentally different kind of response from the generalized, routinized, everyday brand indifference that characterized youths' aesthetics of brandedness. In my experience, such indifference, and even ignorance, was genuine, even if it was a response to a more general contradiction. When such contradictions surfaced, they were met with disavowal. In the everyday of the college, however, they often simply took the form of a habitual indifference.
35. The lower-middle- and middle-class young women with whom I worked often explained that it was rich girls in elite colleges who engaged with such fashion, wearing T-shirts, jeans, and the like. These nonelite women indicated, by contrast, that they could not wear such clothing. Or at least not at their homes, in their neighborhoods, or on their college campuses. When they moved out of spaces regimented by the knowing, patriarchal gaze of "society" (be it on a college "tour," on a trip to a metropolitan city, or for some, out of the country), however, they could more easily wear such cloth-

ing without fear of policing, a claim that I found to be true on the college tour that I went on with the third-year students of a particular coeducational department in the Catholic college where I worked.

36. This is not to say that women's fashion in India has remained or remains static, for it has not and does not. In addition to the nineteenth-century adoption of Western fabrics, women's clothing styles were dynamic during this period, with the spread of blouses, petticoats, shoes, and jackets, to say nothing of the spread of the sari itself for groups who previously wore other styles (Tarlo 1996:46). In the recent history of south India, one major shift in women's dress has been toward north Indian styles—in particular, the salwar kameez and chudhitar among unmarried and upper-class women (Osella and Osella 2007; Lukose 2009:75–76; see note 37 in this chapter).
37. As Ritty Lukose (2009:54–95) has detailed in her ethnography of a Kerala college, such dress indexes (or perhaps we might say, cites) a modern femininity in that it simultaneously eschews "traditional" south Indian dress styles such as the rural-indexing, old-fashioned dhavani (or half-sari) and the sari (associated with adult women and, in the college, female professors) *and* Western dress styles like jeans, T-shirts, and miniskirts. By being associated with dress from elsewhere—most proximately, metropolitan cities, and more distantly, north India—chudhitars and salwar kameezs participate in an aesthetics of exteriority that, while not typified as *style*, resembles it (Osella and Osella 2007). At the same time, such dress is considered demure, comfortable, and appropriately feminine in that it loosely covers most of the body in cloth.
38. See Chatterjee 1993 and Seth 2007:129–58 on colonial representations of this English-educated femininity.
39. See chapter 4 for the story of Gina, a student in a women's Madurai college who was socially ostracized until she changed her dress (from jeans and T-shirts to more "homely" chudhitars) and speech (from English to Tamil).
40. My point here is *not* that brandedness is the brand in drag, nor that it is parodic mimicry. Such glosses fail to describe the complex dynamics, experiences, and pragmatics of youth fashion that I have detailed in this chapter.
41. Here we find resonance with, but also difference from, Michael Taussig's (1993) discussion of mimesis. Resonance because here too we see a play of indexical contact and iconic similitude, difference and sameness, as the grounds upon which young Tamil men sartorially cite the brand to do *style*. Yet this is no straightforward unequivocal attempt to capture the auratic Otherness of the brand, to control it or dominate it, or to become those who authentically and legitimately adorn themselves with it (as I discuss more in the main text that follows). It is, rather, part of opening up another world of youth sociality and fashion, perhaps not unlike some of the Cuna men that Taussig discusses, whose mimetic objects—which also include Western-style clothes—serve other purposes than simply accessing the worlds of those they mime (e.g., curing, crossing over to the spirit world, bringing out Cuna spiritual powers more generally).

42. This form of future-oriented temporality has been emphasized in much work on youth cultures (Liechty 2003; Cole and Durham 2008; Cole 2010; Jeffrey 2010). To this body of scholarship, I would add that the temporality involved here is managed by, and created through, citational acts. Such citationality entails a present whose future is immanent in it and yet partially shunted out of vision, suspended even as it is animated. It is precisely that present-future that *style* simultaneously makes palpable and holds in abeyance (Liechty 2003:241; Lukose 2009:71). Deferrals of time and personhood are only ever expressible by taking material form in some present moment. The brand surfeit and its aesthetics of brandedness is one such example of the materialization of deferral.

CHAPTER THREE

1. While in this chapter I use the singular term "producer," this may include a number of different biographical individuals in a number of different roles: owner of a workshop, copywriter, graphic designer, computer operator, machine operator, tailor, finisher, and so on.
2. For theoretical discussion of the semiotics of trademark and brand, see Coombe 1998; Mazzarella 2003; Moore 2003; Manning 2010; Nakassis 2012a; 2012b; 2013a; 2013c; 2013e; in press.
3. We should not assume that either brand or brandedness is singular or coherent, of course. There are surely many different aesthetics of brandedness, just as the brand ontology itself is variable historically, regionally, and by commodity type, as discussion in this and the last chapter shows. Working out these differences is critical to theorizing the brand, especially given the dissemination, elaboration, and transformation of the brand concept as it has been insinuated into more and more domains of semiotic practice.
4. At the policy level this began with the 1985 Textile Policy, which began liberalizations of the textile industry by easing restrictions (e.g., removing concessions to the handloom industry that constrained powerloom production) and enabling the import of equipment (Roy 2010:271). The New Economic Policy of 1991 further liberalized the textile industry, delicensing production, reducing controls, and encouraging export-led growth. In 1995, with India's signing of the General Agreement on Tariffs and Trade, focus was given to increasing both textile exports and imports. These reforms have further allowed for increases in allowable foreign direct investment, decreases in import and excise duties, removal of the manufacture of readymade woven garments and knitwear from the small-scale industries (SSI) reservation, as well as providing schemes to upgrade the industry's technology and infrastructure, among other changes to promote export-oriented production (Verma 2007). As Sharad Chari (2004:228–37, 240–47, 264–68, 278) shows for Tiruppur, this boom was also contingent on a number of other factors that complexify the simple thesis that liberalization simply led to the export

boom, including the decentralization of production and the weakening of labor unions (which had their own complex internal dynamics linked to the Nehruvian dispensation—e.g., the privileging of handlooms over power-looms; see note 9 in chapter 2 and note 5 in this chapter), as well as other contingencies, such as, for example, the entrance of "a strange character," the Italian capitalist Antonio Verona, who "opened up Tiruppur" to large-scale export in the early 1980s (ibid:236–37).

5. As Sharad Chari (2004) and Tirthankar Roy (2010) point out, one of the effects of liberalization was to further weaken labor unions in the textile industry, creating a highly insecure and lower-paid workforce composed of an increased number of workers from poorer rural areas and women (cf. Vann 2005; Manning and Uplisashvili 2007; Thomas 2009; Luvaas 2010; Crăciun 2012).
6. Of course, it isn't only garments produced for foreign brands that create such overage. There is also overage from garments produced for Indian brands. However, relative to designer Western brands (or brands so construed), apparel brands that are understood to be Indian are not as likely to be seen as aesthetically or commercially viable by local producers for duplication or imitation (see discussion in chapter 2 on the oxymoron "Indian brand" in the context of *stylish* youth fashion). In addition, given that Indian-brand garments compete in domestic markets at prices that are relatively close to the surfeits that circulate therein, we might expect Indian-brand companies to more rigorously police their brand's surfeits. In short, the duplicate and brand-inspired production that I discuss in this chapter rests largely for its designs on brands thought to be "foreign" (and Western in particular).
7. On the emergence and expansion of industrialized textile production in the Madras Presidency in the late nineteenth and the first half of the twentieth centuries, see Baker 1984:338–72.
8. This isn't to imply that all youth fashion originates in Kongunadu or Chennai. It certainly doesn't, with clothing coming from production centers in Bombay, Bangalore, and Ludhiana, to say nothing of China, Bangladesh, and other countries still. At the same time, a significant portion of what circulates in urban Tamil Nadu, as indicated from my research with retailers, finds its origins in Kongunadu or Chennai.
9. It is important to note that not all stores operated in this way. Certain boutiques in Madurai and Chennai operated by more selectively cultivating their selections. Such stores, in my experience, had higher prices and catered to more affluent consumers.
10. "Spread" refers to the distribution of variants of some product, for example by size or color. As the spread of surplus is linked to contingencies in the production process, export surplus is often unevenly distributed with respect to such variables. There may, for example, not be enough medium sizes for a wholesaler to be interested in buying some product.
11. Sharad Chari (2004:80–84) argues that uncertainties in the standardization

and temporality of knitwear manufacture in Tiruppur are a function of (i) an ideology of physicality (that knitwear, given its elastic nature cannot be woven in large, standardized lots but only in small quantities and varieties; cf. the problem of "spread" noted in the main text) and (ii) the fickle fluctuations and seasonality of fashion markets, which buyers attempt to anticipate at the last possible minute, necessitating short, strict schedules that can be difficult for manufacturers to abide. The result is that risk is devolved to outsourced manufacturers, which inevitably increases the circulation of surplus in domestic markets, among other things (e.g., encouraging decentralization and increasing the precarity of labor). As with my discussion in the main text of this chapter, here we see how the global political economy of textile production increases the circulation of brand commodities in local markets, but independently of questions of local demand for particular brands per se.

12. Against this trickle-down account of fashion, we might also suggest that in this case, this pattern is produced by the differential relationship that elites and nonelites have, on the one hand, to the circulation and production of branded forms and, on the other hand, to the metadiscourses that attempt to imbue them with value (Nakassis 2010:393–95). While urban elites are attuned to, and consume, (the metadiscourses of) brands that are fashionable in foreign markets—for which brand-commodity manufacture in India is calibrated—fashion brands also circulate among nonelite youth according to a logic that is partially independent of such elite consumption and the brand metadiscourses to which it is oriented. This isn't to say that a "trickle down" effect doesn't exist; indeed, mass-media representations of elites in television and film are clearly one principle for the movement of brand fashions across classes, as I discuss in chapters 6 and 7. Rather, the point is that, trickle down notwithstanding, the cycling of branded forms among nonelite youth seems to follow more closely the vagaries of export-oriented production schedules and their subsequent uptake in locally oriented garment production than it does the *specific* brand tastes of the elite in India or of consumers abroad.
13. As Diesel's sourcing agent in Chennai told me in 2008, Diesel had no interest in policing brand surfeits at the time; for them, if anything, such surfeits were footpath advertisements for when they would enter the retail market (as they did in 2010).
14. Whether this was sincere or willful ignorance of intellectual property law so as to deny culpability is unclear, though my impression was that many local producers did indeed believe that their modifications and hybridizations were legal. In any case, given the murky and changing status of intellectual property law in Europe, the United States, and India (Gangjee 2008), such stances toward intellectual property law are unsurprising.
15. Here we come up to the limits of legal doctrines like "consumer confusion" and more recent notions like "disassociation," "dilution," and "tarnishment" of brand image (Bently 2008; Davis 2008; Ginsburg 2008; Manning 2010). The brand surfeits I have discussed in this and the last chapter confuse no

one as to their origin. In fact, they are not even read as indexing any (brand) origin except for some vague notion of exteriority (the "foreign"). From this, it follows that they cannot tarnish or dilute particular brands. Without the brand identity to hold together various brand "meanings" or associations, there is nothing to tarnish and no one for whom it can be tarnished. See Nakassis 2012a:715–18 for more discussion.

16. The phrase "brand heartlands" refers not to geographic places but to ideological imaginaries and regimes of brand authenticity, of which certain places are recruited as metonymic emblems. In this sense, to speak of a brand heartland is, to use Bakhtin's (1982) term, to speak of a chronotope of brand, one that may abut and even overlap spatially, temporally, and sociologically with other commodity chronotopes, such as the chronotope of surfeit or brandedness. To give a concrete example, from New York to Chennai, it is not uncommon to find "pirate" roadside stalls near authorized brand retailers, each in their own world and yet also contiguous and in dialogue.
17. For discussion of such examples, see Coombe 1998; Halstead 2002; Vann 2006; Pang 2008; Luvaas 2010; 2013; Crăciun 2012; Nakassis 2012b; Graan 2013; Thomas 2013.
18. The Tamil context described in this and the previous chapter bears resemblances to what Kal Raustiala and Christopher Sprigman (2006) have dubbed "low-IP" environments, the most canonical in the United States and Europe being the fashion industry, organized as it is around rampant citational copying and alterations of others' designs (Nakassis 2013e; in press).
19. At the same time, contemporary brand marketing and legal practice also turn on leaving some slack in this calibration (Mazzarella 2003; Lury 2004; Arvidsson 2005; Nakassis 2012b; 2013a; in press), for it is precisely the disarticulation of the commodity from the brand that, on the one hand, protects the semiotic monopoly of the brand from becoming an actual monopoly of the market (and thus guarantees it legal protection) and, on the other, allows reflexive marketing practices to recoup consumers' value-adding, citational appropriations of the brand back into the cauldron of brand design and marketing.

CHAPTER FOUR

1. Also relevant to the colonial history of language contact, higher education, and the dissemination of English in India are the East India Company taking on the education of its Indian subjects in 1813; the Charter Act of 1833 allowing Indians to be part of the Company's civil service (where English was a practical prerequisite; Annamalai 2004:181); the replacement of Persian with English as the official and court language in 1837; Lord Hardinge's government's 1844 announcement giving preference to English-educated applicants for government appointments (Basu 1991:23); Charles Wood's Despatch of 1854 that de facto made English the official language of higher

education (Seth 2007); and the subsequent expansion of higher education itself.

2. There is, of course, an older history of foreign-produced Tamil dictionaries and grammars extending back to the sixteenth century, though their production and circulation grew dramatically with increasing British governance and availability of print technologies (Blackburn 2003:26–72; Mitchell 2009).
3. While caste inequity and Brahminical domination (in particular, in the state civil service) were the central issues for the turn-of-the-century non-Brahmin movement (see note 17 in chapter 1), by the mid-twentieth century, concerns about Brahminical domination were subsumed by, and in certain ways articulated as, a purist politics of language by the electorally focused Dravidianist parties (Fuller and Narasimhan 2014:10–11).
4. Being motivated by the twin drives of purism and modernization, the lexical composition of pure Tamil (*sen Tamiḻ*) comprises both archaic words recycled from ancient literature as well as new and innovative coinages informed by an aesthetics of the archaic (Annamalai 2011).
5. The "choice" to use (particular registers of) English or Tamil in speech, of course, is also mediated by the topic of conversation, who one's interlocutors are, and the formality of the context, among other variables (see Kanthimathi 2007 for discussion). Here I am mainly concerned with how (particular registers of) English and Tamil are used, or avoided, by youth to do *style* as a function of (i) these linguistic varieties' widely circulating metapragmatic stereotypes and (ii) the dynamics of the peer group.
6. On loans versus (intrasentential) code switching in Tamil and English, see Sankoff et al. 1990. See Gumperz 1982:59–99; Eastman 1992; Myers-Scotton 1992; and Paz 2010:106ff. on the distinction more generally. Beyond questions of phonological, morphological, or grammatical integration, or of folk-etymological reanalysis (see the following main text), my interest here is in the pragmatics of the ambivalent, fuzzy threshold of (non)normalized English speech (as construed and negotiated by speakers), whether it comprises loans or "code switches" (in the sense of Sankoff et al. 1990).
7. This is not to say, of course, that the etymological origins of such words are in fact English (whatever that might mean), but rather that they were often so construed.
8. By contrast to pure Tamil and proper English, my usage of highly *local* Tamil speech often—though not always—caused my friends discomfort. My use of curse words and other highly colloquial speech forms was often seen as a shame to the language and its speakers (because I had learned the "bad" variety). In other contexts, of course, it could function to create intimacy and solidarity, or humor.
9. Indeed, many of the dynamics I discuss here are not particular to youth peer groups. What is particular is the way that pushing and playing on the limits of English and Tamil is linked to forms of youth sociality and identity,

navigating the space of the college, the here-and-now of youth *style*, the egalitarian ethos of the peer group, and youths' future expectation of adult seriousness and respectability. On similar linguistic dynamics in other youth cultural contexts, see Heller 1984; 1994; Rampton 1995; Franceschini 1998; Woolard 1998; Eckert 2000; Smith-Hefner 2007; Mendoza-Denton 2008; Tetreault 2009; Bucholtz 2011.

10. On similar anxieties among Indian youth, see Jeffrey et al. 2008; Rogers 2008; Lukose 2009; Jeffrey 2010; LaDousa 2014; Proctor 2014.
11. E. Annamalai (1991:36) indicates the longer history of the demand for English-medium education (also see Seth 2007), in particular in the postindependence period, where the "exuberant confidence" that English would be replaced as "the medium of the vital functions of the society waned." (On the policy history of this waning, see Annamalai 2004.) Annamalai (1991:39) also indicates that at the time of his writing, tutorial institutions teaching English were "mushrooming everywhere."
12. As I note in the front matter of the book, graphically rendering Tamil and English words in a context where the distinction between Tamil and English may be ambiguous and indeterminate is problematic. Inevitably, putting words that exist across and between codes in either *italic* or normal romanized font (to distinguish, as I do, Tamil and English linguistic forms) simplifies things. In this conversation, for example, note how "*Āṅkilam*" and "*English*" (both meaning 'English,' the former a Tamilized variant of "Anglo" and the latter a normalized borrowing) are both italicized as Tamil words (similarly, "*state*" and "*mānilam*"). At the same time, "*Āṅkilam*" is more likely to be indexically associated with Tamil-medium students (seen as more "pure" and literary), while "*English*" is more likely to index English-medium education (and seen as more "modern"). In this excerpt, Senthil's use of the word "*Āṅkilam*" is triggered by my use of the term at the beginning of the conversation. Tellingly, over the course of the conversation (which is about the globality of English), "*Āṅkilam*" drops out in favor of "*English.*"
13. Similar observations regarding the effacing of caste and regional identity in speech have been made about 'pure' (*sen*) Tamil in DMK oratory (Krishnan 2009:144–47) and "standard spoken Tamil" in college contexts and film (Schiffman 1998).
14. On the meanings of "exposure" in Indian English, see Fuller and Narasimhan 2006; 2014:119–20.
15. This is not to say that speaking in/with Tamil couldn't do *style*, but that this quality was not seen as a default quality of Tamil, as it was with English.
16. This wannabe figure is animated by Sam in contrast to the unmarked English-speaking figure iconically indexed by Sam's seemingly unaffected Indian English "delivery" later in the quote. (This latter delivery's understated citational framing, relative to Sam's hyperbolic reanimation of the gauche wannabe, implicitly imputes this latter figure as Sam's default persona. This contrast belies, perhaps, his own anxiety at being seen as a

"comedy person.") Importantly, this "delivery" implicitly differentiates itself from another affected mode of infelicitously *stylish* speech: that of the overly anglicized "*Peter*," as discussed in the next section of the main text.

17. The use of light-skinned Indian or Caucasian models in such advertisements is common (also see figure 10) and interestingly reverses the stereotypical phenotypic associations with English disfluency. One might suggest that the co-occurrence of whiteness and the silencing tape figurates a trope of transformation, a balanced sameness and difference that connotes before-after, disfluency-fluency.

18. By Bradley's account (I never spoke with Venkatesh about what happened), neither caste nor religion were at play, though these young men were from different communities (Bradley was a Christian Nadar and Venkatesh a Hindu Thevar). Religion, however, wasn't completely unrelated to the event's interpretation by other students. This fight prompted the principal, along with the college's other hostel wardens, to visit our hostel the next day for a meeting with the students. (I came to the hostel late that night while the meeting was in progress; what I report here was told to me by my hostelmates.) During this meeting, Venkatesh was questioned by the warden about the incident in English. He couldn't understand the warden and asked him to speak in Tamil, which enraged the warden. The warden said that having to conduct the meeting in Tamil rather than English was humiliating (*kēvalam*). This prompted the warden to ask the students to raise their hands if they didn't know English; about three-quarters raised their hands. When he asked how many could speak English well, no one raised their hands (including those who could). (Implicitly underwriting the warden's discourse was an association between lack of English competence and an uncultivated rowdy subjectivity, the latter of which was assumed to be the proximate cause of the altercation between Bradley and Venkatesh; indeed, in explaining to me why the warden focused so much on students' English knowledge in a meeting devoted to a fistfight, some of my hostelmates made this connection explicit.) This admission in front of the principal and the other hostel wardens (who answered in the affirmative, of course, when the principal asked if their students were able to speak in English) was shameful to the warden. His head hung when the principal left the meeting. Afterward, the students received a thrashing from the warden for having no guts to speak up in front of the principal. The warden rhetorically asked them, in Tamil, if they were men or women ("*Nīṅka āmbiḷḷaiyā pombiḷḷaiyā?*"). After this, the third-year students lectured the first-years on the necessity for hostel (and year-cohort) unity and solidarity rather than infighting (alluding to what was perceived as "groupism" among the first-years). While some of my third-year hostelmates, like Sebastian, attributed such "groupism" to a lack of ragging (chapter 2), one particular friend, a Dalit Hindu, also speculated on religious divisions among the first-year students. In this context, this friend noted that one first-year student had earlier complained to the warden

that Christian and non-Christian students received differential treatment from the administration for their transgressions; indeed, while Venkatesh was suspended, Bradley received no punishment.

19. The term "*Peter akkā*" incorporates the patrilineal kinterm for older sister ("*akkā*") to project an age/year differential between speaker and addressee/referent—in effect, an ironic trope that voices the higher status that the addressee/referent is imputed to presume through her use of English. That such a kinterm is otherwise incongruous—in particular, when speaker and addressee/referent are year or age equals—hammers home the implied infelicity of the addressee/referent's English use through a sarcastic inversion of honorification. Another attested term for "*Peter akkā*" is "Mary," though I never heard this term during my fieldwork.

20. Friends provided various explanations for the origin of the phrase "*Peter (v)uṯratu*." Those who studied in the 1990s said that it didn't exist when they were in college, indicating its relatively recent emergence in the 2000s. Friends who hadn't studied in college but were college age in the 1990s indicated that the phrase came from college youth. Some students during my research period referenced the film comedian Vivek's stint in the early 2000s as Mirinda's brand ambassador. In his Mirinda commercials, Vivek uses the word "*Peter*," as one friend explained, "on fellows who would show off a pro-Western attitude," "the so-called bandha types ('show-offs')." Some other college friends referenced what they called the "Peter Essay" (which, from its description, sounds like a version of Phoebe Cary's "A Leak in the Dike") that students in Tamil-medium schools had to study in their English classes. Sourced from the protagonist of the story, the *Peter* is a student who tries to come off as knowing English naturally (that is, he who has mastered the essay and thereby himself become its English-speaking hero) but in the end only mimics such English through rote memorization and artifice.

21. Speaking to a group of postgraduate college women in Madurai, they performed the female version of this persona not only by deploying exaggeratedly affected language—"Ok-*vā*?," "isn't it?," "Yeah, I know *ya*," "Oh, it's true," "Exactly," "Bye *ṭā*," "Hi::," "So::: cute"—but also by referencing other modalities of *style*: clothing that glitters (*jiku jiku jiku ṇṇu*), excessive skin-lightening makeup, "free hair" (i.e., hair not tied up in a braid, pony tail, bun, etc.), talking on a cell phone, matching shoe and dress color, and riding on a scooter with one's *duppatta* ('scarf') flying in the wind. Linguistically, what is interesting is how these young women's proffered examples focus not on the denotational mastery of English but on its interactional incursion in tag questions and phatic communications, figurating the speaker's nonmastery of English through their excessive use of denotationally vacuous phrases. And yet, as I suggest in the following main text, this is precisely how English was domesticated for use by students. Perhaps, then, we may see in these young women's parodic performance an anxiety that youths' strate-

gies to do *style* without being *over* were, by the fact of those strategies, always already *over.*

22. Harold Schiffman (1999:8) notes, "If foreigners can learn it [the retroflex frictionless continuant ழ்], it gets them good karma." It was often the case that I would be tested on my pronunciation of this phoneme and, upon passing, receive laudatory praise (see chapter 5 for more discussion).
23. This is not to say that English never sexualizes female speakers, for indeed English as *style* is sometimes aligned with the stereotyped figure of the hypersexualized female, as discussions in chapters 5 and 7 suggest.
24. While sometimes this mixed Tamil-English linguistic style is called "Tanglish," this wasn't how most of the youth I knew spoke about their speech (even if they were familiar with such a speech style through television programming, as discussed in chapter 5). "Tanglish" was more likely to be used by urban elites to describe English mixed with Tamil, or heavily anglicized Tamil. Tanglish, we might say, typifies a particular register within the ambit of the practices I am describing here, though coming from a different default communicative norm: English.
25. However, we might note that the English normalized into everyday Tamil is overwhelmingly from that denoting category par excellence: common nouns (Sankoff et al. 1990; Kanthimathi 2007). My point here, however, is not that English isn't used by youth to refer or predicate but that it is this feature of English that is divisive in peer groups precisely because of its potent performativity (in contrast to affected anglicized pronunciation, which was more annoying and absurd than excluding and insulting). It is this performativity that must be managed in various ways.
26. This aesthetics of Englishness uncannily echoes the modernist typographic projects discussed by Johanna Drucker (1994).
27. Carol Myers-Scotton (1993:70–72) calls such a linguistic pattern a "best strategy" that emerges in "uncertain situations" where multiple conflicting norms may apply to linguistic usage. But as should be clear, the issue is not just that of conflicting norms but rather the reflexivity to that very fact as it guides linguistic usage. This means that the question is not one of quantity or ratio of static codes (code switching merely as a balanced performance of status-raising and -levelling), but one of the intersubjectively negotiated achievement of balance. It is a question of how code itself is reflexively figurated in interaction.
28. Such reflexivity is also at play in Kathryn Woolard's discussion of the "virtual form of simultaneity" (Woolard 1998:16) or "read simultaneity" (ibid.:18). In such cases, simultaneity is not simply the co-occurrence of multiple voices (a temporal notion) but their formulation as simultaneous (a metasemiotic notion).
29. That any linguistic norm implies the possibility, and perhaps necessity, of being troped upon is implied by John Gumperz's (Blom and Gumperz 1972;

Gumperz 1982) original notion that conversational code switches are "metaphorical." Indeed, the intelligibility of a code switch as such presupposes the construal by participants of the tropic noncongruence of two text segments vis-à-vis some notion of denotational/grammatical code (Agha 2009).

CHAPTER FIVE

1. While often the phone operator—who had already spoken with the caller and asked what language he or she was more comfortable in—would let the VJ know what language the caller preferred, he didn't always. Of course, as VJs very well knew, callers' stated preferences and their linguistic ability did not always match up (nor were their linguistic abilities equal to the different genres of talk that such conversations drew on; greetings and dedications in English were easy, but more open-ended chitchat often was not), requiring a delicate negotiation to figure out—within the few minutes in which they spoke—which language would work best.
2. Anglo-Indians are a community in India who have English ancestry and whose native language is English.
3. MTV first entered India in 1991 as MTV Asia, carried by Star TV. Its content was simply transported from MTV US. By 1994, MTV separated from Star TV and was relaunched as MTV India. After being forced to go off the air in 1995, MTV India made a comeback in 1996 by "Indianizing"—which is to say, Hindi-izing—its programming, focusing more on Hindi language and film music, though still framed by the MTV US brand image (Cullity 2002; Juluri 2003). The founders of SS Music, generally born in the mid-1970s, "grew up" on MTV US and drew inspiration from both MTV US and MTV India. As one of the founding producers put it, they used MTV India for "ref[erences] . . . to keep the ethnic touch" while the channel IDs and the like were inspired by MTV US "because of (its) colors and wacky ideas."
4. Channel V is a music-television station that was launched in 1994 by Star TV. Like MTV, Channel V began as an international music-television channel (playing pan-Asian and Western pop music), though it subsequently localized its orientation for its largely Hindi-speaking audience (Juluri 2003).
5. While this desire to be like, and thus to compete with, MTV was founded on the personal tastes of the founders of SS Music (see note 3 in this chapter), it was also a marketing decision. As one of the founders explained, if you want to sell advertisements for multinational brand products, you have to pitch the channel in a mode familiar to advertisers and marketers. By creating a south Indian version of an MTV show—which he characterized as "safe" versions toned down for the more conservative tastes of the south Indian audience—SS Music could more easily sell ad time to the same agencies that advertised on channels like MTV India.
6. While this was usually the case, it wasn't uncommon for VJs to make fun of callers' English, particularly if those callers were attempting to use English in

a (stereotypically) show-offy way (e.g., by excessively using particles like "*ya*" [akin to "like" in American English], cf. discussion of the *Peter* in chapter 4), if they mispronounced the VJs' names (this happened the most to Craig, whose name would often be rendered by Tamil speakers as "Crack," "Cray," or "Crag"), or if they said something particularly infelicitously funny. Such teasing would often seemingly go on unbeknownst to the caller, instead being addressed to the viewing audience. See the following main text for discussion.

7. However, even from the beginning, Tamil occupied a disproportionate place within the channel's linguistic division of labor. This was partly because the station was based out of Chennai. It was also because of the relative popularity and presence of the Tamil film industry and its music across south India.
8. When I worked at the station, there was a significant waffling about language. After I arrived, management decided that their experiment with being a "Tamil station in English" had failed. The channel reverted back to its English focus (with only 10 percent of Tamil-based content) and a "ban" on using Tamil on the channel. This, however, was also short-lived, as the management decided to flip back to its Tamil-based focus. While the original shift to being more Tamil-focused responded to a real crisis in distribution, business model, and personnel, later shifts were seemingly the result of management's lack of creative vision, as well as the inability to resolve the inherent tensions between the station's target market, image, programming content, and linguistic balance. After my research concluded, one by one the main VJs left the station, and in March 2012, the station went off the air, living on as an online blog about Tamil cinema. Friends who worked at the station indicated that its closing was due to the 2011 state-level shift in political regime, which resulted in the arrest of station's owner in a land grabbing case (Indian Express 2011).
9. As this VJ went on to emphasize, however, while this was how she initially felt about the linguistic and content-based shift to Tamil, her attitude had since become more positive, and she "judge[d] less now"; though, as she also noted, if she had a choice, she would "definitely like to go back to how it was."
10. Complicating this, of course, is that VJs had different on-air images and rather different personalities. Craig, for example, was the station's "boy next door." A famously jovial, mischievous, and informal VJ on-screen and off-screen, Craig was able to joke quite easily with callers. This was in contrast to the station's female VJs, whose on-screen images tended toward the sporty, sexy, and sophisticated and whose on-air relationships were comparatively less informal and joking. That there is no "girl next door" screen persona available for such VJs, or that such easygoing joking was generally more problematic for women on-air and in the workplace, is of course indicative of the gender asymmetries at play here, VJs' different personalities and on-air images notwithstanding.

11. Such transgression of the norms of on-air propriety was partial and thus, in a sense, figurative; for example, VJs always used polite second-person plural pronouns and verb endings when speaking with callers in Tamil, an honorificating mode of address that is otherwise anomalous (e.g., in youth peer groups) when used with addressees whom one also addresses with fictive affinal kinterms and other nonhonorificating address terms. This tropically informal style had to be learned by VJs like Craig, who, as he narrated it to me, committed a number of faux pas early in his career by speaking in a truly informal manner in Tamil with on-air guests.
12. As one SS Music producer told me, "VJs" are on MTV, Channel V, VH1, SS Music, and similar caliber stations. All other television hosts—for example, on Sun Music or local stations like Vaigai TV or Media TV in Madurai—could only be called "comperes." And indeed, such hosts were called "comperes" by the youth I lived and worked with, as well as by local television hosts themselves.
13. "*Style*" was not, however, how VJs, or elite English-fluent youth, would describe VJs' speech; for them, the lexical form "style" denoted its standard sense in American and British English (chapter 2). For them, their speech was simply "normal."
14. Craig's initial move into Tamil in line 9 seems to be prompted by Shanmugavalli's pause in line 5 (she fails to excitedly jump into the conversation; cf. the interaction between VJ Paloma and Gomathy discussed in the following main text) as well as by her traditional-sounding Tamil name (Shanmugavalli), which Craig pronounces in line 7 in an emphatically correct way. In line 9, Craig queries Shanmugavalli in Tamil about the meaning of her name (a metalinguistic request for her to perform her Tamil cultural knowledge), which, upon failure, results with his temporary move back into English (the subsequent failure of which triggers his more playful use of both Tamil and English). After the conversation is over, Craig looks off-camera to the Tamil studio technicians and says, in Tamil, that "Shanmugavalli" is 'actually' ("*actual-ā*") a nice name, that it would sound different when you'd hear it called out during school attendance. Looking at the camera, he then quickly wraps up the segment in English as the camera zooms in: "All right, we're going to go now and play you your song. Have fun watching it. Be right back." (I thank John Haviland and Kathryn Woolard for encouraging me to further explicate Craig's initial move into Tamil.)
15. Note, however, how Craig creates this Tanglish verb not with the adverbial participle of the intransitive verb "*bayappaṭu*" ('to be afraid') but with the adverbial participle of the transitive verb "*bayappaṭuttu*" ('to frighten').
16. We might also note how Craig's self-deprecating humor regarding his Caucasian appearance (his queries in lines 20 and 22 as to whether Shanmugavalli is afraid of him because she thinks he looks like a ghost or a demon), like his later query in line 26 as to whether she has ever spoken to a white guy, constratively figures Shanmugavalli as provincial and Craig (and presumably the audience) as not.

17. Of course, Shanmugavalli's silence is produced by Craig's almost cajoling attempts to get her to open up. Indeed, his playful use of Tamil and English and his reflexive jokes uncomfortably put her on the spot (see note 16 in this chapter).
18. As another female VJ, Pooja, said to me on another occasion, along with other deferential address terms like "madam" or "aunty," she "hates" the term "*akkā*," which callers would frequently use with her instead of her preferred first name.
19. As the comperes of a local Madurai television station that I conducted researched at for several months told me, they avoided too much English (though they too noted that they could, and did, use more *stylish* English on-screen than they would otherwise because it was expected by audiences) because the audience would get mad if they couldn't understand them. This difference from SS Music was partially, I would suggest, a function of hosts' different comfort levels with English and the different audience demographics of this local Madurai television and SS Music. It was also, however, due to the different expectations about the stations themselves—that is, this medial distance is mediated by not just the type of programming (call-in entertainment vs. other genres) or the speakers' background (Anglo-Indian vs. ethnolinguistically Tamil) but also the image of the stations (a *stylish* Chennai station with "international" quality programming vs. a local, low-budget Madurai station). While the distance of being on-screen, then, mediates *style*, not all media are equally distant.
20. Here we find an interesting comparison to Erving Goffman's (1981:197–327) discussion of radio talk, where speaker and hearer exist in a common normative frame of fluency. Here, by contrast, professional capacity and pleasurable mass-mediated interaction depend on modes of disfluency and discalibration in both VJs' speech and audiences' understanding, an ironic result of intersecting regimes of standard language in a cross-class, postcolonial context of mediatized youth interaction.
21. One common aesthetic for women's media speech in Tamil Nadu is speaking like a child (e.g., with a high voice, or by mispronouncing words). Such speech was seen by some as "cute." Important here is how this speech style shades into anglicized forms of speech. While I do not know if any media personalities speak in this way on purpose, the VJs on SS Music actively *avoided* such a speech style, both to differentiate themselves from the "wannabes" and to allay their own linguistic insecurities.
22. My college friends often exhibited precisely this ambivalence about the value of English in voicing their desires for English. As one female Madurai student put it after expounding on how much she really liked English, 'Actually, it [this English craze] is a bad thing, a real stupidity, even though everyone think it's something to be proud of. It's because of that that Tamil is in the state it's in now. It's something that's really saddening I think.' ("*Atu actual-ā kuṟe, periya oru muṭṭāḷ tanam, ānā ellārum ate perumaiyā*

neneccikkirāṅka. Atān condition of Tamil *ippa. Varuttappaṭakkuṭiya oru viṣayam appaṭi ṇṇu nān nenekkirēn.*")

CHAPTER SIX

1. Unfortunately, I was unable to see *Pokkiri* in the theater on its opening day. Here my description of audiences' engagement in the theater draws on the opening day shows of other mass-hero films that I have attended. I take this license given the consistency and generic nature of these types of theater practices across such film events (also see Gerritsen 2012:59ff.).
2. My use of the term "hero-star" designates the simultaneous, if virtual, copresence of the on-screen and off-screen image—as hero (character) and star (actor)—that comes to inhere in and be projected by statusful actors in the Tamil film industry. While this on-screen/off-screen confluence in the celebrity figure of the hero-star has a longer history and a diverse set of manifestations in south Indian cinema, my concern here is with contemporary mass films and mass heroes in Tamil cinema. This genre and figure emerge at a particular historical juncture, crystallizing into a recognizable form in the second half of the twentieth century. Scholars have pointed to a number of important developments that are critical to the rise of this genre and figure, including the consolidation of the film market vis-à-vis an emergent Tamil language community (in the sense of Silverstein 1998) and linguistically defined state (Prasad 2014; cf. Srinivas 2009; 2013); the hybridization of folklore and social genres; the emergence of a male-centered star system (Prasad 2014); the emergence of dialogue (in particular, in oratorically embellished, politicized registers of speech), as opposed to song, as the important locus of cinematic affect (Krishnan 2009); and, with time, the conflation of the ideological organization of the text into the body of the hero-star himself (Sivathambi 1981). My discussion in this and the next chapter focuses on those mass films and mass heroes that were cited and talked about by my college-age friends—that is, mass films from the 1990s (and Rajinikanth films of that period in particular) and onward that are part of the generational memory and citational repertoire of contemporary youth and the most current crop of film heroes. These films emerge with, and are rendered economically precarious by, the late-twentieth-century shift of (target) audience demographics and textual organization away from the so-called family audience toward young men. This shift was occasioned by economic liberalization in the mid-1980s and 1990s and the widespread advent of television, home-theater technology, and piracy (see the postscript in chapter 7 for more discussion). My claims in this and the next chapter, then, are not about this historically complex and diverse genre and figure in their entirety but about elements of this more circumscribed subset in this postliberalization moment.
3. When I asked what *style* is vis-à-vis Rajinikanth, my friends inevitably pointed out a set of stereotyped mannerisms or actions performed by Rajini

in the course of his films—for example, the way he twirls his finger, the way he throws a cigarette into his mouth from a distance, his gait, his "punch dialogues." These are the most localizable, most detachable, most framed as *style* by the film text itself (through slow motion shots, double takes, sound effects, and explicit dialogue), and the most repeated elements of *style* (both within the film, across films, and outside the film)—that is, they are the most prefigured for *stylish* citation beyond the text. At the same time, as this book as a whole shows, *style* is much more than these elements and thereby can't be reduced to such "mannerisms" or affectations (cf. Gerritsen 2012:72–73; Rajanayagam 2015).

4. The first day of a big hero-star's film may feature rituals performed on representations of the hero-star—for example, pouring milk, or beer, on an image of him (presumably to ritually sanctify it) or performing *tiruṣṭi* rituals that are conventionally used to remove the 'evil eye' to which he has been subjected (Jacob 2009; Rogers 2011; Gerritsen 2012). The use of beer in such rituals, however, points to the citational nature of such acts and the ways in which we should hesitate in too easily imputing religious significance to them (Srinivas 2013; Prasad 2014). As one former Vijay fan club member explained to me, pouring beer on an image of the hero was a way to show the fan club's *gettu*, to show that they are dominant vis-à-vis other fan groups. Not *sāmi* ('god'), but *talaivar* ('leader'), he said, explaining that such acts are not thought of by fans as religious in nature. Rather, they cite the religious as part of a more particular local politics of status.
5. There are a number of other possible interpretations of *nammakku* and *-mā*: (i) as including and addressing the person Vijay is talking to on the phone (though since he has hung up we might exclude this); (ii) as including and addressing Prabhu Deva, the film's director (when Vijay says this line Prabhu Deva's name comes onto the screen exactly where Vijay is looking); or (iii) autoreferentially—*nammakku* here might simply be a trope of self-honorification. While all these possibilities are at play, the point is that the film plays with its own porous boundaries, attempting to align audience, text, and actor. Compare this with Christian Metz's (1991) refutation of the "deictic" capacity of film.
6. Rajan Krishnan (2009:115–16, 118ff.; cf. Hughes 1996:236–37) discusses an alternative circulating discourse that cinema contributes to the audience's development and exposure, a discourse that I have also come across among older friends from working-class, rural backgrounds.
7. For a historical account of the rise of this elitist entanglement with cinema, see Pandian 1996.
8. See Hughes 1996 on the early history of this discourse in south India.
9. This relation of representation, Prasad (2014) suggests, registers a desire for and lack of ethnolinguistic sovereignty within the context of the Indian nation, a lack that is filled, if only in the imaginary, by the hero. This relation between fantasy and virtual representation may take on a literal function

through electoral politics, as it has in Tamil Nadu, though it need not do so. Indeed, as Prasad points out, these same dynamics emerge in other south Indian states where we see evidence of the cinepolitical before formal association with electoral politics (as with NTR in Andhra Pradesh), as well as cases of cinepolitics without formal politics (as with Rajkumar in Karnataka).

10. Even for Prasad, who does much to undermine the idea that the locus of cinepolitics is in the denotational "content" or "messages" of texts (or how they are taken up, sociologically, culturally, or psychologically), mass-hero films are ultimately reduced to the "aesthetic autonomy" of the text, both in the narrow sense of the narratological text (and its modes of positioning the spectator) and in the more expansive sense of the star's image as text (Prasad 2014:21, 142). The latter, Prasad argues, mediates the former, even as it emerges through it. And yet, even as Prasad points to the ways in which south Indian film complicates the identity of the film text (ibid:151–52)—precisely because every mass-hero film contains reference to a surplus that can only be filled by appeal to the hero-star's "metafiction"—in the end, the star's image *completes* the text, and restores it to autonomy. It is together that this complex textual assemblage comes to represent, in both the political and aesthetic senses, the fan-hero relation. What is potentially problematic here is how commitment to the autonomy of the text, and thus to the autonomy of cinema itself, risks rendering actual empirical viewers and their activities external to the *sui generis* cinematic text. The tension that runs through Prasad's argument, then, is a mode of analysis that presumes upon the text as a quasi-transcendent, autonomous entity even as it argues for its historical emergence—a tension that is necessary to justify the distinction of historically particular cinematic logics from cultural, sociological, or psychological analyses (which are thereby assumed to be nonhistorical). Yet the notion that this relation of representation is demanded by the film's (fan) publics—as Prasad (2014) suggests (also see Srinivas 2009; Gerritsen 2012)—already indicates that both senses of the text are already perforated from without. In drawing on ethnography with fan clubs, alongside text analysis and historical research, S. V. Srinivas's (2009:104) work on Telugu mass films comes closest to what I seek to highlight in this chapter and the next: the ways in which the film text registers and anticipates, and thus mediates, its entanglements with that which is putatively exterior to it (also see Rajadhyaksha 2009:99). Here, however, I want to expand on what such entanglements might entail, moving beyond demands for political representation and fans' cinephilia to a wider range of social actors, pragmatic acts, and contexts.

11. For the youth that I lived with in Madurai and Chennai, films like *Boys* (2003), *Kaadhal* (2004), *7G Rainbow Colony* (2005), and *Paruthiveeran* (2007)—not incidentally, all "realistic" films that attempt to represent the "actual" lives of everyday youth (Nakassis and Dean 2007; Nakassis 2009)—would be referenced in narrativizing their own travails, which is

to say that such realist films anticipate their citation (here, "reception") *as* representationalist texts (cf. Hansen 1991).

12. This phrase ("*Enna koṭumai Saravanan itu*?") now has its own Wikipedia and Urban Dictionary entries. "Enna kodumai Saravanan idhu?" *Wikipedia*, accessed June 1, 2013, http://en.wikipedia.org/wiki/Enna_kodumai_Saravanan_idhu%3F; "Eksi," *Urban Dictionary*, accessed June 1, 2013, http://www.urbandictionary.com/define.php?term=EKSI.
13. P. J. dropped the first-person pronoun possessing the kinterm *maccān* in the original lyric, leaving its referent ambiguous. This ambiguity allowed the lyric to simultaneously (i) refer to himself (without having to shift the possessive pronoun to the second person) while addressing the young woman and (ii) ventriloquate the young woman's first-person desire for him qua referent, as in the original song.
14. This reflexive disavowal is not only a feature of reanimating film for *style*. In the other examples previously discussed—flirting through a film song, teasing through a comedy dialogue—putting the filmic in quotes serves to soften the force of the act. Directly talking to young women provokes intense anxiety (and thrill) among young men, given its highly nonnormative valence, just as directly criticizing someone else easily shades into insult and thus dispute.
15. As Sara Dickey (1993b:6, 2001) reports, the urban poor of the 1980s and 1990s also voiced this discourse, if more ambivalently. Roos Gerritsen (2012:47, 66–67, 75) similarly notes this fractal recursion from her fieldwork among fans in the 2000s, indicating how it is always *other* fans, in particular those of mass heroes (as opposed to "class" hero-stars) who are excessively fanatical.
16. See, for example, the descriptions of fan club practices by Dickey 1993b; 2001; Osella and Osella 2004; Rogers 2011:48ff.; and Gerritsen 2012.
17. In terms of how young women relate to or engage with film, some young women indicated to me that, like young men, they too watch films for the hero, largely because the heroines are supremely uninteresting. There are exceptions, of course. At the time of my fieldwork, actresses such as Simran, Trisha, and Jyothika had managed to carve out their own niches as actresses who played roles worthy of attention. And it is these heroines who ultimately licensed filmic reanimations by young women.
18. As Caroline Osella (2013) has pointed out for Muslim women's dress in Kerala (also see Osella and Osella 2007), only those aspects of film fashion that most peripherally frame the body and that least diverge from patriarchal dress norms are likely to be taken up by young women—for example, accessories, shoes, sari prints, certain hair styles, and the like.
19. Young men also performed in public events such as this with similar displays of tentativeness (stoic faces, still bodies, and the awkward placement of their arms and hands), most often when they were forced to take the stage during ragging (e.g., during welcome functions). During such performances,

students mitigated the status-raising presumptions of the stage itself, playing into the ragging while trying not to provoke any more of it. The gender composition of the audience is important here, however, as is evinced by the fact that functions that took place within women's colleges or within women's hostels (where there were few to no men) had a much different quality to them, with young women performing with much less hesitation and trepidation.

20. For discussion of this large literature in anthropology, see Spitulnik 1993; Ginsburg et al 2002; Hughes 2011 and references therein; in cultural studies, see Morley 1980; Radway 1984; Ross and Nightingale 2003; in film studies, see Straiger 2005.
21. This isn't to say that all the dynamics discussed in this chapter—in particular, the middle-class politics of distinction that explicitly disavows the subaltern fan—find their exact analogue in the textuality of the mass hero. Indeed, fans are considered a major constituent of the mass hero's audience and the texture of his films certainly registers this fact (Srinivas 2009; Rajanayagam 2015). And yet, as previously noted in the main text and in notes 15 and 16 in this chapter, fan practices are also citational and abide the dynamics discussed in this chapter, just as the discourse that characterizes commercial cinema and fan practices as *local* is voiced across social classes. As this indicates, the "fan" is less a demographic category than a discursive function, an enregistered figure that is variably animated, that is, cited in different contexts to variable effect (see Gerritsen 2012:46ff.). Finally, as discussed in the next chapter, the mass-hero figure continually performs a complex voicing of both elite and subaltern subjectivity (to say nothing about voicing the fan relation vis-à-vis other hero-stars). This polyphony acts to delicately position the mass hero as a liminal subject in ways that are not totally dissimilar from—if still not the same as—the class-linked stance-taking performed by young men like Prakash (cf. chapter 5).

CHAPTER SEVEN

1. The back bench is also referred to as the "*māppiḷḷai* bench," where the kin-term "*māppiḷḷai*" ('bridegroom,' 'male cross cousin younger than male ego,' 'opposite-sex sibling's son') invokes the recently married bridegroom who, pampered by his in-laws, takes things easy and enjoys life to its fullest.
2. For the Back Bench Boys, who were young and middle class, the design of their T-shirt—while interdiscursively linked to Rajinikanth—wasn't likely to be seen by them as a reference to him at all.
3. In the late 1990s and early 2000s, there were attempts to render Rajinikanth's celebrity image into a form of intellectual property. The coproducer of *Padaiyappa* (1999), for example, registered a design from the film as a trademark in 1998 for goods like beedis, cigarettes, and tobacco (Dhananjayan 2010:205). In 2002, for the release of his 150th film, *Baba*, Rajinikanth issued notice in

the Tamil and English press prohibiting the imitation of his screen persona or using the signature *style*s from the film for commercial gain (Pandian 2005:61), with an exemption issued to autorickshaw drivers (who popularly use Rajini's image on their vehicles; Gerritsen 2012:73). Yet such attempts to police and brand Rajini's *style* have failed, just as *Baba* was a flop, for citational economies of *style*, as we have seen (chapters 2–3), differ from and are indifferent to intellectual property logics of trademark and brand, just as, as this chapter shows, the (inter)textuality of the mass hero necessarily presupposes and entails the promiscuous peregrinations of his *style.*

4. Venkat Prabhu's 2010 film *Goa* reenacts the "corrected *macci*" scenario from *Manmadhan* (2004) in a parody scene starring Simbu in a cameo appearance. Here the reference is simply to *Manmadhan.* The references to *Pandiyan* and Nike are subsumed to the playful reanimation of Simbu's sociopath role.
5. My Chennai roommate, Sam, interestingly framed the issue of *paḻakkam* in an explicitly age-ranked idiom: "Will I listen to the advice of someone I don't know? Only if he is someone I know, someone who has a good name, someone who is older (will I listen to him). Actors are like that." Here the relationship between hero and viewer is made analogous to that of older and younger individuals. For Sam, that status differential justified the ability of the higher-status person to do *style.* Note how this parallels the relationship between seniors and juniors in the college, the former who have the rights to give "advice" to their juniors, as well as to do otherwise excessive amounts of *style.*
6. Out of Vijay's next eighteen films, his father, Chandrasekhar, produced or directed four, bringing the total between 1992 and 1999 to nine out of Vijay's first twenty-three films.
7. The only exceptions that I know of to this pattern in recent years have been Vishal—whose first several films were typical commercial films with elements of mass heroism—and Simbu—who early on flirted with mass-hero roles. In both their cases, however, their attempts to cement a solid, "mass" standing have failed, and both have taken recourse to work with reputed directors like Bala (as Vishal did in *Avan Ivan* [2011]) and Gautham Menon (as Simbu did in *Vinnaithaandi Varuvaayaa* [2010]) to revive their careers. See discussion in the postscript of this chapter.
8. This is to say not that the narratological organization of films of this genre simply follows from the dynamics of *style* discussed in this book (or even that such an organization is singular) but rather that the narrative of these films registers these dynamics in its textual form.
9. There is a longer history to the connection of "ornamental" poetic language and the hero's valor and status as a leader (Krishnan 2009:164), though typifying that connection as the same as *style* risks anachrony, just as it glosses over the different indexicalities of, for example, earlier DMK-film dialogues and those of contemporary hero-stars.
10. Rajinikanth's roles since the 2000s, which have assayed upper-middle-class

characters (e.g., a psychiatrist in *Chandiramukhi* [2005], an IT professional in *Sivaji* [2007], a scientist in *Enthiran* [2010]), are telling shifts away from this pattern, occasioned as much, perhaps, by new postliberalization social imaginaries as by the stage of Rajinikanth's career (cf. Rajanayagam 2015).

11. While MGR's image tended toward being a great action hero, Sivaji's was the consummate actor able to act in any role (Hardgrave 1971, 1979; Krishnan 2009:208–21). This opposition between the hero and the actor (itself metonymizing a whole order of oppositions such as commercial/realist, populist/elite, action/drama) is longstanding and can be observed in some form or another in every generation of actors in the Tamil cinema since the late 1930s: Thyagaraja Bhagavathar (1910–1959) versus P. U. Chinnappa (1916–1951), M. G. Ramachandran (1917–1987) versus Sivaji Ganesan (1928–2001), Rajinikanth (b. 1950) versus Kamal Hassan (b. 1954), and to an extent, Vijay (b. 1974) versus Ajith (b. 1971).

    In citing and appearing under the names of both Sivaji and MGR, Rajinikanth is portrayed in *Sivaji* as uniting, and transcending, this opposition (see notes 12 and 14 in this chapter). Also to be noted is the fundamental importance of both *Parasakthi* (1952; also produced by AVM Productions) and MGR's DMK films to the populist politics of the Dravidianist parties (Pandian 1991; Krishnan 2009; Prasad 2014; Pillai 2015:99–189) and thus the deep, if not completely spelled out, significance of Rajinikanth taking on these two hero-stars as his namesakes.

12. Here the intertextuality is even thicker, for, as revealed in a shot of his passport, the "M. G." stands for Manickam Ganesan. Manickam is a reference to Rajini's name in *Baasha* (1995), while Ganesan references Sivaji Ganesan, whose first name Rajini appropriates in the first half of the film. In taking on the name of MGR, then, Sivaji has been conserved and sublimated by Rajini as in his name; both stars are thereby transcended by being carried along in/by Rajini (also see notes 11 and 14 in this chapter).

13. Rajinikanth also reanimates this gesture in the song sequence "*Annamalai Annamalai*" from *Annamalai* (1992) and in *Mannan* (1992).

14. In his film *Raja Chinna Rooja* (1989), Rajinikanth explicitly connects himself with other past greats of the Tamil film world. Within the film diegesis, he states, "I can sing like Bagavathar. I can wield a sword like MGR. I can act like Sivaji. I can speak Tamil like Kalaignar" (quoted in Rajanayagam 2015:170). We can also consider the "first night" scene from *Sivaji* (2007), where Rajini asks the heroine what kind of (sexual) experience she wants, parodying and co-opting first-night song sequences from classic MGR, Kamal Hassan, and Sivaji Ganesan films. When she finally asks how he would do it, the song-and-dance sequence for the song "*Athiradi*" begins. In this song, Rajini's *style* surpasses all who have come before him, presenting him as the apotheosis to their historical precedents.

15. For further reflection on the deep intertextual resonances of the name and

attached personas of Sivaji in the history of Tamil Nadu, see Krishnan 2007; 2009:256–57.

16. To see a video of one theater audience's reaction to this scene from *Silambattam*, see "Silambattam Billa Scene Theater Response," ajithfans .com, accessed June 1, 2013, http://www.ajithfans.com/blog/2008/12/21 /silambattam-billa-scene-theater-response-video.
17. Consider how an Ajith fansite explicitly frames Simbu's citational acts in *Silambattam* as "honoring" Ajith and showing Simbu to be an "ardent fan" of Ajith. "Ajith Kumar watches Silambattam," ajithfans.com, December 20, 2008, accessed June 1, 2013, http://www.ajithfans.com/news/2008/12/20 /ajith-kumar-watches-silambattam.
18. In addition to being called by his proper name, indirect reference to Rajini's name is not uncommon; for example, in *Baasha* (1995), Rajini's character is referred to as the one who has a "*kāntam*" ('magnet') in his name, referring to both the "*-kanth*" in Rajinikanth and to Rajini's magnetic attractiveness to audiences (Rajanayagam 2015:171).
19. Similarly consider the 1990 Rajinikanth film *Athisaya Piravi* ('Miraculous Rebirth'). Having been killed in the first half of the film, Rajini travels to the underworld, where he meets the god of death. When it turns out that he wrongly died (in the cosmic sense), Rajini demands to be given a new life with the same face, body, and hair. In choosing this next reincarnation of himself, the lord of the underworld comically provides Rajini with several options, each represented by footage of previous Rajinikanth films (*Apoorva Raagangal* [1975], *Bhuvana Oru Kelvi Kuri* [1977], and *Geraftaar* [1985]). Rather than pick one of these (given reasons linked to the fates of the characters played by Rajini in these films), in the end, Rajini is reincarnated as the otherwise humble hero of the second half of the film, though his previous *stylish* self is conserved in this new avatar, waiting in the wings to be fully reanimated in his confrontation with the film's villains.
20. A telling contrast is an actor like Kamal Hassan (or for the previous generation of hero-stars, Sivaji Ganesan), whose characters are so different that they seem not to add up to any particular star image (at least none beyond that of Kamal as consummate actor). In effect, Kamal Hassan's "image trap" is that he doesn't have one.
21. At the same time, since *Mankatha* (2011) Ajith's image has undergone a shift that augurs, as I suggest in the chapter's postscript, a transformation of the figure of the mass hero. See note 34 in this chapter.
22. In this context, note that the *style* and heroism of the mass hero are not only grounded outside of the narrative but also beyond his own physical body. In contrast to the "new face," whose physical acts must be grounded in realist (or narrative) principles (and hence in his own physical body), the mass hero's on-screen actions are grounded in his off-screen status. Hence his thin or flabby, aging body, the lack of physical effort that his characters expend in

doing amazing physical feats, and his general transgressions of the physical laws of nature (Nakassis 2010:280–81; Jain 2007:321ff.).

23. To see the video of this NDTV interview with Rajinikanth, see "Rajini with NDTV," YouTube video, posted by "Narsi Dude," June 18, 2007, accessed June 1, 2015, http://www.youtube.com/watch?v=-0V04ej6gJg.
24. Ambitabh Bachchan was the biggest actor in Hindi cinema from the 1970s to the late 1980s, and is still a popular actor today. Many of Rajini's early films were remakes of Bachchan's films.
25. It is also de rigueur for fan clubs of film stars to visibly engage in acts of social service (Dickey 1993a; 2001; Osella and Osella 2004:242; Krishnan 2009:234; Srinivas 2009:58ff.; Gerritsen 2012)—for example, giving away food, pens, notebooks, or clothing to the poor during celebrations of the hero-star's birthday or recent film releases. This is often encouraged by the hero-stars themselves. The idea here, as Rajini fan club members in Madurai explained to me, is to spread the good name, the civic mindedness, and the "of the people"-ness *qua* patronage of the hero-star (cf. Mines and Gourishankar 1990; Mines 1994).
26. In this, perhaps, we find the equivalent of Victor Turner's (1967:105) discussion of the "chastening function of liminality" in certain rituals. In cases like Ndembu kingship rites or medieval European knight coronations, the liminality of the rite doubles and splits the sign, inverting kingship in images of the lowly and humble. For hero-stars like Rajinikanth (sovereigns in potentia, if we follow Madhava Prasad's [2014] discussion of cinepolitics in south India), this is a permanent condition of multiplicity rather than a temporary phase.
27. While young men's images may also circulate in graffiti, on "flexboards" (large signs erected in public places for friends' weddings, fan club events, and the like), in gossip, and on stage, the importance of such surrogates to youths' image work is comparatively less than their face-to-face interactions. The difference between the hero-star and the young man who cites him, however, is perhaps not a difference in kind.
28. It isn't uncommon for commercial Tamil films to be recut while they are still in theaters based on audience's reactions. Consider Vijay's recent film *Thalaivaa* (2013), which had twenty minutes cut from it due to being "draggy" and had a fight scene added ("Thalaivaa Gets Trimmed by 20 Minutes," SS Music, August 8, 2013, accessed June 1, 2015, http://ssmusictheblog.blogspot.com/2013/08/thalaivaa-gets-trimmed-by-20-minutes.html). Swarnavel Eswaran Pillai (2015:25–26) reports that in the 1940s and 1950s, the film studio Modern Theaters would send representatives to the initial showings of its releases, gauge audience response, and report back to the distribution office. The studio might then instruct their representatives to shuffle the reels (in particular, comedy tracks) or change the lengths of the films at particular points (on similar practices by AVM Productions in the 1940s, also see Pillai 2015: 112, 176 note 19). See Hughes 1996:103–6 on other forms of in-

teractive, editorial entextualization in exhibition spaces in silent-era cinema in the Madras Presidency (cf. Hansen 1991:42–43 on American silent cinema).

29. Rajinikanth's later films—for example, *Sivaji* (2007) and *Enthiran* (2010)—are seemingly exceptions to this. Both films earned well from exhibitions overseas, television rights, and other ancillary markets. Yet also note how since the 2000s, Rajinikanth has reduced his film output to approximately one film every two to four years: *Baba* (2002), *Chandiramukhi* (2005), *Sivaji* (2007), *Kuselan* (2008; where Rajini appears in an extended cameo), *Enthiran* (2010), the animated feature film *Kochadaiiyaan* (2014), and *Lingaa* (2014). This is a drastic change compared to the fifty-five films he starred in from 1980 to 1989, and the sixteen films he starred in from 1990 to 1999. Given his iconic stature and popularity, Rajinikanth has instead gone for extremely huge budget films (his 2010 *Enthiran* being the most expensive Indian film ever made at the time) that feature the newest in film production technology, marketing strategy, and distribution. And yet, as the box office response to his most recent film to date, *Lingaa* (2014), perhaps suggests, even Rajini is also not immune to such risk.

30. One producer also suggested that these shifts were driven by the entry of film-institute trained technicians and directors into commercial Tamil cinema. The effect of the entry of these holders of diplomas of film technology (DFT) was, to his mind, an increase in budget size and thus risk. This is because the increased technical complexity that they brought to cinema necessitated more expensive technology, an increased number of shooting days, and thereby more film rolls and lengthened call sheets for actors and technicians.

31. Also see Krishnan 2007, Kurai 2012, and Prasad 2014 for discussions that touch on different reasons for this prognostication of the 'death of the hero,' as Rajan Kurai (2012) has put it. Provocative is Madhava Prasad's suggestion that, rather than being reinvested in electoral politics, the cinepolitical surpluses of mass heroes are being deposited in the neoliberal economy, wherein the hero-star has come to represent brand imaginaries (as official spokesperson; cf. note 3 in this chapter) rather than the ethnolinguistic polity (as political leader; also see Pandian 2005; cf. Rajadhyaksha 2009).

32. We might see the separation of the hero-star from the generic form of the mass film (so that the mass hero is simply one genred role available to any particular actor within a wider range of hero-types) as a further step in the generalization and decentering that Rajan Krishnan (2009:238; Kurai 2012:32) notes in the transition from MGR (who developed "an exclusive MGR narrative" within which MGR was irreplaceable) to Rajinikanth (whose associated narrative form was inhabitable by other mass heroes, such as Vijayakanth, Vijay, or Ajith).

33. When I spoke with Jiiva in 2011, he indicated that he had, for the time being at least, given up on doing intensely emotional roles in serious films (such as the role he assayed in the 2007 film *Katrathu Tamil*) in favor of lighter

"commercial" entertainment. This was framed by him as due to the emotional stress of filming such roles rather than a calculated move to further his career. Until that point, he noted, proving his ability to be a serious actor was a major priority of his, especially given his privileged film background (his father, R. B. Choudary, is a noted film producer).

34. Recent changes in Ajith's orientation to his own star image are interesting in this light. In the 2010 film, *Asal*, directed by Saran, Ajith dropped his epithet "Ultimate Star" in the opening credits. (The epithet was first used in the 1999 film *Amarkalam*, also directed by Saran.) With his fiftieth film, *Mankatha* (2011), Ajith not only embraced a decidedly villainous role but also encouraged the director, Venkat Prabhu, to make the role even more negative than originally conceived. His use of the curse words on-screen—silenced, though still intelligible with his clearly articulated mouthing (cf. Sivaji Ganesan in *Parasakthi* [1952], where his articulation of the word "*kal*" ['stone'] is silenced, though still visible and intelligible)—was shocking for a hero-star. One industry insider interpreted Ajith's embrace of a negative protagonist in *Mankatha* as Ajith telling his fans that he is "not a nice guy" with plans to get into politics. Ajith also appeared on-screen in *Mankatha* with his natural salt and pepper hair, explicitly opting not to dye it, a change he has generally maintained in subsequent films. Finally, on his birthday in 2011, Ajith dissolved his fan clubs. Whether these recent actions by Ajith are examples of a hero-star attempting to wrestle free of his own image (cf. Srinivas 2009) or a symptom of a more general shift away from the mass-hero figure as such is unclear, but I would suggest that it is indicative of both.

CHAPTER EIGHT

1. My oscillating usage of the terms "medium" and "media object/form" (also see note 9 in chapter 1) aims to highlight that, first, we don't know what a medium is except through particular media objects/forms. We don't know what cinema as a medium (or institution) is, for example, except through particular films, or even what a camera or celluloid are except through the images they capture—or, more precisely, through the (pragmatics of the) events in which they are used to capture and rerender images to be seen. Second, what a medium is, materially and ontologically, is itself a function of such media objects/forms as they come to be materialized and entextualized over time—circulated, taken up, interpreted, cited, and the like—just as the very possibility of the media object/form is the medium in which it manifests. There is a dialectical relationship between media objects/forms and media, each the condition of possibility of the other. While distinguishable, we can't think or theorize one without the other.
2. On how questions of interactivity emerged out of and as cybernetics and its wider philosophical and practical context, see Halpern 2007.

3. On interactivity as characteristic of new media, see Poster 1999; Silverstone 1999; Bolter and Grusin 2000; Manovich 2003; Lury 2004; Jenkins 2006; Lessig 2006; Bruns 2008; Gane and Beer 2008; Jenkins, Ford, and Green 2013.
4. Lurking behind both the discourse of interactivity and the division of new and old media, one senses a desire for, and politics of, immediation (Peters 2001; Halpern 2007). For discussion and critique of the inherent interactivity of new media, see Schultz 2000; Manovich 2001:55–61, 124–29; Gane and Beer 2008:87–101; Jenkins, Ford, and Green 2013.
5. It is not uncommon for such achievements to be reflexively reanalyzed as "in" the media themselves, ideologically naturalized as inherent to their technomateriality. One ironic effect is that such essentializations—in the case of new media, that usage is production or, in the case of brands, that brand value and image are cocreated with consumers (see chapter 3)—may come to guide events of (re)design and (re)use of the medium and its media objects. Through that reflexive loop, such media may materially, institutionally, and normatively realize those very reanalyses, if only ever partially. What was contingent and emergent over a reflexively mediated history of events of design, use, redesign, and so on comes to seem a necessity, historically and technologically (Hansen 1991; Livingstone 1999:63; Boyer 2008; Manovich 2008:41–42; Eisenlohr 2010).

   To take a familiar example from the history of so-called old media, radio in the United States was first used and construed as a decentralized medium (Peters 2001; Boyer 2008). Only later did the "same" technology come to be used for top-down broadcasting. This shift was an institutional achievement that succeeded in changing radio's norms of use (partly through the punitive force of the law), and thus also the technomaterial and infrastructural properties of the medium. Perhaps this is what we are beginning to see with the Internet today (Lessig 2006). In his discussion of virtual reality simulations and video games, Lev Manovich (2001:85, 129–30, 138–41; 2003:15, 22–23) has shown how ideologies and conventions that govern the cinematic image—itself an institutionalization and sedimentation of a field of usage, mediated by ideology, into a particular, naturalized technological form (Hansen 1991)—among other media (e.g., the human-computer interfaces designed for military operations of the mid-twentieth century and 1920s avant-garde art) have mediated, or "remediated" (Bolter and Grusin 2000), the historical emergence of digital hardware and software. This suggests the ways in which the ideological mediation of events of technological usage, or imagined or desired usages, conditions and materializes technological forms in later iterations (see note 6 in this chapter). More generally, we can't know or specify the technomaterial properties or affordances of any particular medium or media object independently of the pragmatics of events of their engagement and use, even as it is these pragmatics that, as noted above, dialectically mediate and materialize that very technomateriality. This requires us to frame questions of medium design features with respect to this historically emergent and reflexively mediated dialectic.

6. For example, Ien Ang (1991) suggests that central to the operation and organization of commercially driven television channels in the 1980s was the discalibration inherent in how these channels "knew" their audiences. Modes of calibration such as "audience measurement" research, she suggests, are necessarily imperfect; such imperfection served the ends of reproducing the institution itself and, in particular, reproducing it as in "control" of its audiences (such that they could be "delivered" to advertisers). These audiences were thereby rendered distinct and distant from, and in a sense unknown and unknowable by, the institution. This noninteractivity, then, was an ongoing and contingent achievement that was mediated by the very modes of (dis)calibration that characterized the medium's entanglements across the screen (as well as its entanglements with advertisers and the like) and the ideological reanalyses of those very (dis)calibrations. Such reanalyses imputed these complex institutional arrangements, themselves contingent historical achievements, as essential properties of the medium (e.g., that television is top-down, unreactive). This, in turn, guided the very practices and institutional arrangements that unfolded in the wake of such reflexive reanalyses, thereby reproducing, to whatever extent they did, the medium (cf. Hansen 1991 on the achievement of noninteractivity in classical American film). We can compare this with Gabriella Lukács's (2010) discussion of 1990s Japanese television, where industry organization and audience practices achieved a form of interactivity that reflexively registered itself in the medium's changing genres, infrastructures, personnel, and industry discourses (also see Jenkins 2006 on contemporary US television).

References

Agha, Asif. 2007. *Language and Social Relations*. New York: Cambridge University Press.

———. 2009. "What Do Bilinguals Do?" In *Beyond Yellow English*, edited by A. Reyes and A. Lo, 253–58. New York: Oxford University Press.

———. 2011a. "Meet Mediatization." *Language & Communication* 31(3):163–70.

———. 2011b. "Large and Small Scale Forms of Personhood." *Language & Communication* 31(3):171–80.

Alex, Gabriele. 2008. "A Sense of Belonging and Exclusion: 'Touchability' and 'Untouchability' in Tamil Nadu." *Ethnos* 73(4):523–43.

Alvarez-Caccamo, Celso. 1990. "Rethinking Conversational Code-switching: Codes, Speech Varieties, and Contextualization." *Proceedings of the Sixteenth Annual Meeting of the Berkeley Linguistics Society*, 3–16. Berkeley, CA: Berkeley Linguistics Society.

———. 1998. "From 'Switching Code' to 'Code-Switching.'" In *Code-Switching in Conversation*, edited by P. Auer, 29–48. London: Routledge.

Anandhi, S. 2005. "Sex and Sensibility in Tamil Politics." *Economic & Political Weekly* 40(47):4876–77.

Ang, Ien. 1991. *Desperately Seeking the Audience*. London: Routledge.

Annamalai, E. 1991. "Satan and Saraswati: The Double Face of English in India." *South Asian Language Review* 1(1):33–43.

———. 2004. "Medium of Power: The Question of English in Education in India." In *Medium of Instruction Policies*, edited by J. Tollefson and A. Tsui, 177–94. Mahwah, NJ: Lawrence Erlbaum Associates.

———. 2011. *Social Dimensions of Modern Tamil*. Madras: Cre-A:.

Arvidsson, Adam. 2006. *Brands: Meaning and Value in Media Culture*. London: Routledge.

Auer, Peter. 1998. "Introduction." In *Code-Switching in Conversation*, edited by P. Auer, 1–24. London: Routledge.

Austin, John L. 1962. *How to Do Things with Words*. Cambridge, MA: Harvard University Press.

Baker, Christopher. 1984. *An Indian Rural Economy, 1880–1955*. New Delhi: Oxford University Press.

Bakhtin, Mikhail. 1982. *The Dialogic Imagination*. Translated by M. Holquist and C. Emerson. Austin: University of Texas Press.

Barthes, Roland. 1977. "The Death of the Author." In *Image, Music, Text*, translated by S. Heath, 142–48. New York: Hill and Wang.

———. 1983[1967]. *The Fashion System*. Berkeley: University of California Press.

Barucha, Rustom. 2000. *The Politics of Cultural Practice*. Hanover, NH: Wesleyan University Press.

Basu, Aparna. 1991. "Higher Education in Colonial India." In *Higher Education in India*, edited by M. Raza, 22–31. New Delhi: Association of Indian Universities.

Bate, Bernard. 2009. *Tamil Oratory and the Dravidian Aesthetic*. New York: Columbia University Press.

Bateson, Gregory. 1972. *Steps to an Ecology of Mind*. New York: Ballantine Books.

Baudrillard, Jean. 1994. *Simulacra and Simulation*. Translated by S. F. Glaser. Ann Arbor: University of Michigan Press.

Bauman, Richard, and Charles Briggs. 1990. "Poetics and Performance as Critical Perspectives on Language and Social Life." *Annual Review of Anthropology* 19: 59–88.

Bazin, André. 2005. *What Is Cinema?* Vol. 1. Edited and translated by H. Gray. Berkeley: University of California Press.

Bean, Susan. 1989. "Gandhi and *Khadi*, the Fabric of Independence." In *Cloth and Human Experience*, edited by A. Weiner and J. Schneider, 355–76. Washington, DC: Smithsonian Institution Press.

Behindwoods. 2014. "ILAYATHALAPATHY or SUPERSTAR—Which One Does Vijay Prefer?" *Behindwoods*, July 7. Accessed January 1, 2015. http://www.behindwoods.com/tamil-movies-cinema-news-14/vijays-preference-on-titles-superstar-or-ilayathalapathy.html.

Bently, Lionel. 2008. "The Making of Modern Trade Mark Law: The Construction of the Legal Concept of Trade Mark (1860–1880)." In *Trade Marks and Brands*, edited by L. Bently, J. Davis, and J. Ginsburg, 3–41. New York: Cambridge University Press.

Béteille, André. 2010. *Universities at the Crossroads*. New Delhi: Oxford University Press.

Bhabha, Homi. 2004[1993]. *The Location of Culture*. New York: Routledge.

Blackburn, Stuart. 2003. *Print, Folklore, and Nationalism in Colonial South India*. Delhi: Permanent Black.

Blom, Jan-Peter, and John Gumperz. 1972. "Social Meaning in Linguistic Structures: Codeswitching in Norway." In *Directions in Sociolinguistics*, edited by J. Gumperz and D. Hymes, 407–34. New York: Holt, Rinehart and Winston.

Blumer, Herbert. 1969. "Fashion: From Class Differentiation to Collective Selection." *The Sociological Quarterly* 10(3):275–91.

Bolter, Jay, and Richard Grusin. 2000. *Remediation*. Cambridge, MA: MIT Press.

Bourdieu, Pierre. 1991. *Language and Symbolic Power*. Translated by G. Raymond and M. Adamson. Malden, MA: Polity Press.

Boyer, Dominic. 2008. *Understanding Media*. Chicago: Prickly Paradigm Press.

Brecht, Bertold. 1964. *Brecht on Theater*. Translated by J. Willett. New York: Hill and Wang.

Brendon, Piers. 2007. *The Decline and Fall of the British Empire, 1781–1997*. New York: Vintage Books.

Briggs, Charles, and Richard Bauman. 1992. "Genre, Intertextuality, and Social Power." *Journal of Linguistic Anthropology* 2(2):131–72.

Bruns, Axel. 2008. *Blogs, Wikipedia, Second Life, and Beyond*. New York: Peter Lang.

Bucholtz, Mary. 2002. "Youth and Cultural Practice." *Annual Review of Anthropology* 31:525–52.

———. 2003. "Sociolinguistic Nostalgia and the Authentication of Identity." *Journal of Sociolinguistics* 7(3):398–416.

———. 2007. "Shop Talk: Branding, Consumption, and Gender in American Middle-Class Youth Interaction." In *Words, Worlds, and Material Girls*, edited by B. McElhinny, 371–402. Berlin: Mouton de Gruyter.

———. 2011. *White Kids*. New York: Cambridge University Press.

Butler, Judith. 1990. *Gender Trouble*. New York: Routledge.

———. 1993. *Bodies that Matter*. New York: Routledge.

———. 1997. *Excitable Speech*. New York: Routledge.

Caldwell, Robert. 1856. *A Comparative Grammar of the Dravidian or South-Indian Family of Languages*. London: Williams and Norgate.

Canagarajah, A. Suresh. 1995. "Manipulating the Context: The Use of English Borrowings as a Discourse Strategy by Tamil Fish Vendors." *Multilingua* 14(1): 5–24.

Chakrabarthy, Dipesh. 2001. "Clothing the Political Man: A Reading of the Use of Khadi/White in Indian Public Life." *Postcolonial Studies* 4(1):27–38.

Chanana, Karuna, ed. 1988. *Socialisation, Education and Women*. New Delhi: Orient Longman.

———. 1994. "Social Change or Social Reform: Women, Education, and Family in Pre-Independence India." In *Women, Education, and Family Structure*, edited by C. Mukhophadhyay and S. Seymour, 37–57. Boulder, CO: Westview Press.

———. 2013[2007]. "Globalisation, Higher Education and Gender: Changing Subject Choices of Indian Women Students." In *Higher Education in India*, edited by J. Tilak, 408–29. New Delhi: Orient Blackswan.

Chandra, Shefali. 2012. *The Sexual Life of English*. Durham, NC: Duke University Press.

Chari, Sharad. 2000. "The Agrarian Origins of the Knitwear Industrial Cluster in Tiruppur, India." *World Development* 28(3):579–99.

———. 2004. *Fraternal Capital*. Stanford, CA: Stanford University Press.

Chatterjee, Partha. 1993. *The Nation and Its Fragments*. Princeton, NJ: Princeton University Press.

Chatterji, P. C. 1987 *Broadcasting in India*. New Delhi: Sage.

Clarke, John, Stuart Hall, Tony Jefferson, and Brian Roberts. 1977[1975]. "Subculture, Cultures and Class." In *Resistance through Rituals*, edited by S. Hall and S. Jefferson, 9–74. London: Hutchinson and Centre for Contemporary Cultural Studies, University of Birmingham.

Cohen, Phil. 1993[1972]. "Subcultural Conflict and Working-Class Community." In *Studying Culture*, edited by A. Gray and J. McGuigan, 95–103. London: Edward Arnold.

Cohn, Bernard. 1989. "Cloth, Clothes, and Colonialism: India in the Nineteenth Century." In *Cloth and Human Experience*, edited by A. Weiner and J. Schneider, 303–53. Washington, DC: Smithsonian Institution Press.

———. 1996. *Colonialism and Its Forms of Knowledge*. Princeton, NJ: Princeton University Press.

Cole, Jennifer. 2010. *Sex and Salvation*. Chicago: University of Chicago Press.

Cole, Jennifer, and Deborah Durham, eds. 2008. *Figuring the Future*. Santa Fe, NM: School for Advanced Research Press.

Comaroff, Jean, and John Comaroff. 2005. "Reflections on Youth, from the Past to the Postcolony." In *Makers and Breakers, Made and Broken*, edited by A. Honwana and P. de Boeck, 19–30. Oxford: James Curre.

Coombe, Rosemary. 1998. *The Cultural Life of Intellectual Properties*. Durham, NC: Duke University Press.

Cosgrove, Stuart. 1984. "The Zoot-Suit and Style Warfare." *History Workshop* 18: 77–91.

Couldry, Nick, and Andreas Hepp. 2013. "Conceptualizing Mediatization: Contexts, Traditions, Arguments." *Communication Theory* 23:191–202.

Crăciun, Magda. 2008. "Researching Fakes: Practising Anthropology Out of the Corner of One's Eye." *Anthropology Matters* 10(2). Accessed December 1, 2009. http://www.anthropologymatters.com/index.php/anth_matters/article/view/32/56.

———. 2009. "Trading in Fake Brands, Self-Creating as an Individual." In *Anthropology and the Individual*, edited by D. Miller, 25–36. Oxford: Berg Publishers.

———. 2012. "Rethinking Fakes, Authenticated Selves." *Journal of the Royal Anthropological Institute* (N.S.) 18(4):846–63.

Cullity, Jocelyn. 2002. "The Global *Desi*: Cultural Nationalism on MTV India." *Journal of Communicative Inquiry* 26(4):408–25.

Davis, Jennifer. 2008. "Between a Sign and a Brand: Mapping the Boundaries of a Registered Trade Mark in European Union Trade Mark Law." In *Trade Marks and Brands*, edited by L. Bently, J. Davis, and J. Ginsburg, 65–91. New York: Cambridge University Press.

Davis, Richard Harding. 1899. *Our English Cousins*. New York: Harper and Brothers Publishers.

Deacon, David, and James Staneyer. 2014. "Mediatization: Key Concept or Conceptual Bandwagon?" *Media, Culture & Society* 36(7):1032–44.

Dean, Melanie. 2013. "From 'Evil Eye' Anxiety to the Desirability of Envy: Status, Consumption and the Politics of Visibility in Urban South India." *Contributions to Indian Sociology* 47(2):185–216.

de Boeck, Filip, and Alcinda Honwana. 2005. "Introduction: Children and Youth in Africa." In *Makers and Breakers, Made and Broken*, edited by A. Honwana and F. de Boeck, 1–18. Oxford: James Currey.

Dent, Alexander. 2009. *River of Tears*. Durham, NC: Duke University Press.

Derrida, Jacques. 1988. *Limited, Inc*. Translated by S. Weber and G. Mehlman. Evanston, IL: Northwestern University Press.

Dhananjayan, G. 2011. *The Best of Tamil Cinema: 1931 to 2010, Volume 1 (1931–1976)*. Chennai: Galatta Media.

Dhareshwar, Vivek, and Tejaswini Niranjana. 1996. "*Kaadalan* and the Politics of Resignification: Fashion, Violence, and the Body." *Journal of Arts and Ideas* 29:5–26.

Dickey, Sara. 1993a. "The Politics of Adulation: Cinema and the Production of Politicians in South India." *Journal of Asian Studies* 52(2):340–72.

———. 1993b. *Cinema and the Urban Poor in South India*. New York: Cambridge University Press.

———. 1995. "Consuming Utopia: Film-Watching in Tamil Nadu." In *Consuming Modernity*, edited by C. Breckenridge, 131–56. Minneapolis: University of Minnesota Press.

———. 1997. "Anthropology and Its Contributions to Studies of Mass Media." *International Social Science Journal* 49(153):413–27.

———. 2001. "Opposing Faces: Film Star Fan Clubs and the Construction of Class Identities in South India." In *Pleasure and the Nation*, edited by R. Dwyer and C. Pinney, 212–46. New Delhi: Oxford University Press.

———. 2013. "Apprehensions: On Gaining Recognition as Middle Class in Madurai." *Contributions to Indian Sociology* 47(2):217–43.

Dornfeld, Barry. 2002. "Putting American Public Television Documentary in Its Places." In *Media Worlds*, edited by F. Ginsburg, L. Abu-Lughod, and B. Larkin, 247–63. Berkeley: University of California Press.

Douglas, Mary, and Baron Isherwood. 1996[1979]. *The World of Goods*. London: Routledge.

Drucker, Johanna. 1994. *The Visible Word*. Chicago: University of Chicago Press.

Durham, Deborah. 2004. "Disappearing Youth: Youth as a Social Shifter in Botswana." *American Ethnologist* 31(4):589–605.

———. 2008. "Apathy and Agency: The Romance of Agency and Youth in Botswana." In *Figuring the Future*, edited by J. Cole and D. Durham, 151–78. Santa Fe, NM: School for Advanced Research Press.

Eastman, Carol. 1992. "Codeswitching as an Urban Language-Contact Phenomenon." In *Codeswitching*, edited by C. Eastman, 1–17. Clevedon, UK: Multilingual Matters.

Eckert, Penelope. 2000. *Linguistic Variation as Social Practice*. Oxford: Blackwell.

Eisenlohr, Patrick. 2010. "Materialities of Entextualization: The Domestication of Sound Reproduction in Mauritian Muslim Devotional Practices." *Journal of Linguistic Anthropology* 20(2):314–33.

Ellis, Francis. 1849[1816]. "Note to the Introduction." In *A Grammar of the Teloogoo Language*, 3rd ed., edited by A. D. Campbell, 1–31. Madras: College Press.

Fanon, Franz. 2008[1952]. *Black Skin, White Masks*. Translated by R. Philcox. New York: Grove Press.

Farmer, Victoria. 2003. "Television, Governance and Social Change." PhD diss., Department of Political Science, University of Pennsylvania.

Ferguson, James. 2002. "Of Mimicry and Membership: Africans and the 'New World Society.'" *Cultural Anthropology* 17(4):551–69.

Fernandes, Leela. 2006. *India's New Middle Class*. Minneapolis: University of Minnesota Press.

Fleming, Luke. 2011. "Name Taboos and Rigid Performativity." *Anthropological Quarterly* 84(1):141–64.

Foster, Robert. 2007. "The Work of the New Economy: Consumers, Brands, and Value Creation." *Cultural Anthropology* 22(4):707–31.

———. 2008. "Commodities, Brands, Love and Kula: Comparative Notes on Value Creation." *Anthropological Theory* 8(1):9–25.

Fournier, Susan. 1998. "Consumers and Their Brands: Developing Relationship Theory in Consumer Research." *Journal of Consumer Research* 24(4):343–73.

Franceschini, Rita. 1998. "Code-Switching and the Notion of Code in Linguistics: Proposals for a Dual Focus Model." In *Code-Switching in Conversation*, edited by P. Auer, 51–72. London: Routledge.

Frank, Thomas. 1998. *The Conquest of Cool*. Chicago: University of Chicago Press.

Freud, Sigmund. 1938. "Splitting of the Ego in the Process of Defense." *Standard Edition* 23:271–78.

———. 1995[1915]. "Repression." In *The Freud Reader*, edited by P. Gay, 568–72. New York: Norton.

———. 1995[1925]. "Negation." In *The Freud Reader*, edited by P. Gay, 666–69. New York: Norton.

Fuller, Chris, and Haripriya Narasimhan. 2006. "Engineering Colleges, 'Exposure' and Information Technology." *Economic & Political Weekly* 41(3):258–62.

———. 2014. *Tamil Brahmans*. Chicago: University of Chicago Press.

Gane, Nicholas, and David Beer. 2008. *New Media*. Oxford: Berg.

Gangjee, Dev. 2008. "The Polymorphism of Trademark Dilution in India." *Transnational Law & Contemporary Problems* 17(3):611–30.

Ganti, Teswajini. 2002. "'And Yet My Heart Is Still Indian': The Bombay Film Industry and the (H)Indianization of Hollywood." In *Media Worlds*, edited by F. Ginsburg, L. Abu-Lughod, and B. Larkin, 281–300. Berkeley: University of California Press.

Gell, Alfred. 1986. "Newcomers to the World of Goods: The Muria Gonds." In *The Social Life of Things*, edited by A. Appadurai, 110–38. New York: Cambridge University Press.

Gerritsen, Roos. 2012. "Fandom on Display: Intimate Visualities and the Politics of Spectacle." PhD diss., Faculty of Social and Behavioural Sciences, Leiden University.

Gershon, Ilana. 2010. "Media Ideologies: An Introduction." *Journal of Linguistic Anthropology* 20(2):283–93.

Ginsburg, Jane. 2008. "'See Me, Feel Me, Touch Me, Hear Me' (And Maybe Smell Me Too): I Am a Trademark—A U.S. Perspective." In *Trade Marks and Brands*, edited by L. Bently, J. Davis, and J. Ginsburg, 92–104. New York: Cambridge University Press.

Goffman, Erving. 1974. *Frame Analysis*. Boston: Northeastern University Press.

———. 1981. *Forms of Talk*. Philadelphia: University of Pennsylvania Press.

Gondola, Ch. D. 1999. "Dream and Drama: The Search for Elegance among Congolese Youth." *African Studies Review* 42(1):23–48.

Goodale, Mark. 2006. "Reclaiming Modernity: Indigenous Cosmopolitanism and the Coming of the Second Revolution in Bolivia." *American Ethnologist* 33(4): 634–49.

Gorringe, Hugo, and Irene Rafanell. 2007. "The Embodiment of Caste: Oppression, Protest and Change." *Sociology* 41(1):97–114.

Graan, Andrew. 2013. "Counterfeiting the Nation? Skopje 2014 and the Politics of Nation Branding in Macedonia." *Cultural Anthropology* 28(1):161–79.

Gumperz, John. 1982. *Discourse Strategies*. Cambridge, UK: Cambridge University Press.

Hall, Kira. 2005. "Intertextual Sexuality: Parodies of Class, Identity, and Desire in Liminal Delhi." *Journal of Linguistic Anthropology* 15(1):125–44.

Hall, Kira, and Chad Nilep. 2015. "Code-Switching, Identity, and Globalization." In *The Handbook of Discourse Analysis*, 2nd ed., edited by D. Tannen, H. Hamilton, and D. Schiffrin, 597–619. New York: John Wiley and Sons.

Halpern, Orit. 2007. "Dreams for Our Perceptual Present: Archives, Interfaces, and Networks in Cybernetics." *Configurations* 13(2):283–320.

Halstead, Narmala. 2002. "Branding 'Perfection': Foreign as Self; Self as 'Foreign-Foreign.'" *Journal of Material Culture* 7(3):273–93.

Hanks, William. 1989. "Text and Textuality." *Annual Review of Anthropology* 18: 95–127.

Hansen, Miriam. 1991. *Babel and Babylon*. Cambridge, MA: Harvard University Press.

Hardgrave, Robert. 1971. "The Celluloid God: MGR and the Tamil Film." *South Asian Review* 4(4):307–14.

———. 1973. "Politics and the Film in Tamilnadu: The Stars and the DMK." *Asian Survey* 13(3):288–305.

———. 1979. "When Stars Displace the Gods: The Folk Culture of Cinema in Tamil Nadu." In *Essays in the Political Sociology of South India*, 92–114. New Delhi: Usha.

Hardt, Michael. 1999. "Affective Labour." *Boundary 2* 26(2):89–100.

Harvey, Keith. 2002. "Camp Talk and Citationality: A Queer Take on 'Authentic' and 'Represented' Utterance." *Journal of Pragmatics* 34(9):1145–65.

Hebdige, Dick. 1979. *Subculture: The Meaning of Style*. London: Methuen.

Heller, Monica. 1984. "Strategic Ambiguity: Code Switching in the Management of Conflict." *Toronto Working Papers in Linguistics* 5:66–89.

———. 1988. "Introduction." In *Codeswitching: Anthropological and Sociolinguistic Perspectives*, edited by M. Heller, 1–24. Berlin: Mouton de Gruyter.

———. 1994. *Crosswords*. Berlin: Mouton de Gruyter.

Hickey, Raymond. 2004. "South Asian Englishes." In *Legacies of Colonial English*, edited by R. Hickey, 536–58. Cambridge, UK: Cambridge University Press.

Hill, Jane. 1995[1985]. "The Grammar of Consciousness and the Consciousness of Grammar." In *Language, Culture, and Society*, 2nd ed., edited by B. Blount, 398–414. Prospect Heights, IL: Waveland Press.

Hjarvard, Stig, and Line N. Petersen. 2013. "Mediatization and Cultural Change." *Journal of Media and Communication Research* 54:1–7.

Hughes, Stephen. 1996. "Is There Anyone Out There? Exhibition and the Formation of Silent Film Audiences in South India." PhD diss., Department of Anthropology, University of Chicago.

———. 2011. "Anthropology and the Problem of Audience Reception." In *Made to Be Seen*, edited by M. Banks and J. Ruby, 288–312. Chicago: University of Chicago Press.

Indiaglitz. 2007. "Vijay Birthday Celebration." *Indiaglitz*, June 23. Accessed January 25, 2010. http://www.indiaglitz.com/channels/tamil/gallery/Events/12584.html.

Indian Express. 2011. "Jayalalithaa 'Crackdown': Lottery Baron Santiago Martin Arrested in Land Grabbing Case." *Indian Express*, August 23. Accessed December 17, 2013. http://www.indianexpress.com/news/jayalalithaa-crackdown-lottery-baron-santiago-martin-arrested-in-land-grabbing-case/831579.

Irvine, Judith. 2002. "'Style' as Distinctiveness: The Culture and Ideology of Linguistic Differentiation." In *Style and Sociolinguistic Variation*, edited by J. Rickford and P. Eckert, 21–43. Cambridge, UK: Cambridge University Press.

Jacob, Preminda. 2009. *Celluloid Deities*. Lanham, MD: Lexington Books.

Jain, Kajri. 2007. *Gods in the Bazaar*. Durham, NC: Duke University Press.

Jain, L. C. 1985. "1985 Textile Policy: End of Handloom Industry." *Economic & Political Weekly* 20(27):1121–23.

Jeffrey, Craig. 2010. *Timepass*. Stanford, CA: Stanford University Press.

Jeffrey, Craig, Patricia Jeffrey, and Roger Jeffrey. 2008. *Degrees without Freedom? Education, Masculinities, and Unemployment in North India*. Stanford, CA: Stanford University Press.

Jeffrey, Patricia, and Roger Jeffrey. 1994. "Killing My Heart's Desire: Education and Female Autonomy in Rural North India." In *Women as Subjects*, edited by N. Kumar, 125–71. New Delhi: Stree.

Jenkins, Henry. 2006. *Convergence Culture*. New York: New York University Press.

Jenkins, Henry, Sam Ford, and Joshua Green. 2013. *Spreadable Media*. New York: New York University Press.

Jenkins, Rob. 1999. *Democratic Politics and Economic Reform in India*. Cambridge, UK: Cambridge University Press.

Johnson-Hanks, Jennifer. 2002. "On the Limits of Life Stages in Ethnography: Toward a Theory of Vital Conjectures." *American Anthropologist* 104(3): 865–80.

Juluri, Vamsee. 2003. *Becoming a Global Audience*. New York: Peter Lang.

Kachru, Braj B. 1975. "Lexical Innovations in South Asian English." *International Journal of the Sociology of Language* 4:55–74.

———. 1983. *The Indianization of English*. New Delhi: Oxford University Press.

———. 1994. "English in South Asia." In *The Cambridge History of the English Language*, vol. 5, *English in Britain and Overseas*, 497–553. Cambridge, UK: Cambridge University Press.

Kanthimathi, K. 2007. "Code Mixing Tamil and English." PhD diss., Department of Humanities and Social Sciences, Indian Institute of Technology Madras.

Kapur, Geetha. 1987. "Mythic Material in Indian Cinema." *Journal of Arts and Ideas* 14–15:79–108.

Kolappan, B. 2011. "Vijay Certain to Enter Politics." *The Hindu*, January 21. Accessed September 17, 2012. http://www.thehindu.com/news/states/tamil-nadu/article1109328.ece.

Krishnan, Rajan. 2007. "Rajini's Sivaji: Screen and Sovereign." *Economic & Political Weekly* 42(27–28):2861–63.

———. 2009. "Cultures of Indices: Anthropology of Tamil and Other Cinemas." PhD diss., Department of Anthropology, Columbia University.

Kuldova, Tereza, ed. 2013. *Fashion India*. Oslo: Akademika Publishing.

Kulick, Don. 2003. "No." *Language & Communication* 23(2):139–51.

Kulick, Don, and Margaret Willson. 1997. "Rambo's Wife Saves the Day: Subjugating the Gaze and Subverting the Narrative in a Papua New Guinean Swamp." In *The Anthropology of Media*, edited by K. Askew and Richard R. Wilk, 270–85. Malden, MA: Blackwell Publishers.

Kumar, Shanti. 2013. "Unimaginable Communities: Television, Globalization, and National Identities in Postcolonial India." In *No Limits*, edited by R. Sundaram, 256–76. New Delhi: Oxford University Press.

Kurai (Krishnan), Rajan. 2012. *Kathanayakanin Maranam* ('Death of the Hero'). Chennai: Kayal Kavin.

LaDousa, Chaise. 2014. *Hindi Is Our Ground, English Is Our Sky*. New York: Berghahn.

Lessig, Lawrence. 2006. *Code: Version 2.0*. New York: Basic.

Levinson, Stephen. 1977. "Social Deixis in a Tamil Village." PhD diss., Department of Anthropology, University of California, Berkeley.

Liechty, Mark. 2003. *Suitably Modern*. Princeton, NJ: Princeton University Press.

Livingstone, Sonia. 1999. "New Media, New Audiences?" *New Media & Society* 1(1): 59–66.

———. 2009. "On the Mediation of Everything: ICA Presidential Address 2008." *Journal of Communication* 59(1):1–18.

Lukács, Gabriella. 2010. *Branded Selves, Scripted Affects*. Durham, NC: Duke University Press.

Lukose, Ritty. 2009. *Liberalization's Children*. Durham, NC: Duke University Press.

Lundby, Knut, ed. 2009. *Mediatization: Concept, Changes, Consequences*. New York: Peter Lang.

Lury, Celia. 2004. *Brands: The Logos of the Global Economy*. London: Routledge.

Luvaas, Brent. 2009. "Dislocating Sounds: The Deterritorialization of Indonesian Indie Pop." *Cultural Anthropology* 24(2):246–79.

———. 2010. "Designer Vandalism: Indonesian Indie Fashion and the Cultural Practice of Cut 'n' Paste." *Visual Anthropology Review* 26(1):1–16.

———. 2013. "Material Interventions: Indonesian DIY Fashion and the Regime of the Global Brand." *Cultural Anthropology* 28(1):127–43.

Mankekar, Purnima. 1999. *Screening Cultures*. Durham, NC: Duke University Press.

Manning, Paul. 2009. "The Epoch of Magna: Brand and Imagining the Transition in Georgia." *Slavic Review* 68(4):924–45.

———. 2010. "Semiotics of Brand." *Annual Review of Anthropology* 39:33–49.

Manning, Paul, and Ann Uplisashvili. 2007. "'Our Beer': Ethnographic Brands in Postsocialist Georgia." *American Anthropologist* 109(4):626–41.

Manovich, Lev. 2001. *The Language of New Media*. Cambridge, MA: MIT Press.

———. 2003. "New Media from Borges to HTML." In *The New Media Reader*, edited by N. Wardrip-Fruin and N. Monfort, 13–25. Cambridge: MA: MIT Press.

———. 2008. "The Practice of Everyday (Media) Life." In *Video Vortex Reader*, edited by G. Lovink and S. Niederer, 33–43. Amsterdam: Institute of Network Cultures.

Mazumdar, Ranjani. 2013. "Film Stardom after Liveness." In *No Limits*, edited by R. Sundaram, 381–400. Delhi: Oxford University Press.

Mazzarella, William. 2003. *Shoveling Smoke*. Durham, NC: Duke University Press.

———. 2005. "Indian Middle Class." In *South Asia Keywords*, edited by R. Dwyer and S. Sinha. London: Centre of South Asian Studies, University of London. Accessed June 1, 2013. http://www.soas.ac.uk/south-asia-institute/keywords/file24808.pdf.

———. 2010. "Branding the Mahatma: The Untimely Provocation of Gandhian Publicity." *Cultural Anthropology* 25(1):1–39.

———. 2013. *Censorium*. Durham, NC: Duke University Press.

McAlexander, Jim, and John Schouten. 1998. "Brandfests: Servicescapes for the Cultivation of Brand Equity." In *Servicescapes*, edited by J. Sherry Jr., 377–401. Chicago: NT Business Books.

McLuhan, Marshall. 1964. *Understanding Media*. New York: McGraw-Hill Book Company.

Meeuwis, Michael, and Jan Blommaert. 1998. "A Monolectal View of Code-Switching: Layered Code-Switching among Zairians in Belgium." In *Code-Switching in Conversation*, edited by P. Auer, 76–98. London: Routledge.

Meiu, George. 2014. "'Beach-Boy Elders' and 'Young Big-Men': Subverting the Temporalities of Ageing in Kenya's Ethno-Erotic Economies." *Ethnos*. Accessed September 1, 2014. http://dx.doi.org/10.1080/00141844.2014.938674.

Mendoza-Denton, Norma. 2008. *Homegirls*. Malden, MA: Blackwell Publishing.

Metz, Christian. 1982. *The Imaginary Signifier*. Bloomington: Indiana University Press.

———. 1991. "The Impersonal Enunciation, or the Site of Film (In the Margin of Recent Works on Enunciation in Cinema)." *New Literary History* 22(3):747–72.

Miller, Daniel. 1995. "Style and Ontology in Trinidad." In *Consumption and Identity*, edited by J. Friedman, 71–96. Chur, Switzerland: Harwood Academic Publishing.

Mines, Diane. 2005. *Fierce Gods*. Bloomington: Indiana University Press.

Mines, Mattison. 1994. *Public Faces, Private Voices*. Berkeley: University of California Press.

Mines, Mattison, and Vijayalakshmi Gourishankar. 1990. "Leadership and Individuality in South Asia: The Case of the South Indian Big-Man." *Journal of Asian Studies* 49(4):761–86.

Mishra, Vijay, Peter Jeffery, and Brian Shoesmith. 1989. "The Actor as Parallel Text in Bombay Cinema." *Quarterly Review of Film and Video* 11(3):49–67.

Mitchell, Lisa. 2009. *Language, Emotion, and Politics in South India*. Bloomington: Indiana University Press.

Moor, Elizabeth. 2003. "Branded Spaces: The Scope of 'New Marketing.'" *Journal of Consumer Culture* 3(1):39–60.

Moore, Robert. 2003. From Genericide to Viral Marketing: On 'Brand.' *Language & Communication* 23:331–57.

Morley, David. 1980. *The* Nationwide *Audience*. London: BFI.

Muniz, Albert, and Thomas O'Guinn. 2001. "Brand Community." *Journal of Consumer Research* 27(4):412–32.

Murphy, Keith. 2015. *Swedish Design*. Ithaca, NY: Cornell University Press.

Muthiah, S. 2004. "A Town Called George." In *The Unhurried City*, edited by C. S. Lakshmi, 27–36. New Delhi: Penguin.

Myers-Scotton, Carol. 1992. "Comparing Codeswitching and Borrowing." In *Codeswitching*, edited by C. Eastman, 19–39. Clevedon, UK: Multilingual Matters.

———. 1993. *Social Motivations for Codeswitching*. New York: Oxford University Press.

Nakassis, Constantine. 2009. "Theorizing Realism Empirically." *New Cinemas* 7(3):211–35.

———. 2010. "Youth and Status in Tamil Nadu, India." PhD diss., Department of Anthropology, University of Pennsylvania.

———. 2012a. "Counterfeiting What? Aesthetics of Brandedness and BRAND in Tamil Nadu, India." *Anthropological Quarterly* 85(3):701–22.

———. 2012b. "Brand, Citationality, Performativity." *American Anthropologist* 114(4):624–38.

———. 2013a. "Brands and Their Surfeits." *Cultural Anthropology* 28(1):111–26.
———. 2013b. "Citation and Citationality." *Signs and Society* 1(1):51–78.
———. 2013c. "The Para-s/cite, Parts I and II." *Semiotic Review*. Accessed June 1, 2013. http://semioticreview.com.
———. 2013d. "Youth Masculinity, 'Style,' and the Peer Group in Tamil Nadu, India." *Contributions to Indian Sociology* 47(2):245–69.
———. 2013e. "The Quality of a Copy." In *Fashion India*, edited by T. Kuldova, 142–65. Oslo: Akademika Publishing.
———. 2014. "Youth Sociality and Suspended Kinship in Tamil Nadu, India." *Current Anthropology* 55(2):175–99.
———. 2015. "A Tamil-speaking Heroine." *BioScope* 6(2):165–86.
———. n.d. "Bus Routes." Paper presented at the *Chicago Tamil Forum: Margins of Dravidianism*, May 21–23, 2015, University of Chicago.
———. In press. "Scaling Red and the Horror of Trademark." In *Scale: Discourse and Dimensions of Social Life*, edited by E. S. Carr and M. Lempert. Berkeley: University of California Press.
Nakassis, Constantine, and Melanie Dean. 2007. "Desire, Youth, and Realism in Tamil Cinema." *Journal of Linguistic Anthropology* 17(1):77–104.
Nandy, Ashish. 2004[1987]. "Reconstructing Childhood: A Critique of the Ideology of Adulthood." In *Bonfire of the Creeds*, 423–29. New Delhi: Oxford University Press.
Newell, Sasha. 2012. *The Modernity Bluff*. Chicago: University of Chicago Press.
Niranjana, Seemanthini. 2001. *Gender and Space*. Delhi: Sage.
Nisbett, Nicholas. 2007. "Friendship, Consumption, Morality: Practising Identity, Negotiating Hierarchy in Middle-Class Bangalore." *Journal of the Royal Anthropological Institute* (N.S.) 13(4):935–50.
Norris, Lucy. 2010. *Recycling Indian Clothing*. Bloomington: Indiana University Press.
Olivelle, Patrick. 1998. "Hair and Society: Social Significance of Hair in South Asian Traditions." In *Hair: Its Power and Meaning in Asian Cultures*, edited by A. Hiltebeitel and B. Miller, 11–50. Albany: State University of New York.
O'Reilly, Tim. 2005. "What Is Web 2.0?" Accessed July 1, 2013. http://oreilly.com/web2/archive/what-is-web-20.html.
Osella, Caroline. 2013. "Memories of Luxury, Aspirations toward Glamour, and Cultivations of Morality: How South Indian Muslim Women Craft Their Style." In *Fashion India*, edited by T. Kuldova, 121–42. Oslo: Akademika Publishing.
Osella, Caroline, and Filippo Osella. 1998. "Friendship and Flirting: Micro-Politics in Kerala, South India." *Journal of the Royal Anthropological Institute* (N.S.) 4(2): 189–206.
———. 2004. "Young Malayali Men and Their Movie Heroes." In *South Asian Masculinities*, edited by R. Chopra, C. Osella, and F. Osella, 224–63. New Delhi: Kali for Women and Women Unlimited.
———. 2006. *Men and Masculinities in South India*. London: Anthem Press.
———. 2007. "Muslim Style in South India." *Fashion Theory* 11(2–3):1–20.

Osella, Filippo, and Caroline Osella. 1999. "From Transience to Immanence: Consumption, Life-Cycle and Social Mobility in Kerala, South India." *Modern Asian Studies* 33(4):989–1020.

———. 2000a. *Social Mobility in Kerala*. London: Pluto Press.

———. 2000b. "Migration, Money and Masculinity in Kerala." *Journal of the Royal Anthropological Institute* (N.S.) 6(1):117–33.

Page, David, and William Crawley. 2001. *Satellites over South Asia*. New Delhi: Sage Publications.

Pandian, M. S. S. 1991. "Parasakthi: Life and Times of a DMK Film." *Economic & Political Weekly* 26(11–12):759–761, 763–765, 767, 769–770.

———. 1992. *The Image Trap*. New Delhi: Sage Publications.

———. 1996. "Tamil Cultural Elites and Cinema: Outline of an Argument." *Economic & Political Weekly* 31(15):950–55.

———. 2005. "Picture Lives." In *Living Pictures*, edited by D. Blamey and R. D'Souza, 55–62. London: Open Editions.

———. 2007. *Brahmin and Non-Brahmin*. Delhi: Permanent Black.

Pang, Laikwan. 2008. "'China Who Makes and Fakes': A Semiotics of the Counterfeit." *Theory, Culture & Society* 25(6):117–40.

Parameswaran, Radhika. 2001. "Feminist Media Ethnography in India: Exploring Power, Gender, and Culture in the Field." *Qualitative Inquiry* 7(1):69–103.

———. 2002. "Reading Fictions of Romance: Gender, Sexuality, and Nationalism in Postcolonial India." *Journal of Communication* 52(4):832–51.

Park, Joseph. 2009. "Illegitimate Speakers of English: Negotiation of Linguistic Identity among Korean International Students." In *Beyond Yellow English*, edited by A. Reyes and A. Lo, 195–212. New York: Oxford University Press.

Parthasarathi, Prasannan. 2010. "Global Trade and Textile Workers." In *The Ashgate Companion to the History of Textile Workers, 1650–2000*, edited by L. van Voss, E. Hiemstra-Kuperus, and E. van Nederveen Meerkerk, 531–76. Farnham, UK: Ashgate Publishing.

———. 2013[2009]. "Historical Issues of Deindustrialization in Nineteenth-Century South India." In *How India Clothed the World*, edited by G. Riello and T. Roy, 415–35. Leiden: Brill.

Parthasarathy, Anusha. 2014. "Tamil to a Tee!" *The Hindu*, February 28. Accessed September 1, 2014. http://www.thehindu.com/todays-paper/tp-features/tp-metroplus/tamil-to-a-tee/article5733883.ece.

Paz, Alejandro. 2010. "Discursive Transformation: The Emergence of Ethnolinguistic Identity among Latin American Labor Migrants and Their Children in Israel." PhD diss., Department of Anthropology, University of Chicago.

Peck, Harry T. 1904. "Americans Whom Oxford Has Honored." *Munsey's Magazine* 32(3):430–34.

Pendakur, Manjunath. 1991. "The Political Economy of Television: State, Class, and Corporate Confluence in India." In *Transnational Communications*, edited by G. Sussman and J. Lent, 234–62. Newbury Park, NJ: Sage Publications.

———. 2005[1996]. "India's National Film Policy: Shifting Currents in the 1990s." In *Film Policy*, edited by A. Moran, 145–171. London: Routledge.

Peters, John Durham. 2001. *Speaking into the Air*. Chicago: University of Chicago Press.

Peterson, Mark. 2005. "Performing Media: Toward an Ethnography of Intertextuality." In *Media Anthropology*, edited by E. Rothenbuhler and M. Coman, 129–38. London: Sage Publications.

Pillai, Swarnavel Eswaran. 2015. *Madras Studios*. New Delhi: Sage.

Poster, Mark. 1999. "Underdetermination." *New Media & Society* 1(1):12–17.

Povinelli, Elizabeth. 2002. *The Cunning of Recognition*. Durham, NC: Duke University Press.

Prahalad, C. K., and Venkatram Ramaswamy. 2004. "Co-Creation Experiences: The Next Practice in Value Creation." *Journal of Interactive Marketing* 18(3):5–14.

Prasad, M. Madhava. 1998. *The Ideology of the Hindi Cinema*. New Delhi: Oxford University Press.

———. 2003. "This Thing Called Bollywood." *Seminar* 525:17–20. Accessed September 3, 2012. http://www.india-seminar.com/2003/525/525%20madhava%20prasad.htm.

———. 2014. *Cine-Politics*. Chennai: Orient Blackswan.

Proctor, Lavanya Murali. 2014. "English and Globalization in India: The Fractal Nature of Discourse." *Journal of Linguistic Anthropology* 24(3):294–314.

Radhakrishnan, P. 1993. "Communal Representation in Tamil Nadu, 1850–1916: The Pre-Non-Brahmin Movement Phase." *Economic & Political Weekly* 28(31):1585–97.

Radway, Janice. 1984. *Reading the Romance*. Chapel Hill: University of North Carolina Press.

Rafaeli, Sheizaf. 1988. "Interactivity: From New Media to Communication." In *Sage Annual Review of Communication Research: Merging Mass and Interpersonal Processes*, edited by R. P. Hawkins, J. M. Wiemann, and S. Pingree, 110–34. Beverly Hills, CA: Sage.

Rajadhyaksha, Ashish. 2009. *Indian Cinema in the Time of Celluloid*. Bloomington: Indiana University Press.

Rajagopal, Arvind. 1999. "Thinking through Emerging Markets: Brand Logics and the Cultural Forms of Political Society in India." *Social Text* 60(3):131–49.

———. 2001. *Politics after Television*. New York: Cambridge University Press.

Rajanayagam, S. 2002. "Cultural and Political Ramifications of Popular Screen Image in Thamizh Nadu: A Comparative Study of the Films of M G Ramachandran and Rajinikanth." PhD diss., Department of Journalism and Communication, University of Madras.

———. 2015. *Popular Cinema and Politics in South India*. New Delhi: Routledge.

Ramanathan, Vaidehi. 2005. *The English–Vernacular Divide*. Clevedon, UK: Multilingual Matters.

Ramaswamy, Sumathi. 1997. *Passions of the Tongue*. Berkeley: University of California Press.

Rampton, Ben. 1995. *Crossing*. London: Longman.

Raustiala, Kal, and Christopher Sprigman. 2006. *The Knockoff Economy*. New York: Oxford University Press.

Reynolds, Holly. 1980. "The Auspicious Married Woman." In *The Powers of Tamil Women*, edited by S. Wadley, 35–60. Syracuse, NY: Maxwell School of Citizenship and Public Affairs.

Reynolds, Reginald. 1949. *Beards*. New York: Harvest.

Riello, Giorgio, and Tirthankar Roy, eds. 2013[2009]a. *How India Clothed the World*. Leiden: Brill.

———. 2013[2009]b. "Introduction: The World of South Asian Textiles, 1500–1850." In *How India Clothed the World*, edited by G. Riello and T. Roy, 1–27. Leiden: Brill.

Rogers, Martyn. 2008. "Modernity, 'Authenticity,' and Ambivalence: Subaltern Masculinities on a South Indian College Campus." *Journal of the Royal Anthropological Institute* (N.S.) 14(1):79–95.

———. 2009. "Between Fantasy and 'Reality': Tamil Film Star Fan Club Networks and the Political Economy of Film Fandom." *South Asia* 32(1):64–85.

———. 2011. "From the Sacred to the Performative: Tamil Film Star Fan Clubs, Religious Devotion and the Material Culture of Film Star Portraits." *Journal of Religion and Popular Culture* 23(1):40–52.

Ross, Karen, and Virginia Nightingale. 2003. *Media and Audiences*. London: Open University Press.

Roy, Tirthankar. 2010. "The Long Globalization and Textile Producers in India." In *The Ashgate Companion to the History of Textile Workers, 1650–2000*, edited by L. van Voss, E. Hiemstra-Kuperus, and E. van Nederveen Meerkerk, 253–74. Farnham, UK: Ashgate Publishing.

Rudolph, Lloyd. 1989. "The Faltering Novitiate: Rajiv Gandhi at Home and Abroad." In *India Briefing*, edited by M. Bouton and P. Oldenburg, 1–33. Boulder, CO: Westview Press.

Said, Edward. 1979. *Orientalism*. New York: Vintage Books.

Sankoff, David, Shana Poplack, and Swathi Vanniarajan. 1990. "The Case of the Nonce Loan in Tamil." *Language Variation and Change* 2(1):71–101.

Sapir, Edward. 1931a. "Communication." In *Encyclopaedia of the Social Sciences*, edited by E. Seligman, 78–81. New York: Macmillan.

———. 1931b. "Fashion." In *Encyclopaedia of the Social Sciences*, edited by E. Seligman, 139–44. New York: Macmillan.

Saqaf, S. 2009. "Drive against Ragging." *The Hindu*, September 25. Accessed February 8, 2010. http://www.thehindu.com/2009/09/25/stories/2009092550950200.htm.

Saraswathi, T. S. 1999. "Adult-Child Continuity in India: Is Adolescence a Myth or an Emerging Reality?" In *Culture, Socialization, and Human Development*, edited by T. S. Saraswathi, 213–32. New Delhi: Sage.

Schechner, Richard. 1985. *Between Theater and Anthropology*. Philadelphia: University of Pennsylvania Press.

Scherl, Richard. 1996. "Speaking with Mariyāthai: A Linguistic and Cultural Analysis of Markers of Plurality in Tamil." PhD diss., Department of Anthropology, University of Chicago.

Schiffman, Harold. 1998. "Standardization or Restandardization: The Case for 'Standard' Spoken Tamil." *Language in Society* 27(3):359–85.

———. 1999. *Reference Grammar of Spoken Tamil*. Cambridge, UK: Cambridge University Press.

Schultz, Tanjev. 2000. "Mass Media and the Concept of Interactivity: An Exploratory Study of Online Forums and Reader Email." *Media, Culture & Society* 22(2):205–21.

Schulz, Winfried. 2004. "Reconstructing Mediatization as an Analytical Concept." *European Journal of Communication* 19(1):87–101.

Schwartz, Gary, and Don Merten. 1967. "The Language of Adolescence: An Anthropological Approach to the Youth Culture." *American Journal of Sociology* 72(5):453–68.

Sebastian, Mrinalini. 2008. "The Legacies and the Prospects of General and Undergraduate Education in India: A Report." Bangalore: Centre for the Study of Culture and Society. Accessed July 7, 2013. http://www.cscs.res.in/dataarchive/textfiles/textfile.2008-05-23.9247175202/file.

Seizer, Susan. 2005. *Stigmas of the Tamil Stage*. Durham, NC: Duke University Press.

Seth, Sanjay. 2007. *Subject Lessons*. Durham, NC: Duke University Press.

Seymour, Susan. 2002. "Family and Gender Systems in Transition: A Thirty-Five Year Perspective." In *Everyday Life in South Asia*, edited by D. Mines and S. Lamb, 100–115. Bloomington: Indiana University Press.

Shah, A. M. 2013[2005]. "Higher Education and Research: Roots of Mediocrity." In *Higher Education in India*, edited by J. Tilak, 184–203. New Delhi: Orient Blackswan.

Sherry, John, Jr. 2005. "Brand Meaning." In *Kellogg on Branding*, edited by A. Tybout and T. Calkins, 40–69. Hoboken, NJ: Wiley and Sons.

Silverstein, Michael. 1998. "Contemporary Transformations of Local Linguistic Communities." *Annual Review of Anthropology* 27:401–26.

———. 2003. "Indexical Order and the Dialectics of Sociolinguistic Life." *Language & Communication* 23(3–4):193–229.

———. 2005. "Axes of Evals: Token versus Type Interdiscursivity." *Journal of Linguistic Anthropology* 15(1):6–22.

Silverstein, Michael, and Greg Urban. 1996. "The Natural History of Discourse." In *Natural Histories of Discourse*, edited by M. Silverstein and G. Urban, 1–17. Chicago: University of Chicago Press.

Silverstone, Roger. 1989. "Let Us Then Return to the Murmuring of Everyday Practices: A Note on Michel de Certeau, Television and Everyday Life." *Theory, Culture & Society* 6(1):77–94.

———. 1999. "What's New about New Media?" *New Media & Society* 1(1):10–12.

Simmel, Georg. 1984[1909]. "Flirtation." In *Georg Simmel: On Women, Sexuality, and Love*, translated by G. Oakes, 133–52. New Haven: Yale University Press.

———. 1998[1904]. "The Philosophy of Fashion." In *Simmel on Culture*, edited by D. Frisby and M. Featherson, 187–206. London: Sage Publications.

Sivathambi, Kartigesu. 1981. *The Tamil Film as a Medium of Political Communication*. Madras: New Century Book House.

Smith-Hefner, Nancy. 2007. "Youth Language, Gaul Sociability, and the New Indonesian Middle Class." *Journal of Linguistic Anthropology* 17(2):184–203.

Spencer, Herbert. 1900. "Fashion." In *Principles of Sociology*, vol. 2, 210–15. New York: D. Appleton and Company.

Spitulnik, Debra. 1993. "Anthropology and Mass Media." *Annual Review of Anthropology* 22:293–315.

———. 1996. "The Social Circulation of Media Discourse and the Mediation of Communities." *Journal of Linguistic Anthropology* 6(2):161–87.

———. 2002. "Mobile Machines and Fluid Audiences: Rethinking Reception through Zambian Radio Culture." In *Media Worlds*, edited by F. Ginsburg, L. Abu-Lughod, and B. Larkin, 337–54. Berkeley: University of California Press.

Srinivas, Lakshmi. 1998. "Active Viewing: An Ethnography of the Indian Film Audience." *Visual Anthropology* 11(4):323–53.

———. 2012. "Ladies Queues, Roadside Romeos, and Balcony Seating: Ethnographic Observations on Women's Cinema-Going Experiences." In *South Asian Cinemas: Widening the Lens*, edited by S. Dickey and R. Dudrah, 83–99. New York: Routledge.

Srinivas, M. N. 1976. *The Remembered Village*. Berkeley: University of California Press.

Srinivas, S. V. 2009. *Megastar*. New Delhi: Oxford University Press.

———. 2013. *Politics as Performance*. Ranikhet, India: Permanent Black.

Srinivasan, Sriram. 2005. "MTV Not Keen on Stake in SS Music." *The Hindu Business Line*, May 26. Accessed June 1, 2013. http://www.thehindubusinessline.com/todays-paper/tp-marketing/mtv-not-keen-on-stake-in-ss-music/article2178635.ece.

Srivastava, Sanjay. 2003. "Schooling, Culture, and Modernity." In *The Oxford India Companion to Sociology and Social Anthropology*, edited by V. Das, A. Béteille, and T. N. Madan, 998–1031. New Delhi: Oxford University Press.

———. 2007. *Passionate Modernity*. New Delhi: Routledge.

Straiger, Janet. 2005. *Media Reception Studies*. New York: New York University Press.

Sundaram, Ravi. 2013. "Revisiting the Piracy Kingdom." In *No Limits*, edited by R. Sundaram, 121–40. New Delhi: Oxford University Press.

Swigart, Leigh. 1992. "Two Codes or One? The Insiders' View and the Description of Codeswitching in Dakar." In *Codeswitching*, edited by C. Eastman, 83–102. Clevedon, UK: Multilingual Matters.

Tarlo, Emma. 1996. *Clothing Matters*. Chicago: University of Chicago Press.

———. 2004. "Khadi." In *South Asia Keywords*, edited by R. Dwyer and S. Sinha. London: Centre of South Asian Studies, University of London. Accessed August 1, 2014. http://www.soas.ac.uk/south-asia-institute/keywords/file24807.pdf.

Taussig, Michael. 1993. *Mimesis and Alterity*. London: Routledge.

Tetreault, Chantal. 2009. "Cité Teens Entextualizing French Television Host Register: Crossing, Voicing, and Participation Frameworks." *Language in Society* 38(2):201–31.

Thomas, Kedron. 2009. "Structural Adjustment, Spatial Imaginaries, and 'Piracy' in Guatemala's Apparel Industry." *Anthropology of Work Review* 30(1):1–10.

———. 2013. "Brand 'Piracy' and Postwar Statecraft in Guatemala." *Cultural Anthropology* 28(1):144–60.

Thurston, Edgar, and K. Rangachari. 1909. *Castes and Tribes of Southern India*. 7 vols. Madras: Government Press.

Tilak, Jandhyala. 2013. "Introduction." In *Higher Education in India*, edited by J. Tilak, 1–20. New Delhi: Orient Blackswan.

Toffler, Alvin. 1980. *The Third Wave*. New York: Bantam Books.

Trautmann, Thomas. 1997. *Aryans and British India*. Berkeley: University of California Press.

———. 2006. *Languages and Nations*. Berkeley: University of California Press.

Trivedi, Lisa. 2007. *Clothing Gandhi's Nation*. Bloomington: Indiana University Press.

Turner, Victor. 1967. *The Ritual Process*. Ithaca, NY: Cornell University Press.

———. 1982. *From Ritual to Theatre*. New York: Performing Arts Journal Publications.

Urciuoli, Bonnie. 1995. "Language and Borders." *Annual Review of Anthropology* 24: 525–46.

Vaasanthi. 2006. *Cut-Outs, Caste and Cine Stars*. New Delhi: Penguin Books.

Van Gennep, Arnold. 1960. *The Rites of Passage*. London: Routledge and Kegan Paul.

Vann, Elizabeth. 2005. "Domesticating Consumer Goods in the Global Economy: Examples from Vietnam and Russia." *Ethnos* 70(4):465–88.

———. 2006. "The Limits of Authenticity in Vietnamese Consumer Markets." *American Anthropologist* 108(2):286–96.

Veblen, Thorstein. 1899. *The Theory of the Leisure Class*. New York: Macmillan.

Venkatachalapathy, A. R. 2004. "Street Smart in Chennai: The City in Popular Imagination." In *The Unhurried City*, edited by C. S. Lakshmi, 15–26. New Delhi: Penguin Books.

Verma, Samar. 2007. "Indian Textile and Clothing Industry: Economic Policy Reform Experience During 'ATC' Period." In *India's Liberalisation Experience*, edited by S. Karmakar, R. Kumar, and B. Debroy, 134–68. New Delhi: Sage Publications.

Voloshinov, Valentin. 1986. *Marxism and the Philosophy of Language*. Translated by L. Matejka and I. R. Titunik. Cambridge, MA: Harvard University Press.

Weidman, Amanda. 2012. "Voices of Meenakumari: Sound, Meaning, and Self-Fashioning in Performances of an Item Number." *South Asian Popular Culture* 10(3):307–18.

Weiss, Brad. 2002. "Thug Realism: Inhabiting Fantasy in Urban Tanzania." *Cultural Anthropology* 17(1):93–124.

Willis, Paul. 1977. *Learning to Labor*. New York: Columbia University Press.

Woolard, Kathryn. 1988. "Codeswitching and Comedy in Catalonia." In *Codeswitching: Anthropological and Sociolinguistic Perspectives*, edited by M. Heller, 77–98. Berlin: Mouton de Gruyter.

———. 1989. *Double Talk*. Stanford, CA: Stanford University Press.

———. 1998. "Simultaneity and Bivalency as Strategies in Bilingualism." *Journal of Linguistic Anthropology* 8(1):3–29.

Yurchak, Alexi. 2006. *Everything Was Forever, Until It Was No More*. Princeton, NJ: Princeton University Press.

Žižek, Slavoj. 1989. *The Sublime Object of Ideology*. London: Verso.

Index

Page numbers in italic indicate figures.

build up *paṉṟatu* ('to show off'; lit. 'to build up [oneself]'), 175. *See also over style*
bus routes, 243n21, 248n32
Butler, Judith, 24, 59–61, 217, 254n27

calibration: discalibration and, 77, 82–86, 235–36, 269n20, 282n6; garment production and, 82–86, 243n19; interactivity and, 28, 234–35, 249n36, 282n6; mass mediation/media and, 233–37, 248n36, 281nn4–5, 282n6; media's entanglements and, 229–30, 232, 235–37; status of hero-stars and, 216; *style* and, 229–30; television and, 282n6
caste: cosmopolitanism and, 48; fashion and, 252n17; higher education and, 11–14, 20, 240n17, 243n20, 247n31; linguistic practices and, 93, 99–100, 262n13; mustaches and, 3, 5, 239nn1–2, 240n5; non-Brahmin movement and, 91, 243n17; 261n3; peer groups and, 14, 19–21, 247n31; *style* and, 51; women's sexuality and, 58; youth identity and, 17, 19–20, 227, 244n22. *See also* hierarchy
Chandrasekhar, 169, 199, 209–12, 222–23, 275n5
Channel V, 128–29, 266n4, 268n12
Chari, Sharad, 70–71, 257n4, 258n5, 258n11
chudhitars, 58–59, 112, 256n37, 256n39
cinema. *See* films
cinna paiyan ('little boy,' 'child'): college rules and, 17–18, 35, 58; filmic citation/reanimation and, 25, 160, 177–78, 196; hero-stars and, 25, 160, 177–78, 196; "maturity" and, 4, 17–18, 44, 58, 177, 246n6; mustaches and, 4, 23. *See also* hierarchy, and age; *periya āḷ* ('big man,' 'adult')
citationality: definition and description of, 7, 23, 61, 230, 235; aesthetics of brandedness and, 69; ambivalence and, 9, 14, 51, 60–61, 229, 246n24; brand fashion and, 25, 59–63, 84, 256nn40–41, 257n42, 260n18; brand ontology and, 56, 60, 84, 260n18; double-voicedness and, 9, 24, 192; English language and, 24, 26, 62, 94–95, 117, 122–23, 126, 150, 229; exteriority and, 25; film and, 3–5, 7, 8, 23, 25, 26, 27–29, 49, 95, 141–42, 152, 154, 160, 167, 171, 173–74, 205–12, 215–21, 228–29, 230, 236, 272n11, 273n14, 274n3, 277n17; flirtation and, 22–23; garment production and, 75–76, 81, 84; imitation versus, 177, 179, 180, 187, 217; kinship terms and, 23–24, 35, 115, 133–34, 249n3; liminality and, 23–24, 27, 61–63, 123; mass mediation/media and, 8, 9, 25–29, 150–51, 171, 220, 230, 233–37, 241n9; mustaches and, 3–5, 240n6; performativity and, 7, 24, 59–61; reflexivity and, 24–25, 60–61, 229, 235; SS Music VJs' speech and, 28, 126, 134–35, 140, 142, 146–47, 150–52; status of hero-stars and, 190–91, 195, 205–12, *206*, *207*, 275n4, 276n11–14, 277nn17–22; *style* and, 7–9, 22–25, 27, 229–30, 233, 254n27; subjectivity and, 25, 59, 62–63; Tamil language and, 93–94, 117, 122–23, 126, 134, 142, 146, 147, 150, 154–55. *See also* calibration; interactivity; interdiscursivity; quotation; reanimation
class (socioeconomic): *decent* and, 19, 34, 47, 93, 95, 102, 114, 167, 172, 227; fashion and, 3–4, 44–47, 50, 57, 61, 76, 240n7, 252n17, 255n35, 256n36, 259n12; fieldwork sites and, 9–11, 13–15, 95, 127; film and, 168, 172, 177–79, 187, 204–5, 274n21, 275n10; hierarchy and, 5, 13–14, 15, 19, 21, 51, 54, 227–29, 252n17; linguistic practices and, 93, 95, 96–98, 102, 108–9, 113, 114, 117, 265n24; *local* ('low class,' 'cheap') and, 41, 48, 93, 177–79; masculinity and, 46–47, 49, 240n3, 243n21; middle classes, 39, 40, 246n24; ragging and, 34, 36; SS Music VJs' social distance from audiences and, 126, 131, 134, 147, 269n20; *style* and, 6, 14, 15, 50–51, 53–54; youth identity/sociality and, 19–20, 21, 50–56, 227–29, 244nn21–22, 247n28
"class" films, 168, 200, 211–12, 222–23, 273n15, 279nn32–33
code mixing, 95, 120–22, 139, 261n5
code switching, 95, 120–22, 139, 261n5, 265n27, 265n29
colleges. *See* higher education
consumerism: liberalization and, 37–40, 70; national imaginaries and, 39–40
Craig (SS Music VJ on *Reach Out*), 130, 133–39, 142–46, *144*, 147, 153, 266n6, 267n10, 268n11, 268nn14–16, 269n17

Schechner, Richard, 23
Schiffman, Harold, 92, 110, 262n13, 265n22
script, and fashion, 45, *67*, 117–19, 188–90, 253n20
sen Tamiḻ ('pure Tamil'), 92–93, 100–102, 261n4, 262n13
sexualization, and women, 15, 58–59, 113, 183, 189, 265n23
Silambattam (film), 208, 277nn16–17
Silverstein, Michael, 219–20
Simbu ("Little Superstar"): citing other hero-stars and, 192, 208, 277n17; "class" films and 275n7; epithet of, 209; *Manmadhan* (film), 189–90, *189*, 275n4; on-screen/off-screen persona of, 214–16; *Silambattam* (film), 208, 277nn16–17; youth citation/reanimation of, 154, 188–90
Simmel, Georg, 22–24, 61, 63, 76
Singam (film), 4, *5*
Sivaji Ganesan, 205–7, *206*, 276nn11–12, 276n14, 277n20, 280n34
Sivaji: The Boss (film), 152, 160, 174, 205–6, *206*, *207*, 208–9, 213, *213*, 275nn10–11, 275n14, 279n29
"society" (*samūkam, samutāyam*): definition of, 17, 246n25; respectability and, 3–4, 172; women and, 59, 181, 255n35; youth identity/sociality and, 17–21, 24, 47–49, 51. See also *mariyātai* ('respect')
Southern Spice Music. *See* SS Music (Southern Spice Music); VJs on SS Music
spectatorship, and mass film genre, 160–61, 167, 170, 187
Spencer, Herbert, 76
Sprigman, Christopher, 260n18
Sriman, 164, 193–95, 203
Srivastava, Sanjay, 240n4
SS Music (Southern Spice Music): overview of, 126, 150–52; aesthetics of programming and, 124–25, *125*, 128–29, 266n3; ambivalence and English and, 134; anxieties of youth and English and, 134; audience of, 128–29, 131, 134, 147; audience relationship with VJs (close distance) and, 126, 130, 134–35, 139–42, 147–50, 266n6, 269nn19–20; Channel V and, 128–29, 266n4, 268n12; code mixing/switching and, 139; desires of youth and, 134–35; English as station's framing language and, 126, 130, 135, 142, 146; fieldwork sites and, 126; format for call-in shows and, 135, *135*; global imaginary of, 128–29, 132; hierarchy of Tamil and English on, 126, 135–42, 146, 268nn14–16, 269n17; history of, 127–28, 266nn2–6; image of, 130–31, 150; institutional organization of, 131, 147; *Just Connect* with VJ Paloma and, 124–25, *125*, 139–42, 146, 147, 153; kinship terms and, 140–41, 269n18; liberalization and, 38, 127; *local* ('low class,' 'cheap') and, 130, 146; market competition and, 128–31, 134, 147; mass mediation and, 26, 29, 150–51; reorientation of target audience and, 125–26, 130–32, 267nn7–9; MTV and, 127–28, 266nn3–5, 268n12; multilingualism and, 128–30, 266nn3–4; *over style* and, 126, 149, 269n20; *PCO* with VJ Pooja and, 135, 146, 147, 269n18; pedagogy for English and, 132–33; *Peter* and, 147–50, 266n6; proper English and, 133, 151; *Reach Out* with VJ Craig and, 130, 133–39, 142–46, *144*, 147, 153, 266n6, 267n10, 268n11, 268nn14–16, 269n17; *style* and English and, 7, 118, 126, 134, 147–49, 155, 268n13, 269nn19–20; *style* and Tamil and, 125–26, 262n15, 269n22; style (non-Tamil senses of the term) and, 268n13; Tamil cited/put in quotes and, 125–26, 130, 135, 141–42, 146, 147; Tamil slang and, 136, 146; "Tanglish" (mixed Tamil-English speech style) and, 134, 138, 146, 265n24, 268n15; *veḷḷai Tamiḻan* ('white Tamil') and, 153. *See also* VJs on SS Music
status, and youth: brandedness and, 75–77; brand fashion and, 37, 46–52, 54; English language and, 92, 94, 102, 105, 111, 114–16, 149–50; *gettu* (lit. 'prestige,' 'dominance') and, 35, 102, 183, 188–89, 243n21, 271n4; "heroism" and, 175; hierarchy and, 15; *local* ('low class,' 'cheap') and, 14, 48, 146; *mariyātai* ('respect') and, 17, 51, 102; mass film genre and, 176; "maturity" and, 4, 17–18, 44, 58, 172, 177, 246n6; mustaches and, 3–4; *paḻakkam* ('habit,' 'familiarity') and, 275n5; *periya āḷ* ('big man,' 'adult') and, 17; ragging and, 34–35; *rowdy* ('thug') and, 4, 49; sartorial styles for young men and, 45, 47; *style* and, 3, 5–6, 15–18, 21–22; Tamil language and, 94, 99, 101–2, 111; *veḷḷai*

ship with, 126, 130, 135, 139–48, *144*, 266n6, 269n18; calibration/discalibration and, 269n20; citationality and, 28, 126, 134–35, 140, 142, 146–47, 150–52; conversational style and, 133–34, 268nn11–13; English fluency/disfluency and, 127, 129, 132; on-air image of, 124–25, *125*, 132, 267n10; *Peter* and, 147, 150, 152, 266n6; *style* and, 133–34, 147–49, 269nn19–20; "Tamil culture" and, 132; Tamil fluency/disfluency and, 146–47, 149–50, 268n20; women as, 124–26, *125*, 132, 135, 139–42, 267n10, 269n18, 269n21. *See also* SS Music (Southern Spice Music); Craig (SS Music VJ on *Reach Out*); Paloma (SS Music VJ on *Just Connect*); Pooja (SS Music VJ on *PCO*)
Voloshinov, Valentin, 231

women: dance reanimated from film and, 182–83, 186, 273n19; English language and, 112–13, 149, 256nn38–39, 264n21, 269n21; exteriority and, 15; fashion and, 255n35, 256nn36–37, 256n39, 264n21; femininity and, 15, 59, 256n37; film fashion and, 172, 181–83, 273nn17–18; filmic depictions of, 152, 174, 180–81, 203, 273n17; *gettu* (lit. 'prestige,' 'dominance') and, 183, 243n21; *glamour* ('racy,' 'sexy') and, 59, 183; higher education and, 12, 243n16; liminality and, 181; media personalities as, 149; modernity and, 58–59, 181–82, 189; *over style* and, 109, 112–13, 183, 264n19, 264n21, 265n23; *Peter* and, 109, 264n19, 264n21; sexualization of, 15, 58–59, 113, 183, 265n23; SS Music VJs as, 124–26, *125*, 132, 135, 139–42, 267n10, 269n18, 269n21; *style* and, 15, 57, 58–59, 112–13, 180–81, 183; "Tamil culture" and, 58, 132, 149, 182; Tamil language and, 149–50; youth culture and, 14–15, 172, 180, 244n22, 255n35. *See also* sartorial styles for young women
Woolard, Kathryn, 94, 265n28

youth (sociocultural category of): citationality and, 25; enregisterment of, 244n22; exteriority and, 15, 20, 228; gender and, 14–15, 244n22; higher education and, 16, 228, 244n22; liminality and, 15–16, 22–23, 36, 227, 245n23; media forms/objects and, 26, 172, 177, 228; shifters and, 244n22; transgression and, 9, 16–19, 21, 50, 254n23; variability of, 244n22. *See also* peer groups
youth culture, 6, 8, 15–17, 23, 172, 227, 244n22, 245n23, 246n24, 257n42